ROOTS OF REVOLUTION

ROOTS OF REVOLUTION

AN INTERPRETIVE HISTORY
OF MODERN IRAN

NIKKI R. KEDDIE

WITH A SECTION BY YANN RICHARD

NEW HAVEN AND LONDON / YALE UNIVERSITY PRESS

Designed by Sally Harris
and set in Garamond type.
Printed in the United States of America by
The Vail-Ballou Press, Binghamton, N.Y.

Library of Congress Cataloging in Publication Data

Keddie, Nikki R.
  Roots of revolution.

  Bibliography: p.
  Includes index.
  1. Iran—History—20th century. I. Richard,
Yann. II. Title.
DS316.3.K42   955' .05   81-40438
ISBN 0-300-02606-4   AACR2
ISBN 0-300-02611-0 (pbk.)

10   9   8   7   6   5   4   3   2   1

. . . could thou and I with Fate conspire
To grasp this sorry Scheme of Things entire,
Would not we shatter it to bits—and then
Re-mold it nearer to the Heart's Desire!

An eleventh-century Iranian scientist

TO ERIC ROULEAU

Who bridges the worlds

Religious distress is at the same time the
expression of real distress and also the *protest* against
real distress. Religion is the sigh of the oppressed
creature, the heart of a heartless world, just as it is the
spirit of spiritless conditions. It is . . .

A nineteenth-century European socialist

CONTENTS

ILLUSTRATIONS

Map of Iran   *frontispiece*

Following page 182

The 1905–11 Revolution (photos from the collection of Nikki Keddie)
  Sattar Khan, leader of the Tabriz freedom-fighters
  Mirza Jahangir Khan, editor of *Sur-e Esrafil*
  Sayyed Jamal ad-Din Esfahani, popular preacher of the Revolution
  Malek al-Motakallemin, another leading popular preacher

Peoples of Iran (photos by Nikki Keddie)
  Shahsevan tribeswoman of Azerbaijan, 1975
  Baluchi, near the Afghan border, 1973
  Kurd at a town market, 1974
  Arab family, Ahwaz, Khuzistan, 1974

The Qashqa'i of Fars province: old and new ways (photos by Nikki Keddie)
  Qashqa'i tribespeople on summer migration, 1977
  Qashqa'i factory worker, Marvdasht, 1977

Carpet weaving: Iran's primary non-oil export (photos by Nikki Keddie)
  Family weaving at home, Kerman, 1974
  Carpet workshop, Ardebil, Azerbaijan, 1974

Comic and tragic popular theatre (photos by Nikki Keddie)
  Blackface clown of the popular theatre, Shiraz, 1977
  Ta'zieh (passion play) on the death of Ali, the first Imam, Taleqan valley, 1979

Four contemporary leaders (three photos provided by Yann Richard)
  Abolhasan Bani Sadr, first president of the Islamic Republic of Iran
  Ayatollah Mahmud Taleqani (d. 1979), a socially conscious cleric
  Dr. Ali Shariati (d. 1977), leading ideologist of progressive Islam
  Ayatollah Kazem Shariatmadari, moderate constitutionalist from Azerbaijan (photo by Nikki Keddie)

PREFACE

This book embodies elements of research and study on Iranian history and politics done over more than two decades, beginning with my Ph.D. dissertation and continuing until today. So many persons, Iranian and Western, have helped me in this long-term research and writing that it would be impossible to list and thank them all. Most of them have been thanked in my past books and articles. Here will be mentioned only those who helped significantly and specifically with this book, omitting those whose presence might cause them embarrassment.

First, heartfelt thanks are due to my outstanding, omnicompetent, and efficient graduate assistants, Brad Hanson and Julia Clancy. The entire manuscript was read and usefully criticized by Gene Garthwaite, John Gurney, Fred Halliday, John Perry, M. H. Pesaran, and Stanley Wolpert. Parts of the manuscript were read and helpful suggestions made by Shaul Bakhash, James Bill, Juan Cole, Richard Cottam, Brad Hanson, Yann Richard, Barry Rubin, and Andrew Whitley.

Also to be thanked are Nancy Lane of Oxford University Press for giving me an advance copy of Barry Rubin's *Paved with Good Intentions*, and to the following persons who gave me advance copies of their book manuscripts or proofs to read and utilize: Mangol Bayat, Gene Garthwaite, Eric Hooglund, Homa Katouzian, Michael Ledeen, and John Stempel. Yann Richard was especially helpful through all the metamorphoses his section had to undergo to make it fit meaningfully into the book.

Several fellowships for work in Iran, Europe, and the United States have sustained my research on Iran over the years. In chronological order, there have been fellowships from the American Association of University Women, the Social Science Research Council, American Council of Learned Societies (two), the John Simon Guggenheim Foundation, the American Philosophical Society, research units at

UCLA and, directly for this book, from the Rockefeller Foundation, to all of whom, especially the last, thanks are due.

Last but in no way least, my gratitude to my Yale editor, Charles Grench, is overwhelming. He has made what is sometimes a difficult or mixed experience into a wholly pleasant one and has uniformly showed excellent sense, liberality with his time and efforts, and constant good humor. Others at Yale University Press have also been most helpful and efficient, as have my copyeditor, Robert Brown, and all who typed the manuscript.

Transliteration follows a simple system, without diacriticals even in cited works. In this system *o* and *e* are used for Persian short vowels, except in a few, mostly religious, terms well known with the transliteration *u* and *i*. Some names and places widely known in the West under spellings not conforming to my system are left in their more familiar form, including some, generally self-chosen, spellings of Iranians' names. Before Reza Shah many Iranians had both names and titles; herein titles are italicized when they follow names.

In a book embodying research and reading in many languages over a long period it was impractical to list in the notes or bibliography every source used. Hence, except in Yann Richard's section, only selected works, mainly in English, are listed. Most of the listed books and articles have notes and bibliographies that should give enough information to those who want to pursue research on specific topics. The select bibliography of books in the English language is not a listing of works in the notes but is intended to help guide those who want to pursue a more detailed study of particular topics, or of modern Iranian history and culture in general. Part of this book is based on interviews or on observation during eight stays in Iran, 1959–79.

Nikki R. Keddie
Los Angeles, California
March 1981

1 RELIGION AND SOCIETY TO 1800

Background

The 1978–79 Revolution and its aftermath awakened for the first time in twenty-five years widespread public interest in Iran—and, to a large degree, bafflement and incomprehension. This revolution did not fit the patterns and expectations of even the relatively well informed. Where before had one seen a leader of an established religion emerge as the widely popular, charismatic head of a revolution against a royal ruler who stressed his own legitimacy, his ties to the national past, and his reformist plans? And where before had one seen a state bristling with armaments worth billions of dollars, armed forces, secret and open police, all supposedly ready for use, crumble in the face of periodic, rising, peaceful mass demonstrations and strikes? Scholars in the field of Middle Eastern studies are now accustomed to being asked: Was this revolution religious, political, social, economic,—or what? The only good answer seems to be that it was all of these; as will be discussed in this study, economic, social, and political discontents had developed over the decades and coalesced in the past few years, while added to the central Islamic identity felt by the majority of the popular classes were new interpretations of religion that justified revolutionary ideas and became widespread in society.

Several long-term factors in Iranian history have contributed to political and social development down to the present. Among these are geographical characteristics that, as in much of the Middle East, favored the early development of settled agriculture (as the clearing of massive forests and use of the heavy plow so vital in Europe were not necessary). On the other hand, as in much of the Middle East, irrigation led to salination of the soil and deforestation to erosion, so that agricultural difficulties and aridity almost surely increased over the

1

centuries, which encouraged a pastoral nomadic adaptation to arid conditions. Economic fluctuations based in part on geographic conditions also gave rise to rebellions, and in recent times inappropriate imitation of Western agricultural methods led to further ecological deterioration.

Iran's location has for centuries been important to international trade and strategy. It borders on the Soviet Union to the north, Iraq and Turkey to the west, the Persian Gulf to the south, and Afghanistan and Pakistan to the east. Iran encompasses about 628,000 square miles, a far larger area than that of any Western European country, but much of this is now desert, including the two huge eastern deserts, the Dasht-e Lut and the Dasht-e Kavir. Most of Iran is a high plateau strewn with mountains, the two major ranges being the Alborz in the north and the Zagros from the northwest toward the southeast. Seasonal extremes of hot and cold prevail throughout most of the country, and Iran is predominantly dry. The regions touching the Caspian Sea in the north, however, have high rainfall; the province of Gilan has among the highest in the world. This allows for a dense and organized peasant population, which encourages a more rebellious peasantry than where peasant population is sparse and scattered.

Since very ancient times, many different peoples have lived in Iran. The word "Iran" is a cognate of "Aryan"; these words were used by that branch of the Indo-European peoples who migrated southeast before 1000 B.C., the Iranians staying in Iran and the Aryans going on to India. (Persia was the Greek name for Iran, taken from the southwestern province of Fars; Reza Shah did not change the name of the country in the 1930s; rather he asked foreigners to use the indigenous name.) Iran had an important history and culture before the rise of Islam, with two major dynasties, the Achemenian, 559–330 B.C., and the Sasanian, A.D. 224–651, the latter lasting until Iran's conquest by the Muslim Arabs from A.D. 637 to 651. (In this book "Iran" denotes a land with about Iran's current boundaries; after the Muslim conquest, only the Mongols, the Safavids (1501–1722), and rulers since 1796 united this territory as one kingdom.)

Pre-Islamic Iran was fruitful in the development of religions, some of whose ideas and social content continued into Islamic times. The complex and varied religion called Zoroastrianism was characterized by a dualistic struggle between a good deity and an evil power in which the good was to win; and it also encompassed beliefs about rewards and punishments in the afterlife and interceding angels. Many scholars think Zoroastrianism influenced Judaism, Christianity, and Islam. Another type of dualism, viewing matter as evil and spirit as good and praising renunciation of this world, characterized Manichaeism founded in Iraq (then an Iranian culture area) by the third century A.D. prophet Mani. The negative Manichaean attitude toward this world has been seen by some scholars as reflecting economic decline and inequities and the growth of a rigid class system. Manichaeans both before and after the rise of Islam were considered dangerous heretics and were often persecuted by rulers. A more radical Iranian offshoot of Manichaeism in the fifth and sixth centuries was founded by Mazdak, who is said to have preached communism of goods and, along with his large body of followers, revolted against the class rigidities, poverty, wars, and economic decline that characterized his period (and ultimately rendered the Muslim conquest of Iran relatively easy).

Themes of righteous battles between the forces of good and justice and those of evil and oppression, of the economically oppressed and their oppressors, thus go far back into pre-Islamic as well as Islamic times, as does emulation of martyr figures, who are found in the great pre-Islamic Iranian religions. Because of the nature of the documents that have survived, and also of the doctrinal interests of scholars, we know much more about religious doctrines than about the details of socioeconomic life in the past. Even religious documents carefully studied, however, can tell a great deal about the injustices and inequalities that sometimes aroused people centuries ago, much as they do today, to risk their lives for a better world. In the early Islamic centuries several social revolts combined pre-Islamic with Islamic ideas in Iran.

In some ways Iran's recent "Islamic Revival" is very new, with ideas never voiced before. In other ways it follows a long tradition in both Iran and in the Muslim world of expressing socioeconomic and cultural grievances in the only way familiar to most people—a religious idiom arraying the forces of good against the forces of evil and promising to bring justice to the oppressed.

Islam and Society

In Iran as elsewhere, the so-called Islamic Revival does not mean that
most people are more religious than they used to be: for the majority the
degree of religiosity shows no sign of significant change. Rather, it
means that Islam is reentering politics and government in a stronger
and more militant way than it had in most areas for many decades. Very
traditional Muslim governments are not part of this trend, as they are
not becoming notably more religious in orientation than they ever have
been. In terms of governments, when discussing this revival one may
speak in 1981 of some governments by military men, including radical
Libya and conservative Pakistan, which make differing appeals to
Islamic law and ideals. The Saudi Arabian monarchy has had a strict
Islamic raison d'être ever since its eighteenth-century beginnings.
Within this general trend, however, Iran is, to date, a special case, as it
was not a king or a colonel who proclaimed Islamic ideology, but rather
a leader of the regular Islamic *ulama* (a word inadequately rendered by
"clergy," as their role is not to intercede between people and God, but
to carry out Muslim law, eduction, charity, and so forth—a broader
role than that of the Western clergy). This difference between Iran's
religiopolitical movement and that of other Muslim countries (including those, like Egypt and Turkey, where the movement is a broad
oppositional one and not in power) is based in part on the contrast
between the way the two main divisions in Islam, the Shi'is of Iran and
the Sunnis who rule most of the rest of the Muslim world, have
developed. We speak here of development because there has been much
more change and development in both Sunni and Shi'i theory and
practice than is usually realized, and specifically because many points
often made about Shi'ism are really only, or mainly, true during the
past century or two. Although not nearly enough research has been
done to allow any scholar to give a complete history of the relations
between religion and politics in either Shi'ism or Sunnism, enough has
been done to allow a general outline that suggests the directions of
change in Sunnism and in Shi'ism. Some elements in recent Shi'i
politics hark back to the earliest period of Islam, and so some understanding of that period, as well as of later Shi'i history, is necessary to
the understanding of more recent events.

The intertwining of religion and politics, found in several religions, began in Islam with the Prophet Mohammad himself. Among his revelations, later gathered together in the Quran, were a large number that would generally be called political and/or legal. Particularly after the Prophet's migration from his home city of Mecca, where he met opposition, at the invitation of notables of the nearby Arabian city of Medina, which he increasingly ruled, Mohammad received governmental and legal revelations. He led his community politically as well as religiously. After his death in A.D. 632, most of his adherents followed the rule of the first three caliphs, or successors, who had in theory no power to alter the revealed religion. A minority felt that succession belonged to Mohammad's cousin and son-in-law Ali (Mohammad having had no living sons), and this originally political claim within a few generations took on religious content. The group who recognized elected caliphs but without granting them religious powers beyond the protection and spreading of Islam came to be called Sunnis (followers of the practice or *sunna* of the Prophet). The party or "Shi'a" of Ali insisted on the charismatic leadership of the male descendants of Ali and were called the Shi'is (adjective) or Shi'a (noun) and developed a variety of doctrines. At first the split was not as clear-cut as it was later made to seem. Ali was chosen as the fourth caliph, and is still revered by the Sunnis, but he succumbed, through battle, arbitration, and assassination, to the founder of the Umayyad caliphate (661–749). This was the first Sunni caliphate to adopt, in practice, hereditary succession, and was castigated by many pious Muslims, both Sunni and Shi'i, as an illegitimate despotism.

Behind these and later doctrinal developments were sociopolitical changes discussed by recent scholars. The most plausible theory regarding the seventh-century rise of Islam notes that Mecca and Medina, as relatively advanced trading and agricultural cities outside the direct sphere of the Byzantine and Sasanian Empires, were at the point of state formation and needed an ideology to help unify the urban populace and the nomadic tribes around them into a state. Within Mecca and Medina class divisions were replacing tribal solidarity and tribes no longer provided for their weak members. In Mecca the rise and fall of merchant fortunes and the development of a complex, class-divided economy demanded the creation of a legal and welfare system. A full explanation would be more complex, but these factors help explain the rise of Islam and its rapid conquest or winning over of Arabian tribes. In addition, the weakening of both Byzantine and Persian Empires through exacerbated class divisions, persecution of religions considered heretical, and frequent mutual warfare left Arab areas unusually free of their influence.[1] Once Arab tribes adopted Islam they were bound no longer to engage in the raids that had kept population down and helped support many tribes. Tribes were still equipped for warfare and sought to make up what they had lost in raids. Mohammad's spreading of his religion and rule through wars against nearby tribes and the Meccans gave Islam a warlike precedent and theory, suggested by the word *jihad* or holy war. Contrary to what many believe, jihad was not meant to force conversion, and it appears that the concept of non-Arab Muslims did not occur to the earliest Muslims. Rather jihad aimed at extending the territory ruled by Muslims, while allowing inhabitants who were "People of the Book" (monotheists with a scripture) to keep their own religion in return for a special tax. This policy allowed the Arab Muslim armies to offer religious freedom to large Christian groups in greater Syria and Egypt treated as heretics by the Byzantine rulers, and hence to attain peaceful surrender from many Near Eastern cities. This, along with the internal conflicts and problems in the great empires, and the tactical superiority and enthusiasm of Arab armies, helps explain the expansion of these armies in a few decades as far as Spain in the west and Pakistan in the east.

The Arab armies' camp cities soon attracted local populations, whether Iranian, Egyptian, Iraqi, or other, and among them the demand arose for conversion to Islam. Along with conversion and contact there entered into some Muslim groups ideas with Iranian, Christian, Jewish, Manichaean, or other provenance. The Shi'is, who originally had few doctrinal differences with the Sunnis, were, as an oppositional group, more open to outside influences.

After the death of Ali and the resignation of a claim to rule by his first son, Hasan, Ali's second son, Hosain, put forth claims to leadership, but, with a small band of followers was massacred by an armed force under the orders of the Umayyad caliph Yazid in A.D. 680. This event, occurring on the tenth day (Ashura) of the first month (Moharram) of the Muslim year, became the great day of mourning and commemoration of the martyrdom of Hosain, with the previous nine days building up to it. One of Hosain's sons who survived was able to carry on the line of Shi'i leaders (imams), who were increasingly regarded by their followers as infallible.

Under the Umayyads began the religiopolitically sectarian character of Shi'ism. Various groups paid allegiance to different branches of Ali's descendants, or to men who invoked their name in leading revolts, often against the Umayyad caliphs. Certain ideas entered into Shi'ism more than Sunnism that Sunnis and moderate Shi'is labeled as "extremist," such as the incarnation of divinity in the imams, transmigration, and especially messianism. The *Mahdi* or "rightly guided one," who is not found in the Quran, entered particularly into Shi'ism, and Sunnism to a lesser degree, as the figure who will come at the end of time "to fill the world with justice and equity as it is now filled with injustice and oppression." This tag line suggests the social base of messianism: it appealed especially to the uprooted masses and lower middle classes who longed for the equity promised by the Quran but not realized under imperfect governments ruling for one or another social elite. A series of small Shi'i and semi-Shi'i revolts was crushed but Shi'i ideals remained.

The growing unpopularity of the Umayyads, who were closely tied to an early Arab aristocratic group and did not meet the needs of either the middle or the popular classes, led to an underground anti-Umayyad (Abbasid) movement in the first half of the eighth century that included Shi'i elements. Its propaganda was carried out so as to make Shi'is believe that Ali's descendants would come to power if the movement succeeded, but when the Abbasids overthrew the Umayyads in A.D. 749, the new caliphs were not in any Shi'i line and many Shi'i movements were suppressed.

Under the Abbasids (749–1256) the three different lines of Shi'ism that are considered its main divisions took shape. The smallest, moderate group, today predominant only in North Yemen, are the Zaidis or "Fivers," who revere their Fifth Imam. They follow a legal system similar to the Sunnis' and do not claim infallibility for their imams, which could bring conflict with the Sunni caliphs. The larger groups are the "Seveners" or Isma'ilis, and the "Twelvers" or Imamis. These two lines reflect a split in opinion over the legitimate successor to the great Sixth Imam, Ja'far as-Sadeq. The Isma'ilis, who opted for one son, Isma'il, do not believe that he was the last imam, but rather have a continuous line of living imams (although there are disagreements about which is the true line); and in one large group of Isma'ilis the line is alive in the person of the Agha Khan. In the early centuries the Isma'ilis were often radical, especially the Carmathian group of Isma'ilis who had a semicommunist ideology that served for a time as the basis of a state. Another Isma'ili group set up the Fatimid caliphate, which conquered Egypt in 969 and became a rival of the Abbasids. Emerging from the Fatimids was a group known in Europe under the pejorative nickname of "Assassins," although their attempts to reshape Muslim society in the eleventh to thirteenth centuries went beyond the idea of killings as a way to gain power. They lost much power after they were suppressed by the Mongols after the thirteenth-century Mongol invasions.[2]

The Twelver Shi'is followed the descendants of a more moderate son of Ja'far as-Sadeq. The Twelvers believe that the infant son of the Eleventh Imam went into "occultation" in the ninth century leaving behind four successive interpreters of his will. After the death of the fourth, during the "greater occultation" (which continues to the present), there is no infallible interpreter of the Twelfth Imam's will until he reappears as the Mahdi to institute the realm of perfection and justice. Twelver Shi'is and many Western scholars have generally believed that before the occultation there was a unified Shi'i community following the imams, and many also believe that from the time of the occultation trained theologians have been recognized as the best interpreters of the Twelfth Imam's will during his absence. Recently both these views have been challenged. Regarding the preoccultation period, W. M. Watt sees no evidence of a united Twelver community or doctrine, but finds rather a variety of views, with no large unified group giving politicoreligious allegiance to the successive imams.[3] Various views existed even after the disappearance of the infant imam. The doctrine of occultation, which became orthodox, was first put forth by a wealthy Shi'i leader in the Abbasid court in Baghdad. At first this doctrine may have been a way to avoid the consequences of the idea that the imam was both visible and infallible, implying that the imam's orders took precedence over the caliph's. The doctrine of occultation may, in its first phases, have been a way for Shi'is to compromise with the reality of Sunni power, and in this first period Twelver Shi'is in fact tended to be politically quietist and to compromise with Sunni governments. The belief that any orderly government was about equally acceptable (or unacceptable) in the absence of the Twelfth Imam could, however, become a two-edged sword.[4] In more recent periods of hostility between the Shi'i ulama and rulers it was used to assert the illegitimacy of any temporal government, and over time claims began that the ulama were more qualified than temporal rulers to interpret the will of the Twelfth Imam, and hence had superior political claims.

In Abbasid times, however, the blunt side of the sword generally was felt. Not only was the doctrine of occultation put forth by Shi'is in Abbasid service, but the main religious split for most of the Abbasid period was more between the Isma'ilis, who in their various political incarnations often tried to undermine or overthrow the Abbasids, and the Sunni Abbasids allied with the Twelver Shi'is on the other. The one significant dynasty of the Abbasid period with Twelver Shi'i leanings, the Buyids (945–1055), held the Abbasid capital of Baghdad but never tried to abolish the caliphate or to establish Twelver Shi'ism. Hence, Twelver Shi'ism during this period was very different from the militant movement that came to power in Iran under the Safavid dynasty in 1501.

It should be stressed that the idea common among some Muslims and Western Orientalists, that Shi'ism is peculiarly Iranian, has no basis before 1501. Before then, although there were many Iranian Shi'is, the great majority of Shi'is were non-Iranian and the majority of Iranians were Sunni. The Zaidi, Isma'ili, and Carmathian Shi'is are still found mostly outside Iran; the great majority of Shi'i dynasties were outside Iran, with only the Buyids as a major partial pre–1501 exception; and the great majority of Iranian dynasties have been Sunni. This is not to deny the profound modern identification of Iranians with Shi'ism, but only to note that this, like many other "traditional" phenomena, is more recent than is usually imagined. The legendary marriage of Imam Hosain with a Sasanian princess, which has no historical basis, was useful in cementing the identification of Iran with Shi'ism, but such legends are usually available when needed.

In the centuries of the greater occultation there was considerable development of Twelver Shi'i thought and law which, prior to the establishment of Twelver Shi'ism as Iran's state religion in 1501, was carried out mostly outside Iran. For relations between religion and politics perhaps the most important development was that of the *mujtahid*. In Sunni Islam it was widely held that after an early date all fundamental legal principles had been decided on the basis of the Quran, the reported words and practices of the Prophet (*hadith*), and the consensus of scholar-jurists, and that there was no more room for new judgments based on the effort (*ijtihad*) of a qualified jurist. New decrees and interpretations continued to be made, but they remained within the traditional framework and had not the same status as the early lawbooks or hadiths. In Twelver Shi'ism the early centuries had not, in theory, seen the need for juridical effort and interpretation that was felt in Sunnism, as only the imams could give correct, indeed infallible, opinions on all subjects. With the disappearance of the imams, however, the Twelvers were in a position roughly parallel to that of the very early Sunnis; the source of infallible legal judgment had disappeared and yet issues continued to arise on which some trustworthy judgment, even if fallible, was desired. To meet this need there gradually developed mujtahids: legal and theological scholars whose intelligence, training, and following qualified them to make judgments on a range of questions. Although their judgments were fallible, and they lacked the divine qualities of the imams, by their learning and response to popular needs they commanded a respect that increased over time.

While these developments were taking place within the body of learned Twelver Shi'ism, particularly in Asian Arab states, there were different developments with a Twelver Shi'i tinge in Iran, Anatolia (Turkey), and Syria, which ultimately had an impact on "orthodox" Twelver Shi'ism. If from Abbasid times on it was often hard to draw a political line, and certainly not one of enmity, between Twelver Shi'ism and Sunnism, their intermixture appears in a new way among several fourteenth- and fifteenth-century movements, usually with a strong mystical or "extremist" bent. Among these are the Hurufi movement originating in Iran and based largely on a mystical letter-number symbolism; the Bektashi religious order, which became the order of the Ottoman Jannisary crops, and incorporated respect for the twelve imams, Hurufi symbolism, and some Sunni, Turkic, and Christian elements.[5] A number of other orders combined Shi'i and Sunni elements, often along with some of local popular origin, and such groups still exist in various Muslim countries. Such groups were growing in Iran, the Ottoman Empire, and Syria in the fourteenth and fifteenth centuries, even though all these areas were officially Sunni. The intermixture and political cooperation between some Twelver Shi'is and Sunnis before 1501 facilitated the growth of groups combining Shi'i and Sunni ideas. The transformation of some of these diverse groups, many of which expressed popular grievances and provided ideologies for nomad and peasant revolts, into a powerful political movement took place under the leadership of a popular Iranian Sufi (mystic) order, the Safavids. Originally a quietist Sunni order centering in Ardebil, East Azerbaijan, and with ties to the fourteenth-century Mongol rulers, its leaders became militant warriors following a kind of Twelver Shi'ism in the mid-fifteenth century after travels among Anatolian nomadic tribes. The Shi'ism of these Safavids was of the militant "extremist" type reminiscent of the earliest Shi'is; a belief in divine incarnation was important, the Safavid leaders were considered divine, and egalitarianism was strong. Like other Muslim dynasties that came to power at the head of religious "extremists" (such as the Abbasids and Fatimids), the Safavids, soon after gaining power in Tabriz, began to moderate their views and search for orthodox Shi'i books and leaders. An early account relates that the first Safavid ruler of Iran, Isma'il, after entering Tabriz in 1501, ordered a search for an orthodox Shi'i religious book, but that in all Tabriz only one such book could be found.[6] Although this must be exaggerated, as other reports say there were many Shi'is in Tabriz, it suggests how little Isma'il, his followers, or most Tabrizis had contact with official Shi'ism. The Safavid rulers soon turned their doctrine, which they may not have known was different from learned Twelver Shi'ism, from one suitable for popular, enthusiastic, egalitarian revolt and conquest into one suitable for stable, conservative rule. They turned their backs increasingly on their tribal followers, seen with some reason as anarchic (armed nomadic tribespeople have often hindered centralized control), and succeeded in enlisting men from the old Persian bureaucracy, and imported some of the official Twelver theologians from nearby Arabic-speaking lands.

Under the first Safavid rulers such theologians, who were paid directly or indirectly by the government and had few ties with the local population, were a firm pillar of political support. Extremist ideas were

increasingly suppressed, and by late Safavid times the word *Sufi,* which
had once designated a supporter of the Safavids, became a term of
opprobrium as Sufi orders were suppressed as a danger to the state and
the official religion. More than most Islamic dynasties the Safavids
worked for conversion to their branch of Islam and for ideological
conformity. Isma'il demanded that all preachers and mollas publicly
curse the first three (Sunni) caliphs, usurpers of the place of Ali, and
this "loyalty-oath mentality" remained characteristic of many Safavid
rulers. One of the main reasons for such rigor by Isma'il and his
followers was to give Iran ideological distinction and identity vis-à-vis
its (Sunni) military-political enemies, the Ottoman Empire and, for a
time, the Central Asian Uzbeks. Isma'il came to power on the eve of
Ottoman expansion into the Near East by Sultan Selim. The Anatolian
tribes who helped the Safavids were hostile to the Ottoman government
both because they resisted centralization and for religio-ideological
reasons. Isma'il must have considered a new affirmation of the differences between Twelver Shi'ism and Sunnism to be important in
creating ideological identity in Iran as a rampart against the Sunni
Ottomans. (Some speak of the Safavids as setting up a national state but
this is anachronistic; not only were the socioeconomic preconditions of
modern nationalism not present, but there was no national or ethnic
content to the Safavids' ideology. Isma'il, for example, habitually
wrote in Turkish and his enemy, Sultan Selim, in Persian.)

In 1511–12 Selim launched a violent campaign against the Shi'i
"fifth column" in Anatolia, killing thousands and resettling many
more. Then he sent armies to invade Iran, defeating Isma'il at the
Battle of Chaldiran in 1514, but then turned back, partly because of
overextended supply lines and a hard winter, but perhaps also owing to
disaffection among his janissaries who might have felt some identity
with Twelver Shi'is. This was only one of several wars between the
Iranians and the Ottomans, a long struggle providing continual encouragement for the Safavids to strengthen the Shi'i identity of Iran.
Although conversion was not as rapid as Isma'il's forcible policies
might suggest, the vast majority of Iranians did identify strongly with
Shi'ism by the end of the Safavid era in 1722 (an end brought on by
Afghan Sunni invaders).

Little socioeconomic research has been done on the Safavids, but it
appears that by the fourteenth and fifteenth centuries Iran was begin-

ning to recover from the ravages of prior invasions and to find a system
of accommodation to a large nomadic population that could be termed
"tribal feudalism," if one uses the term broadly, recognizing the
absence of serfdom and a manorial system. Under this system military
power was largely in the hands of tribal leaders, who also held revenue
rights to and often administered large peasant and sometimes even
urban populations. Most of the nomads spoke languages other than
Persian, either as descendants of invaders or as longstanding autonomous groups (like the Kurds). Ever since the eleventh-century Seljuq
conquest of Iran, Turkic languages were predominant among rulers,
who were all of nomadic origin or, in the Safavid case, brought to power
by nomads. Nomadic or nomad-backed dynasties included two
fifteenth-century Turkmen dynasties who preceded the Safavids; the
Safavids themselves; various eighteenth-century rulers; and the
nineteenth-century Qajars. However, all major dynasties made use of a
Persian-speaking bureaucratic class with long experience in administration and tax collection. One secret of Safavid success was their early
enlistment of this class and of Persian landlords and merchants, which
involved moving away from the egalitarianism of their early tribal
followers.

The Safavids also benefited from the desire of several European states
for any ally against the Ottomans, which encouraged diplomatic and
trade relations. Even before the Safavid victory there were Western
diplomats and traders in Iran, and relations increased under the
Safavids. The great Safavid Shah Abbas (1587–1629) encouraged
international trade through building roads, caravansarais, and workshops to produce the luxury textiles and ceramics demanded in the
West. Silk was the main export. Disruption by military tribes, the low
level of agricultural production, and the gradual change of Western
trade routes to the Far East from overland to overseas, however,
contributed to economic decline, reflected in political decline, and to
easy conquest by Afghans in 1722. Frequent wars with the Ottomans
also took an economic toll.

An important, seldom studied aspect of premodern social history is
the position of women. The Quran allows polygamy of up to four
wives, provided there is equal treatment for all. It also permits easy
divorce for the husband, and there are a few other unequal measures.
On the other hand it provides for a woman to inherit property (half the

amount granted a man). It does not legislate veiling, a practice that existed in the Byzantine and Sasanian Empires and spread from them to Muslim Arabs. Once veiling spread, two vague Quranic verses were interpreted to sanction veiling. Veiling and seclusion were apparently characteristic of the well-to-do urban classes and did not extend to the majority of women.

The position of Muslim women varied more by time and place than is generally realized, as reports from travelers and scholars regarding the early Safavid period indicate. One scholar concludes that Islamicized Turkish and Mongol women were much freer than the older settled populations and that men and women danced together in the Bektashi order and elsewhere. More dramatic information comes from an Italian traveler at the time of Shah Isma'il, who writes: "The Persian ladies themselves follow in arms the same fortunes as their husbands, and fight like men, in the same way as those ancient Amazons who performed such feats of arms in their time." Another Italian description from the same period says that women wear costumes open at the breast, show their bodies, and are wanton. He appears not to be talking about prostitutes, whom he discusses separately regarding the taxes they pay the government. One more Italian description says that women "wear robes of silk, veils on their heads, and show their faces openly." There seems to be no evidence of the top-to-toe veiling found in late nineteenth-century urban Iran; and the evidence of Safavid miniatures suggests that women dressed colorfully and attractively, with headcoverings as partial and diaphanous as among Iranian tribal women today. By the late seventeenth century, however, Chardin says that women covered all but face, hands, and feet, were very closely guarded, and that upper-class women were idle.[7] Perhaps growing religious "orthodoxy" was tied to increased seclusion of women, as such seclusion has in various periods been considered Islamic.

It is rarely appreciated that the Safavid experience largely created the clear line of political demarcation and hostility between Twelver Shi'ism and Sunnism, even though doctrinal differences had long been recognized. Before the Safavids, as noted, while the Sevener Shi'is were clearly marked off from the Sunnis, who often considered them politically dangerous, the Twelvers for many centuries had mostly accommodated themselves politically to the Sunnis, and numerous religious movements combined Twelver and Sunni ideas.

The aggressive insistence of Isma'il and many of his followers on cursing the first three caliphs (who were regarded by Sunnis as, along with Ali, the holiest "rightly guided" caliphs); forcible conversions of Iranian Sunnis to Shi'ism; and persecutions of Ottoman Shi'is seen as a Safavid fifth column resulted in a clear politico-religious split between Sunnis and Twelver Shi'is. From Safavid times through the nineteenth century each group considered itself to be the true Muslims, with the other group often seen as heretics and enemies, and Safavid Shahs and Ottoman Sultans exchanged insults along these lines.[8]

Most pre-Safavid theological Shi'ism was not highly political, and tended to take the lack of any fully legitimate government in the absence of imams as a sign that existing governments, whether Sunni or Shi'i, could be obeyed. This official Shi'ism was centered in a few Arabic-speaking territories that did not border on the pre-sixteenth-century Ottoman Empire. In areas that did border on the empire or were part of it, as in northern Syria, western Anatolia, and bordering eastern Iran, religious movements classified as Twelver Shi'i because of their devotion to the twelve imams remind us more of some of the "extremist" sects earlier associated with Isma'ili (Sevener), Shi'ism. Incarnation of the divinity in leaders, egalitarianism, and warlike militancy against "heretical" regimes characterized these groups both before and during the rise of the Safavids. Safavid Shi'ism in power stressed the Shi'i law and theology brought in by jurists and theologians partly imported by the Safavid shahs, and also incorporated other elements favorable to the rulers' political position and social convervatism. Few of these elements were tied to the "extremist" religious ideas that had helped bring the Safavids to power. Among "extremist" elements not suppressed was a stress on the semidivine powers of the ruler himself, which in the case of Isma'il and his successor Tahmasp were often considered actually divine by the Safavids' followers. Divine claims were frequent in extremist Islamic movements, and had been voiced regarding several pre-Safavid religious rebels by groups in Anatolia, where the Safavids got their military start. The Safavids, as part of their Twelver ideology, also claimed descent from the Seventh Imam (meaning every preceding imam), which gave them impeccable Twelver credentials. Research has shown that the earliest writings about the Safavids put forth no such claim, but it was inserted later into existing and subsequent works in order, clearly, to shore up the Safavids'

politico-religious claims. Western travelers noted the divine worship of
their rulers by the Safavids' followers, particularly the fighting tribes.[9]
Claims to divinity or incarnation are against the doctrines of Islamic
orthodoxy, both Sunni and Twelver Shi'i, which stress the strict unity
of God. As time went on and orthodox teachings were increasingly
propagated, the divine claims of the Safavids were muted, but their
claims to descent from an important imam continued to give them a
religious aura not held by any subsequent Iranian dynasty.

The theology of pre-Safavid and Safavid Shi'ism has not been
sufficiently studied to be summarized, but something may be said
about the changing role of religious leaders, which bears upon later
politico-religious developments. During and immediately after the
Safavid rise there were high officials, largely from among the Safavids'
original backers, who combined military, political, and religious functions in a way that recalled their origin in a militant sectarian movement that had no specific religious functionaries, and apparently no
Shi'i texts to teach. Soon after taking power, however, the Safavid
rulers entrusted thologians and jurists with various religious roles,
while decreasing the religious duties of other high officials. In the early
Safavid period the theologians and their followers and progeny were
dependent on the financial and political largesse of the shahs, and they
understandably did not give the shahs political or ideological trouble.
This conciliatory position was easy for these ulama to maintain in
periods when shahs did not flout Islamic law or treat them badly and
when, as through the early seventeenth century, the shahs seem to have
been mostly popular and to have contributed to the economic well-
being of Iran.

Over time, however, the factors conducive to an alliance between
court and ulama changed. Economic bases for ulama independence of
the shahs grew; these were not all specifically Shi'i, but in the last few
centuries they have operated more strongly in Iran than elsewhere.
Throughout the Muslim world Muslims may make bequests of their
property or money as *vaqf* (inalienable endowment). There are two
general kinds of vaqf, sometimes called charitable or religious, and
private. Charitable vaqf is given for institutions like schools, hospitals,
mosques, and shrines, all of which are controlled and administered by
ulama. All add to the wealth and power of what we may loosely call the

"church," as well as providing posts for men with religious training. Private vaqf income usually goes to the donor's descendants (it is often used to avoid the strictly regulated inheritance shares laid down in the Quran), but even here a guardian from the ulama is required, and this guardian is paid from the vaqf income. As vaqf is, in theory, inalienable, it should have grown ever larger over the centuries; in fact it tended, even before modern changes, to be subject to confiscation. Under a long-lived dynasty like the Safavids that wished to stress its own piety and itself made vaqf contributions, the size of vaqf property and the number of ulama and religious students supported by it grew considerably. Such inalienable income gave the ulama a strong economic base from which some of its members could, if so inclined, bite the hand that fed them.

More specific to Shi'ism was the ulama's success down to the present in keeping direct control of certain religious taxes, the so-called *khums* (one-fifth) and *zakat* (alms), and not having them pass through the hands of the government. Although this has been little studied for Safavid times, it is known that later the ulama were able to use a combination of moral and minor physical pressure to collect, especially from the merchants and other well off bazaar traders and artisans, the khums. Most of this was supposed to go for welfare and charity, but as these include the support of poor students and sayyeds (men claiming descent from Mohammad) and payment of employees of welfare institutions, the taxes brought a significant net increase in the wealth and power of the religious classes.

With the increasing wealth of the Safavid ulama, the development of a growing ulama of local Iranian origin, and the creation of intellectual and material conditions for the ulama to be increasingly independent of the state, there also grew up a division between two kinds of ulama that, in general, has lasted. On the one hand there were government-appointed and -supported ulama who filled official religious posts, including the *imam jom'eh* or leader of the chief Friday prayer of each city, and various judicial figures. On the "nonofficial" side were those who fulfilled no governmental functions but taught, preached, and made judgments in ulama-run institutions and courts, receiving their income from vaqf revenues and the gifts of their followers. The most learned of the ulama, who had reached the highest level in their studies, became *mujtahids,* who were capable, if they attracted a following, of giving authoritative interpretations on questions of religious law. In Safavid times there were very few mujtahids, but there was gradually an "inflation of honors" so that first the number of mujtahids, and recently that of ayatollahs (originally the leading mujtahids but now encompassing many older mujtahids) expanded greatly over time. The most important function of a Shi'i mujtahid was to exert ijtihad to give new interpretations of law and doctrine in response to new questions. Although the Sunni ulama outside Iran in fact made some new interpretations, the latitude for Shi'i ulama to do this was greater. Like other differences between Sunnis and Twelver Shi'is, the power of the mujtahid to interpret doctrine is not a "purely" doctrinal one but has roots in the greater socioeconomc strength and independence of the Iranian ulama and also in the decentralization of power in Iran, owing to great difficulties of communication, sparse and scattered population, and the independent power of nomadic tribes.

In late Safavid times some mujtahids claimed that they had more right to rule than did the impious, wine-bibbing shahs. They did not yet say they should rule directly, an idea that came forth only with Ayatollah Khomaini, but that the shah should carry out their rulings when given and defend the nation militarily.[10] The political claims of the Iranian ulama developed further from the eighteenth century on.

Another feature of Safavid Shi'ism was the greater development of theology under the Safavids than under contemporary Sunni dynasties. This was largely due to the fact that the Safavids were the first state to patronize Twelver Shi'ism; there was a need to put Shi'i ideas into Persian in order to make them more accessible; and also to deal with new questions arising form the existence of a Twelver state. Along with the development of theology there was also a flowering of philosophy based on combinations of Greek philosophy, mysticism, and Shi'ism. In much of the Muslim world philosophy flourished in the tenth and eleventh centuries A.D., after which it was increasingly suppressed, but in the East, especially Iran, there was a virtually uninterrupted philosophical tradition. Muslim philosophy was based on Aristotelian and/or Platonic and Neoplatonic philosophy, which Muslim philosophers often tried to show as compatible with Islam and the Quran. When philosophy and the Quran seemed in conflict the Quran was interpreted "allegorically" to conform with the natural law themes of philosophy. Iran was the home of such philosophical giants as Avicenna and Nasir ad-Din Tusi, some of whose works have continued to be taught in religious schools down to the present. The Safavid period gave impetus to new efforts of Shi'i philosophers to reconcile Greek philosophy specifically with Shi'ism. Iranian philosophy of the past several centuries is sometimes called "theosophy" because it incorporates a more mystical and religious element than does the philosophy of such early giants as al-Farabi, Averroes, or Avicenna, but some recent scholars have overstated the religious and theosophical element of later figures and understated their natural law rationalism. Great Safavid philosophers like Mir Damad and Molla Sadra were attacked in their own times, and many of the orthodox considered Greek style philosophy dangerous and its practitioners, who were themselves ulama, as claimants to usurp the role of more conventional ulama. The philosophers represented a small intellectual elite, whereas the masses and bazaar classes generally followed the more traditional ulama, as they still do.

One reason, rarely noted, why Shi'is were more open to philosophical rationalism than Sunnis is that Shi'i theology was based on a system of thought closer to Greek philosophical and natural law concepts than was Sunni theology. In the early Abbasid period the Mu'tazilite theological school partly based on Greek ideas became predominant in Sunnism. Mu'tazilites put forth as their central idea the Unity and Justice of God. According to them justice ('adl) was a rational, comprehensible concept and God had to act in accordance with it. The implication that God was limited by natural law, along with other Mu'tazilite concepts, was rejected by more traditionalist Muslims, and another theological school, the Ash'arites, gradually won out among most Sunnis. The Ash'arite school rejected natural law, with some Ash'arites going so far as to say that God recreated the world each moment, so that there were no secondary causes, apparent causation being based on God's mercy to mankind. Twelver Shi'i theology, however, became predominantly Mu'tazilite, with a belief in natural law and earthly causation. In Ash'arite theory justice is, in general, what God chooses to do. Mu'tazilites sometimes say that God must follow the rules of justice; by implication whatever happens on earth that is unjust is the fault of men and women, not of God. Mu'tazilism, as the last point implies, also teaches free will. Although theology is less important is Islam than in Christianity, with teaching centering rather on law and on the Traditions of the Prophet and imams on which law is based, Shi'i theology as it trickled down through sermons and decrees may have had a political impact. The central concepts of justice and injustice or oppression (*'adl* and *zulm*), important to most believing Muslims, are of overwhelming importance to the Shi'is, and the idea that rulers who have abandoned *'adl* for zulm are following their own will, not God's, is natural to Shi'i thought.[11]

The last Safavid ruler, Shah Sultan Hosain, in the early eighteenth century enforced strict Shi'i orthodoxy; philosophers and Sufis were suppressed and orthodoxy enjoined. The internal decline of the Safavids made them easy prey to foreign invasion, however, in this case by Sunni tribal Afghans who sacked the capital, Isfahan, but ruled only from 1722 to 1730. The eighteenth century was to be one of decentralization, rule by tribal leaders, and economic decline. Significant developments, however, occurred in the religiopolitical field.

Religious developments in Iran now as before were tied to Iran's socioeconomic structure. Although Iran had been the seat of strong and prosperous states and empires in ancient times, agricultural decline and aridity apparently grew over centuries. Hence when Turkish nomadic tribes invaded Iran beginning in the eleventh century they did not, as had earlier nomadic invaders, settle or fit into interstices between settled areas, but rather, finding arid lands suitable for nomadism, spread that way of life. The spread of nomadism and decline of settled agriculture contributed to a kind of "tribal feudalism" in which tribal leaders provided the armies and were paid in rights to revenue collection. Real rule in many tribal, peasant, and even urban territories thus rested with tribal leaders and the central rulers had to rule indirectly, playing one urban or tribal faction off against another, and trying to keep on good terms with the ulama, whose ideological and economic power was growing. The strength of the Safavids depended in part on their encouragement and control of long-distance and foreign trade. With the development of overseas trade by Europeans and the decline of overland trade to Asia, however, Iran, aside from regions adjacent to the Persian Gulf, was increasingly bypassed. Eighteenth-century decentralization and tribal rule thus had some economic causes, and there seem to have been declines both in production and in international trade.

After the invasion of the Iranian and Shi'i capital of Isfahan by militant Sunni Afghans, the leaders of the Shi'i ulama moved to cities in Ottoman Iraq built around the tombs of the first imams—Najaf and Karbala. This area remained the center of Shi'i leadership from then until the late 1940s, and this gave the Shi'is a new advantage over the Suni ulama in their growing independence of the government. Financially independent in Iraq, the leading Shi'i ulama were not subject to economic or political pressure from the Iranian government. (Some analogy exists to the premodern popes, who had their own territory and could not be intimidated by temporal rulers; as contrasted with the Orthodox Christian leaders of Constantinople and Moscow, who were subservient to rulers in these capitals.)

In the late eighteenth century the power of the ulama was further increased by the outcome of a struggle between two schools of Shi'i thought—schools whose conflict now sharpened and, for most believers, concluded. The losing school was the *akhbaris,* who believed that each Shi'i could rely on, and interpret, the Traditions *(akhbar)* of the Prophet and imams, and hence ulama were not needed to interpret doctrine. This school represented those who wished to lessen the ulama's role (even though it was expressed by some of the ulama), and hence was unlikely to win out. (Gobineau speaks of nineteenth-century akhbaris as bourgeois, which seems probable.)[12] The winning school of *mujtahidis* or *usulis* said that mujtahids were needed to interpret the foundations *(usul)* of the faith. The role of the mujtahid was defined by saying that each believer must choose one mujtahid to follow as a "source of imitation," and that ordinary believers below the rank of mujtahid were not, as the akhbaris said they were, competent to interpret the faith. One must always be guided by a living mujtahid, whose rulings take precedence over those of a mujtahid who has died. Mujtahids, unlike the imams, were not infallible. The mujtahids strove, via their knowledge, to know the infallible will of the Twelfth Imam, but they might fail on particular points. The need to follow the rulings of a living mujtahid, who was less fallible than any temporal ruler, gave a basis for power in the hands of the mujtahids that was far greater than that of the Sunni ulama. There was now a clear doctrinal basis for appeals to the ulama over the head of a ruler, and for claims by the leading mujtahids to make political decisions, provided they touched on Islamic principles, independently of temporal rulers. These powers were increasingly used from the early nineteenth century on.

Another important mid-eighteenth-century development was Nader Shah's rise to power within Iran and foreign conquests. In part because he conquered Sunni lands to the east and had many Sunnis in his armies Nader tried to deinstitutionalize Shi'ism in Iran, and he confiscated Shi'i vaqfs on a large scale to the economic gain of his regime. He wished to make of Shi'ism a fifth orthodox (Sunni) school of law, but this idea was rejected by both sides and scarcely outlived his death in mid-century. By the mid-nineteenth century Shi'i vaqfs had become as extensive as before.

Although Shi'ism had been spread with much coercion, by the eighteenth century it was deeply and widely embraced by nearly all native Persian speakers in Iran as well as a numerical majority of its ethnic minorities. Within the Safavid and modern borders only ethnic minorities bordering on Sunni conationals abroad—most Kurds in the west, the Turkomans in the north, the Baluchis in the southeast and a minority of the Arabs of the southwest—remained Sunni. In addition there remained more scattered religious minorities: Jews, Armenian and Nestorian Christians, Zoroastrians, and the gnostic Sabeans on the Iraqi border, as well as the semi-Shi'i Ahl-e Haqq ("Ali Ilahis") centered among the Kurds.

The eighteenth century also saw the development of a new, more philosophic school of Shi'ism, the Shaikhi school. As their main political importance appeared in the nineteenth-century Babi movement, discussion will be limited to their role in the formation of that movement, below. In general the eighteenth century, though a period of economic decline, civil war, and decentralization, saw the development of several important politico-religious trends.

In the above summary treatment, only a few highlights of Iranian pre-Islamic and Islamic history could be noted, and stress has been placed on those that tie together religious and social movements in a way that provides some background for recent developments. It should be realized, however, that Iran also has a long history of cultural, scientific, political, and economic developments having little connection with religion, which occupy the pages of many lengthy histories. In the arts Iran has a continuous history of excellence in both poetry and the visual arts, best known in the West through Persian miniatures and carpets and through a felicitous translation of a second-rank poet and first-rank scientist, Omar Khayyam. Iran was virtually the only area in the first wave of Arab conquests that kept its own language rather than adopting Arabic (although the new Persian was and is written in Arabic script and is full of Arabic vocabulary). With the rise of local dynasties in Iran in the ninth through eleventh centuries, owing only theoretical obedience to the Abbasid caliphate, poetry and prose began to flourish in the new Persian language and feelings of special Iranian identity were often expressed. In addition to literary figures, the trained Persian bureaucracy helped keep alive such a Persian linguistic and cultural identity even when Turkish-speaking tribes ruled Iran. Cultural and governmental forces thus preserved an Iranian identity during the pre-Safavid centuries when there was rarely a single state covering the territory of today's Iran.

The development of Shi'ism in Iran gave some focus to feelings of a separate local identity. Until the twentieth century the Shi'i component of this identity was more important than the Iranian one, although it was often unnecessary to distinguish the two. From 1501 until this century, Iranism and Shi'ism were for many people parts of a single blend.

2 FOUNDATIONS OF
NINETEENTH-CENTURY IRAN

In addition to the factors just discussed, other forces were at work in nineteenth-century Iran shaping a political and socioeconomic situation that culminated in revolt and rebellion. During this period the economy and society were gradually transformed through interaction with the increasingly industrialized and imperialist West. Although earlier, via trade, the West had had an impact on Iran as on other Asian countries, the industrial revolution made the West a growing exporter of manufactured goods that could often be sold more cheaply than locally produced handicrafts and hence it undermined local handicraft production. This had partially disruptive socioeconomic effects. At the same time, Western demand for Asian raw materials grew, so that Asian countries increasingly became exporters of raw materials and importers of manufactures, to the detriment of many in the popular, artisan, and trading classes and to the benefit of some consumers, long-distance merchants, and landlords. These changes have not been studied in as much detail for Iran as they have for Egypt and India, but the trends were similar, if less dramatic owing to a lesser Western presence and trade.

Before entering into the vicissitudes of nineteenth-century Iranian politics we will discuss long-term forces at work in this period. Aside from the new strength of the Western politico-economic impact, most of the forces were related to those operating since about the eleventh century. At that time large-scale incursions of nomadic Turkish tribes associated with the invasion and rule of Iran by the Seljuq Turks strengthened the regional, semifeudal power of tribal and other military leaders and weakened central governments. Many nomadic tribes were almost autonomous, owing largely to their military power, and could obtain the products they did not produce themselves through trade with local villages and towns. They were difficult for a central government to control, especially in view of Iran's mountainous and arid terrain, lack of good communications, and dearth of navigable rivers. These factors contributed to considerable local autonomy even for non-nomadic groups in pre-twentieth-century Iran, and to frequent periods of decentralization, often under local tribal rulers, with only a few relatively centralized dynasties—the Seljuqs, Mongols, and Safavids. From the eleventh through the nineteenth centuries nomadic tribes essentially managed their own internal affairs, subject in centralized periods to tribute and pro forma confirmation of tribal leaders by rulers, and tribes often ruled over villagers or even townspeople who inhabited lands in their area.

Beyond this, the tribes constituted the best fighting forces in Iran—their mastery of horsemanship and of the latest weapons gave them a decisive advantage over townspeople, whom the shahs generally did not try to train militarily. The military advantage of the tribespeople probably increased in the eighteenth century, which may be one reason for eighteenth-century tribally based decentralization. In the Ottoman Empire, Iran, and elsewhere, the first introduction of firearms in the form of cannons strengthened the central government, which was the only force wealthy enough to afford cannons and a trained artillery. With the development of efficient handguns, however, small decentralized bands could make good use of them, especially if they owned horses and knew how to shoot from the saddle. Research in this area, and on the impact of trade with the West in the sixteenth through eighteenth centuries, is modifying the older view that the nineteenth-century impact of the West on the Middle East was sudden.[1]

Every important Iranian dynasty from the Buyids (945–1055) through the Qajars (1796–1925) was either tribal in origin or relied on tribal armies to take power. According to one estimate, nomadic tribes made up about half the Iranian population in the early nineteenth century and a quarter at the end of the century; if we make a very rough estimate that Iran's population doubled from about five million to ten million between 1800 and 1914, the absolute number of nomads remained about the same.[2] The impact of this large, semiautonomous, and militarily powerful group of tribes on Iranian life and politics has yet to be appreciated.

In periods of weak government or decentralization tribal or tribally based entities continue to assert their autonomy even today. Although there is no universally agreed-upon definition of what should be called a tribe, in general Iran's tribes identify themselves by distinctive words that translate as "tribe" or "tribal confederation" for their larger units and "clan" for a subunit, and they usually believe their tribes and clans to be related by family ties. Most Iranian tribes either practice, or once practiced, pastoral nomadism, which in Iran generally involves two main tribal migrations, from summer to winter quarters and back, dictated by the need for year-round pasture for their flocks. In addition, most tribes practice agriculture during the months of settlement. Tribal women, like most peasant women, are not veiled, and they usually do more physical labor than the men, including spinning, weaving, cooking, agriculture, and animal husbandry. There is considerable internal autonomy and decentralization among tribes, and the top leaders are needed mostly for war and for relations with the government and other outside groups. Among the important non-Persian ethnic groups in Iran having a partially or totally tribal nomadic background are: the Turkic speaking Turkomans (Sunni) in the north, Qashqa'is in Fars Province, and Shahsevans in Azerbaijan; the Kurds (mostly Sunni) in the west; the Lur speaking Bakhtiaris and Lurs between the Kurds and Qashqa'is; the Arabs in the southwest, the Baluchis (Sunni) in the southeast; and many other smaller tribes. Few tribespeople speak Persian as their first language and this intensifies the decentralizing potential of the tribes, as does the Sunnism of the Kurds, Baluchis, Turkomans, and a minority of Arabs who also have people of the same ethnic group adjacent to them across Iran's borders.[3] These four and the Shi'i Azerbaijani Turks have the most autonomist tendencies of all Iran's ethnic groups.

If tribal leaders with well-armed and devoted followers made up a major element of the Iranian ruling group, there were also other key, often overlapping, elements. Under the Qajars the strongest single ruling group was usually the court, headed by the shah and including legions of royal relatives, among whom the queen mother and favorite wife or wives were often very influential. Qajars were frequently named governors of provinces, including some royal women, whose appointments were, however, for the purpose of receiving revenue only. The central and regional treasurers (*mostaufis*) tended to be hereditary, using a private code writing and techniques that they kept in their families to perpetuate their monopoly. Nearly all offices in the rudimentary central and regional bureaucracy were bought (as they were in much of premodern Europe). As the government needed more money for Western arms and goods there developed a virtual yearly auction where governorships were usually given to the men who bid the most; tax collecting and other positions were also sold or subfarmed. This system, which had the advantage of giving the ruler or governor ready cash in advance, had the greater disadvantage for national prosperity of encouraging officials to overtax, since they were not sure they could hold their posts and hence were not concerned to leave the peasants enough to maintain fertility, investment, and productivity. There were exceptions to the yearly bidding, notably the governor generalship of the wealthy and strategic northwest province of Azerbaijan, which went to the crown prince, with real rule often under a minister; and some princes were governors elsewhere. Even in such areas taxes were increasingly used to extort as much as possible from the peasant majority.

A feature of the bureaucracy was the possibility of rising from humble origins within the royal household to a top position. Two major chief ministers of the long-ruling Naser ad-Din Shah (1848–96), Mirza Taqi Khan *Amir Kabir* and Mirza Hosain Khan *Moshir ad-Dauleh,* as well as the later longstanding chief minister Ali Asghar Khan *Amin as-Soltan* illustrate this;[4] the father of the first was a steward in the royal household, the grandfather of the second a bath attendant who rose in royal service, and the father of the latter a Georgian cup-bearer who rose in this service. (It is, however, wrong to draw conclusions about social mobility outside courtly circles from these examples. While Islam knows no aristocracy or other theoretical privileges based on birth, aside from the pensions and respect due to descendants of Mohammad, the sayyeds, not enough research has been done to say whether there was more social mobility in Iran than in other premodern societies.)

If aristocratic blood, in the Western sense, scarcely existed in Iran, where titles were usually purchased and were not automatically passed from father to son, landholding was of major importance in conferring status and power. It is not certain whether it was more frequent for already rich and powerful courtiers, tribal leaders, ulama, and merchants to add to their power and security by purchasing land, or alternatively for powerful landlords by virtue of their landed wealth to enter into positions of influence. Recent writing tends to favor the former idea, which makes land more an adjunct than an original source of power. Tribal leaders, courtiers, ulama, and merchants tried to control large amounts of land, and might purchase tax-farming rights for lands that they could sometimes convert into property rights, as private property in land grew in the nineteenth century. Despite poor statistics, sources suggest that in the nineteenth century large landownership increased and peasant ownership fell, and by the end of the century most land was held by noncultivating owners and farmed by sharecropping tenants. As the century progressed more merchants bought lands and they, along with some traditional landlords, began to meet Western demand by using their lands increasingly for export crops like cotton and opium, which spread in the course of the century. The spread of export crops meant periodic profits for some peasants, especially the relatively richer ones, but it generally increased stratification in the countryside as poor peasants could not make needed investments, while merchants and landlords could. It also put Iranians more at the mercy of fluctuations in the world market demand and in weather, as the spread of export crops meant a decline in subsistence crops which, in times of export problems, could not be compensated for by foreign earnings. The terrible famine of 1869–72 and later famines were partly due to the rapid spread in opium growing.[5] On the other hand, some peasants benefited from export crops and from cheap imports.

Islamic law, which called for inheritance of fixed shares of the property by each family member, led to some breakdown of family estates, but it was possible to keep estates together through the creation of a family vaqf, and sometimes through outright evasion of Islamic law. Officals who incurred the shahs' displeasure might have their property confiscated and sometimes lose their lives, and total or partial confiscations after an official's death were frequent. Thus there appears to have been much upward and downward mobility for a few at the centers of wealth and power (sometimes as far downward as the grave), while some families show continuity of wealth and public office, and far more show continuity in poverty and powerlessness. Wealthy merchant families sometimes moved into landholding and governmental circles. Regarding mobility, case studies covering the last two centuries suggest considerable continuity in occupations and even town leadership in provincial cities at least until the end of Qajar times, while Tehran saw more social mobility, a normal pattern for a capital city that grew with great rapidity and to which many of the most enterprising, ambitious, and even speculative persons from other towns were attracted.[6]

Governmental bureaucracy and functions were both very limited throughout the Qajar period, although they tended to increase some in the latter part of the dynasty. The chief purpose of the bureaucracy was to collect taxes, including customs duties, and the main use made of moneys collected (as of the money paid for the right to collect taxes) was to support the collectors and the provincial and central courts— especially the shah and his entourage in Tehran. Public works of an elementary kind, such as the building and repair of roads and caravanserais (as had been done by some Safavid and other rulers), were seldom undertaken. Institutions considered governmental in the modern West, like schools, hospitals, and most law courts, were, as in most Islamic states, the responsibility of religious leaders, who collected religious gifts and taxes. Apart from rendering money, governors and other officials were responsible only for keeping order.

Surprisingly, only slight attention was given by the Qajar shahs to the creation of a modern military force that might protect them from external attack and internal revolt. Many Asian rulers had early seen the need of military self-strengthening to protect their countries' independence. Recognition of the need for modern armed forces had encouraged the early nineteenth-century modernization programs of such rulers as Egypt's Muhammad Ali and the Ottoman Empire's Selim III and Mahmud II. They found that modern armed forces required translation bureaus, Western education for some students, modern schools, and local armament factories. Although Iran had less commercial and other contact with the West both before and during the Qajar period than did Egypt and the Ottoman Empire, it remains surprising that Iran did not follow their lead even in the late nineteenth century.

The only Qajar to appreciate the need of a modernized military was Crown Prince Abbas Mirza, governor general of Azerbaijan in the early nineteenth century. Abbas Mirza made use of the French and British instructors provided for by treaties to introduce a Western-style armed force in Azerbaijan which, following the terminology of Muhammad Ali and Selim, he called the *Nezam-e Jadid,* or "New Order" (meaning "New Army"). Like his non-Iranian predecessors he had trouble with ulama who claimed his innovation was un-Islamic, particularly in its use of Western-style uniforms, and like them he found complaisant ulama to justify such innovation as the means to protect the abode of Islam. Abbas Mirza also sent students abroad to study practical subjects, established good relations with Europeans, and encouraged good treatment for religious minorities.

Abbas Mirza died in 1833 before he could take the throne, and subsequently there were only sporadic attempts to bring in Western military instructors from various countries to train parts of the armed forces. Of these only the small, Russian-officered Cossack Brigade late in the century became a serious and disciplined force, but it was used chiefly for protecting the shah and his court. Otherwise the Iranian army was notable for its disorganization, for the sale of rank to men or boys with no military capability who pocketed their soldiers' salaries and then had to allow the men to make a living by following whatever trade they could, to the neglect of drill and training. Apart from the Cossack Brigade formed in 1879, the government could sometimes rely on tribal forces that were not part of the regular army, and in return it allowed them some freedom to loot and plunder. Lacking a strong army or police force, and lacking roads and railroads with which to reach the provinces, the central government had to rely upon indirect means of rule, such as dividing opposing forces, encouraging factional fights, offering bribes, sometimes as gifts or annuities, and holding in Tehran hostages ("guests") from powerful tribes and families.

More dangerous than powerful tribes and families to the power of the government was the great influence of the Shi'i ulama. Whereas the Safavid rulers, through their claim of descent from the imams and through their considerable control of many religious leaders, had been able to escape some of the most dangerous consequences of the growing socioeconomic power and ideological pretensions of the ulama, this was increasingly untrue of the Qajars. The Qajars could claim no religious descent or charisma, though they adopted the Iranian royal custom of calling themselves the "Shadow of God" on earth. Unlike the Safavids they had few important dependent ulama. They appointed the leader of the Friday prayer (imam jom'eh) for each city, as well as certain judges, but these men were outranked in the eyes of the populace by mujtahids not tied to the central government. As noted, the ulama hierarchy was economically self-sufficient through its direct collection of religious taxes and through vaqf donations, while the residence of the leading ulama in Ottoman Iraq continued through and beyond the Qajar period and helped reinforce ulama independence. If a leading mujtahid should speak out in favor of a different governmental policy or against the practices of a ruler, it was the mujtahid to whom his followers owed obedience.

The Shi'i shrine cities in Iraq had enough income, through endowments and donations, to support a large community of religious leaders, scholars, and students, who lived in independence of the Iranian government. Even within Iran various sources of revenue led to considerable wealth for the ulama, some of whom doubled as landowners or merchants. The wealth was unevenly distributed, and there were poor and middling mollas as well as rich ones (the latter often having outside sources of income), but as a corporate group the ulama were well endowed, and this wealth promoted their power and independence. Many ulama and sayyeds associated with them also received governmental gifts and annuities, which, however, did not always assure their loyalty.

Many functions that in modern states are governmental were carried out in Qajar Iran, as in most traditional Muslim societies, by the ulama. These included all levels of education, most forms of judicial and legal activity, and social and charitable services. Iran was almost as late to introduce modern or secular education as military reform, and aside from the Dar al-Fonun of Tehran founded in mid-century by Mirza Taqi Khan *Amir Kabir* to train army officers and civil servants, Iranian education was in the hands of the ulama, and the government had nothing to say about curriculum or anything else. Teaching was traditional and Islamic, concentrating at lower levels on reading, writing, and memorization of the Quran (often without understanding its Arabic), and at higher levels on Arabic and the traditional Islamic sciences. In Iran, Muslim and even some ancient philosophy was taught far more than in Sunni schools to the west. Only near the end of the Qajar period were there a few attempts, largely private, to modernize schools. Some girls managed to get an education, either at school or at home, and a few reached the level of learning and accomplishment considered necessary to be a mujtahid, although these were not generally considered mujtahids, and most Shi'is held that being male was a necessary quality for a mujtahid. There was, and still is, however, a wide network of educated women mollas who cater to women's religious gatherings and ceremonies, giving readings and commentaries on the Quran and telling stories from the lives of the imams.[7]

Unlike education, the administration of justice was de facto divided between ulama-run sharia (Islamic law) courts and administrative courts using 'urf or "customary law," often arbitrary, presided over by the shah, governors, and their representatives. In general, the former dealt with family and personal status law, with wills, contracts, and other legal documents, and with breaches of Islamic law, whereas the latter concentrated on criminals and rebels against governmental authority. Throughout the Qajar period there was a trend on the part of the government, particularly when there were strong reforming chief ministers, to extend the power of governmental courts and legal prerogatives—a trend that was resisted by the ulama.

The ulama had strong ties with the bazaar classes (called in Persian *bazaaris*), including both the bazaar elite of merchants engaged in long-distance and international trade and the larger group of bazaar artisan-shopkeepers, organized into guilds. Ulama and bazaaris often belonged to the same families; much ulama income came from levies paid mainly by bazaaris; the guilds often celebrated religious or partly religious ceremonies for which the services of ulama were needed; and piety and religious observance were among the signs of bazaar standing or leadership. (Even today respectable bazaar shopkeepers and moneylenders are often addressed as "Hajji," whether or not the speaker knows if the addressee has made a pilgrimage justifying this form of address.) Entry into the ulama through study was an avenue of upward social mobility and entailed more respect than entry into Qajar service. Mosques and shrines were a major area of *bast* (refuge) for individuals and groups that feared governmental arrest or harassment. Although some of the ulama, especially those with government appointments, sided with the government, and some might cheat, extort, hoard, or take bribes, in general the ulama were seen as doing this less than government officials. The ulama could also sometimes be appealed to by the popular classes as well as the wealthy to represent grievances before the government. Several times in the Qajar period, and most notably in the Tobacco Protest of 1891–92 and the Constitutional Revolution of 1905–11, an important sector of the ulama helped lead popular movements against a government seen as complaisant to the encroachments of foreign imperialists.

The position of women in Qajar Iran has scarcely been studied, but a few generalizations may be broached on the basis of available material. One is that women's positions varied considerably, as was and is true in other Islamic societies, according to class and social status. In theory, Iran, like other Muslim societies, followed Quranic rules concerning women and the family, with some additions from later Muslim law including a few special to Twelver Shi'i law. The Quran gives men permission to marry up to four wives if they are treated equally (the same chapter of the Quran says that no matter how hard a man tries he will not be able to treat wives equally, which some Muslim modernists argue was meant to outlaw polygamy). The Quran provides for easy divorce for the man and restricted divorce rights for the woman, male guardianship of women and girls, and the evaluation of women's testimony at one half that of a man. Women's inheritance is also half that of a man, but this, plus the fact that a married woman continues to hold her own property, is more favorable to women than were most Western laws before this century. As noted, the various forms of veiling are not Quranic, although many Muslims interpret the Quran as enjoining the veil. Guardianship of children (after an age which varies by school of law but which is young for Shi'is) goes to the father in case of divorce.

In practice, there has been and is considerable variation in women's position. Polygamy has never been widespread, for both social and economic reasons, and in premodern periods it was characteristic mainly of the ruling elite, some of whom had harems and observed strict veiling and seclusion in part as a sign that they could afford numerous wives and servants—a form of "inconspicuous consumption." Even harems were rarely the dens of idleness and iniquity imagined by Westerners.[8] Social custom also restrained frequent divorce, as did the custom of the male bride-price (or dower), most of which was to be paid in case of divorce. Even though men might find ways to avoid its payment, the practice had some restraining effect, as did disapproval of divorce in some social groups and between the families who originally arranged the marriage. Another rare but possible protection was the insertion into the obligatory marriage contract of special provisions, such as that the husband could not take a second wife without the first wife's permission.

Important variations existed among different social groups and classes. In Iran and the Middle East nomadic tribeswomen do most of the tribe's physical labor, are unveiled, and are less segregated than traditional urban women; on the other hand, they tend not to inherit as the Quran says they should. The virtual universality of these nomadic practices in the Middle East and their congruity with the tribal-nomadic way of life, which does not permit women to be idle or segregated but also discourages releasing the family's limited property into the hands of the new family that the bride joins, suggests that such conditions go back in time. Peasant women also do hard physical work and reports from the nineteenth century indicate that they were mostly unveiled. Veiling has been mainly an urban (and hence minority) phenomenon. It is also wrong to take veiling as a sign of a complete lack of freedom or of useful activity. As in the West, running, or helping to run, a household was in every sense an important and productive activity, without which society could not function and children could not be reared. Women in various social groups also engaged in activities more universally considered "productive," such as spinning, and weaving textiles, including important market and export items like Kerman shawls and Persian carpets, for which Western demand began to boom in the 1870s. In tribal and village carpets and textiles most of the creativity in design and color had come from women down through the centuries. There were also professional women who served the needs of other women, like midwives, ambulent saleswomen who visited women at home, healers, and others, including the women mollas mentioned above.

Some women at the court had great power, especially queen mothers and favorite wives. The mother of the teen-aged Naser ad-Din Shah exercised great influence on him after he came to the throne in 1848, and later his favorite wife was also influential. (Her residence became the headquarters of a court-centered conspiracy that brought down the reforming but pro-British chief minister Mirza Hosain Khan *Moshir ad-Dauleh*.) On less elite levels ordinary women were often prominent in bread riots and other urban movements, and this tradition was carried forward in their significant participation in the Tobacco Protest of 1891–92, the Constitutional Revolution of 1905–11, and especially the Revolution of 1978–79.

Even in the area of modesty and sexual behavior, all was not as it seemed either in law or in stereotypes. An early nineteenth-century treatise written by a woman or women of the educated upper class tells other women how to flirt, fool, or get around their husbands, and engage in other dubious pleasurable activities, while another treatise by a man constantly admonishes women not to mistreat their husbands in various ways—admonitions that would not be needed if women behaved according to theory. A mid-nineteenth-century Orientalist wrote that many women followed the precepts of the first book, around which there was a virtual women's cult.[9]

If Shi'ism was somewhat special in Islam in its institutionalization of female mollas, it was also special in another, more controversial feature—temporary marriage. In this form of marriage, early outlawed by Sunnis, the duration of the marriage is stated in the contract— anywhere from some minutes to ninety-nine years. As in all marriages, the husband gives a sum of money. The temporary wife or wives could be in addition to the four maximum regular wives. Temporary marriage flourished in Shi'i pilgrimage centers where mollas might be intermediaries; both Sunnis and Westerners often characterized the custom as "legalized prostitution." It has, however, other uses, and even when of short duration it has the advantage that the children are legitimate and the temporary wives, even when professionals, are not breaking any law and are less stigmatized than prostitutes. (It should be added that, contrary to the view of some apologists, straight prostitution has long existed in the Middle East and was not checked either by polygamy or by temporary marriage.)

Enough has been said to suggest the variability and the productivity of women's roles. As in other premodern and modern societies most women had fewer rights and less power than men of the same social group, who tended to dominate them, but their lives had more variation and possibilities for fulfillment than are acknowledged in the usual Western stereotypes about Muslim women.

As noted, religious minorities consisted mostly of recognized "People of the Book" (monotheists with a scripture)—Jews, Nestorian and Armenian Christians, Zoroastrians, and the small gnostic Sabean community near Iraq. The Jews and Armenians were concentrated in towns, and they, like the Sabeans, were often occupied with certain crafts, such as gold- and silverworking shunned by some religious Muslims, as well as moneylending at interest, which was forbidden to Muslims. Although these communities were recognized and had internal autonomy in many matters under their own religious laws, and although they were better treated than minorities in much of European history, they were often impoverished second-class citizens. Shi'i concepts of ritual purity made intermixture between them and Muslims more difficult than in many Sunni countries. During the nineteenth century, coreligionists of the Jews, Christians, and Zoroastrians abroad, including Christian missionaries, tried to improve the education and position of their Iranian coreligionists with some success. As in many third-world countries, however, the ties of parts of these communities (and later of many Baha'is) to Western groups, and Western intervention on their behalf, made many of them be widely regarded as agents of a disliked Western imperialism. Twentieth-century governments of whatever stripe have all restated protection of the recognized religions, although practice has not always equaled theory.

In the early nineteenth century vertical community ties between richer and poorer in tribe or clan, city guild, faction, or quarter, religious community, including Sufi orders and the ulama corps, were often felt more strongly than were regional class ties between persons with similar relations to the mode of production. By the late Qajar period, however, the development of regional and national markets, improvements in communication and growing sociopolitical crises and grievances made nationwide groups like merchants, artisans, the new intellectuals, and even the leading ulama identify and communicate with each other on a national basis far more than they had before. Thus in late Qajar times we find nationwide mass movements with unprecedented coordination and some self-conscious regional and national social and class groupings.

A new factor in Qajar times was the growing power of a nonindigenous, untraditional group who profoundly affected society— foreigners, and, at long distance, the governments and economic groups they represented. Although Iranian towns had not nearly as many foreign nationals as did the cities of Egypt, the Levant, or Turkey, Iran was nearly as affected as they by the policies of foreign governments and some foreign businesses. Ever since the strategic involvement of France, Britain, and Russia with Iran during the Napoleonic Wars, Iran came to be affected particularly by the policies of Great Britain and Russia. In addition to European interest in Iranian trade, and later in concessions for European economic activity, Britain and Russia had very strong political and strategic interests in Iran. Britain was concerned to retain control of the Persian Gulf, to keep other powers out of it, and to safeguard southern and eastern Iran in order to help hold India. Russia, after taking Transcaucasian territory from Iran in two early nineteenth-century wars, tried to make northern Iran an area of overwhelming Russian influence, and also tried, as did Britain, to control the central government as much as possible. There were at times "forward parties" in Russia who hoped to take more territory and push Russian influence to the point of being able to use, or even reach, the Gulf.

Neither Britain nor Russia wished to allow the other to take further territory in Iran, or to make Iran a protectorate, and this mutual desire to forestall control of Iran by the other party was the most important factor in maintaining Iran's formal independence. This independence was often *purely* formal, as Iran did not dare take a step that might seriously displease Britain or Russia unless it had very strong support from the other country. Even the support of one of the two might be insufficient if the other were displeased enough. Nineteenth-century diplomatic files are filled with accounts of discussions by Iranian leaders with British and Russian representatives trying to get them to approve policies that in a truly independent state would be a matter for internal decision. As most Western scholars read the British but not the

Russian or Persian archieves, they get the impression that British intentions in Iran were significantly reformist and progressive, but a fuller acquaintance with Persian and Russian sources does not support this view. On the whole, the British favored those reforms that would facilitate their trade and the lives of foreigners and those tied to them; when genuinely reforming nationalists became strong, as during the constitutional revolution, and wished to limit foreign privileges in Iran, the British opposed them.

European governments pushed and promoted the commercial interests of their own nationals. Here again the difference between Britain and Russia is smaller than it is often said to be. It is true that the Russian government often offered subsidies and rebates to encourage exporters to Iran and elsewhere, and also promoted banking and railroad schemes in part in order to spread Russian political influence. The British, however, also considered railroad projects mainly from their own strategic viewpoint, and both governments eventually opposed and blocked all railroads, primarily for strategic reasons. The British government also played a large role in encouraging or discouraging investment in other economic schemes; discouraging the vast concession of Baron de Reuter in 1872 but then using Reuter's claims to block Russian railway concessions and officially aiding the compensation of Reuter in 1889 through the important concession for the Imperial Bank of Persia, with attached rights for mineral exploitation. In the late nineteenth and early twentieth century the British government was particularly active in helping its subjects to attain concessions, including the disastrous tobacco monopoly concession of 1890 and the very important D'Arcy oil concession of 1901. (All of this is discussed in more detail below.)

Foreigners were also favored by unequal treaties that freed them from internal customs duties, which Iranian traders still paid, and held customs duties at ports of entry to very low levels. Many factors blocked the development of modern industry and transport in Iran, despite some abortive attempts by ministers and Iranian businessmen in Qajar times. Difficulties of communication, low population, vast and hard to penetrate distances, decentralization, and a lack of modern education and training were among the indigenous factors limiting economic development, and to them were added the legal impossibility under unequal treaties of protecting infant industries or handicrafts, and the lack of interest of the Qajar government in improving industry, infrastructure, or agriculture. The jealously guarded and decentralizing power of tribes, ulama, and certain cities and regions was sometimes exercised against attempts at modernization. If one looks at the Middle East and North Africa as a whole it cannot be an accident that those areas where nomadic tribes, and often religious groups, had the greatest power were the last to centralize and industrialize—besides Iran, Morocco, Libya, Saudi Arabia, the rest of Arabia, Afghanistan, and Central Asia may be mentioned. Iran was in fact less controlled by nomadic tribes than many of these, and hence was able to centralize and begin industrialization before most of them.

Iran's dependence on Western economic forces; its political and military weakness; its government's search for Western advice and approval; and Russian and British protection of the Qajars against revolts made Iran a country with very limited independence. Iranian internal politics in the Qajar period are frequently shadow politics, with real politics often occurring not only, as in many countries, behind the scenes, but even beyond the seas.

3 CONTINUITY AND CHANGE
UNDER THE QAJARS: 1796–1890

Political and socioeconomic developments of the Qajar period may be understood against the above general background. Iran was reunified in the nineteenth century under the Qajar dynasty (1796–1925), which owed its long life, despite unpopularity, largely to repeated support from the two European powers most involved in Iran—Great Britain and Russia. The Qajars were preceded by the late eighteenth-century Zands, who ruled from the southern city of Shiraz and like the Qajars were of tribal origin. The Zands were one of Iran's few very popular dynasties. They protected trade, built bazaars, shrines, and caravan-serais, and were personally benevolent. (Their popularity and their refusal to call themselves shahs, preferring to be called "deputies" either of the Safavids or, even better, of the people, made them the only rulers whose names were not taken off streets and monuments after the 1979 revolution.) The Zands came to power, like most dynasties, at the head of a tribal federation, and their chief rivals were the leaders of another such federation, the northern Qajars. A Qajar leader castrated in boyhood, Agha Mohammad Khan, was captured and kept under house arrest in Shiraz, but on the death of a Zand ruler he escaped and returned to lead his tribal forces in battle, taking over much of Iran by 1790. His cruelty, especially in plucking a reported twenty thousand eyes from men of Kerman, was long remembered. Assassinated in 1797, he was succeeded by a nephew, Fath Ali Shah, who ruled until 1834. Qajar reunification of Iran had at least the virtue of ending the civil and other wars and economic disruptions of the eighteenth century.

During the rule of Fath Ali Shah the first major nineteenth-century European incursions in Iran occurred, as a byproduct of the Napoleonic

Wars. Napoleon, along with the short-lived Russian emperor Paul, wished to invade India, which was also threatened by the Afghans. To forestall this the British sent Captain John Malcolm from India to sign an 1801 treaty with Iran, which promised British military equipment and technicians in return for Iranian support if Afghanistan or France moved toward Iran or India. Soon, however, there was a Russo-British rapprochement, and Iran, still looking for an alliance against Russia, which had taken Georgia from Iranian control, signed the Treaty of Finkenstein with France in 1807. In it France promised to help Iran regain Georgia and to supply Iran with military equipment and training, and Iran promised to declare war on Britain and aid France if it decided to invade India. The French sent a military mission under General Gardane, which began to train Iranian troops in modern methods and also to study Iran in preparation for a possible invasion of India. Again the timing of the treaty was bad for the Iranian government. In the same year, 1807, after Napoleon's European victories, he and Tsar Alexander signed the Peace of Tilsit. This reversal led to a new Anglo-Iranian alliance in 1809, followed by two further treaties by 1814 that together ended Iranian ties to France, and said Britain would give Iran financial and military aid if it were attacked by any European power.

The Qajars' interest in these treaties came largely from their desire to gain Georgia, over which they fought the first Russian War, 1804–13, where the defects of their troops, despite some attempts at modern training and armament, were demonstrated. By the 1813 Treaty of Gulistan, Russia gained important Caucasian territory and exclusive rights to have warships on the Caspian. The nineteenth century thus introduced Iran to the inscrutable ways of Occidentals, who might break treaties within less than a year of signing them, switch allies and enemies at their own whim, and hence behave in ways that Iranians versed in politics could only consider utterly irrational.

Wars with the West and high military expenditures brought economic drains. These began to be felt seriously in Fath Ali Shah's nineteenth-century wars against Russia and continued during later wars with the British and in attempts to arm and improve the Iranian military. When the burden on the state treasury was too great to be covered by revenues, it was traditional to give out tax-free rights to revenue collection on landed or other properties. Such grants were usually called *tuyuls*. The first war against Russia forced Fath Ali Shah to give out much state land and property as tuyuls in return for military aid. As often happened in Iran and elsewhere, such grants frequently tended to become hereditary, while remaining tax exempt, which meant that the rest of Iran had to pay higher taxes in order to produce the same income for central and local rulers.

Whereas the first Qajar, Agha Mohammad, had been able to keep the land tax (Iran's basic tax) to the reasonable level of 10 percent (an approximation given the absence of a good land survey, but considered a rough average), Fath Ali Shah, largely because of his military expenses, doubled this tax to about one-fifth of the harvest, near where it remained throughout most of the Qajar period.[1] Few official measures were taken in the Qajar period to increase agricultural productivity, which might improve peasant income and government revenue; most improvements were made by private individuals involved in export crops.

Aside from widespread nomadism, Iran's rural economy had other features that affected Iran's society and politics through the twentieth century. One was that aridity, which had increased through the centuries for reasons already discussed, limited the number of persons who could subsist in most of Iran. Iran's vast territory supported only five to ten million people in the nineteenth century. Most Iranians had to live and work in the countryside in order to produce enough surplus to feed urban populations. Widely scattered villages and peasant populations are less likely to get involved in rebellious and revolutionary movements than are the denser and more internally organized peasantries of the Far East. Most Iranian protest movements in the past two centuries have been urban-centered, with little peasant participation, except in the well-watered and populous northern regions, where the proximity and closer organization of peasants and the early introduction of capitalist relations in crops like rice and silk created "modern" class divisions and the potential for organizing peasants.[2]

In addition, Iran's aridity and relative lack of rivers suitable for damming have helped encourage an ancient capital- and labor-intensive form of underground irrigation channels, *qanats*. Skilled workmen built sloping underground canals, with periodic airholes to the surface, to convey water down from mountainous highlands until it is brought to the surface to be used by one or more villages. Aside from the technical ingenuity of this system, what must be noted is its fragility (true to some degree of most premodern artificial irrigation systems). Invaders or hostile rulers can starve out villages by ruining the system, and this makes villagers especially vulnerable to the powers that be. Also, unless villagers have enough surplus to hire skilled qanaf diggers, payment is undertaken by a landlord, merchant, or bureaucrat, who in return for supplying water demands a larger share of the crop and may ultimately gain control of peasant land. With a rising demand for trade and export crops in the nineteenth century, it was persons with money to invest in irrigation, in new seeds, and in other improvements who appropriated a growing share of the agricultural surplus. Although some richer peasants were among those who improved their position, many peasants either fell in the socioeconomic scale or remained about the same. Those within and outside the village community with enough capital and knowledge to take advantage of new crops and markets profited, and large landownership, often of a more mercantile "modern" kind, increased.

The European presence in the Napoleonic period, and the first war with Russia, led Crown Prince Abbas Mirza, who ruled in Azerbaijan, to try Western military training of his forces and sending students abroad for training as means to improve the military against foreign threats. Abbas Mirza was much aided in his program by his chief minister, known like many notables by a title, Qa'em Maqam, a statesman, writer, and reformer of great ability. After the death of Abbas Mirza in 1833, Qa'em Maqam worked for the central government. Qa'em Maqam is known both in administrative and in literary history as the first person in modern times to try, mainly via example, to simplify the flowery and elaborate forms of Persian court prose. This reform was continued by several later figures, so that official Persian became, if not a model of simplicity and clarity, at least more broadly comprehensible than before, and literary Persian was in time simplified even more. (Premodern elaborate forms, as in many countries, helped rulers limit the comprehension of governmental writings to a small elite.)

The failure of Abbas Mirza's program of army modernization to expand was due not only to the lack of forceful, reforming Qajar leaders after him, but also to the opposition of decentralizing vested interests, which the center never felt strong enough to suppress. Many tribal and even urban leaders opposed a central army that might limit their role and autonomy; some ulama saw the Western instructors, drill, and especially uniforms of modern armies as infidel encroachments that might lead to greater Western incursions; and army officers and others who profited from the corruption of the old military system opposed reform. These obstacles existed through the Qajar period, and while a ruler might have taken a firmer position on army reform than did any Qajar shah, this would probably have entailed, as it finally did under Reza Shah (1925–41), bringing the tribes to heel, silencing the ulama opposition, and setting up a strong central bureaucracy. (Muhammad Ali's Egyptian army, for example, could only be built up when accompanied by a series of other drastic and centralizing reforms.)

Abbas Mirza's military forces had just been launched when they were faced with a challenge beyond their ability, and this too may have prejudiced people against them. The territorial provisions of the 1813 Treaty of Gulistan were unclear enough to create disputes between Iran and Russia. Negotiations did not settle the issues, and some Iranians began demanding revenge and the retaking of at least those territories they felt the Russians had occupied without treaty rights. Some preachers cited, probably mixing truth with exaggeration, mistreatment suffered by their coreligionists in Russian Caucasia. Influenced in part by leading and vocal ulama, some within the Iranian government encouraged the growing pressure for holy war (jihad) against Russia. Fath Ali Shah then proclaimed jihad, launching an attack on the Russians in 1826. The Iranian army, with only a minority of well-drilled and modernized forces, was decisively defeated. The Russo-Iranian Treaty of Turkomanchai in 1828 brought new gains for Russia. More territory was ceded to the Russians, who also were granted a cash indemnity for the cost of the war (a common policy of Western powers in the nineteenth century; lost wars were paid for not only in land but in "costs"). The extraterritorial and tariff concessions earlier partially granted to Russia were now fixed; Iran could demand no more than a 5 percent import tariff on Russian goods, and no internal duties could be levied on them. Also, Russian subjects and Iranians under their protection (in theory usually consular employees, but these provisions were abused by most powers to protect others) were exempt from Iranian law and to be tried by their own consular courts. Both extraterritoriality and the fixed low tariff later spread to other Western powers; the key treaty being that with Great Britain in 1841. As in other Asian countries where similar provisions came to apply, their main result was to open up the country to Western trade and businessmen, while refusing it protection of its own economic life or, often, of its own subjects.

Extraterritoriality appeared necessary to Western powers whose diplomats and private citizens hesitated to venture into countries whose laws appeared to them capricious, if not barbaric. The other side of the coin, however, was that consular courts were often ludicrously lenient, so that a major crime by a foreign national might go virtually unpunished. On the economic side, free trade was forced on Asia even before it was accepted in the nineteenth-century bastion of free trade, Great Britain. Free trade might benefit a Britain whose advanced industries produced cheaper goods than did those of the rest of the world, but in Asia, including Iran, forced low tariffs had a disruptive effect. Growing quantities of European manufactures that displaced Iranian crafts were freely imported, while the impossibility of protective tariffs under the treaties was one of several reasons why native industry could not develop. Many Iranian merchants were also hurt by the treaties. Unlike the Europeans, they were not exempt from internal tariffs and taxes. As early as the 1830s and continuing from then on, Iranian hand-manufacturers and merchants protested against the rising tide of European imports that were ruining their trades and requested the government to institute protections and prohibitions.[3] Under the unequal treaties, however, there was little the government could do, even had it been so inclined. Some Iranian merchants and enterprises tied to foreign trade benefited from the new situation, as did those consumers whose livelihoods were not undermined but who received cheaper imports.

If the economic effects of the Treaty of Turkomanchai's provisions took some time to make themselves felt, there were more immediate political effects. The two defeats by the Russians led to regional and tribal uprisings, and there is some evidence that the government deliberately helped to turn growing popular discontent against the Russians rather than itself. A Russian mission, headed by the well-known author Griboyedov, was sent to Iran in 1829, mainly to force the Iranian government to pay the Treaty of Turkomanchai indemnity. Generally, what ensued has been, as is frequent with such incidents, treated in the West as a matter of blind and unprovoked Iranian mob action stirred up by fanatical ulama. In fact, it appears that Griboyedov (married to an illustrious Georgian wife as anti-Iranian as he) and his party acted with foolhardy disregard for basic tenets of Iranian behavior and honor.

A report reached the Griboyedov mission that one or more Christian Georgian or Armenian women had been forcibly converted to Islam and brought into the harems of prominent Iranians. The Russian mission, against much that was sacred in Iran, forced their way into impregnable harems and took away such women to question them as to where they wished to live. Some women were allegedly held overnight. In the case of two Georgian women, married to an anti-Russian Iranian notable, the Russians claimed that the women, who had converted to Islam and borne children, wished to leave Iran and return to territory now Russian. The rumor spread that they were being held involuntarily and forced to renounce Islam. The Tehran ulama tried first to influence Griboyedov, but then one of them issued a *fatva* (religious decree) saying the rescue of Muslim women from unbelievers was lawful. The crowd that then went to the mission became uncontrollable. When Russian Cossacks shot a boy an attack by the Iranians followed, and Griboyedov and his whole mission, with one exception, were killed.[4] The episode was significant as the first important anti-foreign incident of religious inspiration, which embodied the resentment of many Iranians against their treatment by Western powers. (The incident was sometimes mentioned during the 1979-81 American Embassy hostage crisis as a precedent for Iranian violation of diplomatic immunity, but in fact, certain incidents in China form closer parallels to these events. In all of them, however, widespread antiforeign sentiment based on real grievances is involved.)

The Iranian ulama's power over the masses and ability to move in ways not thoroughly approved by the government had been shown both in ulama action for jihad, which helped precipitate the second Russo-Iranian war, and in the Griboyedov incident. The ulama also frequently sided with bazaaris in their complaints against the ruin of their trade owing to Western imports. On the other hand, before the mid-nineteenth century the ulama were rarely active in opposing government policies. The shahs of this period tried in general to treat the ulama well and show them respect, while the ulama, in turn, generally limited their political demands to questions they considered of immediate or overwhelming concern.

Further embroilment with a Western power, in this case Britain, was barely avoided in 1833 when Crown Prince Abbas Mirza, having recently put down tribal revolts in eastern Iran, was moving to take Herat. This city in western Afghanistan, with a large Persian-speaking Shi'i population, was then under Afghan rule but considered to be Iranian by Iranians. The British opposed having Iran control Herat and would have come to the aid of the Afghans, but conflict was avoided when Abbas Mirza died. His son and successor, Mohammad Mirza, was recalled by the central government and the war stopped.

The death of Abbas Mirza was a blow to the future of "reform from above" stressing the army, bureaucracy, and new education for both, which Abbas Mirza had launched in Azerbaijan on the model of Ottoman reforming sultans and Egypt's Muhammad Ali. Neither Fath Ali Shah nor his grandson Mohammad Shah made real attempts at modernization or centralization, and both governed in old ways, with the minimum of unavoidable adjustments. Fath Ali Shah was known more for his long beard, tiny waist, and huge harem than for any positive achievements. Because of his hundreds of progeny, an unflattering phrase, alliterative in Persian, became common: "Camels, lice, and princes are to be found everywhere."

Fath Ali Shah died soon after Abbas Mirza, in 1834. Peaceful accession of the crown prince, Mohammad Mirza, was assured thanks to diplomatic and military support displayed by the British, with the consent of the Russians. Subsequent peaceful accessions were similarly guaranteed by a show of support and force by these two powers, both of whom had an interest in keeping on the throne and immune from civil war a dynasty from which they had obtained major treaty concessions. Knowledge that the British and the Russians were behind the dynasty and would back each accession of a crown prince helped forestall revolts and rebellions against a dynasty that was widely considered incompetent and rapacious. Partly in return for their support, the British obtained in 1836 and 1841 treaties that gave them the privileges earlier conceded to the Russians. The British Treaty of 1841 included the famous "Most Favored Nation Clause," and with its subsequent extension to other countries' treaties it meant that all foreign powers were united to extend the treaty privileges of any of them, as new privileges were automatically extended to all.

During the reign of Mohammad Shah the strength of foreign powers, and especially Britain, grew, and it was in this period that the first petitions from bazaaris against Western competition were sent to the Shah. Important religious movements and revolts began in these years, possibly connected to dislocations in Iranian life brought on by foreign encroachments. One of these involved Iran's Isma'ili Shi'i community. In Iran there still existed a small group of Sevener or Isma'ili Shi'is, whose leaders were directly descended from the imams of the so-called Assassins, important in eleventh- to thirteenth-century Iran but then suppressed by the Mongol invaders. The Isma'ili community remained largely underground until the Safavids who, even though they belonged to a different Shi'i line, gave them permission to worship openly. The head of this Isma'ili community, who bore the hereditary title of Agha Khan, became involved in a provincial disagreement and, moved in part by personal ambition, launched a revolt in south-central Iran. He was defeated, and as a result he fled, along with many of his followers, to India, where there were many adherents of his branch of Isma'ili Shi'ism. The followers of the hereditary Agha Khans, based from the 1840s until today in India, believe them to be the descendants of the first imams, via the Egypt-centered Fatimid dynasty, followed by the Nizaris (Assassins). Hence they are considered living imams, the imams of the Sevener line never having disappeared like the Twelfth Imam of the Twelvers. Unknown to most, a small and often semisecret community of Seveners has continued to exist in Iran after the 1840s exile.[5]

Far more important for Iran from the mid-nineteenth century on was the messianic movement known as the Babis, an altered offshoot of which later spread both within and outside Iran as Baha'ism. The founder of Babism, Sayyed Ali Mohammad, later called the Bab ("gate" to the Twelfth Imam), was born in 1819 into a family of merchants in the southwestern city of Shiraz. Early choosing a religious vocation, he went to study with the most learned of the Shi'i ulama in the shrine cities of Najaf and Karbala in Ottoman Iraq. Here he became a follower of a movement within Shi'ism named the Shaikhi movement after its founder Shaikh Ahmad Ahsa'i (1754–1826). Shaikhi ideas included elements both more philosophical and more mystical than those of most orthodox Shi'is, but their most important special feature was a new "fourth pillar," which suggested that there is always a man in the world capable of interpreting the will of the hidden imam (and perhaps of communicating with him). After returning to Shiraz, in 1844 Sayyed Ali Mohammad proclaimed himself this door (Bab) to the hidden imam. Later, as his claims were rejected by most ulama and they began to treat him as a heretic, he sometimes announced he was the imam himself, returning as was predicted to institute perfection on earth. In Shiraz and later in Isfahan he preached against the corruption and venality of the ulama, and when civil authorities turned against him he attacked them also for their sins. The Bab had started with a small but devoted following, and this quickly grew; many at first came from the Shaikhi community, which had expanded in Iran since the late eighteenth century. On the other hand less radical Shaikhis now began, and continued, to insist that the "Bab" spoken of by Shaikh Ahmad Ahsa'i would not manifest himself openly, and that the concept was spiritual, rather than referring to an identifiable man.

It seems probable that the Babi movement, which developed into open socioreligious messianic revolt, can in part be understood as one of several mass religiopolitical messianic movements that appeared under the initial impact of the industrialized West in the third world. This impact tends to make third-world countries subject to new trade fluctuations, to undermine handicrafts, restructure agriculture to the detriment of some, and have other disruptive effects, at the same time as Western examples in law, religion, and custom may suggest new ideas on how to meet new problems. Among such messianic movements occurring after the early impact of the industrialized West are the Taiping Rebellion in China, the Ahmadiya and other groups in India and Pakistan, the Mahdist movement of the Sudan, and a variety of Christian and semi-Christian movements in Africa and Latin America. The new ideological content of most of these, as of the Babi movement, supports the idea that they are not simply "traditional" messianic revolts, but are in addition linked to new conditions brought by the Western presence.[6]

Once he lost hope of becoming the leader of a reformed Islam, the Bab not only denounced both secular and religious authorities, but announced a new scripture, the *Bayan,* which contained laws superseding many in the Quran. In his scripture and preachings the Bab spoke out for greater social justice, and his partially modern, perhaps "bourgeois," content is seen in such points as a high valuation of productive work, a denunciation of begging (not blameworthy in Islam, especially as it provides an occasion to give alms), a call for mild and humanitarian treatment of children and others, and the end to the prohibition of taking interest. He also called, if not exactly in modern economic terms, for guarantees for personal property, freedom of trade and profits, and the reduction of arbitrary taxes. He called notably for a higher position for women, who were to be educated and not to be beaten, and for limits on polygamy. The already educated but formerly secluded Babi poet and preacher, Qorrat al-Ain, was reported to have preached unveiled; most Babi women did not dare go that far at this early time.

Whether he claimed to be the gate to the Twelfth Imam or whether, as he sometimes later said, he was both a prophet and the imam himself returned to institute a reign of perfect justice throughout the world, the Bab aroused messianic sentiments among his followers. The differences of his scripture from the Quran he explained by a theory containing a progressive evolutionism rare in premodern thought. Muslims believe that there were prophets before Mohammad but that each brought an essentially identical revelation, from which some followers deviated and needed to be brought back to the true path by a new prophet. Mohammad, however, was the last of the prophets (even though Shi'is often seem to revere Ali and Hosain more, their messages are not considered to differ from Mohammad's). The Bab, however, said that each prophet brings a new message in accord with the growing maturity of humanity, and that each new message supersedes the last one. Hence the *Bayan* does not just interpret, but supersedes the Quran, while including the essence of its message. Past prophets are respected and their laws were needed during their own prophetic cycle, but those laws that are superseded are no longer valid. This doctrine was regarded with horror by pious Muslims and was seen as a dangerous heretical breakoff from Islam.

Political events now impinged on the Babi movement. Mohammad Shah died in 1848 and British and Russian protection served to assure the throne to the crown prince, the teen-aged Naser ad-Din, who was to reign for forty-eight years (1848–96). In Muslim countries interregna are often periods for disorder and revolt, as when there is no new king ruling from the capital many consider that no legal ruler exists. As crown princes took some weeks to travel from Tabriz to Tehran, interregna could be dangerous times for rulers and propitious ones for their opponents. The Babis tried to take advantage of this period to begin revolts, and they succeeded in establishing enclaves, first in a village in the Caspian province of Mazanderan and later in some cities. The Babi revolts were not well coordinated nationally, however, owing in part to lack of modern transportation and communication, and the government was able between 1848 and 1851 to suppress them cruelly, massacring many who had been offered safe conduct in return for surrender. The Bab himself was arrested even before the revolts began, and his civil and ulama opponents evidently decided that messianic feelings about him, considered a main factor in the revolts, could be dampened by his execution. Hence, he was taken to Tabriz, interrogated by the ulama about his religious beliefs, and sentenced to death by firing squad, in 1850. The first round of bullets sent up a cloud of smoke, which remarkably cleared to reveal no body, though the Bab was then found and executed, the first volley having merely cut his ropes.

After the suppression of the Babi revolts, during which one Babi conclave adopted a semicommunist doctrine, and the repression that followed, a small and desperate group of Babis tried to kill the shah in 1852. After this there were terrible tortures and executions of Babis, including the woman preacher-poet Qorrat al-Ain. The Babis who survived now had either to keep their beliefs hidden or to emigrate, concentrating first in Ottoman Baghdad. The successor as leader of the Babis, apparently chosen by the Bab, was called Sobh-e Azal. He was soon challenged by his more dynamic half-brother, Baha'ollah, who succeeded in attracting the great majority of the community. As part of the Bab's progressive theory of prophets, he had predicted that the future would bring a new prophet, "He whom God shall manifest," whose new scripture would supersede his own. In 1863 Baha'ollah declared himself to be this new prophet, and in his writings introduced a cosmopolitan, pacifist, liberal doctrine that largely replaced the Iranian radical messianism of the Bab.

The Baha'is proselytized outside Iran, but are also almost surely the largest non-Muslim religious minority in Iran, while the followers of the Sobh-e Azal, the Azalis, probably now number only a few thousand, nearly all Iranian. Neither group is officially counted as a religion either in Iran or in other Muslim countries. By Muslim law conversion is permitted to Islam or between non-Muslim religions but not *from* Islam, which is apostasy. Nonrecognition of the Baha'i religion is therefore not new and does not distinguish Iran from other Muslim countries; more significant is the question of how Baha'is and other minorities are treated in practice, which has shown some variation.

After 1863, the Azalis retained a strong radical and rebellious component, as well as a hatred for the Qajars that was stronger than their dislike of the Shi'i ulama, and so a number of Azalis were found among the precursors of, and participants in, the Constitutional Revolution of 1905–11. The pacifist Baha'is, on the other hand, eschewed direct political activity, although some of their acts had political implications, and declared their neutrality in the 1905–11 Revolution (which sometimes objectively meant support to the shahs). Many Baha'is received modern educations, and, like other minorities with ties to the West and sometimes employed by Westerners, they were often considered representatives of Western interests, which added anti-Western feelings to the religious antipathy toward them. As with other minorities, most Baha'is probably did nothing to draw hostility, but the acts or positions of only a few among a minority often suffice to add to hostile ideas about a whole religious minority. Besides having modern educations, Baha'is are often professionals or businessmen.

The chief minister brought with him by Naser ad-Din Shah from Tabriz, Mirza Taqi Khan *Amir Kabir,* was heavily involved in the suppression of the Babis from 1848 to 1850. An extremely able man of humble birth in the royal household, Amir Kabir was the first person after Abbas Mirza to attempt modernization from above. As did most Iranian governmental and other reformers in Qajar times, Amir Kabir followed in part the example of the Ottoman Empire, to which he had traveled, although he was also impressed by what he had seen in Russia. He was primarily concerned, like reformers in other Asian countries, with military reform, beginning his attempt to reorganize the army on Western lines by strengthening the European-style education and training of troops. In order to strengthen the impoverished central treasury, he reduced the number of sinecures and took back many dubious tuyuls, replacing them with small pensions. He founded the first official gazette and the first higher school, the *Dar al-Fonun* in Tehran, which included both technical-scientific and military instruction. It was mainly taught by European teachers with the aid of local translators. For years this was the only modern higher school in Iran, as Naser ad-Din came to fear the upsetting effects of modern education and to discourage both its diffusion in Iran and travel abroad for study. (The effects of these and other unenlightened policies by this long-lived ruler have scarcely been assessed. In general, Iran would have been better off if "modernization" could have been more gradual and indigenous before 1925 instead of being so much imposed from the top in a brief fifty-year period thereafter.) Under the Dar al-Fonun's auspices various Western books were first translated into Persian, the first Persian textbooks were published, and some government officials received their education.

The efforts of Amir Kabir to start modern industries were less successful. Although some factories were begun under his auspices, lack of governmental interest or preparation for factories, treaty preclusion of protective tariffs, and the lack of a prepared labor force, transport, and so forth aborted these enterprises. A few of his schemes for agriculture required less infrastructure and succeeded better.

Some courtiers, landlords, and ulama were threatened by Amir Kabir's reforms, which included measures that hit their economic and judicial powers. They might tolerate him until he achieved success against the Babi menace with his improved military, but once this threat was over many of them worked to get rid of him, aided by the queen mother and also by the imperious tone that Amir Kabir used with Naser ad-Din, perhaps not realizing that the boy had now grown up. A strong defamatory campaign to discredit Amir Kabir finally convinced the young shah that his chief minister was hungry for total power, so the shah dismissed him in 1851, and had him assassinated at his bath in Kashan the following year. Although Amir Kabir was in no way a populist or democrat, and though he lacked the diplomacy needed to keep the shah on his side and build up a reformist party, there seems little doubt that a measure of self-strengthening and centralization could have helped the future evolution of Iran. In most Asian countries self-strengthening from the top was an important prelude to more populist developments, but in Iran such self-strengthening began seriously only in the 1920s.

After the fall of Amir Kabir there was a resurgence of the forces that he had tried to limit in order to strengthen the center. These forces included the tribes and their leaders, landlords of various origins, courtiers, and the ulama. The actions of these groups against reform and reformist ministers, along with the informal guarantees of Iran's territory and of the dynasty given by Britain and Russia, inclined the Qajars to think that it might not be important to centralize and strengthen their military forces, especially as steps to do so called forth counterpressures and actions from vested interests.

The informal entente of Iran with the very powers that were exploiting her economically was not without difficulties, however. In 1856–57 the Iranian government once again tried to take Herat and was pushed back by the British army, and a British fleet also landed in the port of Bushehr, on the Persian Gulf. The British, already having trouble with their army in India, were willing to settle for the fairly mild Peace of Paris in 1857, in which Iran promised to renounce, and stay out of, Herat. After this peace British influence was predominant for a time at the Iranian court.

In the nineteenth century the results of contacts with the West appear to have been more negative than positive for Iran, and many traditional evils were reinforced rather than overcome. The costs of Iran's wars, including foreign arms and instructors, along with the import of new goods that added nothing to health, welfare, or education, whether they were sugar and tea for all classes or luxuries for the elite, meant a growing export of precious metals. Persian exports did not grow enough to pay for these new goods, or for imported manufactures like textiles and household goods. Also, the court itself imported arms and luxuries, and this brought increasing taxes. Although statistics are insufficient to prove whether the real income of the "average" Iranian rose or declined in the nineteenth century, and there are scholars who cite facts on either side, consular statistics and travelers' reports suggest that there were increased inequalities of income, and that the popular classes paid for the increased purchase of tea, sugar, tobacco and machine-made crockery and textiles with higher real prices for such vital items as meat, fruit, grain and bread, and vegetables. Iran became more dependent on Western goods and, in its agricultural exports, on world market fluctuations. These might briefly be helpful, as with the high-priced demand for cotton during the American Civil War, but they also made the country and its people more subject to unreliable markets than ever before. Land converted to export crops like cotton in the north or opium chiefly in the south could not suddenly be reconverted in time of lower demand or a bad harvest, and the conversion of land from food to opium, although usually profitable, contributed significantly to the terrible Iranian famine of 1869–72 and to later scarcities. Scholars who look at growing aggregate import and export figures tend to say that Iran was modernizing and growing more prosperous, while those who study areas of the peasant or urban economy in depth tend rather to find increasing stratification (which usually hurt the poor); growing income-distribution gaps; dangerous dependence on a few Western countries; and a lack of effective governmental steps to strengthen Iran's economy vis-à-vis the West.[7]

Lacking the base or determination to carry through essential centralizing reforms, the Qajars were also unwilling and possibly unable to carry through financial reforms that would have been a necessary concomitant of economic and political changes. Increasingly during the nineteenth century, governorships and subordinate positions were sold to the highest bidder at a kind of annual auction. This led many winners to try to get the most revenue from their lands in the shortest time, as they did not know whether they had any interest in the long-term productivity of the region, which would have required more moderate taxation; but they did want enough cash to win the next auction for a profitable territory. Many tribal leaders paid very little, but only promised to lead their forces in battle if the shah wished. Often the shahs had no way to enforce collection in distant tribal lands. City taxes were also very low, aside from the semivoluntary religious taxes paid by most bazaaris to the ulama, which did not go to the government. Peasants were taxed more heavily than any other part of the population; most of their taxes supported various levels of local or provincial tax collectors and little reached the central government.

Entry into the world market also caused numerous regional and local dislocations that were, on balance, more harmful than helpful to Iranians. In the sixteenth through eighteenth centuries Iran had produced a significant quantity of silk, silk thread, soft Kerman goats' wool (a sort of cashmere), and textiles for export to Europe, and in the nineteenth century these exports declined. The British turned more to India for cashmere. One European firm, probably by design, imported diseased silkworm eggs to Iran in mid-century; silkworm disease spread rapidly, almost killing the export industry as well as the use of Iranian silk for Iranian textiles. Recovery was never complete.

Iran had an extensive textile production from the simplest to the fanciest cloths. Iranian handmade textiles, manufactured by men and women in home and workshop, were severely reduced by the import of cheaper factory-made textiles, chiefly from Britain and Russia. Although handweaving continues on a constantly diminishing scale, it has ceased to be a significant part of the Iranian economy. Many other crafts, particularly those providing housewares, where also increasingly hit by Western competition. The Iranian author of a *Geography of Isfahan* in the later nineteenth century laments how one craft after another had either disappeared or been decimated by Western competition to the detriment of Isfahan's economy,[8] and similar trends were noted elsewhere.

On the other hand, some goods benefited from Western demand. Among them were agricultural products like cotton, opium, and dried fruits and nuts. In addition, Kerman shawls made of handloomed Kerman wool with finely hand-embroidered "Paisley" (Perso-Indian) designs were temporarily popular in the West. More permanent was the popularity of Persian carpets, which, surprisingly, became a major item of Western demand only as late as about 1875. Both Western and Iranian (chiefly Tabrizi merchant) entrepreneurs were involved in their production and export. After the supply of old carpets dwindled, carpets came to be produced either in workshops or on a "putting out" system where dyed wool and often looms were supplied to weavers who worked at home by pattern for piecework rates. Such carpets were and are produced to Western tastes and specifications and often lack the live creativity characteristic of carpets produced for home or local use. Village and tribal carpets continued to be bought up, but even these were increasingly made according to Western demand. Carpet workers were chiefly women and children, usually working for very low wages in unhealthful conditions. Often they now contributed more than they had before to family income and hence raised this income, but at a heavy price. The introduction of early, non-colorfast aniline dyes in the 1870s further lowered quality. (It is wrong to think that the synthetic dyes used today, which do not run if properly used, are a main cause in lowered carpet quality, which, when it exists, is more due to other aspects of commercialization and mass production.)

Interaction with the West on unequal terms thus reduced large areas of economic activity and opened up or increased some others. Based on existing evidence it seems unlikely that the gains compensated for the losses—that carpets, for example, compensated for the decline in a great variety of crafts for internal and external consumption. While many imported consumer goods could be bought more cheaply than their local counterparts, this did not necessarily bring a better life to most Iranians. More sugar, tea, tobacco, and especially opium were consumed, which was detrimental to health, while prices of basic foodstuffs rose.[9]

Further impoverishing the central treasury was the auctioning of customs directorships, like many offices, region by region. Local directors competed to attract the most tade to their own point of entry by offering import duties below the official 5 percent (being accountable to no one since all they paid to the central government was their original bid), so that income from customs taxes was far lower than it should have been.

During the long period after 1857 that passed without wars, owing in part to Naser ad-Din's belief that the British would protect Iran's territorial integrity, military officers including those at the top were allowed increasingly to pocket the pay allotted to their troops, who were very badly trained and equipped and whose numbers were far below their official level. To live, troops had to practice a variety of full-time trades in town, and many did not even possess a rifle or uniform.

Iran's increasingly negative trade balance, deteriorating terms of trade, and the dramatic world fall in the price of silver, which made up Iran's currency, were further factors in Iran's growing economic problems. Some merchants, landlords, and officials were able to profit from new relations with the West by expanding their control of raw materials or crafts that were newly profitable, but this was not true of most Iranians. On the other hand, changes in Iran's economy and the development of merchants, entrepreneurs, and a few governmental people who could see the benefits of modernizing the economic, social, and legal system provided a base for ultimately effective opposition to the old regime, as did the discontents of the classes who suffered from the new conditions. The bazaar included both merchants who profited from new outlets but resented Western competition, and other merchants and artisans who mainly suffered from this competition.

Beginning in the 1850s a new phase of Iran's relations with European powers was characterized by the European drive to receive concessions for particular economic activities. The first important concessions, for telegraph lines, were granted to the British, who felt a need for rapid telegraphic communication with India after the 1857 Mutiny and saw Iran as the best overland link. This international line, begun in the late 1850s, was soon extended, by Iranian governmental desire, into internal Iranian lines, so that the government could learn quickly what was happening in the provinces. (In 1891–92 and after, however, the telegraph became an important weapon of revolt, keeping Iranian cities in touch with each other and with the Shi'i shrine cities of Iraq.)

The most extensive concession ever granted by Iran, and perhaps by any country, came in 1872 when the British subject Baron Julius de Reuter, of news agency fame, received a concession granting exclusive rights for railroad and streetcar construction, all mineral-extraction rights except for a few already being exploited, all unexploited irrigation works, a national bank, and all sorts of industrial and agricultural projects, in return for a modest royalty and initial sum. Lord Curzon, himself a firm economic and political imperialist, later called it the most complete and extraordinary surrender of the entire industrial resources of a kingdom into foreign hands that had probably ever been dreamed of.[10] The chief Iranian promoter of the concession was the reformist prime minister Mirza Hosain Khan. He profited personally from it, but probably also thought that Naser ad-Din Shah and the Qajars were so weak and indecisive regarding economic activity that the only way to modernize, as he thought important, and keep Iran from falling further under Russian control was to have Englishmen lead in promoting transport, mining, banking, industry, and agriculture.

Many modern Iranian reformers have been ambivalent toward the West and Western governments, and in some periods, even within one individual, there have been swings between a positive and a negative reaction to the West. In Iran as in much of Asia the earliest reformers tended to be pro-Western, and Mirza Hosain Khan fits this pattern. Such reformers might have known that Western powers were exploiting their country, but felt that the only way to become strong enough to resist exploitation and Western control was to adopt modern Western methods in many spheres, including education, the military, and the economy.

Mirza Hosain Khan, whose grandfather was a bath attendant who entered Qajar service, rose rapidly in the Qajar foreign service, holding posts in India, south Russia, and as ambassador to the Ottoman Empire. In all these posts he saw how much even relatively under-developed countries might gain by adopting Westernizing reforms, and he helped convince Naser ad-Din Shah to take the first trip abroad of any Qajar ruler, to Ottoman Turkey and Iraq. There he impressed on the shah the virtues of administrative and other reforms in improving the strength and prosperity of a country, and the shah was so impressed that he brought Mirza Hosain Khan back with him to try to introduce reforms in Iran, giving him various ministries. Mirza Hosain Khan made reform efforts especially in the army and judiciary, but like other reformers was opposed by vested interests and ulama. He helped bring on his own downfall by promoting the Reuter concession, which he saw as the most feasible way to economic modernization, but which others saw, with much justice, as a means of handing over Iran's resources to a British subject.[11]

On his first of three trips to Europe, in 1873, Naser ad-Din Shah found that the Russian government was hostile to the Reuter concession, and even the British government did not support Reuter, whose concession had not been their idea. Also, a coalition of Persians had formed against the concession during the shah's absence. The shah had wished to bring his wives on the European trip and they had gone as far as Russia, but affronting incidents such as stares, attempts to greet them, and so forth enabled advisers to convince the shah that offenses to royal ideas of honor might increase and that all women should be sent back to Tehran. The shah's favorite wife, Anis ad-Dauleh, was particularly angry at this, and blamed it on Mirza Hosain Khan, although he denied responsibility. The residence of Anis ad-Dauleh became, after her return, the center where opponents of Mirza Hosain Khan met. They were a mixed group of patriotic or anti-British officials, ulama, and others simply hurt by Mirza Hosain Khan's reforms. When the shah landed at the Caspian port of Anzali, the strength of this anti-Mirza Hosain Khan and anti-Reuter coalition was so strong that the shah felt compelled to dismiss Mirza Hosain Khan and to find a pretext to annul the Reuter concession. The latter was done via a concession provision stating that Reuter must start building his railroad by a certain date or forfeit the £40,000 "caution money" he had paid. By blocking the necessary means for Reuter to start the railroad, the shah was able to declare the concession void, and he kept the money. Soon after, Russian concessionaires began to seek railroad concessions in Iran and only then did the British government step in to back Reuter, who had been pressing his claims. The British said that no railroad concession could be granted until Reuter's claims were met, and this was one of several factors that blocked railroad construction in Iran.[12]

Among the more felicitous changes launched by Mirza Hosain Khan were greater centralization of the judicial system and the introduction of a cabinet system of government with nine ministers, each with defined duties, which most ministers had not previously had. The shah's first European trip, under Mirza Hosain Khan's guidance, also encouraged some reforms, notably a modern postal system. In 1874 Amin ad-Dauleh, next to Mirza Hosain Khan the most important reformist minister of this period, was made minister of posts. Mirza Hosain Khan used Austrian advisers to help reorganize the army, and Amin ad-Dauleh used them to help modernize the postal system. In general, however, the shah was increasingly intimidated by defenders

of the status quo—more so after the successful movement against Mirza
Hosain Khan (who died mysteriously in 1881 after holding less exalted
governmental posts). The long reign of Naser ad-Din Shah was characterized by far fewer self-strengthening measures or steps to promote
economic and social development than were to be found in nineteenth-
century Egypt, the Ottoman Empire, or Tunisia, and though this was
partly due to the strength of decentralizing, traditional forces in Iran, it
was also in part due to the character of the Qajar rulers. (The difference
cannot be blamed on European pressures, which were at least as great
elsewhere.)

     Although the British government successfully used Reuter's unset-
tled claims to block not only Russian railway concessions but also some
other concession seekers (Reuter's concession was so universal that most
requests might be blocked on these grounds), there were nonetheless a
few successful concession hunters. An important concession for fishing
on the southern Caspian Sea bordering on Iran was granted to a Russian
subject, who formed a company that retained a monopoly on Iranian
caviar production until after World War I. Other concessions also went
to Russian subjects, but the real concession fever recommenced only in
1888, when British policy toward concessions in Iran changed from
lukewarm to strongly supportive. A special mission from the British
conservative government under a new Minister to Iran, Sir Henry
Drummond Wolff, was active in promoting economic concessions.
Under pressure from Wolff the shah opened Iran's only navigable river,
the Karun in the south, to international navigation. The Russians had
pressured Iran not to grant transport concessions without their approval
and protested this measure, which favored the British, but the Iranian
government claimed that opening a river was not a concession. Wolff,
along with Reuter's son, also reached an accord with the shah over
Reuter's outstanding claims; the accord gave Reuter two important
items from the first concession, the right to build a national bank (Iran
had no modern banking system) and attached rights for mineral
exploration and exploitation. Although the minerals included oil (also
covered in the original Reuter concession), which some thought could
be found in Iran, mineral exploration soon stopped and mineral rights
reverted to the Iranian government. The bank, however, under the
name of the Imperial Bank of Persia, opened, with its seat in Tehran

and provincial branches, and with exclusive rights to issue bank notes or any negotiable paper. The Russians in return soon got rights to build roads in the north and to open their own bank, which they used largely for loans to important Persians.

In 1879 the shah, impressed by Russian cossacks while in Russia, founded the Iranian Cossack Brigade headed by Russian officers. These soon constituted a small, well-trained and disciplined force on which shahs could count, but at the same time it created one more means of diffusing Russian influence in Iran, and it could be used against Iranian movements that threatened the interests of the Russian government. This series of concessions, which returned only small sums to the government, although bribes to the shah and officials to promote them were quite large, meant that Iran in this period was falling even further under British and Russian control. The Imperial Bank of Persia's exclusive rights to issue notes were unpopular with Iranian merchants and moneylenders who had long issued their own notes of variable nature and circulation. There were several runs on the Imperial Bank's specie organized by Persian traditional bankers (with Russian backing, the British thought), and some of these came close to success. The Russian Bank with its governmental financing had fewer economic privileges than the British bank, but was useful to the Russians in enabling them to influence Iranian notables by making them loans on easy terms.[13] By the late nineteenth century, then, both the British and the Russians had heavy economic and political interests in Iran, amounting in some areas to real control.

4 PROTEST AND REVOLUTION: 1890–1914

The economic and political dislocations brought by the Western impact included the undermining of most Iranian handicrafts, the transformation of carpet weavers into laborers working for a pittance, the fall in prices of Iranian exports as compared to European imports, and a disastrous drop in the international price of silver, the basis of Iran's currency. These developments, along with the difficulty of being a trader independent of Europeans and the impossibility of setting up protected factories, led to growing economic discontents and resentment against European rivals. Even though some rural and urban groups benefited from trade with the West, they often had other grievances. Increasing Western political control of Iran was resented and the numerous Iranian merchants and workers who traveled to India, Russian Transcaucasia, and Turkey could witness reforms and hear liberal or radical ideas suggesting ways that governments could change and could undertake self-strengthening policies of a kind that might better Iran's condition and free it from foreign control.

In the 1880s and after there were also a number of officials who advocated reform. Among ministers the most important was Amin ad-Dauleh, who held a variety of positions, chiefly minister of posts, and was generally considered a sincere reformer who disliked the corruption and foreign dominance he saw around him. Less forceful or powerful than men like Amir Kabir or Mirza Hosain Khan (with whom he had not got along), he could have only a small influence in the face of the power held by the longstanding chief minister, Amin as-Soltan. Mirza Malkom Khan, 1833–1908, a Western-educated Armenian Iranian expelled from Iran for forming a society modeled on Freemasonry, later became Iran's minister to Great Britain from 1873

63

to 1889, and concentrated his reform activities on promoting a modified Persian script and on writing reformist essays with very limited circulation.

In 1889 Naser ad-Din Shah took his third trip to Europe, which was heavily promoted by the British minister in Iran, Sir Henry Drummond Wolff, who hoped to further British financial interest in Iran, and largely succeeded. Among the concessions signed by the shah was one for a lottery in Iran promoted in part by Malkom Khan. After returning to Iran, the shah faced strong opposition to the lottery concession, coming partly from the religious element who noted that gambling was forbidden by the Quran. The shah canceled the concession and so informed Malkom Khan, who hastened to sell what he controlled of the concession for a good price before its cancellation became known. This and other actions resulted in Malkom's dismissal from his posts and the removal of all his titles. The somewhat tarnished but influential reformer now decided to undermine, or perhaps to blackmail, Iran's rulers by producing an oppositional and reformist newspaper, *Qanun* (Law), printed in London and smuggled into Iran. Preaching the virtues of a fixed legal system and the evils of arbitrary and corrupt government, *Qanun* concentrated its attacks on Amin as-Soltan. It was widely read among Iran's elite during its existence, until the death of Naser ad-Din Shah.[1] The only other free newspaper at this time, the older *Akhtar* put out by Iranians in Istanbul, was milder in its reformism, and hence less often forbidden entry into Iran. Within Iran there were only official journals. (The one freer paper launched with the encouragement of Mirza Hosain Khan in 1876, the bilingual *La Patrie,* lasted for only one issue, in which its French editor called for open and fearless criticism.)

Before 1890 most educated Westernizing reformists had been rather hostile to the ulama—as were reformist officials like Amir Kabir, Mirza Hosain Khan, Amin ad-Dauleh, and the Babi and Baha'i reformers. On the other hand, some ulama increasingly emerged as effective opponents of the alarming trend toward the sale of Iran's resources to foreigners. Moreover, the ulama's virtual inviolability and their ties to the guilds could make even secular reformers recognize them as useful allies in a struggle against foreign control. From 1890 through 1912 there was some reconciliation between secularists and ulama opposed to the regime's policies.

One architect of this historically unusual alliance between religious and radical elements was the internationally traveled Muslim reformer and pan-Islamist, Sayyed Jamal ad-Din "al-Afghani" (1839–97). Although he claimed Afghan birth and upbringing, probably in order to have more influence in the Sunni world than he could have had as an Iranian of Shi'i birth and education, Afghani was in fact born in Iran and had a Shi'i education in Iran and in the Shi'i shrine cities of Iraq. Educated in the rationalist philosophical tradition of Avicenna and later Iranian philosophers, who were far more taught in Iran than in the Sunni Near East, Afghani was also influenced by the philosophically oriented Shaikhi school of Shi'ism. In about 1857–58 he traveled to India, where he seems to have developed a lifelong hatred of British imperialism. After activities in Afghanistan and Istanbul and an influential stay in Egypt from 1871 to 1879, he continued his modernist and antiimperialist writing, first in India and then in Paris, where he edited the anti-British and pan-Islamic Arabic newspaper. *al-'Urwa al-Wuthqa.* [2]

After activities in London, Afghani returned to the south Persian port city of Bushehr, whence he had left decades before for India. He apparently intended only to pick up books sent to him there from Egypt and to go to Russia to continue anti-British activities. The Iranian minister of press, E'temad as-Saltaneh, who had read *al-'Urwa al-Wuthqa,* talked the shah into inviting Afghani to Tehran. There he soon offended the shah, probably by violent anti-British proposals, but gathered a group of Iranian disciples. He apparently spoke to them of the need for uniting religious and nonreligious opposition to foreign encroachments. Forced by the shah to leave Iran in 1887, he spent two years in Russia and then rejoined the shah during the latter's third trip to Europe and received an invitation back to Iran. He first went to Russia, believing he had a mission from Amin as-Soltan to calm Russian hostility over concessions to the British, but in Iran Amin as-Soltan denied such a mission and refused to see him. In the summer of 1890 Afghani heard that the shah was planning to exile him and forestalled this by taking sanctuary in a shrine south of Tehran. He continued to gather disciples, to whom he explained such means of organized opposition as the secret society and the secretly posted and distributed leaflet. His contacts in Iran included his Tehran host, Amin az-Zarb, the wealthiest Persian merchant and master of the mint;

Amin ad-Dauleh; some members of the ulama, notably the saintly, ascetic, and progressive Shaikh Hadi Najmabadi; and various reformers and ordinary people, like his devoted servant, Mirza Reza Kermani. In January 1891, convinced that a leaflet attacking the regime for its concessions to foreigners emanated from Afghani, the shah sent soldiers who forcibly dragged him from his sanctuary and sent him on a forced march to the Iraqi border in midwinter. From Ottoman Iraq, and then from London, where he soon proceeded and joined Malkom Khan, Afghani continued to write and speak against the shah and his government, and he left behind disciples, some secretly organized, whom he had instructed in political action and agitation.

Discontent over the shah's concession policy came to a head after he conceded a monopoly over the production, sale, and export of all Iranian tobacco to a British subject, encouraged by Wolff, in March 1890. The concession was kept secret for a time but in late 1890 the Istanbul Persian newspaper *Akhtar* ran a series of articles severely criticizing it. The January 1891 leaflets that brought Afghani's expulsion attacked the tobacco concession among others, and new critical leaflets were issued by Afghani's followers in the spring. The tobacco concession elicited far more protest than any other because it dealt, not with areas that were unexploited, or almost so, by Iranian businessmen, but rather with a product widely grown in Iran, and profiting many landholders, shopkeepers, and exporters.

Massive protests against the concession began in the spring of 1891, when the tobacco company's agents began to arrive and to post deadlines for the sale of all tobacco to the company. The first major protest came in Shiraz, and its religious leader was exiled to Iraq. There he conferred with Afghani, who now wrote a famous letter to the leader of the Shi'i ulama, Hajj Mirza Hasan Shirazi, asking him to denounce the shah and his sale of Iran to Europeans. Shirazi did not immediately take strong action but did write privately to the shah repeating many of the points that Afghani had made to him.

A revolutionary movement now broke out in Tabriz, where the government was forced to suspend the concession's operation, and mass ulama-led protests spread to Mashhad, Isfahan, Tehran, and elsewhere. In December 1891 the movement culminated in an amazingly successful nationwide boycott on the sale and use of tobacco, observed even by the shah's wives and by non-Muslims, which was based on an order either issued by or attributed to Shirazi, which he subsequently confirmed. The government tried to suppress only the company's internal monopoly, leaving it with an export monopoly, but this proved impossible. A mass demonstration in Tehran culminated in the shooting on an unarmed crowd, causing several deaths, and this was followed by even more massive protests. The government was forced to cancel the entire concession early in 1892. The affair left the Iranians with their first foreign debt—£500,000 borrowed from the British-owned Imperial Bank for exorbitant compensation to the company. The movement was the first successful mass protest in modern Iran, combining ulama, modernists, merchants, and ordinary townspeople in a coordinated move against government policy. The movement's coordination throughout Iran and with the mujtahids of Iraq was facilitated by the existence and extensive use of the telegraph. Although many of the ulama were now bought off by the government and some quiet years followed, the "religious-radical alliance" had shown its potential for changing the course of Iranian policy, and the government did not dare grant further economic concessions for several years. The basic alliance of bazaaris (especially merchants), ulama, and secular or modernist reformers continued to be important.[3]

The tobacco movement also encouraged the growth of Russian influence at the expense of the British. To preserve his position, Amin as-Soltan assured the Russians that he would henceforth favor them, and his later policies bore this out. The British policy in 1888–90 of encouraging economic concessions by the shah—which was favored by Prime Minister Lord Salisbury and the Foreign Office but pushed with special energy by the British envoy Wolff—had backfired. Russian counterconcessions and Russian support for the tobacco movement led to an increase in Russian, and not British, influence.

Ulama opposition to the shah temporarily receded and some ulama were quieted by being given increased pensions, but attacks on the government from abroad continued. From London Afghani contributed strong articles to Malkom's *Qanun* and published letters sent to the Shi'i ulama in Iraq and Iran calling on them to depose the shah. Late in 1892 Afghani went to Istanbul as a guest of Sultan Abdülhamid, who kept him from publishing more attacks on the shah but encouraged him to spread pan-Islamic propaganda among Iranians and other Shi'is, asking them to lend support to the Ottoman Sultan, who claimed to be the caliph (leader) of all Muslims. With this aim Afghani formed an Iranian and Shi'i pan-Islamic circle in Istanbul, two of whose prominent members were Azali Babis who had by now become radical freethinkers—Mirza Aqa Khan Kermani, a writer and an editor of the newspaper *Akhtar,* and his close friend the writer, translator, and teacher Shaikh Ahmad Ruhi, also from Kerman. The circle sent out numerous letters to the Shi'i ulama in Iran and elsewhere, bidding them to give allegiance to the sultan-caliph. The Iranian embassy complained of this activity, implicitly directed at weakening the authority of the shah (hence the participation of irreligious radicals). The sultan agreed to the extradition of Ruhi, Kermani, and a third Iranian. While the three were in prison in the eastern Turkish city Trabzon, however, Afghani intervened, and the sultan agreed not to extradite them.

The devoted Iranian servant and follower of Afghani, Mirza Reza Kermani, who had been imprisoned for years in Iran for antigovernmental activities, came to visit Afghani in Istanbul in 1895. There Afghani gave him the idea of killing the shah. After his return to Iran, Mirza Reza made his way to the shrine of Shahzadeh Abd al-Azim just when the shah was planning to visit it in preparation for celebrating the fiftieth lunar anniversary of his reign. Mirza Reza pretended to be a petitioner and suddenly shot the shah on May 1, 1896. The shah was whisked away from public view, and his corpse was propped up in a carriage while Amin as-Soltan pretended to carry on a conversation with him—this in order to avoid the disorders and rebellions that often accompanied a change in monarch. The Cossack Brigade was notified to cover Tehran, and disorder was forestalled.

Further anxiety concerned possible pretensions to the throne by two of the Shah's powerful sons. Zell as-Soltan, the shah's oldest son, who was excluded from succession owing to his mother's low birth, had a long history of political power and ambition. Feared and powerful as autocratic governor of a large group of southern provinces, he had built up a virtual private army of Western-trained soldiers that put most of the regular army to shame, and he had not hesitated to put down anyone he considered a threat. His ambition to take the throne in place of his weak and sickly half-brother, Crown Prince Mozaffar ad-Din, was well known. Concern was also felt about his younger brother, Kamran Mirza Nayeb as-Saltaneh, frequently army chief and/or governor of Tehran, who had the advantage of being on the scene in Tehran. The combination of Amin as-Soltan, the Cossacks, and the clearly expressed support of both Russians and British for the legitimate heir, however, brought expressions of loyalty to the legitimate heir by both brothers.

Naser ad-Din Shah was scarcely an illustrious ruler, but he was a relatively strong one, under whom there were few serious tribal disorders or local revolts. The disorders he faced were more directly political, and he or his advisers at least knew when it was necessary to bend or give in. Unlike his son he did not squander his treasury, and the loan to compensate the tobacco company remained his only foreign loan. His interest in reform was sporadic at best, and he sacrificed or crippled the power of his only two serious reforming chief ministers when faced by the opposition of vested intersts. In his last years he lost all concern for reform—a supposed project for codifying laws after the 1889 European trip came to nothing. Instead, he concentrated on his lifelong interest in women and young boys (one of the latter was said to be a repulsive constant companion) and on acquiring as much money and treasure as possible. He left no legacy of a state machinery that might weather what he must have known was coming—the rule of a weak and sickly successor.[4]

Mozaffar ad-Din Shah's relatively mild nature was shown in his treatment of Mirza Reza Kermani, who was interrogated but not tortured before he was hanged. The Iranian government also demanded from the Ottomans the extradition of Afghani and of his three followers still jailed in Trabzon. Sultan Abdülhamid refused to return Afghani, claiming he was an Afghan and not subject to Iranian jurisdiction. The three unfortunate progressives in Trabzon, however, who had no connection with the shah's assassination, were extradited, and the cruel new crown prince, Mohammad Ali Mirza, had them summarily executed in Tabriz. Continued Iranian demands for Afghani's extradition (Mirza Reza having said that Afghani was the only other person involved in the assassination) stopped when he became ill with cancer and died in 1897. These deaths and the cessation of *Qanun* ended one phase of the important "religious-radical alliance."[5]

Mozaffar ad-Din Shah's weakness was combined with mildness, and he was for a time open to reformist ideas. He permitted renewed activity by a man who had set up a modern type of higher school on the Ottoman model in Tabriz, where it had met with religious hostility. Such schools were now opened for the first time in Tehran. The shah also dismissed the unpopular Amin as-Soltan and later appointed the liberal and reformist Amin ad-Dauleh to be chief minister in 1897–98. The shah, however, also paid off his father's harem extravagantly, and was constantly eager for money to meet the incessant demands of his own courtiers, many of whom had come with him from Tabriz and pressed him to make up for years of lean waiting. The shah's doctors advised trips to European spas, and he wanted money for this too. When Amin ad-Dauleh was unable to raise a new loan from the British, and when his reform attempts in law and education aroused the opposition of ulama and courtiers, he was dismissed and Amin as-Soltan returned as premier.

One of Amin ad-Dauleh's projects was to invite in Belgian administrators to reorganize the customs, which had been farmed out by region, resulting in customs farmers underbidding each other to attract trade and also in farmers collecting far more than they paid in. The Belgian experiment was extended under Amin as-Soltan, and the Belgians' leader, M. Naus, was made minister of customs. This resulted in increased efficiency and collections, but also in widespread complaints by Iranian merchants that they were discriminated against in favor of foreigners, particularly the Russians, with whom the Belgians had close relations. The exact validity of these charges is unclear, but it is clear that many Iranian merchants had to pay more than formerly and that they blamed this on the shah, the prime minister, and the foreigners. Naus's influence soon extended far beyond customs, and he became de facto minister of finance.

Largely to pay for the foreign trips recommended by the Shah's doctors, Amin as-Soltan floated two large loans from Russia in 1900 and 1902. The first loan required Iran to pay off British debts and not to incur any other debts without Russian consent, and the second included major economic concessions. The Russians also insisted on a new customs treaty, signed in 1902, which gave key Russian goods lower rates than the already low 5 percent ad valorem. The income gained from the loans and from customs reform went largely for three extravagantly expensive trips to Europe that the shah and his entourage took between 1900 and 1905. Within Iran both government financial and economic conditions deteriorated.

Discontent with the government was becoming organized again. Secret oppositional societies became active in Tehran and elsewhere, and distributed inflammatory antigovernmental leaflets, called *shabnamehs* (night letters) because of their night distribution. Some members were afterward discovered and arrested. A new coalition among some of the leading ulama, courtiers, bazaaris, and secular progressives began to focus on the dismissal of Amin as-Soltan, who was seen as responsible for the alarming growth of loans and concessions to the Russians that were leading to Russian control of Iran. Even the British, alarmed at the growth of Russian influence, gave some money and encouragement to leading members of the ulama in Tehran and in the shrine cities of Iraq to help arouse activity against the Russian tide. Although they failed to stop the 1902 loan from Russia, the opposition became menacing enough to help force the dismissal of Amin as-Soltan (now adorned with the higher title of Atabak) in 1903. A decree execrating the Atabak as an unbeliever, attributed to the leading Shi'i ulama of Iraq, was widely circulated, although doubts were cast on its authenticity.[6]

The shah now appointed a reactionary relative of his, the Ain ad-Dauleh, as premier, but popular protests continued against the Belgian customs officials and against high prices. Secret societies grew, and some helped educate their members by reading and disseminating critical literature about Iran written in Persian abroad. This literature formed the basis for the idological development of many Iranians who had not traveled abroad or received a modern education. It included works by men of Persian Azerbaijani origin living in Russian Transcaucasia, such as Fath Ali Akhundzadeh. His anonymous *Kamal ad-Dauleh va Jalal ad-Dauleh,* a collection of fictitious epistles describing conditions in Iran, was bitterly critical. This series of Persian letters was imitated by Mirza Aqa Khan Kermani, who also wrote other books and articles critical of Iranian conditions. Also widely read were the educational works of Talebzadeh, an Azerbaijan emigre to Transcaucasia, and especially the *Travelbook of Ibrahim Beg* by Zain al-Abedin Maraghe'i, a book of fictitious travels in Iran that mercilessly exposed the evils of Iranian society. Less known, but not without influence, were other critical works, such as James Morier's *Hajji Baba of Isfahan* in a translation by Mirza Habib Esfahani, which added whole pages of additional and more contemporary criticism to the original, and the *True Dream* by the progressive preachers from Isfahan, Jamal ad-Din Esfahani and Malek al-Motakallemin. Such fiction reinforced the impression created by the reformist political writings of Malkom Khan and others, and by the newspapers published abroad and sent into Iran (with greater freedom under Mozaffar ad-Din than under Naser ad-Din), which were now joined by *Parvaresh* and *Sorayya* from Cairo and *Habl al-Matin* from Calcutta.[7] The only papers that could be legally distributed in Iran continued to be official or semiofficial ones.

Some Iranians now began to plan revolutionary action, and revolutionary sentiment was strengthened by the Russo-Japanese War of 1904–05 and the Russian Revolution of 1905. Iranians knew that Russia would intervene against any attempt to overthrow or undermine the Qajar government, but with the Russian government fully occupied first with war and then with revolution, it was a propitious time to move. Also, the strength shown by the supposedly backward Japanese against the dreaded Russians gave people courage, as did the shaking of such a potent autocracy as Russia by revolution. The sight of the only Asian constitutional power defeating the only major European nonconstitutional power not only showed formerly weak Asians overcoming the seemingly omnipotent West, but aroused much new interest in a constitution as a "secret of strength."

The Iranian constitutional revolution is usually dated from December 1905, when the governor of Tehran beat the feet of several sugar merchants for not lowering their raised sugar prices as ordered, which they insisted were beyond their control owing to high import prices. A large group of mollas and bazaaris then took sanctuary (bast) in the royal mosque of Tehran—whence they were dispersed by agents of Ain ad-Dauleh. A large crowd of ulama then decided, at the suggestion of the prominent liberal mujtahid, Sayyed Mohammad Tabataba'i, to retire to the shrine of Shahzadeh Abd al-Azim and formulate demands for the shah. The crucial demand was for a representative *adalatkhaneh* (house of justice) of which the meaning and composition were left unclear—perhaps in order to maintain the unity of modernizers and traditional ulama. The shah dismissed the unpopular governor of Tehran, and in January 1906 agreed to the adalatkhaneh, upon which the ulama returned to Tehran.

The shah and Ain ad-Dauleh showed no sign of fulfilling the promise, however, and acts of violence against the innocent continued in both Tehran and the provinces. Preaching against the government by the popular radical preachers Sayyed Jamal ad-Din Esfahani and Shaikh Mohammad Va'ez increased, and provided a potent means of mass political enlightenment in the absence of an open oppositional press. Sayyed Jamal was expelled from Tehran. Confronting a strong popular attempt to keep Shaikh Mohammad from being ousted, an officer killed a young sayyed. After this a great mass of mollas and some others left Tehran to take bast in the city of Qom, in July 1906. Even more bazaar merchants and tradesmen in numbers reaching twelve thousand to fourteen thousand took bast in the British legation, and Tehran business was at a standstill. Now the protesters demanded not only the dismissal of Ain ad-Dauleh but also establishment of a representative assembly or *majles*—an idea put forth by the advanced consitutionalists. Although not yet among the agreed-upon demands, a constitution, or *mashruteh,* began to be discussed by the advanced reformers.

At the end of July the shah dismissed Ain ad-Dauleh, and early in August he accepted the majles. The first majles was elected by a six-class division of electors that gave great representation to the guilds (mainly middle-class elements who often chose ulama representatives). Subsequent majleses elected by a one-class system were dominated by the landlords and rich. Early majleses had many elected ulama as deputies. Tehran, the most advanced city politically aside from Tabriz, had disproportionate representation.

The first majles opened in October 1906, as soon as the Tehran deputies were elected. A committee was assigned to write the Fundamental Law, which the shah delayed signing until he was mortally ill, in December 1906; a longer Supplementary Fundamental law was drafted in 1907 and signed by the new shah, Mohammad Ali, in October. These two documents, based largely on the Belgian constitution, formed the core of the first Iranian constitution until its replacement in 1979, although after 1912 the constitution was more often honored in the breach than the observance. The intent of the constitution was to set up a true constitutional monarchy in which majles approval was required on all important matters, including foreign loans and treaties, and in which ministers would be responsible to the majles. Equality before the law and personal rights and freedoms, subject to a few limits, were also guaranteed, despite the protests of some ulama that members of minority religions should not have equal status with those of the state religion, Islam.

The majles quickly showed its patriotism by refusing a new Russian loan and beginning plans instead for a national bank, which, however, ultimately foundered owing to lack of capital. Two conservative constitutional provisions, for a group of mujtahids to pass on the compatibility of laws with Islam and for a half-appointed upper house, were approved but not implemented.

The new freedoms of press and assembly caused a sudden flourishing of newspapers, which not only carried direct political news and comments, but also published some of the best new poetry and satire. Particularly noteworthy was the *Sur-e Esrafil* with its poems and the brilliant political and anticlerical satire of the young writer Dehkhoda. Revolutionary societies or *anjomans* were formed throughout Iran, some of them based on older guilds or fraternal groups that now became actively involved in politics. The word *anjoman* was also used for the town councils, usually elected, which now appeared for the first time in many cities with parliamentary encouragement.

In January 1907 the ineffectual Mozaffar ad-Din Shah died, and was succeeded by his cruel and autocratic son, Mohammad Ali Shah. Although the new Shah had to take an oath to support the constitution, he did not invite any majles members to his coronation, and he recalled as prime minister the Atabak, who had been traveling abroad since his dismissal in 1903. As the constitution was not categorical about who really appointed the prime minister, and the majles wished to avoid a direct clash with the new shah, they accepted the appointment despite hostile telegrams from anjomans and arguments in the majles. Conflicts over the Atabak's return and over the constitution occurred between the conservative party in the majles, led by the two prime mujtahid leaders of the revolution, Sayyed Mohammad Tabataba'i and the less principled Sayyed Abdollah Behbehani and by liberal officials; and the smaller democratic left, represented especially by the deputies from the city of Tabriz led the brilliant young Sayyed Hasan Taqizadeh. Tabriz and its surrounding province of Azerbaijan made up the advanced body of the revolution; more modernized economically, heavily involved in international trade, and in contact through travel and emigration with the similarly Turkish-speaking areas of Istanbul and Russian Transcaucasia (where many thousands emigrated temporarily or permanently every year, and whence arms were imported), Tabriz was uniquely situated to play a vanguard role. Some Tabrizis and other Azerbaijanis even preached socialist ideas, learned in Caucasia, and formed a small Social Democratic party.

The Atabak did not fulfill the shah's hope that he would get rid of the majles, but rather tried to strike a compromise between the shah and courtiers on the one hand and the majles conservatives and moderates on the other. In so doing, he aroused the distrust of both the autocrats and the radicals. He was assassinated by a member of a radical group on August 31, 1907; but there is convincing evidence that the shah was also planning his assassination and may even have penetrated the assassin's group.[8] The shah hoped to use the assassination as an excuse to suppress the revolutionaries, but in fact it encouraged them and increased their strength and boldness.

On the same date, August 31, 1907, the Anglo-Russian Entente settling the two governments' differences in Tibet, Afghanistan, and Iran was signed. The growth of the German threat to Britain encouraged this treaty, which hurt Iranians who had counted on British help against Russian intervention. The treaty divided Iran into three spheres, with northern and central Iran, including Tehran and Isfahan, in the Russian sphere; southeast Iran in the British sphere; and an area in between (ironically including the area where oil was first found in 1908) in the neutral zone. The Iranians were neither consulted on the agreement nor informed of the terms when it was signed.

After an unsuccessful attempt on his life, the shah achieved, following one failed coup, a successful coup d'état with the help of the Russian-led Cossack Brigade in June 1908. The majles was closed and many popular nationalist leaders, especially those of more advanced views, were arrested and executed. The radical preachers Jamal ad-Din

Esfahani (caught while trying to flee), Malek al-Motakallemin and the editor of *Sur-e Esrafil,* Mirza Jahangir Khan (the last two had Azali Babi ties) were among those killed. Taqizadeh along with some others found refuge in the British Legation, whence he went abroad for a time.

While the rest of the country bowed to royal control, the city of Tabriz which, exceptionally, had formed an armed and drilled popular guard, held out against royal forces. The leaders of this popular resistance were brave men of humble origin. One of them, Sattar Khan, had defied the royal order to put up white flags as a sign of surrender to the approaching royal forces, and had instead gone around with his men tearing down white flags, thus initiating the Tabriz resistance. With the help of his coleader, Baqer Kahn, Sattar Kahn and their men held out for months against an effective siege by royalist troops. When food supplies became critical the Russians sent troops into Tabriz ostensibly to protect Europeans, but effectively they took over. Many of the popular forces, known alternatively as *Mojahedin* or *Feda'iyan,* both implying self-sacrificing fighters for the faith, left for the nearby Caspian province of Gilan, where they were joined by a local revolutionary armed force, and together they began a march on Tehran. Meanwhile the Bakhtiari tribe, which had grudges against the Qajars and had some leaders who were genuinely liberal and others who wanted to control the central government themselves, helped liberate Isfahan from royalist forces and began moving northward toward Tehran. The Bakhtiaris and the northern revolutionaries converged on Tehran in July 1909. The shah took refuge with the Russians and his minor son Ahmad was made shah with the moderate Oxford-educated Naser al-Molk as regent.

The second majles was elected under a new electoral law calling for a single class of voters, and was marked by differences between what were now considered parties—the Moderates, led by Behbehani, who was assassinated by a left extremist in 1910, and the new progressive and nationalist Democratic party led by men like Taqizadeh, who was unjustly forced to leave Iran after Behbehani's assassination, with which he was unconnected.

Iran's chief problem remained finances, with the related problem of reestablishing control over the provinces, many of which were more subject than ever to tribal disorders and robberies, and remitted little of their due taxes. Desiring a foreign treasurer general unconnected with the British or the Russians, the Iranians consulted the American government and brought in a young American expert, Morgan Shuster, to control and reform their finances. Shuster planned to set up a tax-collecting gendarmerie, and to head it he proposed an officer in the British Indian army, then with the British Legation in Tehran, Major Stokes, who agreed to resign his commission and position. The Russians protested that the Anglo-Russian agreement meant that they should control any such officials in the north, and convinced the British to support their position. In November 1911 the Russians sent an ultimatum demanding the dismissal of Shuster and the agreement of Iran not to engage foreigners without British and Russian consent. The majles refused the ultimatum, but as Russian troops advanced toward Tehran, the more compliant Naser al-Molk and the "moderate" and heavily Bakhtiari cabinet forcibly dissolved the majles accepted the ultimatum, and dismissed Shuster in December 1911.[9]

These events marked the real end of the revolution, which may be considered a short-term failure, but which left an important legacy. In addition to the constitution itself, a series of financial reforms ending feudal grants and regularizing financial practices remained on the books, as did steps toward greater civil jurisdiction in the courts, and the majles as a guardian against certain foreign encroachments. Another important new feature of the period before and during the revolution was the entry of many women into the political arena. Although women had long participated in bread riots, they now put on political demonstrations, and there were women's anjomans and a women's newspaper.[10] This trend was to grow significantly after World War I. Finally, the ulama-bazaari-secular alliance had again showed its ability to arouse political action and change policy, even though the alliance was strained by internal differences.

Although the constitution was never abrogated, no new majles was elected until 1914, Russian troops continued to occupy the north, anjomans were dissolved, press censorship restored, and power returned to a conservative cabinet under the watchful control of Britain and especially Russia. Despite the constitution and political awakening that remained as positive achievements, many reverted to apathy and cynicism when faced by the restoration of foreign and conservative controls.

In 1901 a British subject, William Knox D'Arcy, had been granted a concession for oil in all Iran except the five northern provinces —Russian reaction being forestalled by the ruse of presenting the (Persian) text of the concession to the Russian legation at a time when the premier knew that the Russians' translator was away. Although the first years' explorations were discouraging, oil was finally discovered in the southwest in 1908. The Anglo-Persian Oil Company was formed in 1909. In 1912 the British navy converted from coal to oil, and in 1914 the British government bought a majority of shares in the company holding the concession. The British backed the virtually autonomous Shaikh Khaz'al, the most powerful Arab leader of Khuzistan province, and also entered into independent relations with the adjacent Bakhtiari tribal leaders.[11] British troops were stationed in this neutral zone region, and the British exercised a control in the south comparable to that held by Russia in the north. Given their decades of experience with the British and Russians, it was no wonder that many Iranian nationalists and democrats turned to the Germans for support during World War I.

5 WAR AND REZA SHAH: 1914–1941

1914–1921

World War I brought new problems and devastation to Iran. It promoted revolutionary and democratic sentiment and fueled the desire among many to reconstruct Iran as an independent country. New movements for social change came to a head in the postwar period.

When war began, the Iranian government declared neutrality, but Iran was strategically located and four powers used it as a battlefield. The Turks moved into Azerbaijan in the fall of 1914, after the Russians withdrew. The Germans played on Iranian anti-British and anti-Russian sentiments. The Kaiser was presented as a partisan of Islam, and Iranians were urged to respond to the Ottoman sultan's call for a Holy War on the Allies. British power spread when that of the Turks, Germans, and Russians declined.

Even before the war the British tried to negotiate with Russia for a new partition of Iran, with Britain to control the neutral zone where the oil was. When war came, England promised Russia postwar control of Istanbul and the Straits in return for British rule in most of Iran's neutral zone, and a secret treaty for this was signed in March 1915. Unlike the 1907 Treaty, this contained no reference to Iranian independence but said that, in the Russian sphere, Russia expected recognition of its "full liberty of action,"[1] and did not limit British activities in its zone.

The year 1915 saw the extension of fighting in Iran, with new hardships for the population. In the south the German agent Wassmuss, "The German Lawrence," organized a tribal revolt against the British, who were also active in the south. The Russians moved more forces into the north and forced the dissolution of the new third majles. Most of the majles nationalists were pro-German and anti-Russian, and they now formed a provisional government at Qom. The young Ahmad Shah continued to reign in Tehran, and so there were two governments, neither of which had much authority in a divided Iran. Later Allied advances forced the nationalist government to retreat to Kermanshah and then to flee Iran, but many of its members continued active in Istanbul and Berlin.

In 1916 the Russians were dominant in the north and the British regained control in the south. That year the British formed a local force, the South Persia Rifles, under the command of Sir Percy Sykes. By late 1917 the British controlled the south.

Nineteen seventeen was a year of turmoil with battles throughout Iran. The power of Iranian nationalists at Qom and in central Iran ended when the Russians moved into the area. British and Russian troops occupied nearly all Iran by late 1917, although the British still fought Qashqa'i tribal forces into 1918. Foreign control was weakened, however, by events in Russia. The March Revolution aroused hopes that Russian troops would withdraw, but this occurred only in the fall, when Russian troops in Iran revolted and were recalled by the new Bolshevik government. This had a liberating effect on the north even though the British moved into some of the positions abandoned by the Russians.

The war had a devastating effect, as the country was a battlefield, on which many were killed, and farmlands were ruined by invading armies. Peasants were taken from the fields and forced to work on military projects. Irrigation works requiring careful upkeep were destroyed, and cultivated areas and livestock were reduced. In some Asian countries, like India and China, the war stimulated industrial and urban development, but in Iran it caused a fall in urban enterprise and population, even though some types of local trade and crafts were stimulated. Central authority declined, and local landowners and tribal chiefs reasserted their independence and rebuilt their power.

The war's disruption awakened many Iranians to the need for strong and independent government. Nationalists' influence grew and there were wartime uprisings. The most serious antigovernmental and nationalist movement was a revolt in the Caspian province of Gilan, from 1917 on. A local leader, Kuchek Khan, led a movement for more democratic and egalitarian rule. The partisans of this movement were known as *Jangalis* (forest dwellers), because they operated in the wooded area of Gilan. By 1918 the Jangalis controlled Gilan and parts of nearby provinces.[2] In Azerbaijan a democratic movement also reached large proportions toward the end of the war. The movements were not separatist but hoped to spread their reforms to all Iran.

When the war was over, Iran faced heightened problems, among which were food scarcity, high prices, the revived power of tribal chiefs and landlords, and the diminished power of the central government. The British, whose troops occupied most of the country, spent money freely in Iran during the war, to ensure the complaisance of tribal and governmental leaders and, by the war's end, had great influence over Iran's rulers.

Late in 1917, the Bolsheviks renounced Russia's unequal treaties, loans, and concessions. Revolution in Russia and the disorders caused by war gave impetus to revived social and nationalist movements, which challenged British supremacy. In 1918 trade unions were formed in Tehran and Tabriz, among postal, printing, and other workers, and there were some successful strikes. Reform movements were especially strong in Tehran, and in the northern provinces of Gilan, Mazanderan, and Azerbaijan.[3]

Adding to discontent was a severe famine in 1918–19, which may have killed as much as one-quarter of the population in the north.[4] The famine was related to wartime Western incursions—a reduced crop area and small harvest, food needs of foreign troops, and worsened distribution. Famine was aggravated by hoarding and speculation by landlords, dealers, and officials.

From 1918 to 1921 Britain moved to consolidate control over Iran. British subsidies to the government helped insure its complaisance. In the summer of 1918 the British made Kuchek Khan halt the advance of his forces and sign an agreement that limited his control to Gilan, letting British troops control neighboring areas. Soon afterward an Iranian government, headed by Prime Minister Vosuq ad-Dauleh and subservient to the British, was formed, and was kept alive by British subsidies. The British government, particularly Foreign Secretary Curzon, wished to formalize British control over Iran by a treaty amounting to a British protectorate. Iran was useful both for oil and against Russia, and British control could make Iran part of a cordon sanitaire around the Bolsheviks.

The Iranian government, hoping to gain popularity by backing a nationalist cause, tried to attend the Versailles Peace Conference to receive restitution for Iran's wartime sufferings. Iran demanded reparations and territory taken by Russia in 1813 and 1828, but the conference did not listen, saying Iran had not been a belligerent.

The Bolshevik government encouraged nationalists in Iran with a note detailing the repudiation of tsarist privileges. All Russian concessions in Iran were renounced, except the Caspian fisheries concession, which was left to further negotiation; capitulations were given up and Iran's debts to Russia cancelled. The Soviets proposed a friendship treaty with Iran, but this was delayed by the pro-British government, which was negotiating a treaty with Britian.

The British sent new troops to Iran, and Iranian complaisance was underwritten by large bribes to the treaty's negotiators. Negotiations were secret, but the treaty was made public after Premier Vosuq ad-Dauleh signed. By the Anglo-Persian Treaty of 1919, the British would supply advisers for the Iranian government; British officers and arms would be sent to the army; a large British loan would pay for the advisers and army; transportation and communications would be developed by the British; and the tariff would be revised.[5] The treaty was interpreted as a British protectorate ensuring administrative and economic control.

The United States and France were concerned that the treaty would give a monopoly to British advisers and interests in Iran. The American minister reported:

> Persian patriots claim that this treaty amounts to a protectorate over Persia by Great Britain but the Persians are prevented from public expression of opinion or giving vent to feelings in any manner by the existing martial law and controlled press, as well as the fact that British Army now occupy Persia. While by the provisions of the Persian Constitution, treaties are not effective until ratified by the Persian Mejliss; nevertheless, it is understood that steps have been taken to immediately put into effect the

provisions of this agreement. Moreover, the current elections throughout the provinces are entirely controlled by the present Cabinet, members of which have been chosen as representatives of provinces wherein they have never been.[6]

In response to American queries whether American advisers would be permitted in Iran, Curzon said that if they met with British approval they could come, and the British tried to keep four French law professors from coming to Iran.

The British acted as though the unratified treaty were in force, sending a mission to take over Iranian finances and also military and administrative advisers. Iranian reaction to the treaty became more hostile through 1919. A nationalist movement with goals counter to the treaty grew. Iranian newspapers attacked the treaty and its signers, and demonstrations against it occurred in many areas. Opposition was met by jailing and the banishment of opponents from Tehran. The government also tried to manipulate the majles elections.

Resistance to the treaty continued through 1920, and in some areas merged with a popular democratic movement. This movement grew especially in Azerbaijan, a region much affected by Western incursions and ideas. A Democratic party was formed there under Shaikh Mohammad Khiabani, a leader of the 1905–11 movement in Azerbaijan. By April 1920, it was strong enough to force the government's agents to quit Tabriz. The movement was reformist and also expressed newly awakened national sentiments of the Turkish-speaking Azerbaijanis, some of whom felt oppressed by the Persian central government. Khiabani formed an autonomous local government and renamed the province Azadistan (*Azad*=free). Reforms like price control were undertaken to counteract continued inflation. The success of the Azerbaijan movement encouraged similar forces elsewhere.

The British, however, continued to act as if the treaty were in force. They sent experts to reorganize the armed forces, got an option for a railroad from Iraq to Tehran, took much control over Iranian finances, and brought about a revision of the Iranian tariff. The tariff law of 1920 was favorable to British imports, letting them enter at lower rates, and, hence, providing less protection and revenue. The tariff was unfavorable to Russia. Russo-Iranian trade almost stopped; goods formerly imported from Russia were in short supply, while those exported there lost markets. Reliance on British trade made the trade balance more negative. The justification for British financial control—solving Iran's fiscal problems—did not materialize: inflation continued, and tax reform was not tried.

Inaction was dangerous, given Iran's increasingly rebellious mood. Growth in discontent and its more leftward orientation appeared in the consolidation and changes in Kuchek Khan's movement in Gilan. The movement had shrunk when British and White Russian forces occupied much of north Iran, but grew again in the winter of 1919–20. In the spring of 1920, Red Army troops landed at Anzali to chase out White Russian troops there, and this helped clear out forces hostile to the Jangalis. Kuchek Khan got increasing leftist support and was encouraged by the Bolsheviks. In June 1920, Kuchek Khan's forces, in control of all Gilan, declared the establishment of an Iranian Soviet Socialist Republic, although the measures taken were more democratic-reformist than socialist. A Communist party was formed in the area, but Kuchek Khan and many other governmental leaders had disagreements with the Communists. The Jangalis aimed at changing all Iran on the Gilan model and threatened the conservative central government.

Middle-class nationalists often did not sympathize with Kuchek Khan's movement, but it bolstered their desire to change the government. Conservative nationalists wanted to divert attention from internal problems and hoped that an anti-British display would reduce demands for social change. Radical and antiradical forces were thus united against the pro-British cabinet, and this brought the resignation of Vosuq ad-Dauleh, in June 1920. A government formed under a moderate nationalist, Moshir ad-Dauleh, announced the suspension of the Anglo-Persian Treaty until British and Russian troops quit Iran and the majles could debate freely.

The British and their Iranian allies forced the resignation of Moshir ad-Dauleh in the fall, and the new prime minister, Sepahdar, was more complaisant to the British. He put British officers in command of the Cossacks and prepared to submit the treaty to the newly elected majles. The Sepahdar government was never able to put the treaty to the majles, however, owing to continued opposition.

The government suppressed the Azerbaijan movement through use of the Cossack Brigade. Khiabani was killed and reprisals taken. There were, however, outbreaks of violence in Azerbaijan in the next two years. The Kuchek Khan forces extended their control to the province of Mazanderan, but split internally. The left wanted confiscation and nationalization of land, which Kuchek Khan refused. After the Congress of the Peoples of the East in Soviet Baku in the fall of 1920, in which Iran got much attention, the Iranian Communist party adopted a more moderate program. Iran was seen as between feudalism and capitalism, and socialist measures were rejected; unity with bourgeois groups and winning of the peasants through land reform were stressed. Some of the Jangali left, particularly those leading the army, rejected this approach, but the Communist party leadership began negotiations with Kuchek Khan to reestablish a united program.

Iran's government now turned to the United States for backing and aid. The United States was showing new interest in Iran and its oil; and, in August 1920, the State Department instructed its Tehran representative:

> It is assumed that . . . you have discreetly and orally conveyed to the Persian Foreign Office information to the effect that the Department believes that American companies will seek concessions in the northern provinces and that the Department hopes that American companies may obtain such concessions. . . . The Department has taken the position that the monopolization of the production of an essential raw material, such as petroleum, by means of exclusive concessions or other arrangements, is in effect contrary to the principle of equal treatment of the nationals of all foreign countries. [7]

Iran's government wanted American advisers for ministries, including Finances and War; and an American manager for an Iranian national bank, and oil and transport concessions to the United States.

In the face of hostility, the British became doubtful about their treaty, and the United States began to consider taking over some of England's former position. Late in 1920 the Iranians requested a loan from the United States. The American government did not respond immediately, but negotiations for advisers and concessions continued.

In 1920 and 1921 negotiations were also proceeding for a friendship treaty with Soviet Russia. A treaty was needed to formalize the Russian renunciation of concessions; to reestablish normal trade broken off during civil war in the Caucasus; and to define future relations between the two countries. Negotiations broke down when Iran insisted on the return of territory taken by Russia in the nineteenth century.

By early 1921, there had been no attempt at basic solutions to problems that had been aggravated by the war. The economic crisis had abated, owing to a revival in agriculture and the end of fighting. Problems of economic structure remained as before. A British observer noted that landlords had independent armies for rent collection, peasants were like serfs, and in the villages, "a parasitic group of underlings . . . were growing rich by robbing their master, and also by bleeding the poor farmer."[8] Only in Azerbaijan and Gilan were economic reforms like price control and rent reduction begun. There was, however, a new breadth and intensity of nationalist and reform movements. These movements could take much credit for keeping Iran from becoming a virtual British colony. By early 1921 the British ceased to press for their treaty, owing to strong Iranian opposition, backed by American and Russian official opinion.

The postwar social movement in Iran had a rather sporadic and regional character. The negative effects of the war help account for both the genesis and the limitations of this movement. The war did not stimulate urban development or national economic cohesion, but furthered regionalism and disunity. The popular movement was disunited, and there was no cohesive group with a national program that could challenge the government or exercise strong influence on national affairs. Western intervention also lessened the effectiveness of popular movements.

1921–1925

Dissatisfaction with Iran's postwar governments, along with absence of any strong national party, made it possible for a small group of men to overthrow the Sepahdar government. Sayyed Zia ad-Din, known as a pro-British moderate, led the civilian side of this movement. More important was participation, along with his troops, of the self-made

Cossack Brigade commander, Reza Khan. While there is no written evidence of British civilian involvement in the coup, it is now known that the commander of British military forces in Iran, General Ironside, backed Reza Khan's rise to power in the Cossack Brigade and encouraged him to undertake a coup.[9] Sayyed Zia became prime minister in a new government following the Cossacks' entry into Tehran in February 1921, with Reza Khan as war minister. Control over the only modern armed force in the country, the Cossack Brigade, was a power base for the new government, and particularly for Reza Khan. By 1921 the British saw a protectorate was impossible and favored a strong government that could suppress the Jangalis and other threats from leftist or autonomist movements.

The accession of this government marks a turning point in Iranian history. The government showed a new independence of the West in many matters, and Western interference became more indirect. Reza Khan had no interest in fundamental social reform to help the popular classes, and his reform efforts were mainly measures for centralization and efficiency, including suppression of tribal and autonomist movements and strengthening the army and bureaucracy. Middle-class demands were partly met through centralization, the growth of trade and of the civil service, and the rejection of open British control.

Despite his moderate and pro-British background, Sayyed Zia issued a proclamation promising land reform, national independence, a plan for a modern, industrialized economy, and other social reforms. This program suggests the power of the reform movement, which influenced Sayyed Zia's words. Sayyed Zia also announced the annulment of the Anglo-Persian Treaty. He hastened to conclude the Russo-Iranian Treaty, signed on February 26, 1921, which led to the restoration of normal relations with Russia.

Articles I and II of the treaty contained Russia's renunciation of imperialist policies and all tsarist treaties with Iran. Article III recognized the Russo-Iranian border of 1881, which meant a small cession of territory acquired after 1881 by Russia. Article IV promised nonintervention by Russia in Iran's internal affairs. Articles V and VI, much discussed since, prohibited any armed organization in Iran or Russia whose aim was to "engage in acts of hostility" against the other, and allowed Russia to intervene against the troops of any power using Iran as a base of operations against Russia. Ratification of the treaty by the majles was delayed for a year, partly owing to these clauses, but ratification came soon after a statement by the Russian minister in Tehran that "Articles V and VI are intended to apply only to cases in which preparations have been made for a considerable armed attack . . . by the partisans of the [tsarist] regime which has been overthrown or by its supporters."[10]

Further treaty articles renounced Russian loans, ceded to Iran ownership of all assets of the Russian Bank, and also of Russian roads, telegraph and telephone lines, and all other concessions and property. Russia retained rights to the Caspian fisheries, and a new contract for them was later negotiated. Extraterritoriality was renounced. The Iranian government promised not to cede any former Russian concessions or property to a third party.[11] The Russo-Iranian treaty helped promote Iran's independence and reopened trade with the Russians, which helped restore some prosperity to the north.

Some economic recovery came with the resumption of more normal trade. Reza Khan began modernizing and strengthening the army, which increased his power. Personal ambition and policy disagreements led Reza Khan to force Sayyed Zia's resignation and make him flee Iran. A new cabinet was formed under Qavam as-Saltaneh, a powerful official with more liberal leanings than most of his class, but real power was increasingly in the hands of Reza Khan.

The first concern of the Qavam-Reza government was to put down movements that threatened the established order. Particularly urgent for them was Gilan. In May 1921, a government was established in Gilan including both Communists and the non-Communist forces of Kuchek Khan, who continued as prime minister. There was discord over the extent of reforms, and by late 1921, Kuchek Khan turned against the left and expelled them from the government. Internal discord made it relatively easy for the Tehran government to march in and take over at the end of 1921; Kuchek Khan was not taken but froze to death.

That same year there was revolt among Kurds and others in Khorasan, in northeastern Iran (separate from the majority of Kurds in the West). Anti-foreign and anti-government feeling were high enough among the tribespeople and peasants to permit the temporary establishment of a new government in the area, based on a program of radical social reform. The government used its superior armed forces to put down this movement in the fall of 1921.[12]

There were further popular outbreaks in late 1921 and early 1922, but then the postwar social movement was suppressed. It had suffered from geographical disunity and lack of a national program or party, owing to the backward economic and social state of Iran, its territorial disunity, and the absence of strong urban leadership groups. The popular movement helped prevent the retention of power by men who were open tools of the British. The new government was, however, more effective against protest movements than the older pro-British government had been. This was partly because middle- and upper-class nationalists were split off from protest through fear of radical consequences. Partly due to Reza Khan's efficient armed forces, by the early 1920s all protest movements were put down and trade unions and opposition propaganda were increasingly suppressed.

Reza Khan undertook the organization of the army on the British model and created the first sizable modern armed force Iran had seen. Tax collection and finances were centralized. The government also reopened negotiations for American advisers. The American government was interested in Iran but did not want to act counter to the British, who were seen as "an antidote to Bolshevikism."[13]

In the summer of 1921 the Iranian government sent the diplomat Hosain Ala to Washington to discuss an oil concession and a program for American advisers. The Iranians requested American technical advice, a loan, and investment for modernization to stop the threat of communism. The United States government was cautious about British interests but talks progressed. Standard Oil Company of New Jersey negotiated a concession for the oil of north Iran, excluded from the Anglo-Persian Oil Company (APOC) concession.

The Standard Oil concession was ratified by the majles in November 1921, but brought protests from Britain and Russia. The APOC objected to the breaking of its monopoly on Iranian oil, while the Russians said the concession violated the terms of the Russo-Iranian treaty, as a Tsarist subject had claimed a northern concession, and the treaty renouncing Tsarist concessions said they could not be given to another. Also, many Iranians objected to American influence. The

Standard concession forbade transfers of rights to other companies, but, to assuage the British, Standard agreed to share oil with APOC on a fifty-fifty basis, in return for compensation elsewhere. This violation of terms made the government heed objections to the concession, which was de facto nullified. In August 1922, negotiations began for a northern concession to the Sinclair Oil Company.

Negotiations for American advisers, particularly to reorganize finances, continued. When the State Department recommended Dr. A. C. Millspaugh, then in charge of oil affairs in the department, the British told the United States they did not object.[14] The British apparently felt that since Iran would not allow British advisers, Americans would be next best.

Millspaugh signed a contract with the Iranian government by which he had full control of the Iranian budget and financial administration. The Iranians would grant no concessions and make no financial decisions without securing Millspaugh's agreement. Several Americans accompanied Millspaugh's mission. His program was mainly to increase taxes and the efficiency of collection and attract more foreign capital investment. He used the army to insure tax collection. His main contribution to taxation was to introduce, with the approval of Reza Khan, indirect taxes whose collection was assured but which hit the poor. Millspaugh sponsored a tobacco tax, a match tax, and a government sugar and tea monopoly, all of which affected the lower classes the most. Sugar and tea were purchased by virtually all families, and tobacco and matches were items of mass consumption.[15]

Regarding foreign investments, while Millspaugh and the Iranian government were eager to attract American capital, Great Britain, still the most influential power, was hostile to inroads by others. Negotiations with Sinclair reached fruition in 1923, but Russian and British opposition, as well as strained relations with the U.S. after an American vice-consul's death at the hands of a crowd in Tehran, caused Sinclair to drop the concession.[16] This left Iran without the $10 million loan which accompanied the concession. Iranians who had wanted foreign investment became disillusioned with the American financial mission, and much press comment was hostile.

Millspaugh tried to prevent Russo-Iranian agreement on the Caspian fisheries and a new tariff law. He claimed Russia had given up rights to the fisheries and said the pro-British tariff of 1920 should be applied to Russia, although both these claims went against the 1921 treaty. No agreement on these issues was reached while Millspaugh was present, and Russo-Iranian trade suffered. Millspaugh's failures made him increasingly unpopular in Iran, and disagreements with Reza Khan led to Millspaugh's resignation in 1927.[17]

The British, rebuffed in their attempt to control all Iran, continued to try in the south. They took four years to evacuate their troops from there, and considered contingency plans for an autonomous state, including Khuzistan, the main oil province. These plans centered around Shaikh Khaz'al, the powerful Arab tribal chief. The British negotiated with Khaz'al and promised support against the central government. At the end of 1923, Khaz'al formed a group aiming at an independent south Iranian federation and got some Bakhtiari and Lur groups to follow him. The government put down the Lurs, but Khaz'al and his allies declared independence. The central government was now too strong for the rebels, however, and Khaz'al was met by Reza Khan's army and forced to surrender in 1924. Soon after this, Reza Khan negotiated with the British, who saw it was in their interest to come to terms with the newly powerful regime. The British henceforth usually supported Reza Khan.

Reza had taken over real control of Iran and persuaded the weak shah to leave for Europe, in 1923. Reza wished to insure his control against any possible revival of Qajar power. He now favored a republic and encouraged the dissemination of republican propaganda. This movement was opposed by many ulama and landlords, however, some of whom associated a republic with the secularist and relatively radical policies of Ataturk in Turkey. Both the clerical majles leader, Modarres, and the young political leader, Mohammad Mosaddeq, vocally opposed Reza Khan's plans to increase his power. Reza Kahn did not want popular control and was not averse to changing his aim to the installation of himself as shah. His power was insured by 1925 with the crushing of all tribal revolts and centers of separation or left opposition in the cities. In 1925 there was a growing anti-Qajar campaign and in October the majles deposed the Qajars. Reza's assurance that he would fulfill Islamic law and not institute radical reforms meant many ulama, landlords, and middle-class and professional persons supported his rule. Modarres, Mosaddeq, and Taqizadeh were among the few majles deputies to oppose the change. A constituent assembly, in December 1925, declared the foundation of the new Pahlavi dynasty.

Under Reza Shah, Western incursions became far more indirect than before. Socioeconomic structure had changed little from the prewar period until 1925. A Western observer in 1926 noted Iran's backwardness as compared to most Asian countries and claimed that the position of Iran's women was lower than in almost any other Muslim country, adding, "There is a tremendous gulf between the women of Cairo and Constantinople and the women of Teheran, even those of the very highest position."[18] Backwardness also continued in agriculture, and the wartime fall in agricultural production was not completely overcome by 1925.

There was little economic development before 1925. The poor had a growing tax burden, while the rich evaded taxes. Army and budgetary reform were the sole important reforms during this period. The only real development took place in the British-owned oil industry. Production shot up from the prewar low of 80,800 tons a year to 4,556,000 tons in 1926.[19] Iran had several complaints against the British, claiming manipulations that lowered royalties and a failure to train Iranians for skilled jobs. Aside from royalties and the employment of some Iranian workers, the oil industry had little effect on Iranian socioeconomic life. It was in an isolated area, wherein the British supplied almost all the economic needs. Before 1925 Iran failed to make productive use of royalties. Throughout its history the oil industry was a virtually isolated enclave that had little effect on the rest of the Iranian economy beyond what was contributed by royalties, which were low for several decades.

If industry and agriculture remained backward in the postwar period, so too did other sectors, like health and education. Foreigners, especially missionaries, ran the first modern hospitals and schools, and Iranian governments did little. Only a bare minority of Iranians were educated.[20] The position of women hardly changed, although some pioneering Iranian and foreign women and men introduced female education in new subjects and ideals of more equal treatment for women. Muslim family law was still enforced, and most middle- and upper-class urban women were heavily veiled in public and segregated

from men. Office jobs were not open to women, and they were subject
to the worst exploitation in carpet and textile workshops. Some
pioneering women leaders had begun to work for women's education,
welfare, and rights. Certain male intellectuals and poets ever since the
late nineteenth century wrote for these causes. The resulting schools,
orphanages, and organizations laid the foundations for later improvements in women's position.[21] Down to today, however, improvements
have affected mainly the middle and upper classes.

For all its relative backwardness, Iran in 1925 felt great pressure for
change. To exist as an independent nation, Iran needed a civil service,
army, and efficient tax system. The middle classes grew after the war,
and many of them wanted new outlets for their talents and capital. The
revival of foreign trade meant a growth of Iranian merchant capital,
while profits achieved by speculators and others in the war were also
potential sources of investment. Before 1925, there were bare beginnings of industry, notably textile mills, mostly in Isfahan, but this was
insufficient to meet the middle class and modernizers' desire for investment and modernization. Pressure mounted for industrial tariff
protection and for modern transportation to develop a national market
and insure central control over the provinces. Also, the government
wished to break down the tribal-nomadic way of life in order to end a
threat to state power.

Thus, there were pressures to industrialize and modernize, although
these were based mainly on top-level nationalism. Reza Shah soon
began an impressive program of modernization largely by superimpos-
ing new institutions on the old agrarian structures. Interaction with the
West influenced the direction of change. In addition to pressures from
the small middle class, "modernization from above" was seen by Reza
Shah and those around him as the only way to make Iran a strong,
self-respecting nation that could hold its own in the modern world.

1925–1941

Political life under Reza Shah was extremely limited, owing to the
Shah's despotic controls and suppression of opposition. The prominent
poet Eshqi was early assassinated for his opposition to the new ruler.
The fiery clerical opposition leader Modarres was imprisoned in 1929

and killed nine years later. Mohammad Mosaddeq, a high-born Western-trained liberal nationalist intellectual who started his Iranian official career as a teen-ager, continued briefly to attack Reza Shah's programs in the majles. He was soon put out of office and retired to his estate, reemerging to prominence in World War II. Other high-level oppositionists either kept quiet or were, at least for a time, co-opted by the regime, as was the former democratic leader of the constitutional revolution, Sayyed Hasan Taqizadeh, who became minister of finance and minister to England.

More striking was the fate of some of Reza Shah's top advisers and aides. Abdol Hosain Taimurtash, a highly able adviser and negotiator on whom the shah depended heavily, died in prison after the oil negotiations of 1933, in which the shah suspected him of double-dealing. Sardar As'ad Bakhtiyari, whose national power dated back to the constitutional revolution, became a leading supporter of Reza Shah, but was arrested and murdered in prison. Lesser men suspected of disloyalty were similarly treated, although some old and new politicians continued to serve Reza Shah throughout his reign. The majles became a rubber stamp and the constitution was paid lip service only. Communist and socialist groups and propaganda were outlawed, and effective censorship meant that only official nationalism stressing national homogeneity, anticlericalism, and a modernity and strength that were read into the pre-Islamic past could flourish.

The years 1925 to 1941 saw the partial fulfillment of a far larger modernization program than had ever been attempted in Iran. In these years Western incursions were mostly indirect, but the continued alliance between the regime and certain Western interests influenced the nature of reform. If the emphasis below seems critical, this may be a counterweight to the more usual listing of impressive changes, which may easily be found in various publications.[22]

Between 1925 and 1930 foundations were laid for a program of modernization from above. The income from high taxes on sugar and tea was saved for use on a railway. In 1925 a uniform land tax was established, to be based on a new land survey.

A conscription law, with universal service, was enacted in 1926. Army reform and strengthening was a primary concern of Reza Shah, and military expenses were for a time the largest budget item. This meant that the armed forces were large and modern enough during Reza Shah's reign to maintain governmental authority. Civil service reform in 1926 established a bureaucracy with certain ostensible educational standards. Like the army, the bureaucracy grew prodigiously and was a force supporting the government. The civil service became the major outlet for educated young men, and there was pressure to create more jobs, to which the government often responded.

The growth of the army and the bureaucracy contributed to urbanization, and Tehran's population grew greatly. Nearly all civil service jobs were in the capital, owing to a policy of rigid centralization, with all important decisions made in Tehran. The growth of Tehran created new jobs for most urban groups. The army and civil service were channels for the spread of new ideas, although censorship and government propaganda limited published ideas largely to official nationalism.

From 1925 to 1928 three new codes of law, largely based on French models although incorporating parts of the sharia, were approved. These replaced religious and customary law, which had served in premodern society, but which many saw as a brake on economic development. Religious law had, for instance, forbidden trade by Muslims in some goods and the charging of interest, and had left certain commercial rulings to the ulama. The joint-stock principle was not recognized. A new Commercial Code in 1925 curtailed ulama influence in commercial matters and recognized joint-stock companies and other principles of modern Western commerce. In 1926 a Criminal Code was approved, and in 1928 a Civil Code.[23] Some ulama objected , but they had little strength against the bureaucracy, the army, and the commercial middle class.

Preparation for a railroad, centralization, and provision for modern economic enterprise were measures that permitted the establishment of a more modern economy. Most important was Reza Shah's declaration, in the spring of 1927, that Iran would take control of its tariff policy within a year and not be bound by tarriffs negotiated under duress. It was also announced that other "capitulations" favoring foreigners would be abolished. (This was more easily accepted by the West, given Iran's new legal codes, which were adopted partly to end the capitulations.) In 1928 new commercial treaties were signed with most Western nations, raising tariffs on many goods. Tariff policy was primarily based on revenue needs, however, and protective tariffs on goods that competed with existing or projected industries were not yet enacted. No distinction was made between luxury and essential imports, aside from duty-free agricultural and other machinery.

If some reforms encouraged capitalism, others strengthened the position of landlords. Any village in the possession of one person for thirty years became his private property. This legalized expropriations that had occurred since the nineteenth century. In many areas there was still a division of ownership, with peasants and nomads having some traditional rights to the land they worked. Laws of 1928–29 requiring registration of property strengthened doubtful claims to land. The wealthy might register land to which peasants had titles, as the upper classes influenced the courts and government.[24] Land registration laws, as in many countries, were a modernizing step taken at the expense of the poor.

The 1928 Civil Code also strengthened landlords. Although the code shows French influence, it largely restated Muslim principles, updated where modern exigencies required. The Civil Code recognized de facto ownership as proof of ownership, thus confirming usurpations.[25] Lacking articles that protected peasants, the code was weighted toward landlords. Tenants were liable for keeping the harvest up and carrying out the terms of the sharecropping agreement, despite obstacles. The code assumed a contract between landlord and tenant but did not require one. Generally tenants had to comply with the landlord's interpretation of an oral agreement. According to Ann Lambton: "It will . . . be clear that very little attention is paid by the Civil Code (or any other body of legislation) to the regulation of the relation of landlord and tenant. In general the scales are weighted in favour of the former, and little or no protection is afforded to the latter."[26]

The only pre–1930 laws encouraging agricultural modernization were the exemption of agricultural machinery imports from tariffs and of industrial crops from taxes. These laws favored the development of mechanized capitalist farming, but, in fact, few mechanized farms were inaugurated. The old system remained profitable, as labor was cheap.

The early years of Reza Shah's rule also saw a successful effort to disarm and settle the nomads. This was done primarily to suppress power centers that might be a threat. Many tribes were forcibly settled by government troops. No alternative way of making a living was provided, and most tribes had to continue their husbandry and agriculture on inadequate land. Ex-nomads could support much less livestock when deprived of the chance to move from summer to winter grazing quarters, and horses and cattle died from severe winters and lack of grain. Tribes were settled at the cost of impoverishing nomads, and of decreasing livestock production. Many tribespeople awaited only the demise of Reza Shah to resume migrations. Tribal uprisings that protested this policy were cruelly suppressed.

The years 1925–1930 marked the beginning of educational reform. Earlier some Western technology, ideas, and languages had been taught in foreign missionary schools, private schools, and a few government schools. Although a public school program had been provided for after the constitutional revolution, internal troubles prevented its being carried out. Only in 1926 did the majles vote that one-half percent of the land-tax receipts should go to a public elementary school system—still a very inadequate sum. A uniform school curriculum on the French model and emphasizing academic training was adopted. In 1928 foreign and private schools were required to teach in Persian and follow the public school curriculum. Another 1928 law provided for sending Iranian students abroad each year. Exemption from military service was a strong motive for attending secondary and higher schools. Still, it was mostly the wealthy who went to school, and education was almost nonexistent in rural areas. Under Reza Shah an average of 4 percent of the budget went to education[27] and inadequate funding continued under his son.

An active movement for the emancipation and education of women, led by several courageous women campaigners, existed in Iran even before 1925.[28] Reza Shah's early modernization program relaxed somewhat the social restrictions on women, and encouraged the adoption of European dress and manners at home, although the government moved slowly in this matter in the 1920s. Modern dress was decreed for all Iranian men in 1929, but urban women continued to wear their traditional outer dress in public for several years more. For most urban women this consisted of the chador and a face veil. The Civil Code retained most of the sharia provisions: divorce easy for men but difficult for women; guardianship of children by the man in case of separation;

consent of the father for a daughter's marriage; and polygamy and temporary marriage. A husband could kill an adulterous wife and her lover with impunity and could keep a wife from a job "degrading" to him or her. The only reforms were a rise in the legal marriage age,[29] and a requirement that all marriages be registered in civil bureaus. By 1930 the foundations for a program of economic modernization from above had been laid. Most important was centralization, accomplished via a growing bureaucracy and a strong army. In the Reza Shah period, the main public expenditure was on the armed forces, which took over half of the government budget. The army was used primarily to strengthen the government's authority within Iran, over peasants, tribes, and urban dissidents. The privileged classes now included more government employees, army officers, students, and merchants. The status of nomads was lowered when they settled, while urban unemployment, the outlawing of trade unions and leftist groups, and laws strengthening landlords helped keep the peasants and workers impoverished. Reza Shah terrorized or jailed potential opponents, and there was no chance for organized oppositional politics.

Earlier Western activities had supported traditional ruling groups, but Western influence on the socioeconomic structure undermined old relations and gave impetus to the introduction of reforms and economic changes. The West continued to influence Iran's economic structure via world market conditions. Western demand and Iran's economy limited Iran's exports to oil, carpets, and agricultural goods, while expensive manufactured goods were imported, and Iran's balance of trade continued to be negative.

From about 1930 to his abdication in 1941, Reza Shah embarked on an ambitious modernization program, with government control over the economy. Many of his measures, as in other spheres, were modeled on the reforms of Ataturk in Turkey; often Reza Shah would inaugurate a reform a year or two after a nearly identical one had appeared in Turkey. Basic causes of reform can be found within Iran, however. The world economic depression increased Iran's economic and social problems, and there were several peasant and tribal risings in the early thirties. The depression, by lowering demand for Iran's products, threatened Iran's trade and production. Partly to meet these threats, the government began a strong program of state-centered economic development.

Given the existing social structure and low purchasing power of most Iranians, the state was the logical initiator of development. Private capital was too undeveloped and too attracted to "safe," quickly profitable fields like land and usury to be directed to industry, which often involves high initial investment, slow returns, and competition with Western goods. Purchasing power was too low and transport too undeveloped to ensure a large internal market. Even those willing to invest in modern enterprises were eager, as elsewhere, to have the government carry infrastructural costs and to guarantee their companies against losses.

In transport Iranian and Western interests had formerly differed, and Britain and Russia had discouraged the development of railroads. After 1925, however, when Iran became unified with no Western spheres of influence, Western and Iranian interests coincided here. It was in the West's economic interest to have modern transport to facilitate the sale of Western goods, and it was in Iran's interest to encourage internal trade. Since the late 1920s Western powers have backed efforts to improve Iran's transportation. Military-strategic considerations also motivated both Iran and Western powers.

In 1920 Iran had a very backward transportation system, with about two thousand miles of usable roads, designed more to facilitate Western penetration than to link Iran internally. Road construction, with the help of foreign firms, increased road mileage over ten times from the mid-twenties to the late thirties. In 1920 it cost two hundred dollars a ton and took two months to take goods from southern ports to Tehran; by 1929 motor transport of goods was general, and the same trip took one or two weeks and cost fifty dollars a ton. Motor vehicles in Iran rose from about six hundred in 1928 to twenty-five thousand in 1942.[30]

Reza Shah was determined to build a railroad to connect north and south Iran, and funds for this were collected from 1925 on. In 1928 an agreement was signed with a German and American syndicate to survey the ground and build a trial section. The contract was annulled in 1931, and in 1933 a new contract was signed with a Scandinavian consortium, who worked until the railroad was completed in 1938. Work and material orders were divided among many countries, partly to avoid control by any one power. Railway construction created the first Iranian work force numbering in the tens of thousands outside the Anglo-Persian Oil Company.[31]

As in many countries, the railroad was largely an instrument to ensure the political, economic, and military control of the government. It also provided an economic link between north and south, but its high cost, estimated between $150 million and $200 million for a single track road, was a great drain on national wealth.[32] The bulk came from those least able to afford it, through regressive taxes. A national road system could have been cheaper and more useful.

Shipping remained in foreign hands as Iran had no ships, but an air service was inaugurated. Telegraph, telephone, and radio communications, although still small, expanded under government auspices. Transport and communication were a major achievement of the Reza Shah regime, whose expenses were borne mainly by the poor, with road building financed largely through a road tax levied on common consumer goods.

In industry as in transport, government encouragement and financing brought rapid growth. Various forms were used, including government ownership, partial or total ownership by the shah or a bank, and private ownership, often with governmental guarantees or subsidies. After World War I industry had been limited to a few power plants and match factories. In the 1920s, small, privately owned textile factories expanded, but real growth came only in the 1930s. Then approximately thirty modern large factories owned by the government were built, plus another two hundred small factories, with both government and private owners.[33]

Nearly all cities had electric light and power plants by the late 1930s. Large sugar refineries, spinning mills, and weaving mills were built. Meat and fruit processing factories were built along the Caspian, and several soap and vegetable-oil plants were constructed throughout Iran. Wheat and barley were cleaned and milled in government plants. The state Tobacco Monopoly operated a highly profitable plant in Tehran.[34] Industry was concentrated in textiles and agricultural processing, in which capital outlay was relatively low and the savings from producing close to the market or source of supply were great. Iran still remained dependent on the West for heavy industry. The one cement factory built in Tehran was inadequate to meet Iran's needs. Mining and smelting barely progressed.

Industry was guaranteed by government monopolies on some items, government licensing of industry to ensure against competition, and government financing and loans to companies. To promote Iranian goods the government required civil servants to dress in Iranian-made clothes. Another potential aid to industry was high tariffs. Tariffs might have helped the Iranian economy had they been used to protect the building of efficient industry. However, they mostly raised profits by allowing manufacturers to raise prices without improving productivity. Government and semiprivate monopolies also charged high, noncompetitive prices. There was an inflationary rise in the Iranian price index in the late thirties, caused largely by the encouragement of high prices.[35] Reza Shah's industrialization apparently rested more on the capture of existing or reduced markets than on the creation of expanding ones, which would have required higher incomes for the majority and increased, efficient production.

Reza Shah's policy toward city workers was similar to that toward peasants. Strikes were broken and unions outlawed, and low wages were perpetuated by agricultural poverty and chronic unemployment. A gesture toward factory regulation came in a 1936 law creating standards of construction, hygiene, and workmen's compensation, but these were mostly ignored, as there was no inspection. The only provisions carried out well were those outlawing strikes and unions. Long hours with low wages remained the lot of workers, with women and children the most exploited.

The economic enterprises launched by Reza Shah suffered from overcentralization and bureaucratic inefficiency. He and many of his subordinates profited from government-sponsored enterprises by both legal and shady practices. Government protection and financing of industry often discouraged efficiency. The practice of paying out all profits as dividends and then turning to the government for funds was, and remained, characteristic of Iranian enterprise. Government help and guaranteed high profits to semiofficial trade monopolies favored investment in commerce, rather than in the more essential industry, as commerce required less capital and promised quicker returns. In 1940 there were twice as many commercial as industrial corporations, and their total capital was twice as high. Management and control of enterprises was lodged in Tehran, with little local initiative or decentralization. Economic development centered in Tehran, which, by 1940, was the scene of 58.5 percent of all domestic capital investment.[36] Development of industry and other economic enterprises was an important step toward modernization, but was often done in ways that led to inefficiency, corruption, and exploitation.

In the 1930s there was also extensive urban construction, especially the modernization of main streets and of downtown Tehran. In general, the middle and upper classes benefited most, whereas the more populous classes bore the major cost of the fine new buildings and streets.

Finance in the 1930s was characterized by a large increase in government income, expenditure, and financial control. Banking came under national control with the provision for a National Bank in 1927. The role of the National Bank as Iran's leading financial institution was ensured in 1930 when the right to issue bank notes and other national banking privileges were withdrawn from the British Imperial Bank. All banking in Iran came under government control; the Agricultural and Industrial Bank was formed in 1933 and the Loan Bank in 1939. These banks provided a large share of the capital used for Iranian industry, trade, and transport. Their capital came from tax monies provided largely by the poor, while profits from the enterprises they helped went to private individuals, officials, or the government. Credit on reasonable terms went to the upper classes, while peasants, smaller bazaaris, and workers remained subject to usurious rates. No cooperatives or group credit institutions were started. The Agricultural and Industrial Bank gave low-interest loans only to landholders who were good risks, who might lend the same money to tenants at higher rates.

The Reza Shah regime avoided foreign debt by means of large increases in indirect taxes. Government expenditure, in terms of the pound sterling and not the deflated rial, rose tenfold from 1923/24 to 1941/42.[37] Oil royalties provided only about 10 percent of the budget, the rest coming mostly from indirect taxes. Rial income of the poorer classes in the 1928–40 period was stationary. The government budget in rials, however, rose over elevenfold.[38]

By the late 1930s and early 1940s half of government income was going to industry, transportation, and trade, while the ministry of war was the third spender, after the ministries of transport and industry.[39] A large part of government outlays went to maintain a swollen bureaucracy. Expenses for education, health, and public works were low. The regime's strategy meant that the profits of modernization accrued mainly to the enlarged, but still small, middle and upper classes.

A key to Iran's problems remained its agrarian structure, which encouraged low productivity, medieval methods, and investment in land and usury. A 1934 study of agriculture shows the growth of traditional evils, with the government strengthening the old system. According to this account, private landholders had about 80 percent of the cultivated land, the state 10 percent, and 10 percent was vaqf. Large landlords with several villages owned about half the land, yet 95 to 98 percent of the agricultural population was reportedly landless.[40] Peasant proprietorship was rare, found mainly on marginal lands, and even these peasants were under the thumb of landlords. Their economic position was little different from that of tenants. Sharecropping was prevalent on the vast majority of land. Contracts were oral, unclear, and designed to keep tenants from accumulating a surplus.[41]

In the more prosperous northern provinces of Gilan and Mazanderan, some peasants paid fixed rents. This allowed them to accumulate a surplus and was disliked by landlords. More prevalent throughout Iran was renting by an intermediary. This involved a short-term contract from a landlord by a renter who subcontracted to peasants. This system was partly a result of increasing large properties, for which a landlord could not be responsible. Most state and vaqf land was rented like this.[42] The system hurt agriculture by encouraging high short-term profits and discouraging investment. Peasants were often more abused by renters than by landlords, who at least had a long-term interest in their cultivation. Land was periodically redistributed, so that peasants had no permanent stake in a plot. They were supervised by landlord-appointed agents. The village headman (*kadkhoda*), who had once represented in part the villagers' interests, was now a landlord appointee, as was the man in charge of water distribution.[43]

Tradition based the crop division on five factors—land, labor, water, seed, and animals—with the provider of each to get one-fifth of the crop. In practice the weight allowed to each factor varied. The peasant's share might vary from one-fifth to seven-eighths of the crop, depending on where he lived and what he supplied.[44] Many peasants were also subject to landlords' dues and taxes, to state taxes, and to a share in the pay of village officials. Peasant conditions were best in the northwest, but were bad elsewhere. Housing and health conditions were primitive and unsanitary. Peasants were often hungry, diseased, and malnourished. Although migrating tribes were generally better off than peasants in health, food, and independence, settlement reduced them to the level of the peasant, which is one reason it was resisted.

In the 1920s and 1930s there was no agrarian reform, although an attempt was made to bring in a few technical improvements. The regime's policy strengthened the position of large landowners. Unprofitable state lands were put on the market in 1934, but on terms that only the rich, officers, or officials could afford. Thus even a painless way to begin reform through the sale of land to peasants was avoided.[45] Through expropriation and forced sales, Reza Shah made himself by far the biggest landlord in Iran.

The later 1930s saw little change. A 1935 law concerning kadkhodas said they were landlords' representatives and responsible for enforcing law and order. No provision was made for consulting the villagers. A law of November 1937 made landlords responsible for proper cultivation of their estates on pain of confiscation, but no regulations for enforcing this law were drawn up, owing to landlord opposition.

In Sistan province, where landlords were notably unproductive, state lands were to be sold to peasants in 1937. So many complaints were made of the law's being flouted that Reza Shah set up a commission to investigate, but it did not ensure that peasants got the land. Landlords and officials used their power to take over the land. Through pressure, such as withholding needed water from the land, many peasants were expropriated.[46]

Almost the only agricultural measures taken were aimed at increased productivity. A 1937 law encouraged the improvement of badly cultivated lands or wastelands through agricultural loans. A few agricultural schools and experimental stations were founded, notably the Agricultural College at Karaj, near Tehran. These measures had few results, and, in 1940, a Five-Year Plan for agriculture was launched. Its operation was interrupted by the war, but its success was always problematic. The lack of measures to improve the lives of the poorer classes hindered fundamental economic change. Few landlords and merchants were moved to invest in modern enterprise when traditional exploitation of land and peasants continued to be profitable. Improvement in agricultural methods was unlikely as long as peasant labor was so cheap that landlords had little desire to encourage innovations. In the depression, prices for agricultural goods sold by peasants fell more than the prices of the manufactures they bought.[47] The peasants got no protection against dispossession or rent increases. The extension of police and army control, allowing rapid suppression of any movement for better conditions, also helped keep down the peasants' economic and political status.

Landlordism and declining rural standards were the weakest point of Reza Shah's modernization. If Iran were to develop large-scale industry an expanding national market was needed to provide purchasers for industrial goods. In fact, however, the consumer-goods market declined in the 1930s, except for expensive luxury products.[48] This was partly owing to the world depression, but also to Iran's unproductive agrarian system. Agricultural productivity and peasant living standards could not be raised without reform.

Toward the tribes, Reza Shah continued a policy of military control without economic solutions. With the Kurds and other major tribes he pursued a policy of forcible disarmament, arrest of tribal leaders, and control through military rule. The Iranian government also tried to suppress autonomist sentiments among the Kurds and other tribal peoples and national minorities. Some tribes like the Lurs were decimated by governmental policies.

Foreign trade under Reza Shah shows both the problems and the achievements of Iran's new relations with the West. Iranian foreign trade surpassed its prewar level by the 1920s. Trade with Great Britain prospered, more than counterbalancing the fall in trade with Russia, which reached only three-fourths of its prewar level in 1928.[49] British trade accounted for the majority of Iranian trade in the 1920s, disregarding APOC imports and exports. Trade with Great Britain was encouraged by APOC royalties, much of which were left in England during the 1920s and 1930s to pay for military equipment. British-Iranian trade ties were also strengthened by Reza Shah's emphasis on construction of southern roads. Iran's trade balance with Britain continued to be negative, while that with the Soviet Union was about even.

In 1929 and 1930 a crisis developed in Iran's foreign trade. The country could not sell its exports, or had to sell at ruinous prices, after the 1929 crash.[50] Also, trade with the Soviet Union was down, owing to disagreements. Dependence on Britain and the impossibility of exporting Iranian goods at the old prices contributed to a disastrous drop in the sterling value of the Iranian rial. Although the rial value of trade scarcely fell in the early 1930s, its real value fell to less than one-third the 1929 level. This fall was greater than the world average, despite efforts to encourage trade.[51] The import decline was sharpest in some articles of mass consumption, such as plain cotton and woolen cloth, while luxury imports remained as before and goods needed for industry and transport rose. The government continued to levy both import duties and excise taxes on items of mass consumption so that Iranians could buy fewer of them in the depression years.

The regime tried to overcome Iran's negative trade balance and to halt the rial's drop in value. This policy was embodied in the Monopoly of Foreign Trade Law of 1931. The government took control over imports and exports, with the aim of balancing them. Some imports were reserved to the government, and others could be authorized only by proving exports of greater value. The exchange rate between the rial and the pound was fixed. Smuggling and evasion limited the monopoly's effectiveness, and it was soon relaxed, mainly in the interests of big merchants whose exports had been restricted. The law provided a favorable trade balance only in its first year, although the negative balance was reduced. Control of currency exchange was abandoned, largely under foreign pressure, and the rial dropped further.[52]

The world economic crisis, characterized by a sharper drop in agricultural than industrial prices, hurt Iran. The price of manufactured goods from the West remained high, while the price of Iranian goods on the world market fell by two or three times. Iranian workers and peasants might have to put out twice as much work in order to buy a manufactured item. By 1932 the 1929 price level of imports had effectively doubled.[53] To maintain a more equal trade balance, Iran cut its imports, especially in mass-consumption articles. The dearth of local industry meant that few items could be produced and consumption fell. Large merchants shifted the burden of the crisis to consumers and smaller merchants. The government and large merchants formed several joint semiofficial trade monopolies, which had exclusive control of foreign trade in items including silk and cotton. These monopolies were often partially financed by the National Bank, and their exclusive control put many smaller merchants out of business. Monopoly profits were often government-protected and high.[54] Guaranteed profits enabled the monopolies to withstand exchange-rate fluctuations and other uncertainties that undid small traders, and trade became increasingly concentrated in the hands of large Tehran merchants. Trade monopolies discouraged price competition, and import prices were kept at levels guaranteeing high profits to the monopoly. Protection of big traders, as of big landlords, limited the capital going into manufacturing.

Increasing the prices of necessities were customs duties, which equalled an average of 30 percent in the early 1930s, and even more later.[55] Prices were further raised by guaranteed monopoly profits, which were in reality taxes, as the largest share went to the government, and by excises. Recovery of import and consumption of the basic items in the late 1930s was incomplete. In the late 1930s industrial goods were imported more as new industries were built, and arms imports grew. Imports of medium-priced and luxury goods increased but mass-consumption imports remained low. By the end of the decade, the Soviet Union had overtaken Great Britain in Iranian trade, the United States had an important trade position, and Germany had become Iran's leading trade partner.[56]

Capital invested in commercial corporations by 1940 was greater than that in industrial, transport, and banking corporations combined.[57] Merchant capital, with strong Western ties, continued to be the dominant form of capital.

Political and social life in the 1930s had many of the same features as the economy. Strict centralization was the rule in politics as in the economy. There was no elected self-government in villages, towns, districts, or provinces. Officials were appointed from and accountable to Tehran. In 1938, local administrative units were reorganized into a nationwide hierarchy, with divisions often cutting across traditional cultural and ethnic lines. Control was autocratic and distant, separating the administrator and the subject, who might literally speak different languages and have different educations and values.

Education saw important advances, although these affected mainly the upper and middle classes. The government for the first time put a regular and increasing share of taxes into education, so that educational expenses rose from £100,000 in 1925 to £2 million to £3 million in 1940—still a very low percentage of the budget.[58] Less than 10 percent of the population received any elementary education, and, for secondary education, the figure was under one percent. In 1935 Tehran University was founded, giving Iran its first modern university, and it was opened to women. Students were also sent abroad by the government in increasing numbers. However, traditions of contempt for manual and technical work and the effects of overcentralization hurt education. Control over details of education remained in Tehran, and the course of study was formal and academic, aimed at producing an intellectual elite, with little relation to practical needs. Official nationalism propagated an emphasis on Iranian history and literature, with stress on the pre-Islamic empires and de-emphasis of Islam. As the legal and educational positions open to those with religious educations declined, sons of the ulama tended increasingly to get secular educations and jobs. Social welfare, including public health and hospitals, also registered some advance under official auspices for the first time.

The partial emancipation of Iranian women was one of the most important changes occurring during the Reza Shah regime. A growing women's movement since the early twentieth century and the Westernization of middle- and upper-class life, as well as women's entrance into factory work, teaching, and nursing, helped relax traditional restrictions on women's lives. A gradual lessening of restrictions took place through the 1930s. In 1936 the use of the veil was outlawed and women were ordered to dress in Western-style clothing. (Although many people think Ataturk had passed a similar law, this is untrue; Iran was the first country to outlaw the veil.) The brutal enforcement of this law until 1941 was one reason for a later pro-veil backlash, and many now doubt that legislation is a useful approach to veiling. Women's education was also encouraged by the regime, although over three times as many boys as girls continued to receive education.[59] There was a de facto decline in upper-class polygamy and in inequality in marriage and divorce in the modernized classes, and a rise in paid work for women. These trends affected primarily middle- and upper-class women, who nevertheless did not obtain political rights or complete economic and social equality, though their advance in a decade was considerable. Women's organizations, also mainly middle and upper class, continued to work, provided their aims were considered consonant with those of the regime. Women working on carpets and textiles may have had a harder life than before, however.

The Reza Shah period, for all its apparent independence of Western control, was affected by the Western powers, as can be seen particularly in Reza Shah's economic program and foreign relations. Foreign investment grew at a rapid rate, notably in the oil fields, but also in transport and communications. In foreign policy, Reza Shah was friendly first to the British and later to the Germans. For all his nationalist talk, he did not end Iran's dependence on the West or undermine foreign interests in Iran, although he acted with considerable independence.

The major Western power in Iran continued to be Great Britain, whose capital investment in the oil fields during the 1930s overshadowed all Iranian investment in trade and industry. There were more workers employed in the oil fields than in all other industries combined.[60] Although the British had to give up their banking privileges, the main center of their economic power and profit remained inviolate. There was a major dispute over the terms of the oil concession, but this did not end with any real loss to APOC. A series of accumulated postwar grievances caused Reza Shah to cancel the APOC concession in 1932. British threats and Reza Shah's fear of internal revolts were among the factors bringing Reza Shah to accept a revised concession in 1933, which did not significantly improve Iran's control or royalties. The concession's area was reduced but its termination was changed from 1961 to 1993, by which time most of the oil could be gone. Great Britain continued to reap huge profits and pay low royalties, to be the economic masters in Khuzistan, controlling retail trade as well as the oil industry, and southern politics were still largely British controlled.

Reza Shah chafed under British influence, and the British were unpopular with Iranian nationalists. This hostility, combined with a German drive for economic and political influence in Iran, led to a rise in Germany's position in the late 1930s. German firms had a large role in the Trans-Iranian Railroad. The Germans opened sea and air communication with Iran and provided most of the machinery and contractors in Iran's industrial, mining, and building program. Germany was the leading country in Iran's foreign trade from 1939 to 1941, controlling about half of it.

Seen as a base against the Soviet Union, Iran was penetrated by the Germans militarily and politically. Nazi ideology and agents were prominent, and the Germans declared Iran a pure Aryan country. Reza Shah was not averse to Nazi phrases and methods, as they suited his dictatorial and nationalistic inclinations. On the eve of World War II, Iran housed German economic and political agents, and the government had economic and political commitments tying it to a pro-German policy.

During the Reza Shah period, economic self-determination could only have come to Iran if the regime had followed a policy of fundamental socioeconomic reform. Instead, Reza Shah took a path to modernization that did not integrate the economy, which remained unbalanced. Economic dependence on the West and on the fluctuations of the world market remained crucial.

Despite its limits, modernization did have an impact on the Iranian socioeconomic structure. For the first time, a significant modern bourgeoisie was created, albeit with strong traditional features. Most Iranian capitalists or factory managers used old methods of nepotism, bribery, government aid, and quick high profit, but they were also interested in industrialization. The middle class was augmented by several new groups: a growing bureaucracy, increasingly influenced by Western education and ideas; army officers, who became a feared and privileged caste; doctors, lawyers, and teachers, imbued with Western ideas and methods; a limited number of technical specialists and engineers; and some journalists and writers. As these groups developed in the cities, the service trades there also grew—the bazaars expanded and new retail stores were built to accommodate new needs. A rapid growth of the urban classes was characteristic of the Reza Shah regime. The new urban working class was a product of this period. Migration to, and modernization of, Tehran made it the center of working and middle classes, often at the expense of provincial cities. Economic structures were changed through a reinforcement of private property and of the position of large landlords and traders, along with an increase in the relative weight of more modern enterprises, transport, banking, and industry. A breakthrough had been made toward economic growth. Nevertheless, agriculture still employed almost 90 percent of working Iranians. Traditional methods in agriculture and trade left productivity extremely low. In the countryside the impact of the Reza Shah regime was both least apparent and least happy. Nothing was done to improve the conditions of the peasantry, and the government's demands on peasants, in the form of taxes and military services, were greater than before.

The Reza Shah regime widened the gap between the growing, but still quite small, middle and upper classes, and the vast majority of the poor. If new opportunities existed for entrance to the privileged classes and the scope of these became wider, these opportunities scarcely affected most of the population. Reza Shah's work for rapid modernization from above, along with his militantly secularist cultural and educational program, helped create the situation of "two cultures" in Iran, which became more acute in recent decades. The upper and new middle classes became increasingly Westernized and scarcely understood the traditional or religious culture of most of their compatriots. On the other hand, the peasants and the urban bazaar classes continued to follow the ulama, however politically cowed most of the ulama were in the Reza Shah period. These classes associated "the way thing should be" more with Islam than with the West or with the new myth of pre-Islamic Iran, whose virtues were essentially Western.

Under Reza Shah, the social structure continued essentially to be one where a small minority lived off the labors of the rest. The Reza Shah program of modernization, and the growth of the privileged classes, were largely financed by exactions from the majority. In these exactions, the West also participated, as more and more Iranian goods were needed to pay for Western industrial products. Iran's economic development and reform program produced some striking results, which have been catalogued in a generally accurate fashion by both Iranian and Western writers: industry, transport, education, women's and minority rights all grew.

Although the total gross national product rose under Reza Shah, so did inequalities, and one careful observer wrote that, owing to the new expense caused by Reza Shah's program, "by the time of the outbreak of World War II, the economic position of the average Iranian was considerably and chronically worse than it had been in 1925."[61] Even though further research may show this to be an overstatement, there appears to be no doubt that Reza Shah's reforms were financed mainly by the poor and mainly benefited a relatively small elite.

6 WORLD WAR II AND MOSADDEQ: 1941–1953

World War II, 1941–1945

With World War II, Reza Shah and his development program came to a sudden end and new problems appeared. During the war the United States became a key influence, while Russian and British activity in Iran continued.

At the outbreak of war, in September 1939, German influence in Iran was paramount. German agents were active, and the shah's sympathy for the Germans was no secret. This sympathy caused concern once the Nazis invaded the Soviet Union in June 1941. After that the Germans wanted to use Iran as a base against the Soviet Union, and the Allies needed Iran as a supply route to the Soviets, which would be impeded by a German fifth column. The British and Russians sent a note to the Iranian government demanding the expulsion of the Germans. When Reza Shah procrastinated, on August 25 Russian and British troops entered Iran.[1]

Allied pressure forced the shah to abdicate in September 1941, and he was deported and died in 1944. Iran was once more divided into three zones by the British and Russians, although now the division was for war purposes. Soviet troops were in the north, British in the south, while Tehran and other important areas remained unoccupied. In January 1942, Great Britain, Iran, and the Soviet Union signed an alliance. The Allies guaranteed to help safeguard Iran's economy from negative effects of the war and to withdraw their troops within six months after the war's end.[2]

Reza Shah's abdication put the kingdom under his Swiss-educated son, Mohammed Reza (b. 1919), who was for years less brusque and dictatorial than Reza Shah and did not imitate his policy of bypassing constitutional government. With Allied encouragement, cabinet-led government revived, the leadership coming mostly from politicians who antedated Reza Shah. For the first two years of occupation, the majles remained the same as before 1941, and hence was filled with Reza Shah's appointees and conservatives.[3]

The occupation, the abdication of Reza Shah, and new economic and social problems created by war meant growing instability and unrest. Internal trade was disrupted by the use of the Trans-Iranian Railroad mainly to send supplies to the USSR. The demands of Allied troops contributed to an urban boom but also made inroads on supplies. As prices for scarce staples rose, these were bought up by speculators, which forced prices higher.[4] The Iranian government took little effective regulatory action. Difficulties grew with a bad harvest in 1942, which brought famine in many areas.

In 1942 the government asked for an American financial mission to bring order into finances and the troubled economic situation. Dr. A. C. Millspaugh was again called upon, and he writes that he was urged by the State Department to accept: "I was informed . . . that the United States after the war was to play a large role in that region with respect to oil, commerce, and air transport, and that a big program was under way."[5]

The government's industrial and commercial activities remained inefficient, and the Persian government was seen by Millspaugh as more corrupt than it had been twenty years before.[6] Bureaucratic capitalists and landlords with business interests worked in the majles to continue the government's policy of high subsidies to businesses and government-sponsored monopolies. Inflation tended to demoralize civil servants on low, fixed salaries, who had to take bribes to live. The government was the instrument of the upper classes, and regressive tax and other policies continued to hit the majority.

Although the government took few steps to meet wartime problems, the political and social situation did change. In September 1941, the survivors of fifty-three men who had been arrested in 1937 for communist activity were released from jail. They joined with others to form the Tudeh ("masses") party in late 1941. In 1942 the party held its first conference, electing a central committee and adopting a provisional program, which was at first moderate and liberal, but the party's initial united-front character was undermined in part by its consistently pro-Soviet line.[7] During the war the Tudeh grew and recruited some prominent liberals. Its main center was the north, where it was favored by the Russians, who, like the British, were ready to use their position to support favored political movements. The North was also an economically advanced region and the locus of the large Azerbaijani and Kurdish minorities. The party was strong as well in the Isfahan textile area, in the oil fields, and in several cities.[8]

Inflation, scarcities, and dissatisfaction with the government led to a growth of oppositional organizations and protests in 1942 and 1943. From 1942, trade unions reappeared, and were able to operate openly. Most were Tudeh-led.[9] The revival of a free press led to a flowering of newspapers, which were often advocates of political and economic change. In Tehran in December 1942, there were bread riots, owing to the acute grain shortage, aggravated by hoarding and speculation.[10] War and Reza Shah's abdication gave a chance for tribes to reassert some independence and to rearm. The British, who followed their policy of backing southern tribes, found tribal leaders useful allies in protecting conservatism in the south.[11]

Various American advisers were called into Iran in 1942 and 1943. After the United States entered the war, American troops came to Iran to help transport war supplies across the Trans-Iranian Railroad. In the war years the American role in Iran became greater than ever before. A major American activity was the second Millsapaugh mission. Millspaugh was engaged as administrator general of finances in November 1942, and in May 1943, his extensive control over Iranian finances and the economy was clarified by the so-called Full Powers Law. His purview included finances, banking, government industry, commerce, and emergency wartime controls. Americans were put in charge of all key economic departments.

Millspaugh's chief measure was to introduce a progressive income tax bill in 1943. This could have helped the government balance its budget and begin to equalize the tax burden, but it was largely vitiated through nonenforcement.[12] Some of Millspaugh's efforts were less constructive. He worked to improve grain collection and storing, but ended government subsidies, which had allowed some cheaper bread to be sold, thus increasing bread prices. Little was done to maintain government enterprises, as Millspaugh was concerned to rid the government of these and promote a free-enterprise policy. Millspaugh's efforts brought opposition from both conservatives and reformers, the former objecting to controls that interfered with their interests, and the latter to his failure to cope with high prices or industrial inefficiency. When Millspaugh tried to fire the head of the National Bank in late 1944, Iranian opposition grew. This opposition caused the misssion to resign, with most of its program having had little effect.[13] Millspaugh attempted some important changes, but these could only have succeeded had he followed a consistent reform policy and brought Iranian reformers into the administration of this program.

In 1942 and 1943 the United States missions sent to advise the Iranian army and gendarmerie took substantial control of these forces.[14] Colonel H. Norman Schwarzkopf was put in charge of the Iranian gendarmerie, and he reorganized this internal security force along American lines. American influence in these two branches continued throughout the postwar period, and the contract for military and gendarmerie advisers was renewed several times.

The later war period did not see any solution to Iran's wartime economic problems. Allied troops spent large sums, which contributed to inflation. The disruption of supply was serious, and famine broke out in some areas. Speculation, hoarding, and black-market operations multiplied, often causing great suffering. The cost-of-living index issued by the Iranian National Bank rose from 100 in 1939 to 269 in 1942, 650 in 1943, and 757 in 1944.[15] In some parts of the country the rise was even greater.

The war brought new opportunities for profit to those in the middle and upper classes who dealt in goods or credit, but caused suffering to the popular classes and those on fixed incomes. The war also stimulated urbanization and created larger groups of merchants, professionals, and others occupied in urban services for the Allies. The working class also grew, as railroads, construction, and expansion of the oil fields and refinery led to new demand for workers. Journalists and writers also flourished, and discussion of a variety of political ideas became the order of the day.

The war's disruption of the economy appeared in state finance, which encompassed almost all the modern economic sector. In wartime, current expenditures absorbed most government outlays, leaving little for development activities. Most state enterprises operated at a loss during the war, and funds had to be poured in to meet this deficit. Foreign technicians were scarce and equipment hard to replace. This, along with self-seeking and inefficient management of many state enterprises, meant that plant and production declined. From 1930 to 1941 government expenses on economic projects had been 30 to 40 precent of total government outlays, but by 1945–46 this was down to 7 percent.[16] Revenue from income taxes rose a little after the Millspaugh mission, but not enough to meet needs. No new non-AIOC factories were established, although efforts were made to improve the output of some existing factories.[17]

From 1943 to 1945 political activity increased greatly, owing to economic and social disruption, new political freedom, and the encouragement of various political groups by the Allies. German agents were active among southern tribes, and reached an agreement with General F. Zahedi to lead a southern tribal revolt should German troops reach Iran's frontiers. The British arrested Zahedi and stopped most of this activity, however, and British influence with the southern tribes became paramount.

In 1943 several parties emerged, most of which had nationalist programs and a small middle-class and intellectual following. The British allowed Sayyed Zia ad-Din, the old exiled prime minister, to return. With British encouragement, he formed a party finally called the National Will party. This soon became the focus of right-wing politics and the main opponent of the Tudeh. The party advocated a return to old Islamic customs and the abolition of many of Reza Shah's reforms—making a largely traditional and religious appeal. Its main support came from ulama, merchants, landlords, and tribes.[18]

Elections to a new majles were held in 1943, resulting in a large conservative majority, partly because of dishonest elections. Sayyed Zia and his party were a key conservative influence. On the left were eight Tudeh deputies and about twenty-four sympathizers. Between the Tudeh and the right was a nationalist group led by deputy Mohammad Mosaddeq, a political leader known for his early opposition to Reza Shah and to foreign control.

Political struggles with international implications occurred even before the war's end. In the north, the Russians encouraged left-wing officials and kept out many non-Russian foreigners. The Russian presence encouraged demands by Azerbaijanis and Kurds for autonomy and the use of their own languages. The Tudeh and leftist trade unions also grew in other areas. In the south, the British encouraged conservatives: tribal leaders, landlords, and religious leaders. Tudeh headquarters in several southern cities were destroyed by agents of the National Will party. While the British and Russians concentrated on their own spheres, the Americans had advisers to several key government departments and the military. Thus all the Allies tried to influence Iranian politics to their own advantage.

The interests of all three, although partly strategic, centered on Iranian oil. The Anglo-Iranian Oil Company (AIOC) expanded its facilities during the war. The British wished to preserve their concession intact and keep out competition in the face of growing Iranian nationalist feeling and interest by other powers. Two American oil companies and then the Soviet Union opened negotiations for oil concessions in Iran during the war. The majles, however, passed a law, authorized by Mosaddeq and directed primarily against a Soviet concession, making it a crime to enter into such negotiations with foreigners for oil concessions. Although the Soviet Union and the United States remained interested in oil they achieved nothing during the war.[19] The bill against new oil concessions was one indication of Iran's increasing belief that oil should be used for Iranian ends. Nationalists, seeing the profits coming from oil, along with a relative drop in the value of Iran's fixed royalties as the value of the pound sterling fell and the price of oil rose, wanted new concession terms to give them a better return.

The war period in Iran was one of ferment. It saw a growth of economic problems: inflation, famine, deterioration of the modern sector, and disruption of government finances. According to an American expert who was then in Iran, the war "widened the already yawning gulf between the staggering poverty of the long-suffering masses and the wealth of the privileged few."[20] There was also an increase in urbanization and new urban groups, at the same time as traditional ways of tribes and religious leaders reemerged. Acute economic and social problems led to a growth of political organizations. Competing groups and ideologies—religious, nationalist, and socialist—vied for the allegiance of Iranians as never before. And, to compound internal problems and rivalries, foreign powers showed a stronger interest in Iran, with concern to control her politics and her oil.

Postwar Socioeconomic Problems

After the war, Iran's social and economic problems intensified, as did social conflicts and foreign interference. The immediate postwar years were characterized by a series of dramatic events that surpassed in scope the movements after World War I. Wartime and postwar crisis conditions contributed to the appeal of movements aiming at a radical change in social and economic life. As after World War I, the strongest radical movements were in the north, where they were now encouraged by the Soviets.

The center of postwar leftist activity, Azerbaijan, was the province with the most radical traditions, and resentment against the central government was strong for many reasons. Azerbaijan paid more taxes than any other Iranian province without receiving commensurate benefits. The Azerbaijani Turki language was not taught or permitted for official business, and there was resentment against forced Persianization. Russian presence in the province encouraged leftist forces and discouraged the right, especially as many large landlords fled when the Russians came in.[21]

The Tudeh party was strong in Azerbaijan, but in mid-1945 it was replaced by a new united front party called the Democrat party, which included a larger coalition of groups and classes and stressed autonomist demands. (The Democrats were not simply the Tudeh with a new name, as is often said.) The Democrats took over military posts, and a provincial assembly was elected in Azerbaijan in November 1945. Most of the seats were won by the Democrats, the rest going to those who collaborated with them. Many posts were held by veteran Communists, some of whom had spent time in the Soviet Union.[22] The new provincial government, headed by Prime Minister Ja'far Pishevari, declared for autonomy, but not independence of the central government. A large portion of tax receipts was to remain in the province, local administration was to be based on self-government and not Tehran appointment, and the Turki language was to be used in the schools, including a new university. A land reform program included the lowering of rents and the distribution of land belonging to the government or to landlords who had fled the province. The presence of Soviet troops had allowed the Democrats to take over Iranian army posts without intervention by government troops. Otherwise, the Soviets avoided obvious interference.[23]

Similar events occurred in Kurdish territory, some of which was Soviet occupied, and much of the rest close enough to be under Soviet influence. The Kurds are divided chiefly among Iran, Iraq, and Turkey, and have strong nationalist sentiments. They resented the centralizing policies of the government and wanted provincial autonomy. In December 1945, a Kurdish autonomous republic was set up and, although its leadership was non-Communist, it was supported by the Soviets.[24]

The Soviets kept the Iranian government from sending in troops to suppress the new governments. The central government asked Soviet troops to leave and, with American encouragement, placed a complaint before the United Nations Security Council regarding Russian interference in Iranian affairs when Soviet troops remained beyond the date they were to leave, six months after the war's end. The Security Council decided to leave this to be negotiated between Iran and the Soviet Union. Troop withdrawal was agreed upon at the end of March 1946, in negotiations between the Iranian premier, the clever Qavam as-Saltaneh, who had been prime minister before Reza Shah, and the Soviets. Qavam promised not to use force against the autonomous regimes and approved, subject to majles confirmation, a concession for a joint Soviet-Iranian oil concession in the north. Qavam probably knew that neither of these agreements was definitive. Soviet activity in the north apparently violated the Russo-Iranian Treaty of 1921, promising noninterference by the Soviets in the internal affairs of Iran, as well as the troop-withdrawal limit agreed on by the Allies in 1943.

In 1946 internal leftward pressures continued and Qavam had to take account of them. No immediate action was initiated against the Azerbaijan and Kurdistan autonomous governments. Rather, Qavam and Pishevari reached an accord in June 1946, granting most of the Azerbaijani demands, including the province's keeping 75 percent of the taxes collected there and using the provincial language.[25] The left was also powerful in the south, as was shown by a major Tudeh-supported general strike in the oil fields in July 1946, which took out tens of thousands of organized workers in oil and other AIOC enterprises. Qavam took into his cabinet three Tudeh ministers in August.

The continued growth of trade-union and popular movements, as well as of the Tudeh and of reformism, were reflected in new social measures passed by the Qavam government in 1946. Most important was a new labor law, which limited hours of factory work to forty-eight, with overtime to be voluntary and better paid. Children could not work over six hours a day, and no child under ten could work in a factory, which suggests the previous child-labor conditions. Women were to have twelve weeks' maternity leave with full pay. Unions were allowed, and labor-management factory councils were to be set up in all factories. A minimum wage was established, along with higher skilled minimums, based on subsistence costs for a family of four.[26] In 1946 the government also issued a decree that landlords should give 15 percent of their share of the crop to the peasants.

Subsequent right-wing resurgence negated much of these laws' effect (although minimum wages remained), but their very passage by a landlord-controlled government indicates the strength of demands for change. There was an attempt to enforce the labor law, although inspection provisions were inadequate. The growth and strength of trade unions in the war and postwar period helped ensure their position, and AIOC, the biggest employer, complied with factory-council and minimum-wage provisions, so as not to be accused of breaking the law. However, increasing numbers of AIOC jobs were contracted out to small firms that did not comply.[27] The law increasing the peasants' share was hardly enforced. A landowners' conference in 1947 attacked the decree, and there was no attempt to compel obedience.

The growth of Tudeh influence was disliked by many Iranians and by Britain. After the Tudeh-led general strike in the Khuzistan oil area, British troops were ordered to Basra, Iraq, near Iran's border, and a British-supported exile, the son of Shaikh Khaz'al, raided Khuzistan from Iraq. Several southern tribal leaders, often allied with the British, announced their opposition to the Tudeh cabinet members. In September 1946, a southern tribal revolt began under the leadership of the Qashqa'i, whose chief demand was the dismissal of the Tudeh ministers. The revolt was backed by ulama and landlords, and probably the

British. On October 17, 1946, the Tudeh ministers were dismissed. The new American Ambassador to Iran, George V. Allen, was a major supporter of an Iranian anti-Communist policy.[28] Since the withdrawal of Soviet troops the Russians had less influence in Iran than the United States, and only the Tudeh and its allies were effective instruments of a pro-Soviet policy. Soon after Allen's arrival, in November 1946, the Qavam government sent troops north to put down the Azerbaijani and Kurdish autonomy movements, which was done very brutally. Some leaders fled, some hid, but others were executed. In Kurdistan the leaders were shot, and numerous jailings also occurred in both areas. The economic and social problems of Azerbaijan and Kurdistan grew after the reestablishment of central government control, and there was a severe famine in Azerbaijan in the winter of 1949.[29]

Part of the 1946 agreement between Qavam and the Soviets had been a promise of a joint concession for northern oil. The Tudeh was vociferously in favor of this, as were some others, but Iranian deputies were wary that it might be a wedge for Soviet influence. The support given by Ambassador Allen for rejecting the concession is generally considered an important factor in the majles's rejection of it.

Soviet influence in Iran thus suffered a decline in 1947, although the Tudeh remained active, particularly among trade unions, students, and intellectuals. The United States assumed a position of major influence, strengthened by 1947 agreements to extend the American military and gendarmerie missions, to provide for the purchase of military equipment in the United States, and a 1948 military-aid program giving Iran sixty million dollars worth of military equipment. Colonel Schwarzkopf was considered particularly valuable in maintaining the power of the Iranian government. "Schwarzkopf was tireless in inspecting all those places where trouble was brewing. He helped in no small degree to ensure firm government control in Azerbaijan and the northern provinces."[30]

By the end of 1947 conservative rule seemed well established, but discontent was still strong. The problems created by the war and previous developments had not been met. The peasants in postwar years suffered extreme poverty. Peasant landownership was down to a bare minimum as landlords and speculators had bought up much of the remaining peasants' land in hard wartime conditions. Debts, rents, and taxes tended to increase, and peasants had to borrow for capital requirements and current expenses. High interest rates and low income made it hard for peasants to repay the principal on loans.[31] High interest rates not only impoverished peasants (and urban dwellers), but kept capital from productive ventures and directed it toward the profitable but often unproductive field of money-lending.

Many peasants borrowed from their own landlords, and some lost their land for inability to repay debts. According to an extensive survey of Iran done by an American advisory group, "The villages and, for all practical purposes, the peasants are the property of the landlords, most of whom live in the larger cities or even abroad."[32] The growth of large landholdings and the immense holdings by the royal family multiplied the kind of middleman operations described for the 1930s. Renters and subcontractors took ever more of the surplus.

Sharecropping remained the main form of tenancy. By now many tenants had nothing to offer but their labor and could expect little better than one-fifth of the crop, unless this was too small for bare subsistence. The family income realized under such rentals may be imagined: "Under normal conditions each farmer can produce about 200 bushels of grain per year. Since most farmers own nothing, they get only the labor fifth, which amounts to 40 bushels. This means that the average farmer must live and support his family on approximately $110 per year."[33]

Tenants could be evicted or their rents raised without compensation for improvements. Although tenants were rarely forced off the land when traditional labor-intensive means of cultivation were employed, they were with the growing use of agricultural machinery. Machinery benefited landlords, since far fewer laborers were required.[34] Many peasants still owed dues and services. The most onerous was free labor service, and in many areas regular "presents" to the landlord were still demanded.

Most Iranian taxes were indirect, hitting those least able to afford them. After 1941 indirect taxation increased and other economic conditions became more difficult. Government monopolies, which made large profits from sugar, tea, tobacco, and other items of mass consumption, continued to be the largest single source of government income in the postwar period, accounting for one-third of the government's revenue in 1948–49. Customs duties, which were also felt by peasants and workers as they covered such items as sugar, tea, and cloth, accounted for 27 percent of the government's income in the same years. Income taxes, despite increases, accounted for only 8 percent of the government's income.[35]

Besides taxes, the government had a monopoly on the purchase and sale of wheat, Iran's principal crop. The price the government paid was below the free-market price, and this disparity grew in the war and postwar years. By 1948 the government was buying grain for one-third of its free-market price. This not only hurt peasants but led to a decline in wheat production, forcing Iran to import wheat in the postwar years.[36] (Similar policies and results occurred in the 1970s.)

Wartime and postwar inflation increased the pressures upon peasants. Scarcity meant profits for middlemen but hunger and debt for the peasants. Not only did wheat fields go out of cultivation when wheat was needed, but the production of cotton, the second major crop in Iran, fell by 1948 to about 14 percent of its 1937 level.[37] War also made great inroads on Iran's livestock. The postwar period saw some recovery, but little of it was reflected in peasant living standards. Although there were various announcements of sale of some government land to the peasants, before 1962 there was scarcely any practical outcome.[38] The government was known to peasants mainly through agents who bought grain, collected taxes, and recruited for the army. Most of them were underpaid, and tried to make up for their salaries by taking what they could from the peasants. It is not surprising that the social and health conditions of the peasantry were among the worst in the world. Peasants used primitive tools and suffered from lack of water or good seeds. Technological improvements under postwar conditions of land tenure offered them little.

The agrarian structure incorporated medieval features—feudal dues, primitive methods, and strip farming—with an exploitation facilitated by the development of a national and international cash market and the strengthening of the central government. The situation was pushing many peasants toward bare subsistence, tenancy, and rising debt. Major improvements seemed impossible under the pre–1962 structure, as most peasants had no capital and no guarantee that the fruits of improvements would not go to the landlord. Profiting from the agrarian structure were landlords, middlemen, overseers, headmen, officials, and moneylenders. They enriched themselves in various ways; by buying peasant goods cheaply, by lending at high interest, by selling goods at high prices, and by collecting rents. Peasant poverty encouraged the development of a hierarchy that reduced agricultural productivity.

The second important rural group are the tribes. During and after the war many returned to nomadism, although some remained settled. The tribal peoples were no longer necessarily better off than the peasantry. The destruction of livestock during the Reza Shah period and the war hurt the tribespeople, although the khans and a few other privileged tribespeople often remained wealthy. Some tribes continued to be a politically unstable force, capable of rebelling with deadly effect. There were also conflicts between nomadic tribes and the peasants and landlords whose land they cross and whose agriculture they occasionally disrupt. Among the settled tribes, conditions are much the same as with peasants, if not worse, the khans owning villages and tribespeople being reduced to the status of landless tenants.[39]

The chief beneficiary of the exploitation of tribal peoples and peasants was the large landlord. The crown, which confiscated vast areas under the Reza Shah regime, continued to be the largest single landholder in Iran, but there were other landlords with hundreds of villages. The composition of the large-landlord group changed more radically after World War I than before, as Reza Shah confiscated vast properties, while rising groups of merchants, contractors, bureaucrats, and especially army officers increasingly bought up land. Thus, although old families, religious groups, and tribal khans continued to own much land, there was extensive ownership by new groups, which also include overseers and kadkhodas who enriched themselves enough to buy up holdings. In general the new landlords were reputed to be not more modern in their methods, but often to seek short-term profit at the expense of both land and peasant.[40]

Landlords were mostly city-dwelling absentees, concerned to profit with little investment. Landlords were heavily represented in the government, as the scarcely secret or honest election practices ensured their election to the majles, and officials and army officers continued to buy land. Various schemes for irrigation and technology, the destruction of insects and disease, and rural education, tried since the war under such auspices as the Near East Foundation, Point Four, and the Seven Year Plan, brought some improvements, notably in eradicating the scourge of malaria, but were limited by peasant poverty. Poor peasants and agricultural laborers increasingly migrated to cities, where they made up an impoverished and politically volatile subproletariat. A very high rate of postwar demographic growth, about 3 percent annually, required new avenues for employment in both village and city that were rarely provided.

The towns' social structure presented a more complex and variable picture than did the countryside. A fair idea of living standards in towns may be gained from available statistics. More important, an assessment can be made of the crisis in urban life that has helped make Iranian cities, particularly Tehran, the scene of many major disturbances since World War II. Urban economic problems cannot be separated from rural ones. Low village living standards held down the internal market, thus limiting the expansion of consumer-goods industries. Also, rural poverty made it easy to pay low wages to industrial workers, whose ranks could be filled from the mass of unemployed and semiemployed city poor who came to the towns to escape a hopeless rural existence. The agrarian situation also contributed to the shunning of industrial investment by those with capital in favor of investment in land, speculation, moneylending, and quickly profitable trading ventures. Agricultural poverty and backwardness continued to be a major obstacle to Iran's postwar modernization.

The shaky foundations of Reza Shah's modernization showed up in World War II, which also aggravated problems. Maintenance of Iranian industry virtually stopped, equipment deteriorated, production declined, and capital sought other outlets. Wartime and immediate postwar scarcities and high demand meant that industries could operate inefficiently and still make profits. After 1947, however, a new flood of relatively cheap European goods led to crisis for Iranian industry. At the same time, export markets for Iranian goods shrank.[41] The bazaar classes also suffered from a postwar decline in demand. While wartime demand had encouraged expansion of the major urban bazaars, bazaar producers suffered from the end of Allied purchases and the revival of Western imports.

Modernization and economic reform were undermined during and after the war. Inflation, which leveled off slightly from its 1944 peak, became a growing problem again after 1947. The goverment foreign-trade monopoly, which allowed some control over imports, became inoperative in postwar years, as Westerners assumed more control in Iran and opposed any limits on their countries' exports. Widespread corruption in the customs administration brought falsification of receipts and of import and export permits, and foreign trade was no longer regulated.[42]

The small scope of industry is shown by the fact that only fifty-three thousand were employed in Iranian enterprises in 1950, or less than one-half percent of the population. This contrasts with sixty-seven thousand employed in the efficient British-owned oil industry, and one hundred and thirty thousand (or more) in hand carpetmaking.[43] As Iranian industry used mostly antiquated and inefficient machinery, and was said to employ many more people than necessary, industry's small place in Iran's economy can be appreciated.

Transport facilities, despite the expansion of the Trans-Iranian Railroad by the Allies, suffered a severe setback in maintenance during the war. In 1949 the condition of railroads and seaports was judged to be "approaching a point where it may seriously cripple the entire economy of the country."[44] A sudden drop in railway traffic after the war meant a great economic loss for the railroads. The cost of transporting freight rose and was five times as high per ton-km. in postwar Iran as in the United States, despite the much lower wages on Iranian railways.[45] After 1950, with American aid, some improvements were made in transport, but it remained underdeveloped.

Other aspects of Iran's economic backwardness in the postwar decade are indicated by the fact that no Iranian city had a modern water system before the 1950s and that per capita consumption of electricity and cement were well below that in Egypt and Turkey, not to mention more developed nations.[46] There was little modernization or expansion of the Iranian educational system. The number of university students per one thousand population was far below that of Egypt, Turkey, and other Asian countries.

The social structure of postwar urban Iran was not static, and increasing urbanization together with the emergence of new urban social groups meant the development of social unrest in cities. The growth of cities was stimulated by the World War II demand for urban goods and services, the expansion of the professions, and the continued growth of the army, gendarmerie, and bureaucracy. The accumulation of capital by Iranians who profited from the war helped to create a new middle class. Some of them wished to invest in productive industry, and the privately owned sector of Iranian industry expanded after the war. The new middle class tended to favor reforms that would improve economic stability and government efficiency. Its members wanted also to limit the power of foreign capital in Iran, represented chiefly by the AIOC.[47] The bazaar middle classes and parts of the new middle classes were a nationalist bourgeoisie who were increasingly willing to fight for Iranian economic and political independence and reduced foreign competition and control in Iran's economy.

The growing intelligentsia was also a newly significant social group. Educated in Tehran or abroad, the young Iranian intellectuals had little outlet for their talents. The demand, as distinct from the need, for professionals and scholars in Iran was outstripped by the supply. There was intellectual unemployment, and both students and mature intellectuals tended to identify their troubles with those of the Iranian nation. Intellectuals and students were in the forefront of many social protest movements, and they often spoke out for Iranian independence and fundamental social reform. The only major employment outlet for Iranian intellectuals was the bureaucracy, whose lower ranks were a seedbed of discontent at the same time as its top levels were known for their stake in the old regime. Dislike of foreign interference was characteristic of the young government employee.[48]

The lower-middle-class groups, the artisans and shopkeepers of the bazaars, have been a major focal point of postwar social and nationalist discontent. This group profited from wartime demand, but later suffered from the postwar economic crisis. Although it was not a new social group, its outlook changed in postwar years. Its members saw their position threatened by the competition of foreign goods and services, by governments' favoring of the new middle and upper classes, and by economic conditions that reduced Iranians' purchasing power.

These people tended to identify Iran's problems with the operations of foreign interests. They were tied to a revived religious class that took advantage of the end of anticlerical despotism to reassert Islamic views and practices and to regain some of their former sociopolitical status. The industrial working class, though small, became increasingly important after World War II. The war and postwar period saw the formation of numerous trade unions, finally grouped into three federations. Most unions owed their inspiration and leadership to the Tudeh party, but some were affiliated to other, including governmental, parties, and some were formed by employers to counteract true unions. Workers became a major radical force in Iran. Economic crises directly affected their welfare, and they led agitation for social reform and the nationalization of the oil industry. There were several important strikes in the postwar period, the majority of which had political as well as economic repercussions. Most famous was the strike of oil workers in the Anglo-Iranian fields in 1951.[49] Postwar unemployment was large—in absolute terms larger than before—owing to the wartime growth of cities. The unemployed were an element leading to social instability, and supporting movements for change.

At the opposite end of the scale were those few but powerful persons with a stake in the social structure. These included the upper bureaucracy, those who profited from the peasants, and some traders who profited from the underdeveloped distribution system to buy cheap and sell dear. Some industrial shareholders, many army officers, and those in the middle class who profited from foreign industry and trade were also among the "satisfied" group. Economic conditions in the towns were better than in the countryside, although the income-distribution gap was also greater. In the late 1940s it was estimated that 60 percent of town dwellers lived in slum conditions.[50]

Another largely dissatisfied group were the ulama, who took advantage of Reza Shah's abdication to reassert their position in many spheres. Most urban women went back to chadors, though without face veils, but the ulama wanted more reassertion of Islamic law and many also opposed growing foreign influence and control. Although most of the leading ulama were not then political activists, the active anti-British Ayatollah Kashani had a growing influence. He had variable ties to the small terrorist fundamentalist group, the Feda'iyan-e Islam, founded around 1945. The discontents and demands voiced by such men were to have increasing importance.

The postwar crisis in Iran, and the demand for change from many parts of the population, led even the landlord-dominated majles and government to undertake economic development. American influence in Iran grew, and as the United States was largely responsible for stabilizing the postwar Iranian government, it was natural to turn to an American firm for development aid. On Iran's invitation, the American engineering firm Morrison-Knudson made a survey and suggested a development program in August 1947. They put heavy emphasis on agricultural technology and little on industry. Raw cotton and wool production were to increase, but no new plants were planned to process them. Some Iranians, who felt that Iran's role as supplier of raw materials to the West and buyer of expensive finished goods was to be perpetuated, criticized the report. An Iranian economist prepared a specific plan late in 1947. Transport and agriculture were the two chief beneficiaries of his plan, but industry was allotted almost three times as much money as by Morrison-Knudson.[51]

A Plan Commission was set up to draft a bill for what was called the Seven Year Plan. The Commission's report to the majles in August 1948 showed the pressure of circumstances which had pushed the government to the plan. The report began:

> It is not concealed from anybody that the economy of the country is passing these days through a critical phase which has resulted in the weakening of the productive power of the country, the decline of exports, necessitating the importation of primary living needs from abroad, lowering of the purchasing power of the rial, increase of the cost of living, poverty and unemployment.
>
> The extent of this crisis is such that indivdual means and power, private initiative and undertakings, and even sporadic measures of the Government agencies will not be able to overcome it.[52]

At the same time, Americans had a large role in the Plan. Max W. Thornburg, oil executive, consultant, and an adviser in Iran, was one of the most influential. In 1948 Thornburg secured the services of Overseas Consultants, Inc. (OCI), a United States oil-related consortium, for the Iranian Plan. OCI was to do a survey of Iran's needs and help administer the Plan. In February 1949, the Development Plan Act was passed. OCI published a large report based on a survey it had conducted, emphasizing technical improvements, particularly in agriculture and transport. The report ignored the potential benefits of land reform, which Thornburg specifically denied.[53]

Neither the government nor OCI envisioned reforms in the social structure or land-tenure system. Improvement in agriculture was to come purely by technical and educational means. OCI recommended major improvements in communications and transport. Regarding industry, OCI noted that plants were inefficient, overstaffed, overcentralized, and technically backward. Most of these ills were attributed to government ownership, which was seen as always inefficient. "Fundamentally the profit motive must be present if efficiency and quality of management and production are to be achieved," the report stated.[54] The government was told to get rid of industry, and some expansion of private light industry was recommended. (Although the faults of government ownership in Iran were real, this might have been the only way to mobilize capital.)

The Plan as approved by the majles and the government had modest aims, and the rate of governmental development expenditure was to be far below that of prewar years.[55] Even the limited aims set for the first year and a half were not met, however, and after the loss of oil exports in 1951 the Plan was in effect suspended. Even sooner, most government agencies tried to get a share of the Plan funds, so that little could be spent on Plan projects.[56]

Scant accomplishment during the Plan's first year brought criticism from the Iranian press. It was charged that old ruling groups had passed the Plan only to allay unrest, and that they had no intention of working for economic change. The United States and Britain were blamed for backing men who cared little for Iran's economic development. The Tudeh, although outlawed after a man of doubtful affiliation tried to assassinate the shah in 1949, still controlled newspapers that attacked the Plan and its foreign advisers.

In June 1950, OCI made a stateme . detailing the Plan's failures and the old, corrupt forces that had .sed it. The Plan administration was accused of having no serious ir .ent of carrying through the Plan.[57]

No projects were being systematically followed, while funds were spent on unplanned projects. Owing to disagreements, the contract between OCI and Iran was terminated in January 1951. The Iranian Plan director stated that the main dispute centered on Iran's desire to industrialize much faster than OCI recommended. It is often said that the cutting off of AIOC royalties finished the Plan, but its de facto demise was assured before oil nationalization.

Industrial rehabilitation was the only part of the Plan with significant results. Government plants were revamped and sold to private owners, so that the majority of Iranian factories became private. Production rose from its postwar nadir. Increased foreign competition and continued low consumption meant, however, that ambitious expansion plans were abandoned. Some textile factories had to close again. Industrial rehabilitation was limited and would probably have occurred without a plan.

The Seven Year Plan and later United States-supported planning efforts in Iran assumed that the very groups with the most to gain by keeping the existing social structure could bring economic reform and development. The assumption that development was possible and desirable without a basic change in social structure fundamentally weakened planning in Iran. The Plan did not even provide for a basic change in tax structure, which might have mobilized the savings of the rich and made the poor better able to purchase Iranian manufactures. The economic and social crisis that the Plan was to overcome deepened during the Plan period.[58] This crisis and the profound discontent it engendered provided one basis for the powerful nationalist movement that characterized the years of the oil dispute.

The Oil Crisis and Mosaddeq

To summarize the involved postwar oil crisis, one may note that the Iranians had many grievances against the AIOC, and feelings about them became increasingly inflamed after the war. The fixed royalties provided for in the 1933 agreement had suffered a relative decline, as prices and profits had increased over three times. The AIOC was paying out an ever smaller percentage of its growing income as royalties. This was particularly galling in light of more favorable oil agreements between American oil companies and other countries. Iran also objected to having no say in the company, not even the right to see its books; to paying high prices for Iranian oil; and to the small number of Iranians trained for skilled jobs. The total net profits of the AIOC from 1945 to 1950 after deducting high British taxes, royalties, and exaggerated depreciation figures were £250 million while royalties were £90 million. The AIOC paid much more in income taxes to the British government than it did in royalties to the Iranian government. In addition, the increase of nationalist and radical sentiment after the war inflamed Iranian resentment over the political and economic control exercised by the AIOC. The AIOC was seen as a major cause and channel for British influence and control over Iran.[59]

The Iranian government began negotiations with AIOC for a different concession in 1947. The AIOC finally offered a "supplemental agreement," which was far from meeting Iranian demands, but which Iran's conservative government agreed to accept in July 1949. The agreement was highly unpopular, however, and was not passed by the majles. Elections to a new majles in 1950 centered around oil, and the nationalist National Front coalition of groups and parties opposed to the supplemental agreement and to subservience to foreign interests and led by Mohammad Mosaddeq scored major gains. The new premier, General Ali Razmara, delayed trying to push through the oil agreement, as he saw that majles and popular sentiment were against it. His pro-agreement position, however, was generally regarded as responsible for his assassination in March 1951, by a religious nationalist of the extremist Feda'iyan-e Islam group. (This was a small group of young fundamentalists who assassinated men they regarded as enemies of Islam.)

Popular sentiment and demonstrations were so marked that the majles turned completely to a pro-Mosaddeq position. Nationalization of the oil industry was approved by the majles on the recommendation of a majles committee in March 1951, and soon thereafter Mosaddeq became premier, replacing the shah's choice, Hosain Ala. Mosaddeq headed a coalition of secular and religious nationalist parties, the National Front. Earlier in negotiations with the British, Iranian demands had been backed by the American ambassador, Henry Grady, and by other American officials, who did not want to see British oil companies achieve a competitive advantage over their own. Later, however, American officials became increasingly alarmed at the radical implications of Iranian actions. The illegal Tudeh party gained strength through the nationalization period, after a decline of influence in the late 1940s, and Tudeh-led strikes and demonstrations helped push Iran toward anti-British and anti-American policies. The refusal of AIOC to meet the 50–50 profit-division pattern seen in new American oil agreements until it was too late, and its obstinacy on other issues, moved many moderates to favor nationalization, as did pressures from street demonstrations and threats of assassination.

The British early referred the dispute to the International Court at the Hague. The Court ruled it had no jurisdiction, implying that the matter came under Iranian law, and that Iran had the right to nationalize (compensation was always promised by Iran). In both Britain and the United States, however, Mosaddeq was pictured increasingly but inaccurately as a dangerous fanatic, likely to deliver Iran to the Soviets. In fact he was an anti-imperialist nationalist who intended to keep Iran from being controlled by any foreign country or company.

After nationalization Mosaddeq and his followers apparently expected to find the United States a neutral party that would make loans to, and purchase oil from, Iran. In fact, however, after some failed attempts by the Truman administration at mediation, the United States was increasingly hostile to nationalization, and American oil companies joined an unofficial but effective worldwide major-oil-companies' boycott of Iranian oil, sparked by the AIOC after nationalization was declared. The AIOC enforced the boycott with gunboats, saying the oil belonged to them, as it was stolen. The National Iranian Oil Company, set up to handle the AIOC fields and refinery and other oil in Iran, was able to produce some oil, but was not allowed to sell it during the nationalization period, except for a few late sales to Italian and Japanese "blockade busters." Thus, oil revenue was cut off from Iran, while the government continued to keep Iranian Oil Company employees on its payroll, in order to keep them from losing their income. Numerous attempts to negotiate, in which the United States often participated, came to nothing as AIOC, and even a later compromise World Bank plan, would have kept control and most profits in foreign hands.[61]

The new government was thus faced with economic problems even greater than those that had plagued Iran in the preceding crisis-ridden postwar years. To make matters worse, the British placed major restrictions on Iranian trade and on the convertibility of Iranian sterling balances in England. To counteract financial troubles, the Mosaddeq government introduced trade controls to encourage exports and discourage imports. Mosaddeq also hoped to get a sizable loan from the United States, which had previously been informally promised. He traveled to the United States in the fall of 1951 and tried to convince the Truman government that a loan was urgently needed if the left were not to gain power in Iran. The government refused a loan, however, on the grounds that Iran should settle the oil question before expecting aid. American hostility to Iran on oil nationalization, and American backing of the British position, produced animosity in Iran towards the United States, whose aims had generally been thought different from Great Britain's. Later Iranian loan requests from the United States were similarly rebuffed, although some military and Point Four aid continued.

In the years of oil nationalization, the social and economic crisis in Iran intensified, and popular unrest, organized into different movements, increased. The oil issue was to a degree used by some Iranian leaders to divert attention from social problems, and there was little basic reform in the early Mosaddeq period. On the other hand, pressure for reform continued to mount, and the government and majles had increasingly to heed the demands of the people; in the latter part of Mosaddeq's rule more social reform measures were introduced. The reform aspect of the government might have continued to increase had it lasted longer.

The general line of the Tudeh in this period was to tie in popular nationalist demands and slogans with arguments suggesting that Iran would be better off if it would sever its ties with the West and rely on Soviet trade and good will. Pressure from both leftist and nationalist opinion was strong enough to encourage reforming economic and social measures. In the summer of 1952 Mosaddeq signed a decree saying that

all landlords must give up 20 percent of their share of crop; 10 percent
was to go to the peasant and 10 percent to newly created rural banks
that would help the peasants with credit. To collect the unpaid back
taxes of the rich, commissions were created throughout Iran that were
entitled to jail, and confiscate the property of, those in arrears.[62]

Although Mosaddeq was very popular in Iran, the shah and his
foreign advisers wanted him out, as did the AIOC and the new British
conservative government under Churchill. In mid–1952 the shah
dismissed Mosaddeq and appointed Qavam as-Saltaneh as prime minister. Mass demonstrations and sentiment for Mosaddeq were so great,
however, that Mosaddeq soon returned to office with new plenary
powers. It was widely believed in Iran that the United States was
behind the attempt to replace Mosaddeq with Qavam.[63] Mosaddeq's
charisma and lifelong courage and honesty made him vastly popular
with most Iranians.

The restoration of Mosaddeq was a sign of new strength and determination by the nationalist coalition, and the signal for some serious
reforms. In 1952 came efforts to enforce tax collection and reduce the
landlord's share of the crop. Several irrigation dam projects were
launched, and also a rural development program, along with the
United States Technical Cooperation Administration, which carried on
agricultural education and pest control. Import limitations and government planning resulted in the first substantial postwar expansion of
industry. Output of refined sugar, textiles, and minerals rose. The
government began four large textile mills, several dry-fruit processing
plants, a cement factory, and sugar refining plants. Measures to
encourage exports actually produced a growing favorable trade balance
in 1952 and 1953.[64]

The loss of oil revenue, decline in oil-related employment, and
deterioration of economic relations with the United States and Britain
continued to strain the Iranian economy, however. Lowered imports
and scarcities contributed to inflation. There was still no basic agrarian
reform nor enough taxes on the rich, which might raise living standards
and capital for economic expansion. Iran suffered both from direct
discrimination by Western governments and from a continued trend
for prices on imported manufactures to rise while international prices
of Iran's exports fell. Iran's terms of trade (the relation between export

and import prices), which had already deteriorated in the 1930s, fell further. Taking 1948 as 100, they went to 90 in 1949 and to 69 by 1952.[65]

The United States continued to support the AIOC call for a worldwide boycott on Iranian oil. A letter from Max Thornburg to Clare Booth Luce, United States ambassador to Italy, in May 1953, which spoke of his response to an Italian desire to import Iranian oil, gives some idea of how Americans helped enforce the boycott:

> My own comments on oil import request are summarized as follows: . . .
>
> 1) While Italian companies are inhibited from selling oil without a government license, no such bar exists in the U.S. where there are thousands of independent oil companies, and which is a net importer of oil. Nevertheless, they have not chosen to buy Persian oil. This fact should throw some light on the American attitude.
>
> 2) For Italy to clear this oil and take additional cargoes would definitely indicate that it had taken the side of the oil "nationalizers", despite the hazard this represents to American Foreign investments and vital oil supply sources. This of course is Italy's right. It is only the prudence of the course that is in question.
>
> 3) The American people made generous contributions to Italy's rehabilitation after the war, and might regard this proposed act as ungracious.
>
> 4) Major oil companies, British and American, would be likely to resent it strongly—and remember it. The Caltex-Aramco group alone spends around $13 million a year in Italy for supplies which are sent all over the world . . . in addition to using Italian crews, and Italian families (in Arabia about 1000 plus families). At a guess this might be multiplied by 5 or 6 to include all major oil companies. The total volume of trade the Italian Embassy representative in London mentioned at stake in Persia was $20 million a year. Italy could scarcely expect to keep both.[66]

In 1953 the struggles in Iran reached new proportions, with the government allowing the Tudeh party, whose popularity was increasing owing to the continued economic and social crisis, the growth of anti-Western sentiment, and the Tudeh's partial support for Mosaddeq, to operate more openly. The religious revival forces of the leader of the majles ulama, Ayatollah Kashani, who had a long record of opposition to Western, and particularly British, incursions in Iran, also became stronger. Oil negotiations were stalled. The British and Americans involved were unwilling to allow Iranians really to control their own oil, while the Mosaddeq government would not settle for less.

In late February 1953, General Fazlollah Zahedi, a former collaborator with Nazi Germany, was arrested for plotting with foreigners to overthrow the government. In March there were serious conflicts between Mosaddeq and the shah in which Mosaddeq emerged victorious after large popular demonstrations in his favor. The government released Zahedi as a conciliatory gesture, but there continued to be apparent military and foreign-inspired plots against the government.

In the first half of 1953, relations became increasingly embittered between Iran and the United States government. In January Mosaddeq wrote to President Dwight Eisenhower saying that the United States had supported the British in the AIOC controversy, had withheld aid from Iran, and had helped the British enforce an economic blockade. After a letter from Mosaddeq requesting economic aid, Eisenhower responded in June that the American people felt: "it would not be fair to the American taxpayers for the United States Government to extend any considerable amount of economic aid to Iran so long as Iran could have access to funds derived from the sale of its oil and oil products if a reasonable agreement were reached. . . . Similarly, many American citizens would be deeply opposed to the purchase by the United States Government of Iranian oil in the absence of an oil settlement."[67]

Although many Iranians knew from the first that the United States Central Intelligence Agency (CIA) was involved in the overthrow of Mosaddeq in August 1953, only gradually did details of these events become available in the Western world. The idea of overthrow became stronger in British and American official and oil circles over time. It gained some impetus from the replacement of the British Labor government by the Conservatives and, in early 1953, the replacement of the Truman government, which had hesitated to join schemes for Mosaddeq's overthrow, by the Eisenhower administration, with John Foster Dulles as secretary of state. Specific plans for Mosaddeq's overthrow apparently originated with British Intelligence, but were

modified by the CIA. According to various sources including Kermit
Roosevelt, he simplified the British plan and helped get it accepted by
the very willing Dulles brothers (Allen, head of the CIA, and John
Foster); by other high-ranking officials, and, via John Foster Dulles, by
President Eisenhower. Roosevelt then traveled to Iran to put it into
effect via Iranian contacts developed through American and British
sources.

The period was relatively propitious, as there had been important
defections from Mosaddeq, including some leftist leaders and groups in
the National Front, and especially Ayatollah Kashani and some of his
religious nationalist followers. Most of Mosaddeq's support, including
the rest of the ulama deputies, remained, however, despite discontent
over economic problems. A major cause of dispute between Mosaddeq
and the shah had been Mosaddeq's attempts to get control of the army,
which was still mostly loyal to the shah and influenced by its American
advisers. Mosaddeq failed in this, although there were some Mosaddeq
supporters at the top of the army, which remained a crucial weak link in
Mosaddeq's control of the situation. During his premiership Mosaddeq
had worked to limit the shah's powers as intended by the 1906–07
constitution, but although he succeeded in other spheres, he did not in
the military.

The Anglo-American overthrow plan (in which the British could not
participate on the scene as British officials had been expelled from Iran)
involved telling the shah of the plan and its foreign backing and getting
him to dismiss Mosaddeq as premier and appoint his own favorite,
General Zahedi. According to Roosevelt, the orders for dismissal and
appointment were delayed. Mosaddeq learned of them (some say via the
Soviets or a leftist general) and mobilized effectively to stop the planned
coup. As had been agreed in case of failure, the shah and queen flew in
their plane from the Caspian to Baghdad, but when the Iranian
ambassador there, a Mosaddeq man, moved against them, they went to
Rome.[68]

There was now major antiroyalist rioting, much of it sponsored by
the Tudeh party, which went to the point of overturning statues of the
shah and calling for a republic. Seeing that this was alienating some
supporters and threatening the regime's control, the Mosaddeq government ordered the rioting suppressed by the army and police, which
it was. This probably caused the crucial split between the two most

powerful forces that could have united against a foreign-inspired overthrow of Mosaddeq—the Tudeh party and the Mosaddeq coalition. It
also brought the army effectively into the streets.

On August 19, 1953, a crowd led by the strongmen (in a literal
sense) of the bazaar in south Tehran and including religious leaders
began to move northward, and were joined by military forces. Both
Kashani and especially the leading Tehran Ayatollah, Behbehani,
actively supported the coup. Roosevelt states that the crowd was
inspired by his Iranian agents, and he had also received the cooperation
of key men in the military. He speaks of the expenditure of less than
$100,000 by the CIA, although Loy Henderson and others have said
millions were spent, and there may have been British expenses.[69]
Partly because of its recent bad experiences with Mosaddeq's government, the Tudeh did little or nothing to call out its masses of followers
to defend Mosaddeq, a policy for which it later engaged in strong
self-criticism. Between the crowd and the army the Mosaddeq regime
had no chance, and although the premier escaped he soon gave himself
up. He was later tried by a military court, defended himself brilliantly,
and escaped the death penalty asked by the prosecution, being sentenced to three years in jail, followed by house arrest in his village. His
foreign minister, Hosain Fatemi, was killed, however, and there were
massive arrests, jailings, and executions in subsequent years.[70] There
appears to be no doubt that the coup was CIA-planned on the basis of
British and American proposals, although Roosevelt may have taken
the initiative himself the second time. The coup could not have
succeeded without significant internal disaffection or indifference, but
without outside aid it would not have occurred.

The 1953 coup, which culminated a year later in an oil agreement
leaving effective control of oil production and marketing and 50
percent of the profits in the hands of the world oil cartel companies, had
an understandably traumatic effect on Iranian public opinion, which
has continued down to the present, with varying intensity at different
times. Although most Iranians understood almost from the start that
both the British and Americans were involved, by most the Americans
were and are especially blamed. Not only were the Americans more
directly involved, but Iranians expected little more of the British,
especially since their oil company was in question, whereas America
had raised high hopes among some Iranians in the past. In the early

stages of the oil dispute, men like Ambassador Henry Grady and Max Thornburg had expressed support for Iran's stand against AIOC's proposed terms, partly because they were unfair in comparison to those that the United States had to give elsewhere, and both they and Truman and Secretary of State Dean Acheson had aroused some hope that the United States might be a counterweight to the British. Iranian reaction to the progressive American betrayal of these hopes, accompanied by American media attacks on Mosaddeq as a virtual madman whose "support" for the Tudeh party and obstinacy over oil were supposedly driving Iran into the Soviet sphere, was rather parallel to Iranian reaction to the Anglo-Soviet 1907 entente dividing Iran into spheres of influence. In both cases a power that had been seen by nationalists, on the basis of some experience, as a possible counterweight to a more dangerous foreign power ended up by combining with that dangerous power and undermining a popular nationalist movement. After 1907 it took a few years for the Iranian constitutional revolution to be overthrown by Russian pressure and troops, combined with British acquiescence and troops in the south. In 1953 the joint overthrow by two powers of a major Iranian nationalist movement was quicker, but the pattern was similar. In both cases the foreign power formerly favored by Iranian nationalists was especially blamed, as it was seen as a betrayer and not just an old enemy. Although both nationalists and leftists were long discouraged and persecuted, they did not forget or give up hope.

Mosaddeq's defense of Iran's independence, his defiance of AIOC, his charisma, and his overthrow with American and British support helped make him an enduring national hero. Oppositionists of the most varying views—Marxists, leftists, liberals, and rightists, both secular and religious—invoked his name and example, cherished his picture, and found appropriate quotations from him to support their views. These groups and Mosaddeq were united in their continued desire to lessen foreign control and influence and increase Iran's independence. As the post-1978 years showed even more than did 1951–53, reducing foreign control, necessary though this is, neither solves all important problems nor preserves the unity of coalitions that lack clear constructive programs and embrace a range of ultimately incompatible elements.

7 ROYAL DICTATORSHIP: 1953–1977

General Character of the Period

The overthrow of the nationalist Mosaddeq regime in August 1953 by an American- and British-supported coup changed postwar Iran's situation in several basic ways, most of which remained important for the quarter century of ensuing dictatorial rule. First, the United States, which had had in the early postwar period an uneasy partnership with Britain in influencing Iran—the British monopolizing oil while the United States dominated in military and governmental advice and support—now became the dominant foreign power in Iran. This was reflected in the United States taking a 40 percent share in the oil consortium in 1954—the same large minority percentage as was held by the AIOC, now redubbed British Petroleum (BP). It was also reflected in America's ever-growing lion's share of military supplies and advisers and in civilian and governmental programs, as well as in various forms of investment by the United States government and companies that now entered Iran in greater numbers.

Second, as a result of United States involvement in Mosaddeq's overthrow and continuing American support for the shah, however dictatorial he might become and however many persons were jailed and tortured, earlier hopes that the United States might help in supporting a more democratic government in Iran declined. There remained some Iranians, however, who thought Americans were being fooled by the British or by the shah and would pressure their government to change its behavior if it only knew the truth. Older National Front leaders followed this line, but from 1961 on, the successors of the National Front concentrated increasingly on opposing the shah.[1]

Third, the shah himself, who had earlier struck outsiders as an uncertain young man who had grown up fearing his harsh father, was increasingly prepared to engage in repressive and dictatorial acts, however much they might be covered over by superficially democratic or Western forms. Not only age and experience explain this change. During World War II the Allies had pressured the shah to adopt more liberal and democratic forms than had his father, but after the Mosaddeq threat to the interests of the world oil cartel, dominated by American and British companies, Western governments and corporations felt safer with a centralized government under a pro-Western ruler who would not again allow into power a regime that might threaten economic and political relations with the West. While many in the United States and Britain spoke mainly of a Communist threat, in which they may have believed, the source of most of their outrage in 1951-1953, as with Nasser's 1956 nationalization of the Suez Canal, was a non-Communist nationalist government taking over, in defiance of the West, economic and strategic resources important to the West. Occasional Western pressures to mitigate his dictatorship, as in the early 1960s, were finessed by the shah, who probably knew where the real priorities of American governmental and business interests lay. Such pressures were in any case rare. In the widely read American press between 1953 and 1973 there is very little basic criticism of the Shah or of United States policy in Iran; the shah was overwhelmingly presented as a progressive, modernizing ruler whose problems lay in a backward population and some Iranian fanatics. Only after the shah pioneered in the OPEC oil-price rise in late 1973 did part of the American press and a few officials begin to note some of his faults. Some, usually secret, official documents were more critical and realistic, but they rarely resulted in action.

Fourth, beginning in the 1950s and increasingly in the next two decades, the shah showed a growing interest in modernizing Iran's economy and society and in making the country Western in character and militarily strong. In this he followed his father's precedent, but whereas Reza Shah, with fewer economic resources and much lower oil income, had minimized economic dependence on the West in his modernization program, Mohammad Reza greatly increased it. This was partly owing to an emphasis, common in the Third World but here carried to extremes, on big showy projects, supersophisticated and expensive weapons, and fancy consumer goods, all of which put Iran in a position of long-term dependence on Western countries, especially the United States, and which were profitable to American companies. ("Dependence" here is a relative concept, unconnected with Dependency Theory, which understates the possibility of independent action by the Third World.)

Fifth, under the dictatorial regime that developed after 1953 there were increasingly only two ways to deal with opposition, whether religious, nationalist, or Marxist. One was repression, including jailing, torture, and killing (the latter two especially in the 1970s). The other was co-optation of oppositionists, used especially in the 1960s and 1970s. Oppositional students and other ex-opponents were brought into the ever-widening network of governmental jobs on the understanding that they would not talk or act out of turn. The increase in good governmental jobs, salaries, and perquisites as oil income grew made this an effective strategy for a time, but did not bring about real loyalty to the shah. Participation in decision making was not broadened and freedom of expression actually declined over time.

Sixth, after the Mosaddeq experience the shah decided he wanted an effective internal security service and set up the large organization known by the acronym SAVAK in 1957. Aid to SAVAK from the American CIA and the Israeli Mossad assured some efficiency, but added to feelings against the countries that helped train SAVAK. One part of SAVAK was involved in the jailings, beatings, and tortures that became notorious in the years before the revolution, but there were also suave, educated operatives in coats and ties who persuaded people of the dangers of speaking or acting out of turn. In addition, the shah maintained other intelligence services, partly to check on each other.[2] Numerous intelligence agents infiltrated opposition groups, and many informants, as in American and other intelligence services, worked part time for SAVAK. With jail, torture, or even death as the possible stakes, it is not surprising that even underground or exile oppositional groups were decimated and suspicious or that within Iran people were increasingly hesitant to discuss politics at all.

Seventh, as the shah (with some variation in different periods) built up his autocratic powers and associated opposition with disloyalty or treason, his retinue hesitated to confront him with uncomfortable facts. Without anyone to contradict him, he may have really believed the picture he presented in his words and books of himself as an enlightened ruler leading his people to a better life in a strong, independent Iran, opposed only by "black and red reactionaries" (religious fanatics and Communists). It is not credible that he did not know of the tortures he often denied, and he cannot have believed all he said, but did believe his beneficent picture of himself, underestimated Iran's problems, and overestimated his ability to solve them.

Eighth, the suppression or co-optation of much of the opposition over the years, including both its leftist and its more liberal or moderate elements, along with the growing gap between the masses and elite, made it increasingly likely that eventual effective opposition would come from those who could appeal to the traditional disaffected masses more than from Westernized liberals or leftists. Western values did not trickle down to the popular classes any more than did significant benefits from the modernization program. Ultimately the vast majority of Iranians became more anti-Western, more anti-shah, and more open to oppositionists who stood against the shah, the West, and Western ideas.

1954–1960

After the overthrow of Mosaddeq, the shah and those around him were determined to ally with the West and try to develop the Iranian economy along Western lines. The Mosaddeq experience of boycott and the refusal of foreign aid made the new regime believe that economic development depended on settling the oil dispute, which had been an implicit condition of American and British backing of the coup. Development was also seen as dependent on loans and direct aid from the United States.

From the time of his restoration, the shah was determined never to allow a Mosaddeq type of situation to recur. This meant emulating Reza Shah in ignoring the main thrust of the 1906–07 constitution, which had foreseen government by a cabinet responsible to a freely elected majles and had reserved few powers for the shah. It also defended freedom of speech and the press, with minor exceptions.

Elections to the eighteenth majles early in 1954 were firmly controlled and candidates were chosen by the regime so that it, like subsequent majleses, was subservient to the shah. In 1955 the shah dismissed Prime Minister Zahedi, whom the Americans had seen as Iran's real strongman, and the shah became Iran's single ruler.

In the face of arrests and persecution, most opposition groups went underground, especially the Tudeh party, which was the most persecuted and most of whose leaders had to flee Iran. Iranian security forces uncovered a network of Tudeh or pro-Tudeh officers in the army, whose extent they may have exaggerated but whose existence was real. There were many executions and a widespread purge of the armed forces, and new legislation against oppositional organizations was passed by the majles.

The United States, particularly after the shock its government and business interests had received from the Mosaddeq years, was prepared to give extensive financial aid and advice to a regime that they knew to be strongly anti-Communist; which was making the right noises about economic development, social progress, and reform; and which seemed eager to take American advice regarding the use of United States aid. Also, the United States and Iran anticipated a new oil agreement pleasing to both regimes and to American oil companies, whose payments could provide some extra development funds. Immediately after Mosaddeq's overthrow the new government received a $45 million emergency loan from the United States. In December 1953, diplomatic relations with Britain, broken off during the Mosaddeq period, were restored.

A miscalculation by Mosaddeq and his backers had been that Britain and the West would face a shortage of oil if the large Iranian oil production were cut off. In fact, fields in Iraq and Kuwait, largely controlled by the AIOC, soon made up for this production, thus depriving Mosaddeq of his only real weapon (his attempt to scare the United States with a potential Communist takeover was counterproductive). Now, however, an opposite problem existed of reintegrating Iranian oil into a world system that was producing enough without it. Given world control of production and prices by the cartel of major oil companies, "the seven sisters," this turned out not to be difficult, especially since all seven companies were dealt in on Iranian oil and hence were not hurt if their production elsewhere was lowered. Discussions between AIOC (renamed British Petroleum) and other major cartel companies, and the United States government's renunciation of antitrust barriers to American companies' participating in an Iran consortium, paved the way for an agreement. In April an international consortium was established and began negotiations with the Iranian government. The consortium included: BP, 40 percent; Royal Dutch Shell, 14 percent; Compagnie Française des Petroles, 6 percent; 8 percent each to Standard Oil of New Jersey, Standard Oil of California, Gulf Oil Corporation, Texas Oil Company, and Socony-Mobil. The five United States majors later gave up one percent each of their share to a group of American "independents," who thus held a 5 percent share together.

The consortium reached agreement with the Iranian government in August 1954; it passed the majles with little opposition, and came into force in October 1954. The agreement was essentially for 50–50 profit sharing, which was the common in the Middle East, with nationalization retained only in theory. In order to claim nationalization, the new forty-year concession took the form of a lease of most of the 1933 concession area. The concession was operated for the consortium by two companies for exploration and producing and one for refining. Nonessential housing and service functions were to be handled by the National Iranian Oil Company. All major decisions, such as production levels and the sale price of oil, remained in the hands of the consortium and its constituents, and the agreement was in essence similar to those in operation in nearby countries. A secret consortium accord that in effect limited production and income became known to Iran only in the 1970s. Soon Iranian oil began to regain its share in world markets and new income began to accrue to the government.

Iran was again able to embark on the now fashionable road of economic planning. Abolhasan Ebtehaj, governor of the National Bank (Bank Melli) and a widely respected economist and administrator, was appointed head of the Plan Organization (PO) in September 1954, and a second Seven Year Plan was scheduled to start in 1955. The final expenditure figure for this plan was $1.16 billion. At first all oil revenues were to go to the PO, but owing largely to characteristic corruption and mismanagement an increasing proportion of oil rev-

enues was diverted to general expenses, and the proportion going to the
PO fell to 55 percent. This plus inflation necessitated cutting down on
several projects and having recourse to foreign loans. Of proposed Plan
expenditures about 26 percent was allocated to agriculture, 33 percent
to communication and transport, 15 percent to industry, and 26
percent to social services.[3]

In this and later plans large amounts of money, materials, and labor
were devoted to building large dams for irrigation and power generation. Most dams have been poorly planned and wastefully expensive;
more seriously, the stress has been overwhelmingly on the dams
themselves, which are showy and spectacular, and on power generation. Often the subordinate local irrigation systems, without which the
dams serve no agricultural purpose, were not built for years, if ever, nor
have the areas been adequately studied to see if the planned types of
irrigation and field allotment are suitable to the regions. Dams formed
a part of the later agribusiness disasters in the province of Khuzistan.
Planners, the shah, and many foreign advisers preferred large, impressive projects to those that would increase the output of the intensive
labor of peasants, nomads, and small-scale workers. In addition to
inexperience, corruption, and sometimes bad foreign advice, Iranian
plans suffered from jealousies between ministries and government
departments that wanted the PO to give them the money and let them
implement projects. The PO, on the other hand, wished to have
ministries act under its instructions on development projects. This
unresolved and continuing dispute, punctuated by currying of favor
with the top by the involved parties, was one cause of Ebtehaj's forced
resignation as head of the PO in 1959 and his replacement by more
pliable and less competent directors in the next few years. Ebtehaj also
disagreed with economically irrational royal interference with the plan.

The influx of foriegn exchange after 1954, chiefly from oil revenue
but also from loans and aid, helped finance PO development projects,
which progressed, however skewed they often were. The foreign-
exchange influx also encouraged private investment, and investment
and GNP both grew. Increased corruption and the lack of control of
imports or credit led to serious inflation, while the impossibility of real
trade-union organization, or effective strikes or collective bargaining
helped keep wages down, thus widening the disparity between rich

and poor. Price rises were concentrated on necessities like grain, which particularly hit the poor. With no control on imports or on the export of currency there was a bad fall in foreign exchange reserves, which helped precipitate a financial crisis in the autumn of 1960.

Before the early 1960s the regime was apparently deluded by the rise in GNP, the efficiency of the army and security forces in suppressing opposition, and by American economic and military support, into thinking that no major structural reforms were needed. The shah may have thought that enough other landlords would follow his example of selling land relatively cheaply to peasants so that no government-enforced land reform would be needed. The shah's case was, however, very special. His father had acquired, mostly by dubious means, about two thousand villages, and after Reza Shah's abdication there was a clamor for the return of these lands to their former owners. When this appeared almost impossible the shah turned over the land to the majles for disposition, but later took it back and inaugurated his own sale of these lands to cultivating peasants. It was not widely known that the money realized from these sales remained under the shah's control or that about a third of the land was given to wealthy favorites and members of the royal family.[4] (Mosaddeq's opposition to the shah's distribution program was not based on opposition to land reform but on his conviction that these lands did not really belong to the shah, and that any reform program should be initiated by the government.) The shah's example was not followed, and the majles and senate (an upper house half appointed by the shah included in the constitution but instituted only in 1949), representing mostly big landlords, blocked land-reform legislation.

By 1960 the shah and his American advisers were convinced some kind of land reform was needed and a bill was drafted for the division of large estates. Opposition by big landlords, represented in the legislature, and also by important ulama, led by the top "source of imitation" (*marja'-e taqlid*), Ayatollah Borujerdi at Qom, brought the amendment of this bill so that by the time it passed, in May 1960, it was so full of exceptions as to be virtually meaningless. Borujerdi's declaration against it helped make it a dead letter.[5]

Among the signs of the shah's pro-Western orientation was Iran's joining the Baghdad Pact in October 1955, along with the other

"Northern Tier" countries, Iraq, Turkey, and Pakistan, and also Great Britain. The United States stayed behind the scenes and joined several of its committees but was not formally a member. The pact was considered a hostile alliance both by Nasser's Egypt and by the Soviets, who began to beam hostile broadcasts in Persian into Iran. National Front sympathizers opposed the pact as a means of increasing Anglo-American control of Iran.

In 1958 three new oil agreements ratified by the majles and covering areas outside consortium territory paved the way for more control by Iran over its oil. The first was with the Italian governmental AGIP company, and the other two with private American and Canadian independents; all of them provided for an essentially 75–25 percent profit-sharing deal in Iran's favor, with the foreign companies to bear most of the exploration costs. NIOC also carried out some explorations on its own. The vast majority of production continued to come from fields under consortium control, however, as AIOC had been careful in 1933 to retain all the promising areas in its concession.

In response to pressures for more democracy the shah introduced a two-party system with the hope of making elections appear more real, and also of giving himself leverage against the dominant party should he need it. The governmental Melliyun (Nationalist) party was headed by Prime Minister Manuchehr Eqbal, and the "opposition" Mardom (People's) party was led by Asadollah Alam, one of the shah's oldest confidants and a large landlord. There were no real differences between the two, and both parties were creatures of the shah.

1960–1963

In early 1960, with the approach of elections, problems such as serious inflation, growing corruption, and signs that the economic boom of the late 1950s was about to burst brought to the surface a real opposition outside the two official parties. When campaigning began in June 1960, opposition became strong and vocal. It included a number of prominent personalities, among whom was Dr. Ali Amini, a descendant of the late-nineteenth-century liberal minister, Amin ad-Dauleh. Minister of finance during the consortium negotiations and later ambassador to Washington, a post from which he was dismissed, he became a critic of Eqbal and, by implication, of the shah. Although he was, then and later, widely associated by Iranians with the United States, he was considered to represent a liberal wing of American policy makers, like John Kennedy, who did not want to rely on the shah's dictatorship and wished to institute some serious reforms. At the same time National Front leaders began to speak out for free elections and against the government.

The formation of a second party and some official statements implying that the 1960 elections would be free also encouraged various oppositional groups and individuals. Prime Minister Eqbal, however, announced that no pro-Mosaddeq or Tudeh candidates could be elected, and he appeared determined also to exclude independents of Amini's stripe. Eqbal, probably with the shah's connivance, apparently arranged a pact between the two official parties by which each would get a certain number of majles seats, with a majority for his Melliyun party.

As the election results began to come in and evidence of vote fraud grew, open discontent mounted sharply. By late August 1960, the shah decided to dissociate himself from the obvious vote rigging and from Eqbal's growing unpopularity. The shah therefore voiced displeasure with the conduct of the elections and "advised" elected deputies to resign, to pave the way for new elections. With this expression of no confidence from the ruler, Eqbal and his cabinet had to resign. The shah named as prime minister Ja'far Sharif-Emami (who was called to this post again in the 1978 crisis). The elected deputies resigned, with reluctance.

The new government appointed a committee to draft rules for the conduct of elections, which were announced for January 1961. But popular discontent began to be expressed on other matters. Sharif-Emami had to admit Iran's bad financial condition and its low foreign-exchange reserves. A stabilization program was announced that sounded serious, but which was regarded skeptically by those who knew the Iranian elite's skill in curcumventing rules. Under this program many import duties were increased in order to discourage nonessential imports; the Central Bank (Bank Markazi) was given powers to limit domestic credit; and strong restrictions were placed on buying foreign exchange. Inflation had been triggered largely by too much credit, little control on foreign currency, purchases of too many nonessential imports, and too little productive investment. But those affected by controls often had enough influence to evade them. Many in the middle and popular classes had been seriously hurt by inflation and saw it as one means by which those with power or influence became enriched at their expense. Hence discontent grew.

The new elections were again considered dishonest, although they were not as flagrantly so as the previous ones. Several independents were elected, including even one National Front leader, Allahyar Saleh of Kashan, despite the strong pressure against National Front candidatures, and official exclusion of such a candidate in Isfahan.

Notwithstanding these difficulties the shah evidently felt reassured by the birth of his first son and heir in late 1960. The shah's first marriage to Princess Fawzia, sister of King Faruq of Egypt, in 1939 had produced one daughter, Shahnaz, but in Iran as in many countries women were not allowed to inherit the throne. Fawzia apparently left the shah. His second wife, Sorayya Esfandiari, with a Bakhtiari father and a German mother, bore no children and the shah divorced her in 1958. His third wife, Farah Diba, he married in early 1960 and she later had two sons and two daughters. She also gained power and influence in cultural and social welfare matters, which did not interest the shah particularly, and acquired her own circle of patronage and influence. Although growing opposition to the shah encompassed many of his blood relatives, especially his powerful twin sister, Princess Ashraf, and her progeny, Farah was not generally implicated in the corruption and repressive actions of the court. It was, however, noted that in traditional style the (queen's) Diba family was widely represented in the leadership of cultural and social welfare institutions. In the case of the queen's cousin Reza Qotbi, the young head of National Iranian Radio Television since its foundation in the mid-1960s, the appointment was justified by ability and intelligence, shown in choice of staff and in patronage of innovative theatre and musical groups and film projects unconnected with radio or television (although radio and television were media for government propaganda). Not all the queen's relatives had such justification for their influence, however, and even less did many of the shah's.

To return to the crisis of the early 1960s: the 1961 majles was faced by major problems. The National Front, seeing the growth of popular opposition and the disarray of court and government, denounced the recently completed elections, with much justification, as fraudulent, and demanded the dissolution of the majles and a new round of truly free elections. The majles, seeing that it had to identify to some extent with the growing opposition, became the scene of numerous denunciations of corruption in the PO, NIOC, and other government departments. More seriously, strikes were threatened, and Tehran's school-teachers, led by a member of Tehran's independent opposition, Mohammad Darrakhshesh, went on strike and demonstrated before the majles for higher pay. During the demonstration two teachers were killed by the police. This was the breaking point, and there were rumors of a military coup backed by the shah or, alternatively, of serious royal concessions. The shah apparently considered bringing National Front members into the government and had a long interview with Allahyar Saleh. They were unable to reach agreement, and the next day the shah sent for Ali Amini, the ablest member of the independent opposition, asking him to form a government. Amini apparently made two conditions, both granted by the shah: that Parliament be dissolved, and that the shah give him an unequivocal statement of support.

Amini succeeded Sharif-Emami in April 1961, at a time when it was widely believed that the survival of the government depended on its ability quickly to implement major social and administrative reforms. Amini, despite, and in some cases because of, his American ties, was for a time in a relatively strong position with various sectors of the population. His voiced opposition to the governments of Eqbal and Sharif-Emami gave him some credibility with National Front and other oppositional groups, except for the underground or exiled Tudeh party. It was known that, unlike other prime ministers, he had imposed terms on the shah, and this added to his prestige. The dissolution of the majles at first also pleased the National Front and other oppositionists, who expected new elections soon; when it was seen that Amini expected to rule by decree without a majles, however, much of this support dissipated. Some National Front militants also distrusted Amini because of his part in negotiating the consortium agreement and his ties to the United States.

Amini settled the teachers' strike by awarding the teachers a pay raise and making their leader, Darakhshesh, minister of education. More dramatic was his appointment of Hasan Arsanjani, a lawyer with a radical background, as minister of agriculture. Amini had two ex-ministers arrested for corruption and promised a vigorous anticorruption drive. He needed the shah's support in view of potential opposition from the army and, in the case of land reform, from landlords and some ulama, and the shah needed Amini in order to recoup some power and popularity, but he did not want Amini to become strong or popular enough to undermine a return to his one-man rule.

Amini felt that strong government and reform were possible only with a lengthy, and technically unconstitutional, period of rule without elections or a majles. He and the shah agreed to undertake this and to rule by decree. The unconstitutional failure to call for new elections within a month of the dissolution of the majles led to demonstrations headed by the National Front. In July 1961, a demonstration resulted in the arrest of several National Front leaders and strong restrictions of National Front political activities, which had been open for only about a year. In November a royal decree allowing the government to legislate by decree without a majles brought on further pro-election agitation both from the National Front and from groups opposed to anticipated land reforms. In January 1962 came both the first major land-reform decree and a major riot by Tehran University students, brutally suppressed by the police and army. The students used National Front slogans, but other groups may also have been involved. The government chose to blame "right-wing elements" and arrested several rightist personalities. One man who had been stirring up trouble was the dismissed director of SAVAK, General Taimur Bakhtiar, who saw himself as a potential prime minister if Amini were forced to resign because of disturbances. Amini persuaded the shah to exile Bakhtiar, who went on to plot against the regime until he was finally killed by the shah's order in a "hunting accident" in Iraq. Partly to broaden the base of popular support, from late January 1962, the Amini government devoted itself seriously to implementing the land-reform decree (which, to retain some semblance of constitutionality, was presented as an "amendment" to the toothless 1960 law, but in fact was a wholly new law).

In its relations with the United States, the Amini government was in a relatively strong position. Whereas in the cold-war atmosphere of the mid–1950s the United States government was concerned mainly that Iran be anti-Communist, anti-Soviet, and have a large military force, there were by now some moves toward United States detente with the Soviet Union and war was not considered imminent. It was increasingly seen in the United States, especially during the Kennedy administration in 1961–63, that it might be important to American strategic and economic interests in the area to have an Iranian government with a broader internal base, greater efficiency and popularity, and less corruption than existed in the 1950s. From the unconditional support of the shah, provided he stayed firmly on the American side of the Cold War, United States policy shifted somewhat during the Kennedy years. The shah was asked to deal with corruption and inefficiency, and United States loans and grants decreased. Amini was, as was recognized in Iran, welcomed by the United States, whose officials urged the shah to support him and his reform program. A stress on certain reforms abroad by the Kennedy administration led to some of these changes. The shah was unhappy with American reform pressures, especially as they threatened his one-man rule, but felt he had to make some concessions. Amini had the immediate problem of improving the financial situation. The existing stabilization program had not accomplished a great deal. In its fifteen months in office the Amini government moved toward improving Iran's foreign-exchange position via drastic cuts in nonessential imports and restrictions on foreign travel and purchases of foreign currency by Iranians. But serious problems came in April 1962 when Amini and his new finance minister, Dr. Jamshid Amuzegar, tried to get all ministries to reduce their budgets. The shah refused to reduce the army budget, and so in July Amini resigned, giving as his reason the inadequacy of American aid. Clearly the shah would allow powerful and partially independent ministers to exist only so long as the alternative appeared even more dangerous to his own power. Now Asadollah Alam, the shah's old friend, became prime minister.

Amini never had the cooperation of the National Front forces, who mistrusted him for having accepted the Finance Ministry and the ambassadorship to America from the shah, and they opposed his decision to rule unconstitutionally without a Parliament rather than holding the free elections that they demanded, which would surely have resulted in major National Front and oppositional gains. Prime Minister Alam met with National Front leaders, who asked for free elections and other freedoms, which were refused. In December 1962 the National Front created a new unified central council and began open attacks on the shah. Most of the central council and many other National Front leaders were arrested soon thereafter, and the shah simultaneously tried to create a reformist image by adding other reforms to the land reform of 1962. To demonstrate his own and his regime's popularity he called early in 1963 for a national plebiscite on a combined six-point reform program including (1) land reform; (2) sale of government-owned factories to finance land reform; (3) a new election law including woman suffrage; (4) the nationalization of forests; (5) a national literacy corps, mainly for rural teaching; and (6) a plan to give workers a share of industrial profits. The vote, which was boycotted by the National Front on the grounds that such programs should be referred to a freely elected majles, was held in January 1963, and, like most such referendums, was overwhelmingly favorable. (Later other reform points were added to these. The program was called the White Revolution, and later by a phrase best translated as "The Revolution of the Shah and the People," but nearly always referred to in the regime's publications as "The Shah-People Revolution"—perhaps awkward style was less important than putting the word "shah" *first*.) The most important of the reforms in practice—land reform and the sale of factories to private industry—helped move landlord capital into industry and other urban projects and to lay the base for a state-dominated capitalism in city and countryside. Land reform also undercut landlord political power to the benefit of the central government.

Although one constituent wing of the National Front, soon to develop into the Freedom Movement, included both lay and clerical religious leaders, notably engineer Mehdi Bazargan and Ayatollah Mahmud Taleqani (who became prominent revolutionary leaders in 1978–79), in general the National Front now had little connection with the large ulama-led opposition movement that developed especially in 1963.

In the Mosaddeq period and subsequently some leading ulama had at first been pro-Mosaddeq but had then backed off from opposition to the shah's regime and had become relatively pro-shah because they had feared the rise in secularist and Communist power under Mosaddeq. Also, Ayatollah Borujerdi of Qom, who became the sole marja'-e taqlid (source of imitation) until his death in 1961, was not unfriendly to the shah and his only important antiregime fatva came in opposition to the land-reform proposal of 1960. Pressure by prominent ulama may have helped reshape this land reform into innocuousness.[6] Since Borujerdi's death there has not been a single, universally recognized marja'-e taqlid, but several men emerged as leading ayatollahs: among them Mohammad Hadi Milani in Mashhad; Kazem Shariatmadari, an Azerbaijani residing in Qom; and later Ruhollah Khomaini, also living in Qom, who first came to prominence in 1963, because of his oppositional activities. The economic and political crisis that had increased open opposition to the autocratic regime and to its subservience to Western powers affected religious leaders and their followers as it did other groups. The shah's regime labeled the religious opposition as a purely reactionary and largely selfish response to reform, particularly land reform and the woman suffrage included in the new electoral bill. Others have responded that Khomaini and Shariatmadari did not oppose land reform and that woman suffrage was not an important issue, given Iran's rigged elections; rather the crucial issues for Khomaini and others were dictatorship, subservience to the United States, and good relations with Israel.[7] It seems there is some truth and some exaggeration on both sides of the argument; although the latter points apparently were stressed by Khomaini, he and his colleagues also attacked the electoral law, in part but not exclusively for its woman-suffrage provision (he and his associates have not recently opposed woman suffrage), and some religious leaders, although possibly not Khomaini, also opposed land reform.[8] As on many questions in many periods, it is wrong to characterize the outlook of the ulama leadership at this time either as purely "reactionary," as did the regime and most of the foreign press, or as "progressive," as did some Iranian students abroad. Those opposed to dictatorship and to Iranian dependence on the United States may say that the ulama-led forces played a positive role in weakening both of these in 1963 and since, but this does not mean that the ulama were partisans or even nonopponents of many reforms that might help the majority of the population. In the event, land reform turned out to be not very helpful, but had Arsanjani's original plan been carried out it could have been so, and ulama arguments against it in 1962–63 were not based on an economic analysis of how the regime and vested interests would manipulate it in the future. Later, however, Khomaini did criticize the faults in practice of land reform.

Ayatollah Khomaini (see chapter 8) had written a work attacking Reza Shah and highly critical of monarchy as early as 1944, but in the late 1950s he was closely associated with Ayatollah Borujerdi at Qom and politically rather quietist.[9] He did not moderate his views, however, and in early 1963 began to preach against the shah in the chief, Faiziyeh, *madrasa* (religious school) of Qom. In March 1963, on the anniversary of the martyrdom of the Sixth Imam, Ja'far as-Sadeq, the madrasa was attacked by paratroopers and SAVAK, a number of students were killed, and Khomaini was arrested. Released after a short detention, Khomaini resumed his denunciations of the government and its policies. He attacked United States control of Iran and denounced America as an enemy of Islam, partly because of its support of Israel. Interestingly, even in a violent attack on the shah delivered on June 3, he, like most of his colleagues, at this time presented himself as a defender of the (monarchical) constitution: "the constitution has been bought with the blood of our fathers, and we will not permit it to be violated."[10] The next day, on the anniversary of the martyrdom of Imam Hosain, Khomaini was arrested before dawn. When the news became known in Tehran processions of mourning for Hosain turned into demonstrations. Demonstrations spread the next day to the university and to Shiraz, Kashan, and Mashhad. Despite heavy deployments of troops on Friday, June 7, the uprising continued, with one pamphlet calling for Holy War against the regime. The demonstrations were finally suppressed after several days, with loss of life in the hundreds or more.

Although the National Front wing that had religious and bazaar ties participated in the later days of rioting, the National Front had not expected riots and there was not prior collaboration with Khomaini. After the 1963 riots there was to be more cooperation between religious and nationalist opponents of the shah both within Iran and among students and exiles abroad. As was the case in 1977–78, discontent was sparked in part by a few years of painful economic crisis and inflation following several boom years that had helped the rich much more than the poor or the petty bourgeoisie. As in 1977–78 the shah responded to the crisis and to discontent by partial reforms, which were far from meeting the demands of opposition groups and encouraged them to voice their demands more openly. The crisis of 1960–63 was less serious than that of 1977–79, however, and the shah was able to restore his autocratic power by beefing up his security forces, shooting demonstrators, arresting large numbers in the religious and nationalist opposition, and putting forth a program of reform that for a time appeared to have substance. Partly owing to governmental controls and new policies encouraging industry, and partly for cyclical reasons, immediate economic problems were overcome and Iran soon entered a new phase of rapid growth that made many forget that a whole range of basic problems remained untouched and new ones had appeared.

The religious opposition movement continued after June 1963. Khomaini was released from arrest in August 1963 and SAVAK issued a statement saying agreement had been reached with him and the other leading oppositional ayatollahs that they would stop interfering in politics. But Khomaini asked his followers to boycott the parliamentary elections of October 1963, and was again arrested and held until May 1964. At that time SAVAK announced another understanding with him but he denounced this. In October 1964 the majles passed, with an unusual number of negative votes and speeches, a bill to grant diplomatic immunity to American military personnel and advisers. Shortly afterwards the majles agreed to a $200 million loan from the United States for the purchase of military equipment. Both the connection between the two bills and the capitulatory nature of the first were publicly and strongly denounced by Khomaini, who saw them as signs of bondage to the United States. After Khomaini's attack was circulated as a pamphlet, he was exiled to Turkey by the government in 1964, whence he went to Iraq in 1965. There he taught and spoke, with many of his words eventually brought into Iran as writings or cassettes, until his exile, probably under Iranian pressure, from Iraq to France in 1978.

Reform, Boom, and Bust: 1963–1977

The socioeconomic policies of the consolidated autocratic regime in the later 1960s and early to mid–1970s appeared to many, especially outside Iran, as a great success story, and in support of this contention they could point to large increases in Iran's GNP, impressive industrial, agricultural, and infrastructural projects, and a number of social welfare activities. On the other hand, many opponents of the regime proclaimed that all the reforms were fraudulent, that growth benefited mainly the rich, and that there were no structural changes. In fact, the social and economic changes and projects undertaken by the shah's regime in this period may be seen as contributing to a capitalist type of agriculture and of industrial growth, with a natural emphasis on state capitalism, given the autocratic nature of the regime and its monopoly control of the ever-growing oil income.[11] For purposes of brief analytic treatment the years 1962–77 may be seen as a unit in this building up of a predominant state capitalism, undermining of semifeudal forms of landownership seen as a bar both to development and to central government control of the countryside, and encouragement and subsidy to private capitalists. (Some authors, reacting against simplistic equations of Iran and other countries, reject terms like "capitalist"; in fact *every* area is unique but one needs general terms to indicate comparable structures.) Instead of proceeding year by year or five-year plan by plan in discussing the basic features of the economy, it seems more enlightening, within the short compass of this chapter, to deal with developments in key economic sectors over the whole period after 1962 and to stress analytic conclusions rather than details that may be found elsewhere.[12]

Land reform, which was legislated early in 1962, was the earliest phase of new economic policies and of an agricultural program which, by 1977, was clearly going in directions very different from those envisaged by the original architect of land reform, Agriculture Minister Hasan Arsanjani. The first phase of land reform, passed in 1962 and implemented over several years, sold to peasants, on the basis of (usually low) tax evaluations by their landlords, villages held by landlords with over one village. The landlord was allowed to keep one village or, and this was often the option chosen, the "equivalent" of one village by holding, say, the best of the traditional one-sixth divisions of the village in each of six villages. The latter option not only gave the landlord more and better land, but gave him some say in the running of six villages instead of one. Within Iranian villages some sharecroppers had cultivating rights which assured them of a certain share of the crop, and one family might own more than one such right, or might, if they owned oxen or parts of an underground water channel, hold a right without actually being cultivators. On the other hand, about 40 percent of the cultivating villagers were laborers paid in cash, kind, or both according to hours of work done and without cultivating rights. Those who drafted the reform may have been unaware of the number of laborers without cultivating rights who would be left out of reform, but, on the other hand, the shah had spoken out in favor of small landlords, whom he did not wish to buy out and who he said were more productive than large ones. A division that included the laborers would have been possible only with a far more radical taking over of land and equalization of landholding, with cooperative farming where appropriate, than the shah's regime wished to carry out.[13] Hence the reform, like most capitalist land reforms, was unequal even in its relatively progressive first phase supervised by Arsanjani, and even on the level of villagers in the same village; some got more, some got less, and some got nothing.

A widely praised feature of the Iranian land reform was Arsanjani's pragmatic solution to the lack of cadastral surveys for most villages, which would have made very slow any reform based, as in most countries, on acreage limits for landlords. By making the top limit the traditional village unit, the expensive and time-consuming problem of surveying was avoided. As in many countries, some landlords found ways to evade the top limit. Since land reform had been mooted for some years before 1962, and particularly since the government's abortive attempt in 1960, landlords had a chance to make partly fictitious sales or gifts to relatives or friends in order to lessen their legal holdings in return for real control or compensation. Moreover, the bill, with some economic reason, excluded orchards, pastures, plantations, and mechanized farms. It was easy to convert much of one's land to one of these. Although in some areas land-reform officials, who in the first period tended to be young and enthusiastic, tried to disallow any such changes made after passage of the law, this was often not done. In the end, despite many previous reliable estimates that well over half of Iran's land belonged to large landlords with over one village, the best estimate is that something like 9 percent of Iran's peasants got land in this first phase.[14] This is not an insignificant figure, especially as peasants affected by the first phase, unlike those in later phases, usually got whole farming units, i.e., an amount of land equivalent to that which had previously supported their families, and their payments to the government were generally lower than their former rent in kind. By law all peasants receiving land had to join a credit cooperative, and many such cooperatives were formed. These cooperatives were supposed to provide for the credit needs of peasants who formerly resorted to landlords and usuerers (who might be peddlers or traders who theoretically charged no interest but instead overcharged for their goods). Studies have shown that the cooperatives were grossly under-capitalized and could not provide enough low-interest loans to those who needed them, so that usury continued at almost the same rate as before, and richer peasants who could borrow more from the coopera-tives often re-lent money at high rates to poorer villagers. Also, there were no adequate controls to ensure that loans were used for productive purposes, as they were supposed to be, while the provision that only landowning peasants could be members and receive loans discrimi-nated, amongst others, against credit-worthy village craftspeople, particularly female carpet weavers.

Despite these problems the early record of those who got full shares in the first stage of reform was rather good. Many peasants began to invest in improvements, including deep wells with motor pumps. There has never been any adequate agricultural education or extension service in Iran, however, and the assumption has been that problems can be solved by a combination of tinkering with property rights and agricultural units and using modern and often expensive equipment from the West without testing its appropriateness to Iran. The traditional means of irrigating much of Iran has been the underground water channel, or qanat, which gets its water from the mountains. It involves a great amount of skilled labor but allows for a democratic division of water and does no ecological harm. The deep wells and pumps, however, after working well for a few years, were found often to lower the water table significantly and some areas that were once cultivable no longer are. Modified qanat construction might be a better approach.

Related problems have arisen, or will arise, in some areas from the use of tractors for plowing (their import has been favored and sub- sidized by the government). Large amounts of thin topsoil are plowed up in this fashion and in some cases deposited into streams and rivers, which then flood more often and may even change their course. The whole relationship between pasture and farmland has similarly been upset for the worse by new technology. Although American and other Western companies and governments are to blame for overselling such technology, the Iranian regime and many Iranian specialists who should know better were caught up in the idea that what is modern and Western is good. They should rather have studied the difficult prob- lems of an arid country with few remaining forests and thin topsoil, and tried to meet Iran's specific conditions, which may involve modifica- tions of traditional methods rather than straight borrowing from the West. Little has been done even with such a proven reliable method as reforestation; the old regime preferred buying tractors to planting trees. Western agricultural machinery was given preferential treatment over Iranian equipment, and little research went into improving exist- ing methods.

In short, even for the favored peasants of the first phase of reform not enough was done to make available to them appropriate means to increase production for most of them to become significantly more prosperous. As government price controls increasingly favored city dwellers, considered politically volatile, and in effect subsidized foreign grain growers by paying them, but not Iranians, world market prices, peasants became a disfavored class, although there were excep- tions. As for the laborers who got no land in villages affected by the first reform phase, they were less likely to be hired by cultivating peasants than by the old landlords, and most of them joined in the swelling migration to the cities, which reportedly reached over 8 percent of the population per year in 1972–73, although this was well above the average 1956–76 rate.[15]

In the spring of 1963 Arsanjani was forced to resign as minister of agriculture, largely because the shah never allowed another man to become too popular and pose a potential threat to his autocracy, and Arsanjani was clearly popular among Iran's peasants. Arsanjani wanted to transfer as much landlord land as possible to the peasants and promoted slogans and expectations of this kind. After his departure, subsequent phases of land reform were far more conservative than the first, and little was done to supplement the first phase, as Arsanjani and many peasants wished, with adequately capitalized multipurpose cooperatives or extension programs with new seeds and other aids to improving peasant output.

The second phase of reform, after its revision under conservative pressure, amounted more to a regularization of the existing system than redistribution of wealth. This stage was to cover, in theory, all remaining villages not in the excluded categories, except for vaqf villages, which were put on ninety-nine-year leases. The landlord owning one village or less was given a series of five choices, among them cash rentals, division of the land based on the former crop division, and sale to the peasant (which very few landlords chose). In a later phase, applied in 1969, all peasants were to get land through installment purchase, but since this generally meant only a percentage of the land they cultivated equal to the percentage of the crop they received under the old system, the majority of Iran's peasants did not get enough land for subsistence and had to find additional farming or other work. In the majority of Iran's villages covered by the second and third phases there were thus far fewer peasants who could make a living than in phase-one villages, and migration to cities by both laborers and poor peasants grew. These villages were also hit by the problems of inadequate loan funds, no extension services, and manipulation of prices by the government, which favored the towns and foreigners and disfavored the countryside.

Most government economic and technical aid and encouragement from the late 1960s on went into a small number of large agricultural units, while the small and middle peasant, to say nothing of the improverished agricultural laborer, were increasingly starved of government help and discouraged from managing their own affairs on a comprehensive cooperative basis. The government bias toward big units was shown within a few years of agrarian reform especially in two policies, embodied in two major programs. One was the law for the creation of farm corporations. In these units one, or usually more, villages were combined into a corporation, with peasants "persuaded" to turn over their recently received lands to the corporation, in return for which they got one or more shares, according to how much land they gave in. Wages were based on a combination of land and labor, but since farm corporations use modern machinery not all shareholders could be employed, and former farm laborers could hardly ever be employed. These groups contributed to the massive migration to overcrowded cities. Farm corporations were run by government specialists sent from Tehran, and required large expenditure for machinery, and for salaries, housing, and other buildings for the nonfarmers. Farm corporation directors often claimed that their enterprises were profitable, but their basis of calculation did not include the government's initial and overhead expenses, and the claim of profitability was not credible. It is clear that, in the early phases at least, peasants generally disliked the farm corporations, although there are no known studies of their attitudes years after joining. It would be surprising, however, if a peasant would put in as much productive effort into a farm corporation as he would on his own farm. About one hundred farm corporations were created by 1978. After the revolution they were mostly dismantled, suggesting both their unpopularity and unprofitability.

The other form of large production that was favored, at least until 1977, was huge agribusiness, partly owned and operated by multinational corporations. These farms of five thousand to twenty-five thousand hectares were generally built below new dams, especially in Khuzistan. Despite their supposed concentration on "new" land, they too cleared off many small peasants, and those who did not become agricultural laborers joined the rural exodus. Agribusinesses generally farmed only a small part of the land they held, and their relative contribution to the Iranian economy was seen as dangerously small by Iranian experts. Before 1978 some of the largest agribusinesses, especially in Khuzistan, were taken over by the government in part because of poor performance. Both agribusinesses and farm corporations have been proven to be far less productive than middle peasants.[16] This is largely because they have involved huge expenses in preparing the ground for irrigation and heavy machinery in a land of low-cost labor suited to cheaper home-manufactured implements. They appear to have been favored both by foreign farm equipment manufacturers and by Iranian special interests who skimmed off large sums, which they invested in more profitable ventures. They often concentrated on unproven export crops and hence lowered Iran's food production and contributed to a growing dependence on food imports.

Government policy also favored private mechanized farming. Toward the reformed villages, however, the government did little in terms of economic or technical aid, or aid in forming multipurpose cooperative societies. In some spheres there was progress in a minority of villages, as in the military-service literacy corps, supplemented to a small degree by health and development corps. In the more direct problems of production, however, the government did little. Few of the technical benefits of the "green revolution" were diffused; there were scarcely any efforts to pool resources for machinery; and extension services and technical education remained extremely inadequate. Most cooperatives remained purely credit societies, instead of giving the aid in marketing and production that a multipurpose society could give. Restrictive cooperative loan policies described above favored a growing disparity of income within the village, also favored by the digging of deep wells, which often monopolize water that once was more democratically divided from underground channels. The well-owner can sell a precious resource.

In favoring mechanized extensive farming and disfavoring the small and medium peasant, despite the latter's proven higher productivity per person within Iran itself, the Iranian government adopted a policy that might have been economically rational in a country with large cultivable territory and a shortage of labor. In Iran, however, the present cultivable surface is too small for a heavily underemployed rural labor force, and to push ahead with large mechanized farms rather than more intensive techniques operated by peasants with a personal stake in their own lands was counterproductive. The production record of

agribusiness was miserable; farm corporations contributed less than
would the same amount of government capital and effort spread over
reformed villages, and increases in agricultural production were low.
Although official statistics on the annual rise in agricultural production
state that it was about 4 percent a year, this figure is almost universally
considered unreliable and based on the need to mask the shocking
reality that agricultural production rose more slowly than population.
A more reasonable estimate is that agricultural production rose about
2–2.5 percent a year, population 3 percent, and consumption of
agricultural products about 12 percent. With rising mechanization,
the unemployment or very low income of agricultural laborers, and the
rise in rural population, there was a rapid stream of rural migrants into
the cities, especially Tehran—cities without the housing, amenities, or
even jobs to cope with them. The agrarian situation plus a growth in
food consumption meant a rapid rise in agricultural imports, which
would create a major problem when oil income began to run out. The
government also reduced sheep production, forcing ever more imports
of meat and wool. Despite the huge migration to towns rural population grew slightly, owing to natural increase,[17] but migration was
concentrated among men of working age, leaving agriculture further
weakened.

If the government favored the big over the small in both city and
countryside, it also favored the cities—already wealthier and more
powerful—over the countryside. This was shown particularly in price
controls on basic food products, which for a time kept down the vocal discontent of the volatile urban masses. These controls were often
based on fixed low prices paid to producers for certain agricultural
products—prices that further depressed agricultural incomes relative
to urban ones.

Similar problems were felt by tribal-pastoral peoples. Although it
was probably tribal khans who instigated a revolt related to land reform
among the Qashqa'i and Boir Ahmadi of Fars province in 1963,
ordinary tribespeople also suffered from the government's agricultural
policies. First, townspeople and wealthy farmers were more likely to
take advantage of loopholes in the land-reform law to lay claim to
disputed tribal land than were tribespeople who had less influence with
the authorities. Second, the nationalization of pasture, one of the points

added to the White Revolution, took away tribal control of pastureland and made tribes increasingly subject to governmental whims, policies, and gendarmes. Agricultural and other projects spread at the expense of pasture, and tribespeople were less and less able to support themselves by a primarily pastoral existence. In the 1970s especially the government became increasingly convinced, partly persuaded by American businessmen, that instead of relying on the nomads' sheep for much of Iran's meat the government should underwrite the creation of large meat, poultry, and dairy farms, with expensive imported equipment, cattle and feed. Like other large agricultural projects these were both costly and unproductive, besides the fact that Iranians prefer fresh sheep and lamb to the beef and imported frozen meat that the government's policies toward pastoralists increasingly forced on them. Mohammad Reza Shah, like his father, in fact pursued a policy of settling the nomads—not by force of arms but by depriving them of their livelihood so that they had increasingly to become agriculturalists or enter the subproletariat of the urban slums.[18] As in the case of peasant farming, the regime felt that nomadism was not modern whereas big American-style animal farms were; and wealthy Iranians and Americans profited from the latter. In both cases a way of life in which ordinary people had learned to make maximum use of marginal resources, and which could survive with tested modifications, was increasingly sacrificed to a wholesale use of inappropriate modern Western imports. (Since 1979 some nomads have moved back into lands taken from them, and the last chapter in this old struggle has yet to be written.) Although in both agriculture and industry large mechanized enterprises made up a minority of total units, the important point is that investment and efforts were heavily concentrated on such units while small producers were disfavored. Land reform may never have had primarily economic goals; a major aim was to cut landlord power and bring peasants and nomads under direct government control, and this was accomplished.

The industrial sphere has been somewhat more connected to Iran's Five Year Plans than have major agricultural changes (land reform, in particular, was not suggested in the plan that covered the period in which it was launched). The defects of the first Seven Year Plan have been noted above. Later plans have become increasingly sophisticated in technique and personnel and increasingly comprehensive in coverage, although a running battle between the "independent" Plan and Budget Organization and the ministries that were supposed to carry out its projects but preferred to control their own, was a continual cause of delays and immobilization. In the late 1950s an Economic Bureau was set up for the Plan Organization assisted by a group of Western advisers under the auspices of Harvard University. The only general evaluation published by a member of this bureau is almost totally negative about planning in Iran, and notes that the main economic advances experienced by Iran in the past half century have occurred not through planning but because of nationalism—such as the increasing control over oil, tariffs, and relations with foreigners.[19] It is thus best to be wary on the subject of planning in Iran. The regime indeed followed a general economic strategy, which was much influenced by increasingly large oil revenues. It is likely, however, that much of this strategy might have been followed without the mechanism of a Plan Organization, although the latter had some effect and played the ideological role of indicating that the government was thinking ahead for the benefit of the whole country, and using the most modern mechanisms to ensure rapid economic and social progress. Often the dictates of the shah in fact determined economic policies.

Governmental strategy toward the economy since the 1960s included rapid development of import substitution industries, especially large enterprises that used much modern and labor-saving technology. Despite a few showy "crackdowns," mainly on retailers or vulnerable targets, extremely large profits were encouraged for both domestic and foreign companies, while less was done for those on the bottom rungs of the economic scale. The above policy was justified by some according to the theory that in early stages of development, income distribution must worsen, and that those at the top of the scale should be favored since they save and invest more than those at the bottom. The rival theory that, at least in the stage Iran had reached, much greater equality of incomes is needed for self-sustaining development if a mass consumer market where people could buy back what they produced were to be achieved, was rarely stated. The regime's race for greater size, military strength, and modernity, with its concomitants of unemployment, waste, corruption, and poverty, affected both agriculture

and industry. In both spheres heavy inputs of foreign capital, personnel, and imports were favored by official policies. The shah in the
1970s voiced the expectation that Iran would become one of the world's
five top powers in this century: such a fantasy encouraged heavy
collaboration with multinational corporations and short shrift for the
everyday needs of most Iranians. The essential mechanisms of the above
economic strategy are fairly simple, although not well known to
nonspecialists. Oil income was one factor in a generally regressive tax
structure, encouraging the government not to enforce its mild income
tax and not to institute other progressive taxes. The government could
essentially do without tax income and did not try seriously to use
taxation either as one means for more just income distribution or to
prepare Iranian tax collectors and citizens for the day not long hence
when oil will start to run out.

More seriously, the impetus given by oil to the dramatic economic
boom experienced by Iran from 1963 until the late 1970s, with per
capita GNP rising from about $200 to $1,000 in real terms, and with
one of the highest growth rates in recent history for a sizable country,
did not lessen the income disparity between the rich and the poor, but
the contrary. Gains were concentrated at the upper levels, owing
largely to government policies.

In industry, government policies, at least since the 1960s, favored
both the private production of relatively expensive consumer durables
with a large foreign component and a concentrated market in Tehran,
and also the concentration of economic enterprises in or near Tehran.
This helped both Iranian and foreign investors, who by law were free to
repatriate their profits. (Foreign direct investment outside oil was,
however, not very large; foreign sales and personnel were far more
important.) Because of its oil income, the government could renounce
industrial taxes to favor certain industries or itself build industries or
infrastructure that favored large industries; and the government was
able on the basis of oil income to pay higher salaries to the higher
administrative echelons, thus enabling them to purchase consumer
durables.

The relevant government policies included preferential high tariffs,
prohibition of certain imports, very low rates for bank loans to large
industries, tax holidays, licensing of only a few industries in each field,

and preferential treatment for foreign capital. High tariffs and prohibitions may have been needed in some cases at an initial stage in order to launch an industry, but tariffs were seldom lowered, so that there was little incentive to operate efficiently or to direct capital toward those branches of production using local inputs. An unneeded variety of automobiles were assembled and partially produced, while many goods that could be made for popular use in small plants were either imported or handmade in insufficient quantities. Lowered tariffs could rationalize production by reducing the production of complex goods requiring many imported elements and encouraging production of simpler, more popular goods, which should need less tariff production as their manufacture is relatively less expensive. Capital-goods production could also have been encouraged by new tariff policies.

Credit policies were designed to favor large enterprises and the rich Iranians and foreigners who owned and ran them. In general, subsidized rates considerably below the market price of money were available only to large enterprises, whereas small shopowners and craftspeople were starved even for unsubsidized bank credit, since their plants did not provide sufficient collateral for loans. They were generally not eligible for normal bank rates of about 12 percent, but had to borrow in the bazaar at 25 to 100 percent. More employment and less income inequality could have come from an opposite loan policy, with higher commercial rates charged to the big industrialists and subsidized rates to the small owners. (Difficulties in getting bank loans were probably one factor in mass attacks on banks in 1978, although other factors were more often mentioned.)

Tax holidays of various kinds were given to encourage foreign investors, or investors in certain regions. Although this policy was publicized as a way to decentralize industry out of the Tehran region, by offering tax inducements to factories built at least 120 km. from Tehran, it was found that the concentration of industry in the Central province where Tehran is located increased after the policy was enunciated, with a ring of industries built about 120 km. from Tehran.

Although legally a company did not need a license in order to operate, any sizable company did need one to import, export, or deal with the government. Government licenses were given out only to a few companies in each field, their main theoretical rationale being to keep a field from getting so overcrowded that plants overproduced and could not operate to capacity. The need to get and keep a license, like many other government rules, required that top persons in a company spend much time in Tehran cultivating one or more leading people in order to insure the receipt of a license or other needed favors. Regarding licenses and other matters, credible stories circulate of the highest-ranking Iranians (including Princess Ashraf and her son Shahram) who took 10 percent or more of a new company's stock gratis in return for insuring the delivery of a license. Such practices, along with other industrial practices listed above, and other forms of corruption, significantly increased the sale price of Iranian goods, thus limiting their domestic and ultimately needed foreign market. They also further skewed income distribution. Corruption, which mushroomed with the growth of oil income, is in part one more mechanism that pushes wealth up and out. It also made the culpable more subject to royal control. Besides the shah's growing fortune, in the 1970s corruption in the court, royal family, and the elite was so massive as to add significantly to the opposition. Many foreign firms were also involved in payoffs to individuals.

As to foreign capital, although foreigners could legally own only a minority share in Iranian industries, they were subject to few other restrictions and could repatriate profits freely. Brochures for foreign investors proclaimed that profits on capital of 30 percent were normal in Iran. Economists who know the country often spoke of 50 percent, and profits in trade and industry of 100 to 200 percent were not unknown. Hence the "traditional" Middle Eastern reluctance to invest in "unprofitable" industry gave way to an industrial boom concentrating on the assembly of consumer goods and aimed largely at a restricted, relatively wealthy market. Such a boom carried within it major problems.

Foreign investment in Iran was much smaller than was the import of foreign goods, and foreign corporations encouraged the shah's mania for the ultramodern and sophisticated. In armaments the shah bought billions of dollars worth of the latest weapons, often while they were still on the drawing board. Imported high technology computers and other instruments were fed primitive statistics and controlled semi-automatic factories. Iran became a huge market for American grain, some of which was used to feed the imported American cattle and poultry that were supplementing and replacing the nomads' sheep. Sophisticated foreign equipment demanded foreign technicians and workers, who in the 1970s streamed in by the tens of thousands. Americans and Europeans were concentrated in the high technical posts, Far Easterners often held skilled labor positions, and Afghans came in for unskilled jobs, often depressing wage rates. The skilled foreigners, to the contrary, got higher salaries than Iranians— sometimes several times higher—and this, plus their behavior and their pushing up the price of scarce housing, helped make them objects of resentment.

It is within the context of industrial policies favoring large profits by a few capital-intensive industries that the occasional campaigns against "profiteers," or in favor of shareholding by factory workers, which were given more publicity than the above policies, should be evaluated. Such measures were either scapegoating or palliatives in face of rising profits, income inequalities, high inflation, corruption, and a failure to meet government promises of greater economic and social equity. Along with certain other policies they were designed to allay the discontent of the class that evinced, through fairly frequent, illegal, and unreported strikes, its continued discontent—the factory workers. Partly through government favoring of workers in large factories by shareholding and other measures, which were, however, less dramatic than their announcements would make it seem, and partly through rising wages for qualified workers, workers in large factories and in certain trades became a relatively favored group in the mid–1970s. One cannot, however, take reports regarding groups of workers whose wages, say, tripled in a few years, as typical of the popular classes en masse. As for the jailed or exiled "profiteers," they were more often disfavored bazaar merchants or members of minorities than rich modern Muslim businessmen.

All this does not mean that the government's industrial policies produced only negative results. The rate of industrial growth was one of the highest in the world, and rose further with the impact of huge oil revenues since 1974. What was questionable was the continuation of preferential policies toward Western-style industries; the disfavoring of small crafts and industries, which contribute to production, to employment, and to greater income equality; the favoring of foreign investments and the kind of production requiring a huge foreign presence; and the underwriting of heavy consumer durables. These contributed to the overcentralization of the national market in Tehran, and to the development of a kind of demand which meant that "import substitution" led to a rise in imports of food, capital goods, and many consumer goods. Thus, many of the problems often noted by Iran's own planners—such as overcentralization in Tehran and a few large cities, too many automobiles and luxury imports, too much dependence on foreigners, and above all the growing income-distribution disparity —were fed by the government's own policies.[20]

With what has been said, it is not surprising that income gaps widened in the 1960s and 1970s. Although no good income survey exists, there are family expenditure surveys, and on the basis of these Iranian and foreign economists have made studies with similar conclusions. Briefly, since the 1960s, income inequalities in Iran, which were already great on a world scale, increased, and this increase was particularly dramatic after 1974, when oil income shot up after the great price rise. The size and increase in Iran's distribution gap is notable whether the top decile or two are compared with the bottom decile or two, or whether one takes the Gini coefficient, which measures deviation from the norm all along a normal distribution scale. In addition, an important Iranian study shows increases in income inequality in all major dimensions: between the top and the bottom, between the cities and the countryside, within the cities, and within the countryside.[21] All this occurred despite a repeatedly expressed government determination to reduce income inequality. However, as noted, overall it was primarily the rich who were subsidized by oil and other governmental money, and the poor much less.

This does not mean that most of the poor literally got poorer. Given the huge increase in GNP per capita, the rich could get much richer and many of the poor get somewhat richer. The poorer classes started from such a low income level, however, that even doubling or tripling their effective income would not bring them to anything like European working-class standards. Also, they saw the conspicuous consumption of the elite all around them, and this gave rise to increasingly vocal discontent. The consumption patterns encouraged by this distribution along with the dizzy oil-based growth of the 1970s created a host of national problems: constantly increasing spending on imports; orientation of the economy toward dependence on foreigners; the huge population flow into overcrowded cities; and a lack of urban low-cost housing and skyrocketing housing prices, exacerbated by the growing presence of foreigners whose high wages added to rising prices and scarcities, particularly in housing. More equitable income distribution could both be aided by and contribute to a policy of economic decentralization and dispersion of the population, and could create a market for goods with greater Iranian inputs. A policy favoring peasants and small producers could boost production, add to employment, and encourage population dispersion, especially if crafts and small industries were developed in or near villages. Only diversified investment including towns and villages can humanely meet the needs of Iran's rapidly growing population.

The oil component of Iran's economy became increasingly important over time. Even before the OPEC quadrupling of oil prices led by the shah in late 1973, oil provided a steadily rising income as production went up, and also an increasing percentage of plan funds, rising finally to 88 percent of these. In the late 1960s and early 1970s Iran was able to renegotiate the terms of its agreement with the consortium so that Iran took some control of production levels and pricing, leaving a guaranteed supply to the consortium companies for marketing. Although this involved a partial return to nationalization, it did not hurt the consortium companies; to the contrary, they have profited immensely from every OPEC price rise.

The 1973 Arab-Israeli War led to an Arab oil boycott on Western suppliers of Israel and an effective doubling of oil prices. At the OPEC meetings late in 1973 the shah pushed successfully for a redoubling of prices, arguing with some justice that oil prices had been kept low while prices on all other commodities had risen. Later there were grandiose statements by the shah that Iran would soon become one of the world's five great powers with average incomes equal to the best. The shah seemed not to realize that huge sums could not simply be thrown into the Iranian economy without serious results in terms of inflation, shortages, and overheating the economy. In early 1974 he presided over an official conference where, in the face of feeble opposi-

tion from some planners, he vastly expanded the expenditures pro-
grammed for the current Five Year Plan.[22]

Ironically, the shah was in part undone by his OPEC triumph and its
consequences within Iran. The processes described above—stress on
big industry and agriculture with the resultant overrapid migration
and shortages in housing and other goods and services—increased to
crisis proportions. In cities shortages of food items, power blackouts,
traffic jams, overcrowding, and pollution made life increasingly
difficult, and loud arguments and physical fights in the streets were
one sign of the strain.

The shah's virtual mania for buying large amounts of up-to-date and
sophisticated military equipment from abroad had free rein from 1972,
when the Nixon administration underwrote the shah as the policeman
of the Gulf, and agreed to sell him whatever nonnuclear arms he
wished. Western governments and corporations, with the United
States in the lead, were happy to sell, with little consideration on either
side of possible negative consequences. Western eagerness to sell
billions of dollars of military equipment to Iran each year was reinforced
by the economic drain on the West caused by the OPEC price rise; arms
purchases seemed a fine way to recycle petrodollars. After the British
pullout from the Gulf, the British and American governments were
happy to see Iran become the gendarme of the area, fighting leftist-led
rebels in Oman's Dhofar province and threatening other potential
disturbers of the status quo. The British provided Iran with more
Chieftain tanks than they had in their own armed forces, and the
United States let the Shah be the first to buy a series of sophisticated
fighter planes, often before they were in production or their reliability
had been proved. Iran also began to construct a sophisticated
American-designed electronic intelligence network called IBEX for
American surveillance of the Soviet Union. Along with all this equipment, as well as numerous less sophisticated items like Bell helicopters,
went a large number of expensive foreign technical advisers and instructors and their families, who contributed to inflation and whose behavior often caused justified indignation among Iranians.

American military suppliers like Grumman, Lockheed, and
Westinghouse took over key positions in the economy. Many potentially productive Iranians, including a high percentage of the techni-

cally trained, were increasingly concentrated in the armed forces and in building projects for army and naval bases and for facilities to transport and house military equipment. New housing starts, and particularly the use of cement, were at times outlawed or rendered impossible because of the heavy demands on cement and other building materials for sheltering military equipment. Thus the growing housing shortage and rise in home prices was tied to military spending, and foreigners' and foreign contractors' willingness to pay high rents added to the problem. The stress on big and complex projects increased, and as there had never been any adequate program of technical education there were not enough Iranians for skilled and technical jobs, much less scientific or managerial ones. Hence the importation of foreigners grew, further contributing to overcrowding, shortages, inflation, and anti-American feeling.

Inflation and other economic problems contributed to the appointment of Jamshid Amuzegar as prime minister in mid–1977. He immediately launched a deflationary program, which brought a sudden growth in unemployment, especially among the unskilled and semiskilled, and this, coming after rising expectations, helped create a classic prerevolutionary situation. The combination of inflation, shortages, and large and evident income-distribution inequities probably contributed more to growing discontent than did the standard factor cited in the West of "too rapid modernization." It was mainly *how* modernization was carried out, and the results of these policies, that were important.[23] Cultural uprooting was also important in the late 1970s, when Westernization was challenged by radical new interpretations of Shi'ism, associated particularly with Ali Shariati (see ch. 8).

While some of the American press and even some government officials began to criticize the shah after he pioneered the OPEC price rise, major United States business interests became more closely tied to, and even dependent on, the shah's regime than ever. This was especially true of three key sectors of American business: armaments, oil, and banking. Producers of high technology, grain and agricultural equipment, and consumer goods also had large sales in Iran. Iran's huge advance orders were more than once responsible for bailing out an American arms manufacturer, some of whom spent vast sums, often illegally, lobbying Iran for business.[24]

The several American oil companies who together marketed 40 percent of the large consortium sales of Iran, the world's second largest oil exporter, profited increasingly from Iran and from high oil prices. Finally, several American banks received and helped invest huge amounts of Iranian money, both from the Iranian government and from funds sent abroad by the shah, the royal family, other rich Iranians, as well as the Pahlavi Foundation, which was an effective charitable front for many profitable royal investments. American banks also owned percentages of Iran's banks and held shares in Iranian businesses. Given these and other Western business interests in Iran and the Anglo-American desire to use Iran strategically in the Gulf, against Russia, and against possible trouble with bordering radical movements in Muslim countries, it is no surprise that United States representatives in Iran predominantly went along with the shah's reported desire that they not contact the opposition, and with his rosy assessment that the opposition consisted of small and unimportant groups of Marxists and religious fanatics. Although the United States under Carter may have influenced the shah some concerning human-rights violations, neither the United States government nor major American business interests wanted to see a fundamental change in Iran's orientation in the direction of nonalignment, reduction of arms and other deals profitable to Americans, or the building up of a more independent, self-sufficient economy. American government and business interests thus preferred the shah to any truly popular alternative, which would have had to reduce American economic and political influence, and might alter Iran's pro-American foreign policy. The only reforms favored by the United States were ones that would not change Iran's pro-American oil, strategic, and economic policies.

To add a brief word about major political developments since 1963 which, until 1977, had none of the drama or importance of the early 1950s or the early 1960s: as the Melliyun party of Eqbal was discredited by the electoral fiascoes of the early 1960s, a new party called Iran Novin (New Iran), was encouraged by the shah. Some of its leaders reputedly had Freemasonic ties, which Iranians often associate with the British. The first prime minister from this party, Hasan Ali Mansur, like Amini and Alam from an old, rich landholding family, ruled only from March 1964 to January 1965, when he was fatally shot by a religious terrorist. There was also an attempt on the shah's life in 1965. Another Iran Novin leader, Amir Abbas Hoveyda, was appointed prime minister in 1965 and held the post for an extraordinary twelve and a half years, owing to the lack of economic and political crises in this period, the apparent success of the government's economic and social policies, and Hoveyda's ability to carry out the shah's wishes without appearing as a threat to the shah's power. In March 1975, the shah announced that the legal parties would be merged into a new single Rastakhiz (resurgence) party headed by Hoveyda. Membership was required of most government and university employees, as well as many others. (At the same time the shah's first autobiography, called in English, *Mission for My Country,* was withdrawn from circulation and a new edition minus the passage saying that only Communist and fascist countries used one-party regimes was later issued.) The Rastakhiz party was allowed to have two wings, but each was headed by a loyal pretender to succeed Hoveyda. Instead of mobilizing most Iranians for the regime, the Rastakhiz added significantly to discontent.

The economic and social development of the 1960s and 1970s, of which a critical assessment is given above, was not without positive features, and an early minister of the economy of this period as well as various figures in the PO's high quality staff and in some other departments are generally credited with a number of useful projects and policies. Some industrial, infrastructural, educational, and social welfare achievements were net gains for Iran. Although his low opinion of women as expressed to the journalist Oriana Fallaci is well known, the shah was apparently convinced that it was economically beneficial and would contribute to his modern image to have more women educated and in the labor force. Just as organizations like trade unions and chambers of commerce could exist only under official control, but nonetheless managed to express some of the needs of their members, so independent women's organizations were merged into a single Iranian Women's Organization under the patronage of Princess Ashraf.

Owing partly to pressure from this organization a Family Protection Law was passed in 1967 (repealed and passed in stronger form in 1975). The law introduced a number of important reforms into marriage, divorce, and family law, which until then had been rather strictly based on the sharia and the Quran. To try to make the new legislation

Islamically legitimate, a feature of Shi'i (and some Sunni) law was utilized whereby special provisions can be inserted into the required marriage contracts, such as one saying that a husband cannot take a second wife without the first wife's consent. Reform provisions were henceforth to be inserted into all Muslim marriage contracts. According to the new law men could no longer unilaterally divorce their wives, but all divorce cases had to go to court and grounds for divorce by husband or wife were similar. Guardianship of children, which in Islamic law goes to the husband after an age that varies by school of law but in Shi'ism is young, was now to be awarded according to the merits of the case by the courts. No man could take an additional wife or wives without the permisssion of the previous one(s), and if he did so this was grounds for divorce. While opponents of the shah are right to say that this law was neither totally egalitarian nor universally applied, especially mong the popular classes, this is true of such reform legislation everywhere, and is not a good argument against such legislation as one important step toward changing the unequal treatment of the sexes. Even the real problem of lengthy and complex court procedures could have been met by further reform. Unluckily for women's rights, this cause and the Family Protection Law became associated with an increasingly unpopular regime and with Western-style mores disliked by religious traditionalists.[25]

Such displays as the shah's coronation and especially the huge celebration in 1971 of a mythical 2,500th anniversary of the Persian monarchy (which had not existed between A.D. 640 and A.D. 1501) showed up the discrepancy between the seemingly unlimited wealth the shah could throw around and the poverty, however slightly mitigated, of most of his subjects. It was hard for many to give the shah credit for any achievements when so much more could have been done with his oil billions (ca. $20 billion a year after the price rise), and when there was little freedom of speech or press and opposition was so ruthlessly suppressed, particularly after the rise of guerrilla groups in the 1960s and 1970s. The effective suppression of the Tudeh after 1953–54 and of the National Front after 1963 as well as the exile or jailing of Khomaini and other oppositional figures helped change the character of the opposition. In part it became more than ever concentrated abroad, particularly among the tens of thousands of Iranians studying in the West, many of whom belonged to various leftist groups, while an increasing number combined leftism or Third Worldism with their interpretation of Islam. The increasing circulation by cassette and leaflet of the talks and writings of Ayatollah Khomaini in exile in Iraq encouraged the religious oppositional trend both outside and within Iran.

With the improvement of relations between Iran and the Eastern European countries in the 1960s and later with China, both the pro-Soviet reformism of one wing of the exiled Tudeh party and the pro-Chinese position of the other wing seemed increasingly unattractive to antishah radicals inside and outside Iran. Beginning in the late 1960s there was a rise in small urban guerrilla groups who carried out a number of assassinations, hitting a few American military personnel and advisers. These groups came to coalesce primarily into two important ones: the Marxist Feda'iyan-e Khalq and the Islamic leftist Mojahedin-e Khalq, both of which became, toward the end of the 1978–79 revolution, large and open revolutionary groups. Guerrilla activities contributed something to the increase in political repression, jailing, tortures, and executions from the late 1960s on; many of those executed were tied to these groups. On the other hand, they also suggested to many oppositionists that it was still possible to act against the regime despite its formidable repressive machinery.[26] At the same time religious and bazaar opposition to the regime continued to be expressed indirectly in sermons, meetings, and ceremonies. The bazaar economy was hurt by the regime's favoring of big, ultramodern enterprises and of foreigners and disfavoring of bazaaris, who bore the brunt of attacks on "profiteers." Given the economic dependence of the ulama on bazaaris and the political influence of each of the two groups on the other, governmental attacks on both helped create a strong oppositional coalition.

By 1977 an economic recession, inflation, urban overcrowding, government policies that hurt the bazaar classes, glaring income gaps, and conspicuous Western-style consumption by the elite and the lack of political freedom or participation were all widely felt and belied the numerous official predictions that the "Great Civilization" was just around the corner. The effective suppression of secular oppositionists, whether from the National Front or Tudeh, left room for the religious opposition, whose sermons, processions, and plays with themes like the martyrdom of Iman Hosain by tyrants were understood to refer to contemporary tyranny, but could not be suppressed.[27] In addition the association of the shah's regime with Western culture, commodities, and vices brought on a traditionalist reaction even among many former Westernizers, which often took an Islamic form.

Clockwise from top left: Sattar Khan, leader of the Tabriz freedom-fighters; Mirza Jahangir Khan, editor of *Sur-e Esrafil;* Sayyed Jamal ad-Din Esfahani and Malek al-Motakallemin, leading popular preachers. All but Sattar Khan were killed following Mohammad Ali Shah's 1908 coup.

Clockwise from top left: Shahsevan tribeswoman Azerbaijan, 1975; Baluchi, near the Afghan border, 1973; Kurd at a town market, 1974; Arab family, Ahwaz, Khuzistan, 1974.

Above: Qashqa'i tribespeople on summer migration, 1977.

Below: Qashqa'i factory worker, Marvdasht, 1977.

Above: Family weaving at home, Kerman, 1974.

Below: Carpet workshop, Ardebil, Azerbaijan, 1974.

Right: Blackface clown of the popular theatre
Shiraz, 1977.

Below: Ta'zieh (passion play) on the death of
Ali, Taleqan valley, 1979.

Left: Abolhasan Bani Sadr, first president of the Islamic Republic of Iran.

Below: Ayatollah Mahmud Taleqani (d. 1979), a socially conscious cleric.

Left: Dr. Ali Shariati (d. 1977), leading ideologist of progressive Islam.

Below: Ayatollah Kazem Shariatmadari, moderate constitutionalist from Azerbaijan.

Above: Women's section, prayer meeting at the University of Tehran, 1979.

Below: Men's section, Mehdi Bazargan (at right) and Sadeq Ghotbzadeh (second from left) in front row.

8 MODERN IRANIAN POLITICAL THOUGHT

Intellectual and Literary Trends to 1960

Before coming to contemporary Shi'i though it will be useful to discuss briefly literary and intellectual trends that formed part of the background for more recent writers and thinkers. (Premodern religious trends—majoritarian and dissident—were discussed in chapter 1 and will be given relatively minor attention here.)

The "two-cultures" phenomenon in Iran (that is, different cultures for the elite and the masses) is largely a phenomenon of the Pahlavi period, before which there was a gradation but no sharp break between elite and popular cultures. This can be seen in such elementary spheres as dress, homes, styles of furnishing, means of locomotion, and mosque attendance. It also appears in literary forms; "folk culture," which in the nineteenth century and before cut across classes, has increasingly been relegated to the popular classes. Such folk culture includes the folktale, a widespread genre now most important to the popular classes, especially in the countryside.

Better known to outsiders is the "passion play," or *ta'ziyeh,* in reality a series of plays centering around the martyrdom of the imams, especially of Imam Hosain, whose small forces were slaughtered in Iraq by the army of the Umayyad caliph Yazid. In the first ten days of the holy month of Moharram, a series of these plays are performed, today mostly in rural and popular class areas (though in the nineteenth century they were also patronized by Qajar shahs and notables). A variety of personal and political feelings are expressed by the audience—comprising men, women, and children—in the course of such plays. For example, spectators, especially women, who see inno-

183

cent children die in the play as they do in reality can find an outlet for their grief; while many, particularly during periods of political discontent, find in the ta'ziyeh stories of Imams Hosain and Ali a paradigm of just struggle against unrighteous tyrants, a theme often given explicit political resonance. The themes of the martyrdom of Ali, Hosain, and other imams are reiterated in less elaborate ways in other forms of popular religious culture, notably by the *rauzeh-khan* who tells these stories with the aid of a few pictures and props. This can be a woman molla at women's gatherings, and props may include puppet shows.[1] Sermons in mosques can also be political.

There is a gradual gradation between the "religious" ta'ziyeh and the "secular" humorous folk play. Some plays have both elements. The predominant form of secular folk theatre does, however, differ from most ta'ziyehs in its choice of secular subjects, and its comic, rather than reverent, view of its characters. Like the ta'ziyeh the folk theatre in the pre-Pahlavi period was a multiclass phenomenon, with middle-class urban families as well as peasant villages hiring theatre troupes for special occasions such as weddings. The folk theatre, like that in much of the world, is characterized by stock characters, notably the black- or white-face clown who can defy social convention with impunity. Like many folk theatres it is also openly or subtly obscene and in other ways too represents the "World turned upside down"; the respectably pompous merchant bested by his wife and/or a poor youth; the hypocritical molla unmasked, and so forth.[2] In this theatre as in ta'ziyeh women's parts are taken by men, but the audience includes men, women, and children. There is also a lesser known form of popular theatre found in women's theatre games, performed by groups of women in their homes. As in public folk theatre the world is turned upside down, and the follies and weaknesses of the dominant group (men) are revealed—whether it be hypocrisy, impotence, or whatever. The women in these plays, much like the poor in the others, often succeed in outwitting their husbands or other male oppressors.[3] Like the ta'ziyehs the popular theatre may have very different effects in different periods; in politically quiet periods they may just provide an outlet for feelings against sexual, political, and personal repression; as crises approach, however, people's attention turns increasingly to the evils of such injustices and the need to combat them, and the plays and rauzeh-khanis increasingly become a political medium for expressing such ideas, and the character traits stressed in their heroes change accordingly.

Reza Shah banned ta'ziyeh performances, which were allowed a limited comeback under Mohammad Reza under whom, however, limits were put on folk theatre by demanding (nonexistent) licenses, scripts (for improvised comedy), and so forth. But the major assault on such theatre, as in much of the world, came from Western-style film, radio, and TV, which helped limit popular theatre increasingly to villages and small towns.

Beyond popular literature there were also other manifestations of the multiclass nature of pre-Pahlavi culture, even though some cultural forms were limited to the secular and religious elites respectively. Among the multiclass cultural forms that have declined visibly even in the past twenty years is knowledge and recital of the best classical poetry, including poets like Hafez and Sa'di, by unlettered men and women in both city and countryside. Western visitors knowing Persian frequently remarked on such long recitations with amazement. Related were coffeehouse poets who generally gave dramatic recitations from the *Shah-nameh* (*Book of Kings*), the Persian national epic composed by the poet Firdausi; these continued to exist, but in smaller numbers. (It should be noted that Persian has one of the world's outstanding poetic traditions, often of great difficulty and subtlety, so that the phenomenon described is the equivalent of English peasant men and women being able to recite very lengthy passages of Shakespeare, Milton, and John Donne.) This phenomenon, perhaps because of modern schools and distractions, has declined notably, and Iran's poets have become mainly the property of (one part of) the propertied. Folk poetry, rarely written, continues to exist, but it too has a reduced role.

Even "mystical" Sufi orders, which brought members together for special religious practices outside the usual ulama-mosque network, were both more important and more of a channel for interclass cultural communication in the past than they have been since the cultural and religious changes of the Pahlavi era.

In view of the changes that have occurred in Iran since 1978, it is well to remember that both folk and high literature had strong anticlerical features; in folktales and popular plays the molla or *akhund* (the same as *molla* but more often pejorative) is most often showed negatively—as money-loving, hypocritical, and so forth—and hypocritical ulama are also found in written belles lettres more often than good ones.

As suggested in chapter 1, reformist thought did not begin in Iran after interaction with the West; rather Islamic Iran has always had important reformists and dissidents in such fields as philosophy, poetry, religion, and politics.[4] What is new about the nineteenth century is that Iran's weaknesses vis-à-vis the advanced West became clear to many, and that interaction with the West hastened and altered the nature of socioeconomic change, producing both new problems and new possibilities of development. The main concern of many Iranian leaders and thinkers came to be catching up with the West. Although they differed somewhat regarding which elements of Western civilization must be adopted in order to do this, nearly all believed that much must be borrowed.

The earliest reformers were practical political leaders, a breed that has continued. The main ones have been mentioned; Abbas Mirza, crown prince and governor of Azerbaijan in the early nineteenth century, brought in Western advisers, sent students abroad, and got local ulama to validate his acts. His minister Qa'em Maqam contributed to the process of early Westernization and to the reform of writing style. Under Naser ad-Din Shah (1848–96), not a consistent reformist, there were two reforming prime ministers: Mirza Taqi Khan *Amir Kabir* and Mirza Hosain Khan *Moshir ad-Dauleh* (whose reforms are discussed in chapter 3). After Naser ad-Din's death, another reformer, Amin ad-Dauleh, became prime minister and attempted tax and other reforms. All these man were hindered, pushed from office and sometimes to their death by vested interests at court and among the ulama. There were many who gained in wealth and power from the old decentralized governmental system, which encouraged local power and corruption, and Iran was not economically as ripe for centralization as were countries with a greater Western impact and trade like Egypt, Turkey, or Tunisia. Also, Great Britain and Russia preferred the weak Qajar government, from whom they had favorable treaties, to the strong one desired by reformers and nationalists.

There also developed in the later nineteenth century unofficial, or predominantly unofficial, reformers, known primarily for their writings. They built on Iranian reformist traditions, including philosophy, Shaikhism, and Babism, more than has usually been realized, so that it is wrong to see them as pure and uncritical Westernizers, as some recent Iranian critics have done. Naturally, in view of the poverty, corruption, mismanagement, and lethargy seen in many aspects of Iranian life, most of them sought Western-style solutions to many of Iran's problems. This they did in somewhat different ways, which can only be outlined very briefly.

The first important such intellectual was Mirza Malkom Khan, discussed in chapters 3 and 4. It seems clear that he was the most complete Westernizer of the reformers in this period, having spent most of his life in the West and having only a nominal commitment to Islam. Before his dismissal from government service in 1889, he kept his Westernism somewhat disguised, and in reformist essays distributed in manuscript generally limited himself to calling for a rationalization of government departments, spending, and so forth. In the newspaper he formed after being dismissed from the government, *Qanun* (London, 1890–96), however, he called for the rule of a rational codified law, and at one point called for a constitution. He also attacked the long-lived prime minister, Amin as-Soltan, and did not spare the shah. His newspaper was smuggled into Iran, and along with the earlier moderately oppositional paper *Akhtar* from Istanbul, and the later *Parvaresh* and *Sorayya* from Cairo and *Habl al-Matin* from Calcutta, formed one of the bases for a reformist, and eventually revolutionary and constitutional group in Iran.

The story of most late-nineteenth-century reformist and revolutionary writers suggests the importance of residence abroad and foreign influence on Iranian enlighteners of this period. Although it is true that those who spent their whole lives in Iran had little opportunity to circulate reformist writings, but might consign their views to later-published diaries (as in the case of the minister Amin ad-Dauleh), foreign travel and experience did change the views of many. This travel was not always in the West. There were Iranian merchant communities in Russian Transcaucasia, in Istanbul, and in India, all of which areas were more modernized than Iran, and Iranian reformers were very often tied to merchants, both within and outside Iran. Sometimes they themselves were merchants, as in the case of the author of what may be called Iran's first novel, *The Travelbook of Ibrahim Beg* (vol. 1, ca. 1900). Merchants were a particularly dissatisfied class in the late nineteenth and early twentieth centuries; they felt increasing competition from Western merchants, whom they firmly believed were favored by Persian customs being under the control of a Belgian team from 1898–99. Although some profited from Western trade, they were subject to disabilities that Westerners were not, and capitulatory trade treaties made almost impossible the manufacturing ventures that some of them tried and others would have liked to. Thus numerous Iranian merchants at home and abroad supported reformers who called for an end to favors to the West, the rule of law, and the like.

A number of oppositionists with religious training and even functions can now be shown to have been secret secularists (or at least opponents of the leading ulama), who used a religious guise in order effectively to arouse large masses of people. A pioneer in this technique was Sayyed Jamal ad-Din "al-Afghani," whose brief biography was given in chapter 4. Until the early 1880s Afghani had more of a reputation for heterodoxy than religiosity, but after then, sensing a new pro-Islamic mood in the Muslim world, he began to speak more and more of Islam and pan-Islam, the unity of all Muslim countries, preferably under the leadership of the sultan-caliph of the Ottoman Empire, against an encroaching West. Although the term "pan-Islam" and the basic idea of it as a mass movement seem to have been coined earlier by the Turkish Young Ottomans, particularly Namik Kemal, Jamal ad-Din was more responsible than anyone for spreading the idea. This pan-Islamic movement, which involved some Iranian ulama and others and continued into the 1920s, has some significant points of comparison with the recent "Islamic Revival." Both may be seen more as political than spiritual reactions against Western imperialism and control in Muslim lands: in the 1880s following Russian, British, and French conquests, and today following frustrations about internal weaknesses, Western strength, and Israel, seen as a Western colonial enclave. Both tend to idealize Islam by going "back to the sources," particularly the Quran, and reinterpreting them. With Jamal ad-Din

and his followers, who lived in largely traditional societies, this rein-
terpretation had a modernist and reformist bent: Western-style law and
science, sometimes constitutions, and other reforms were found in the
Quran. Today, however, the movement in Iran is only in part reformist; it is carried out more by ulama than by independent intellectuals
and stresses the literal following of many Quranic rules. This greater
conservatism after a century may most briefly be explained by saying
that Jamal ad-Din and his Iranian followers were reacting against a
traditional, scarcely reformed governmental and religious structure and
naturally thought that Iran's problems might be solved by interpreting
Islam in ways to bring it closer to the more successful, stronger, and
better functioning West. Khomaini and his followers, however,
reacted to a situation where Iran was felt to be a junior partner or puppet
of the West, particularly of the United States, and in which cultural
and economic Westernization of a certain type was occurring at break-
neck speed with little regard for human consequences. When no
traditional or Islamic government had existed for a long time and the
formal power of the ulama had been curbed, it was easy to imagine that
a return to an idealized Islam, so far past that no one remembered it,
could solve Iran's problems: hence, in brief, the more "traditional"
nature of thought and action in 1978–80 than in 1905–11.

Afghani's appeals to unity around Islam to fend off the West had a
multiclass appeal, as do many nationalist and Third Worldist ideas,
which see the Third World as uniformly exploited by an imperialist
West, without drawing real class distinctions. Afghani was invited to
Tehran in 1886 by the quite conservative minister of press, and stayed
at the home of Iran's leading merchant, Amin az-Zarb, who was close
to the prime minister and no radical. His son, like other unradical
merchants, was very important in the constitutional revolution. Afghani scared the shah by his anti-British talk, and had to go to Russia,
though he returned briefly later. Although Afghani is now known for
fighting despotism, in fact his main target was the British, and his
record on despots is ambiguous; he tried frequently to get into the
counsels of rulers, succeeding with one in Afghanistan, but only
tenuously in Egypt, Iran, and Turkey. He attacked the shah only after
his expulsion from Iran in 1891. Although there is one recorded
Egyptian talk in the 1870s where Afghani supports a constitution,

none of his major writings or talks thereafter supports this or any other clear institutional brake on despotism. He was rather an apostle of self-strengthening against the West, whether by kings or not, and most of the reforms he advocated had this goal. His use of religious language and of lines from the Quran as more effective than secular arguments was vindicated in the alliance of ulama, merchants, and intellectuals that led the successful tobacco protest in 1890–91, although it is wrong to see him as the sole architect of this natural alliance.

After 1890, even formerly anticlerical writers like Malkom Khan and some radicals at Istanbul began to emulate Afghani's tactics. There is not space here to document the fact that Afghani's own Islam, which appears to have come from Iranian deist-philosophical traditions with a heavy Shaikhi influence, was very different from orthodox Islam, but that has been done elsewhere.[5] Clearly he was successful in his tactic, which was traditional in Shi'ism and in Islamic philosophy, of appealing in different ways to an unorthodox "elite" and the orthodox "mass." His name is venerated among both religious and irreligious in Iran today, and republication of his writings in Iran with new introductions was one means used by the oppositional but still "orthodox" religious forces to promote their ideas in the 1950s and 1960s.

The Iranians abroad with whom Afghani was closest had little claim to Islam, much less orthodoxy; nonetheless after 1891 they went along with Afghani's pan-Islamic program. Afghani and Malkom worked together in London in 1891, with Afghanj contributing to *Qanun*, which now began to adopt a pro-ulama line. In 1892 Afghani accepted an invitation from the Ottoman Sultan Abdülhamid to go to Istanbul, where he remained largely under a kind of glorified house arrest until his death in 1897 from cancer. There he worked with a group of Iranians and Shi'is to write to Shi'i ulama suggesting they follow the (Sunni) Ottoman sultan-caliph. This would of course weaken the shah, whom Afghani now hated. Among the group were men in no way Muslim, even though they wrote their appeals and other antishah works in the most orthodox terms; specifically the writers Shaikh Ahmad Ruhi and Mirza Aqa Khan Kermani, who had been Babis of the original, Azali line, but by now appear to have been atheists. (Ruhi is photographed in one book leaning on a tablet that says "There is nothing but nature.") Kermani, a prolific writer, was also one of the first representatives of a trend that grew in importance among twentieth-century intellectuals: rejection of Islam and the Arabs for having ruined Iran, and a glorification of pre-Islamic Iran. This he began to do before meeting Afghani and adopting his pan-Islamic tactics.

Although Kermani now worked with Afghani, the nationalist trend rejecting Islam was quite a different line of thought: both trends have continued to today. Both can be said to represent kinds of nationalism (or, in the case of pan-Islam, a "proto-nationalism" that fed later individual nationalisms). Both had the typical nationalist feature of glorifying a period in the distant past when one's own people were stronger, more successful, occupied more territory, and had more scientific, artistic, and cultural achievements. Afghani (at least after circa 1881—before that he often spoke in Egyptian, Indian, etc., nationalist terms) and those in the Islamist line to the present identify this past with the early age of Islam, and blame decline on influences (usually foreign) corrupting or undermining true Islam, as it is interpreted by a given ideological school. This line of thought sometimes advocates unity among all Muslims, although even in Abdülhamid's time few imagined real political unity could be achieved. There are various ideas of federation and cooperation, and uncooperative Muslim leaders can be denounced as being not truly Islamic. This trend is strong in Iran today.

Kermani, influenced by the Iranian-born north Azerbaijani thinker, Mirza Fath Ali Akhundzadeh, saw the ideal past very differently, in the period of the great pre-Islamic Persian Empires that appeared populous, prosperous, and strong. Islam and the "inferior" Arabs were seen as destroying this greatness. Kermani even denounced all the great Persian classical poetry, except for the warlike and pro-Persian *Shah-nameh*, for inculcating passivity and corruption. Both the *Shah-nameh* and popular literature and attitudes do reflect considerable past anti-Arab ("lizard-eater") and even antiorthodox feelings, sometimes also expressed in poetry, art, and so forth. The radical anti-Arab and anti-Islamic ideas of Kermani were expanded by a number of twentieth-century writers and intellectuals—notably two of the greatest, the writer Sadeq Hedayat and the wide-ranging intellectual

Ahmad Kasravi (see below). Both pan-Islam and its apparent opposite, anti-Islamic nationalism, are multiclass (some would say bourgeois) phenomena; both have been used by intellectuals and rulers with different emphases for their own ends. The Pahlavi shahs picked up pre-Islamic Iranian nationalism, cut off the radical elements that were central to its chief intellectual advocates (especially the communist religion and revolt of the fifth-century-A.D. heretic Mazdak), and made it a foundation of anticlerical monarchism. This use of it was possibly no more forced than the other, as the two great pre-Islamic empires were strong monarchies; on the other hand popular elements could be found in pre-Islamic religions like Mazdakism, Manichaeism, and Zoroastrianism, as could evidence that women and agriculturalists enjoyed higher respect in some pre-Islamic periods than in the nineteenth century. The main appeal of an idealized distant past, however, whether Islamic or pre-Islamic, was and is that a great variety of values may be read into it, while the evils of the present can be ascribed to deviation from the true Iranian or true Islamic essence. In a period when all society was at least formally Islamic, it was natural for many thinkers to blame Iran's problems on Islam and the Arabs, and to see in a nationalist interpretation of the distant Iranian past virtues that were often modern or Western ones. As Iran became more modern and Westernized, the evils of indiscriminate Westernization became more obvious, and Islamic ways for many receded into the background, it was natural for many after 1960 to blame evils on Western ways and to turn for salvation to an idealized Islamic past. Ironically, many in both trends, especially the Iranist one, were really Westernizers, understandably unwilling to admit wholesale borrowing from the West.

Before 1960, most recognized Iranian intellectuals with a following outside traditional religious circles were to a high degree Westernizers. The desire for rationalized law, rule, and economics was expressed both in the emigré newspapers published before the Constitutional Revolution of 1905–11 and the great majority of papers published in Iran during that revolution, of which *Sur-e Esrafil* with its brilliant prose satire by the writer Dehkhoda and *Iran-e Nau* led by the outstanding socialist Caucasian Rasulzadeh may be singled out. In addition to news, these numerous newspapers were full of new poetry and satires that spoke out against corrupt and hypocritical officials and ulama, and also took as a main theme criticism of the veiling, seclusion, and enforced ignorance of women. Before and during the revolution longer prose forms with themes similarly critical of Iranian mores and looking, at least implicitly, to Western models for improvement, played a role in enlightening Iranians. These, like the newspapers, were often read aloud and discussed to groups. The most famous such early twentieth-century work was Zain al-Abedin Maraghe'i's *Travelbook of Ibrahim Beg,* exposing a myriad of Iranian evils. There were also the improved translation of James Morier's *Hajji Baba of Esfahan* by Mirza Habib Esfahani, which was more savage and political about Iran's faults than the original, and the works by men of Iranian origin living in Russian Transcaucasia, notably Mirza Fath Ali Akhundzadeh and Talebzadeh.[6] The victory of Japan in the Russo-Japanese War aroused interest in Japan's secret of rapid self-strengthening, which many saw in the fact that Japan had a constitution and Russia did not; hence a spate of writings on Japan, some of which stressed for the first time the virtues of constitutions.

As to the ulama in the constitutional revolution, there were varying degrees of support for a constitution and of awareness of its implications. Among the popular preachers there were a number in the tradition of Afghani—men brought up with a religious education and filling, more than Afghani, religious functions, notably preaching, but who were not themselves believers in any usual sense. These included most notably two preacher friends from Isfahan—Malek al-Motakallemin and Sayyed Jamal ad-Din Esfahani, the former the father of the historian of the constitutional revolution, Mehdi Malekzadeh, and the latter the father of Iran's first great modern short-story writer, Mohammad Ali Jamalzadeh (still alive as of 1980). Malek al-Motakallemin was long an Azali Babi, although by the time he became a preacher in the revolution he appears to have lost even this belief, while Sayyed Jamal ad-Din Esfahani was described by his son as a freethinker.[7] They both recognized the appeal of Islam to the masses and bazaaris, however. Before the Revolution they helped, with the participation of Isfahan businessmen, to set up and publicize an "Islamic company" that would boycott foreign cloth and goods and promote local products. In Tehran, the two became major preachers of the revolutionary and constitutional cause, explaining it in familiar Muslim terms emphasizing such Islamic concepts, particularly central in Shi'ism, as Justice and Oppression. Mohammad Ali Shah considered them among the most dangerous of his enemies and had them both killed in 1908, as he did the editor of *Sur-e Esrafil,* Mirza Jahangir Khan, also of Babi background.[8]

Among the more powerful ulama there was a variety of views, but the most prominent ulama of Iraq and many prominent ones in Iran remained proconstitutional throughout the revolution, although there were defections as the social revolutionary and even "anti-Islamic" potential of the constitution became clearer. The two main ulama constitutional leaders within Iran were very different types: Sayyed Mohammad Tabataba'i, who appears to have had genuinely liberal proclivities and considerable contact with other liberals, believed that a constitution would be the best way to limit the power of uncontrolled autocrats who were selling Iran to the Western powers. The more wily and powerful Sayyed Abdollah Behbehani had a long record of pro-British activity; he had been almost alone in refusing to back the anti-British tobacco movement, had taken personal presents and money from the British to organize movements against the Russians, and had helped arrange the use of the British Legation for the bast of 1906. To a degree his early participation in the revolution may be seen as part of his pro-British policy with an aim of advancing himself as he weakened the Qajars. He also wished to keep the constitutional movement conservative, while not openly turning against it. The third main leader of the Tehran ulama, Shaikh Fazlollah Nuri, did turn against the movement once it became clear that the constitution was not going to reinstate the sharia, but bring in many Western-style institutions and laws. The constitution and its form reflected more the ideas of Westernizing secularists, backed financially especially by merchants, than the ulama, although, as noted, provisions were inserted to protect ulama power. However, in 1909, a defense of the constitution was written by a younger mujtahid, Na'ini, that was endorsed by leading Iraqi ulama.[9] It does not appear to have been very influential when it was written, however; its real fame and importance came with its republication with an introduction by Ayatollah Taleqani in 1955, as part of the struggle against Pahlavi despotism, a struggle that until the very end based itself largely on the idea of true application of the 1906–07 constitution.

The revolution saw writings and activities reflecting a wide range of political tendencies that went on to have an important future in Iranian politics. Quite early in the constitutional revolution, a Social Democratic party was founded in Tabriz. It was influenced by Iranian returnees and immigrants from the Russian Caucasus. In the second constitutional period, from 1909, this was mostly merged into the well-organized, nationwide Democratic party, whose program included land reform and other major social reforms. The Democrats dominated the World War I pro-German nationalist government that was forced from Iran in 1915, whence some of its members went to Istanbul and some to Berlin—both anti-Allied capitals. In Berlin the Democrat leader Sayyed Hasan Taqizadeh edited two series of the important newspaper *Kaveh* (named after a lengendary blacksmith who liberated Iran). The first series, published during the war, aimed largely at getting Iranians to support the Central Powers against Britain and Russia, while the second was the main organ of the new Iranian nationalist culture. In addition to supporting new young writers like Mohammad Ali Jamalzadeh, it contained striking editorial features by Taqizadeh, in one of which he said that Iran must become wholly Western in every way if it were to progress; this is perhaps the high point of the Westernist view of nationalism, which Taqizadeh himself later modified.

The Constitutional Revolution also saw the beginnings of socialist writings by Caucasian immigrants like Rasulzadeh and Haidar Khan Amu Oghlu (the latter responsible for a few assassinations during the revolution and later a prominent Communist in the Gilan Jangalis). Iran was also involved in the Communist Congress of the Peoples of the East, 1920, and socialist and Communist writings and activities developed after World War I. These were, however, outlawed under Reza Shah and during most of his son's rule, so that this line of thought was far less expressed in writing especially within Iran than it would otherwise have been; like the Democrats the socialists and Communists were Westernizers. Already in the 1940s and 1950s there were socialist offshoots from the Tudeh, and in the 1960s and 1970s the number of socialist and Marxist movements, especially abroad, multiplied, and all expressed their positions in writing.

As was the case in Tsarist Russia and other autocratic countries, thinkers who wished to publish within Iran their criticisms of government and society usually had to do it indirectly, especially via poetry, fiction, and literary criticism, which involve ambiguity and are hard to pin down, rather than through directly critical essays, whose publication in most periods of modern Iranian history was not permitted. Such essays can be found in the relatively freer periods, like 1906–11, 1918–21, and 1941–53, and to a degree 1978–80, but most of the time it is the poet and author, not the editorial writer, who is the chief social critic. (This did not prevent the poet Eshqi from being killed by Reza Shah or numerous writers from being jailed, and often tortured, under his son.)

Literature is particularly well suited to criticize social customs the author considers unjust or outworn, and such social criticism is rife in modern Iranian literature from the *Travelbook of Ibrahim Beg* to the present. Significantly, one of the strongest points of attack by both male and female authors, in both prose and poetry, is the position of women, although authors of different periods and views differ somewhat on proposed solutions. In the poetry of the Constitutional Revolution and after there are strong attacks on the veiling that cripples women's activity, on the lack of education that cuts down women's contribution to society and harms their children's education, on their mistreatment by ignorant husbands, and on other aspects of their subordination. In the same first decades of the twentieth century, a number of women from upper-class and upper-middle-class backgrounds worked with some success to set up girls' schools and orphanages. By writers and activists alike, Reza Shah's opening of schools and universities to girls and his unveiling of women were welcomed as in part an outcome of their struggles. In the Pahlavi period there were a number of excellent women writers and essayists, as well as important women in other fields. Among the poets the two most outstanding were, under Reza Shah, Parvin E'tesami, a brilliant poet in the classical style; and, under Mohammad Reza, Forugh Farrokhzad, who lived the kind of free and varied life usually reserved for men, and dared write about her sexual feelings and activities in her poetry, shocking some of her contemporaries. The life and writings of Forugh may properly be classified as "feminist" (without any hostile implication to men).[10] Unfortunately, both these highly talented poets died very young.

It should be noted that before Shariati no significant recent writers complained about the too rapid Westernization of Iranian women. Although miniskirts, tight jeans, and makeup may offend some, attacks on them in recent decades turned out, predictably, to be a prelude to partly successful attempts since 1979 to return all women to restrictive clothing and to aspects of strict Muslim law.

Another area of literary attack going back to the first modern Iranian prose is the intellectuals' view of unpleasant aspects of Iranian mores as seen by Iranians themselves: hypocrisy, pretentiousness, unreliability, untruths, venality, and opportunism. These themes are stressed in the pre–1906 books discussed above and in revolutionary satires. They are also found in the groundbreaking collection of realistic short stories published by Jamalzadeh in 1921, *Yeki bud yeki nabud,* in which, among other things, the verbal pretensions of both the old-style ulama, with their incomprehensible Arabized talk, and the young European returnee, who fills his Persian with French, are mocked.

Sadeq Hedayat, generally considered the greatest modern Iranian prose writer, wrote in a variety of styles, optimistic and pessimistic, realistic and mystical-paranoid, which can be tied both to Iran's political state and his own fragile mental state. His more realistic and satirical works appeared between 1941 and 1947, when there seemed to be hope for democracy, and when he, like many other writers, was close to the Tudeh party. A number of short stories about rural and urban common people present with sympathy their hard life, their courage, and their subjection to irrational customs and superstitions. His masterpiece in the realistic-satirical genre is the novel *Hajji Agha,* an exposition of political, financial, personal, and religious hypocrisy in which Hedayat presents in the person of his title character many of the main faults that have kept Iran from progressing soundly.[11] Although Hedayat's surrealistic and drug-influenced *The Blind Owl* was translated much sooner into English and other languages, *Hajji Agha* is more important, or at least more comprehensible, as social criticism.

The two English-language Iran-centered novels of F. Esfandiari, *Day of Sacrifice* and *The Identity Card,* reflect this Iranian self-criticism. The former vividly portrays the father-son tensions characteristic of many Iranians, as well as an attempted political assassination; the latter shows the unending labyrinthine bureaucracy that keeps an Iranian from returning to America, where he lives, because he does not have an Iranian identity card. In all these prose works, the situations are socially important because they are seen by the authors and readers as typical of the situation in Iran.

Although a large number of authors in the 1941–53 period, including such famous ones as Sadeq Hedayat and Jalal Al-e Ahmad, had close ties to the Tudeh party, the one great author firmly associated with the party and its predecessors is Bozorg Alavi, who for over twenty-five years now has lived and taught in East Berlin, having been educated in Germany at the time when many Iranian nationalists were there. Alavi was one of the circle of "53" whose Marxist discussion group was arrested by the Reza Shah regime and sent to jail until Reza Shah's forced abdication. He, like the others in the group, became one of the founders of the Tudeh. Close to Hedayat and some other leftist authors, he considerably influenced literature and literary criticism. One of his well-known Persian works tells the story of the "53" and other novels and stories deal with social themes, including women. From Germany he has written especially nonfiction about Iran and its modern literature. Unlike Jamalzadeh, who spent most of his life outside Iran but continued to write stories set there, he has preferred more analytical writing in recent years.[12]

Space does not permit extensive discussion of many writers of recent decades. Among the well known are the Azerbaijani Samad Behrangi, whose early death under mysterious circumstances was widely blamed on SAVAK, as were deaths of men discussed in the next section, Al-e Ahmad and Shariati (the heart attacks of the latter two are, however, attested by persons close to them). Behrangi was especially known for his adaptation of Azerbaijani folktales, most of which were censored, but one of which, *The Little Black Fish,* was widely read and published despite its symbolic progressive implications. Another progressive author persecuted by the shah's regime is the playwright Gholam Hosain Sa'edi, best known in the West for his story *The Cow* in its film version directed by the new wave film director, Daryush Mehrjui. Better known in the west for his English writings is Reza Baraheni, who in his essays reprinted in *The Crowned Cannibals* castigates not only the monarchical system but also male supremacy and other evils of Iranian culture. Like the majority of well-known Iranian writers since the late nineteenth century, these three and many of their contemporaries were *both* antiregime and *secularist.* Again like most writers, they were leftists of different persuasions.[13] Only recently did religious publications come to outnumber secular ones and were there more than a few modern writers who stressed religion. On the other hand the authors mentioned above were read chiefly by a minority of the modernized elite, while religious preachings were heard by the popular classes.

Outside the belletristic category was the highly influential scholar, jurist, and essayist Ahmad Kasravi, who developed the trend of an anti-Shi'i Iranian nationalism. In his writings he coined numerous new terms from Persian roots, avoiding words of Arab origin, and openly criticized most Iranian religions. He developed a considerable following, became a natural target for the polemics of the religious, and was assassinated by a member of the Feda'iyan-e Islam in open court in 1946.[14]

The activities of the Feda'iyan-e Islam can serve as a reminder that there was also a continuous, albeit changing, tradition of Islamic thought and activity throughout the nineteenth and twentieth centuries that has perhaps not received the attention it deserves. The great nineteenth century Muslim philosopher Sabzavari developed further the tradition of original Shi'i philosophic thought, teaching, and writing represented in the Safavid period by such major thinkers as Molla Sadra and Mir Damad. The developing tradition of Shi'i thought, influenced both by philosophy and by Sufism, was represented in the twentieth century by such thinkers as Jalal ad-Din Ashtiyani and Allameh Tabataba'i, and reflections of this tradition may be found in recent ulama activists, including Ayatollah Khomaini, himself well versed in Muslim philosophy.

More directly political thought among practicing Muslims was also important. The Islamic defense of constitutionalism written by Na'ini has been mentioned, and other mujtahids wrote briefer and less comprehensive statements along the same lines. Under the Pahlavis, however, many ulama and other religiously oriented thinkers became less concerned with the constitution, which proved to be a feeble defense against autocracy, and more worried about the diminution in ulama positions and prerogatives on the one hand and the complaints of the ulama and their constituents against Pahlavi autocracy on the other. There was also growing concern about increasing deviations from what were seen as Islamic norms and about subservience to Western ways and Western powers. Such concerns could not be published under Reza Shah's censorship, but they were voiced in the early 1940s by Ruhollah Khomaini, who, as noted below, attacked Reza Shah's autocracy and the secularist influence of men like Kasravi. A less erudite attack in the 1940s and 1950s came from the Feda'iyan-e Islam, a group of young men of popular origin who published a fundamentalist program calling for a return to pure Islamic ways and laws and an end to Western influence, and who also assassinated their chief enemies. The most politically influential of the ulama in the early 1950s was Ayatollah Kashani, known especially for his anti-imperialist and particularly anti-British speeches and activities, and at times allied with the Feda'iyan-e Islam. At first cooperating with Mohammad Mosaddeq in the oil nationalization crisis, he later broke with him and backed his overthrow. The later 1950s were primarily a quietist period for the ulama, led by the conservative Ayatollah Borujerdi, but new trends began in the 1960s.

As was suggested above, most modern Iranian literature, especially until about 1960, has been anticlerical insofar as it touches the subject. Even Al-e Ahmad's attempts to rediscover religion in the 1960s resulted mainly in his anticlerical attack on hypocrisy witnessed during his pilgrimage. Shariati was also far more opposed to the average cleric than is often admitted.[15] The poems and writings mentioned above that defend the rights of women often attack ignorant mollas; so too do many satires from preconstitutional times on down, and many realistic writings. Further, the great majority of Iranian writing to which any significant attention has been given by lay readers (only a small sample of which could be noted here) has been explicitly Westernist and modernist, again at least until 1960, and in many cases much later. The evils depicted are, explicitly or implicitly, seen more as owing to Iranian customs and traditions than to Western imperialism and encroachments, and the solutions, if they are suggested at all, are seen as coming from Iranians finding ways to change their customs and traditions. It may be surmised that had literary publication been uncensored, more would have been said about the responsibility of the government in bringing or perpetuating certain evils, and along with this would have gone recognition of the government's considerable dependence on Western states, especially the United States.

It is almost impossible to imagine, however, that an honest writer would devote himself to showing how Iranian internal conditions must be changed, and how these changes were held back by powerful and hypocritical lay and clerical leaders if what the writer *really* meant was almost the opposite; namely, give more power to clerical leaders and put the entire blame for all evils on the court and foreigners, and then problems will be solved. If that had been the intended message, there would have been prudent ways in which it could be implied, just as Al-e Ahmad and Shariati found ways to put forth not exactly that message but still one that put much or most of the blame for Iran's problems on blind imitation of the West.

Twentieth-century Iran has also seen a number of directly political thinkers and writers, whose works have been read mainly by their own followers, and who have rarely been the subject of scholarly analysis. Like the writers discussed so far, political writers have been primarily secularist until quite recently. Socialist and Communist writings go back as far as the Constitutional Revolution of 1905–11 and in their main line of the post–World War I Communist party and the post–World War II Tudeh party they tend to follow closely the Soviet line, although with variations and internal struggles as to how it should be interpreted. Leftist guerillas from the late 1960s on rejected the Tudeh line of sharing power peacefully in favor of armed struggle to overturn the system, although there were and are numerous tactical differences within and between guerilla groups.

Mosaddeq-style nationalism, directed mainly at freeing Iran from great-power control, has continued to inspire Iranians of varied political tendencies, including the bourgeois National Front, socialists of various shades (like those in 1979's National Democratic Front led by Mosaddeq's grandson, Hedayatollah Matin-Daftari), and some of the more secularist members of the current regime. This varied following suggests both the broad appeal of Mosaddeq's nationalism and anti-imperialism and the fact that the rest of his program was not specific or detailed enough to disqualify Mosaddeq as a source of inspiration for any of the above groups. A leader of one of the groups in Mosaddeq's coalition, Khalil Maleki, is regarded by some as Iran's most original and astute socialist thinker, who successfully adapted his ideas to the special conditions of Iran, although those belonging to other parties might contest this view.[16]

We thus arrive at the perhaps startling conclusion that the main lines of Iran's literature and political thought in the past century have been radically different from the culture most visible in 1980, and even quite different from the complex, and *not* proclerical emphasis of the "anti-Westernists" Al-e Ahmad and Shariati. To understand the rapid changes in culture after 1961 we must remember the concurrent intensification of a Westernizing despotism, closely tied to dependence on the West, and especially the United States. We must also remember the overrapid rural-urban migrations, increased income disparities, socioeconomic problems, and *anomie* that lead people to go back to familiar traditional moorings and to associate Westernization with suffering and dictatorship. The religious and secular popular culture discussed at the beginning of this chapter persisted, in modified form, for the majority. For the mass of people traditional and religious cultural forms were supplemented by Western films and TV, not by Sadeq Hedayat. Hence the ta'ziyeh, the rauzeh-khani, the mosque sermon, and the religious club, plus the folktale and folk theatre formed the words and literature that expressed most closely the world view of the popular classes. It was to the educated strata of the urban (or newly urban) bazaar classes and youth that Shariati first appealed. It was he, more than all the poets and writers who made such brave attempts to employ the simple language of the masses in order to change their consciousness, who most touched their sensitive nerve. Once dependence on theWest was associated with Western culture, and Western culture with moral decay, it was natural to seek Iran's salvation not in the Westernization pushed by the shah's regime but in a return to an idealized indigenous Islam.

Contemporary Shi'i Thought

After the 1960s, new trends of thought questioned the governmental image of progress and Western rationalism. Jalal Al-e Ahmad inspired a theory of alienation among new intellectuals, and the question of identity was later raised by a variety of writers. Some themes found among Iranian thinkers are similar to those in contemporary Arab thought.[17] Muslim ideologists prefer arguments taken from the Quran or Islamic Traditions—a preference found both among popular preachers and sophisticated intellectuals. When something is demonstrated with Islamic arguments it is more easily accepted. When Abolhasan Bani Sadr demonstrates with Quranic citations that property belongs only to God, and hence that Iran should nationalize enterprises that could enslave people, his demonstration is more effective for Muslims than are arguments taken from *Das Kapital*. The weakness of Shi'i ideologies is that of all apologists—namely, they try to show that their religion has provided in advance the key to all difficulties. A theme held in common with many Arab ideologists (for example, Anouar 'Abd al-Malek)[18] is Islam as the basis of anti-imperialist action. From a knowledge of the profound popular influence of Islamic slogans, and from a belief that Islam has a revolutionary aspect, Muslim ideologists associate Islam with struggles against colonialism and great-power domination. Here it is possible to present only a few trends, all with Shi'i overtones, but it should not be forgotten that various secular trends also continued to exist in Iran.

Iranian Identity in the Face of Westernization

The increasing cultural Westernization of the Pahlavis was resented by the popular classes, especially the bazaaris, and by the ulama, whose prestige and positions were attacked. Westernized habits were associated with Western politico-economic domination, and anti-Westernism and antiregime ideas turned increasingly to the masses' Shi'i outlook. In the 1960s thinkers began to discuss defense against westernization and returning to Iran's cultural identity. For this they denounced "Westoxication" (*Gharbzadegi*).[19] This reaction can be understood in the context of the anti-imperialist struggle of Mosaddeq, and of rapid Westernization after the 1953 coup d'état.

Jalal Al-e Ahmad was, in the 1960s, the intellectual leader of a new generation of Iranian thinkers. Born in 1923 into a clerical family in the Taleqan Valley near Qazvin, he witnessed his father's ruin after the laicizing reforms of Reza Shah. The father did not accept state control over his work as a notary, a post formerly reserved for ulama. Al-e Ahmad had to quit his family and work to pay for his studies. At twenty he became a Communist, in the years when occupied Iran was undergoing great social crises. Ahmad Kasravi's influence on him was very strong.[20] He quit the Tudeh party after the Azerbaijan events in

reaction against Stalinism, and joined nationalist and socialist movements while teaching, translating, and writing stories with social
themes. He was also an essayist, ethnologist, and critic. In the 1960s he
became the conscience of many intellectuals, and wrote a classic essay
against Iran's "Westoxication."

When the ulama became leaders of the opposition he returned to an
interest in Islam and went on pilgrimage to Mecca in 1964. Until his
death in September 1969 he defended Islam against the policy of
Westernization at any price championed by the regime, although his
conversion was more political than religious.[21] Al-e Ahmad found
cultural roots and ties to the Iranian people in Islam. This feeling is
found in a new way in Ali Shariati. After Al-e Ahmad died, Shariati
took up the part of his work that was devoted to giving an Islamic
response to the modern world.[22]

Two books by Al-e Ahmad will be discussed: *On the Loyalty and
Betrayal of the Intellectuals,* a work of historical sociology where the
author judges the attitude of educated Iranians by their services to the
Iranian nation; and *Westoxication,*[23] a violent pamphlet directed against
this terrible malady that alienates Iranians from their identity and
bewitches them with the West.

Al-e Ahmad's viewpoint on Shi'ism was both critical and positive.
The Shi'ism imposed by the Safavids crushed the independent spirit of
the ulama and encouraged the religiosity of martyrs (the vanquished).
The popularity of the Twelfth Imam arises from his being the hope and
refuge of believers against the insurmountable inequities of this world.
Islam, weakened by divisions between Sunnis and Shi'is, by mystical
groups, and by Babism-Bahaism, was vulnerable to imperialism.
Iranians succumbed to the image of "progress" and played the game of
the West. Al-e Ahmad attacks nineteenth-century Westernizers like
Mirza Aqa Khan Kermani, Malkom Khan, and Talebzadeh, and
defends the anticonstitutional Shaikh Fazlollah Nuri for upholding the
integrity of Iran and Islam in the face of the invading West.[24]

This does not mean that Al-e Ahmad was reactionary. His struggle
was for the identity of the Shi'i Iranian. What he asked of Islam, at the
moment (ca. 1963) when it again became the symbol of a national
struggle against monarchy, was to raise politics to its just position. The
ulama should cease their interminable ratiocinations over details and

externals and consider real problems. Then Islam might again be a liberator as it was for the seventh-century Iranians.

Al-e Ahmad's revolt, in part by its exaggerated tone, aroused the conscience of many Iranians. The Pahlavi regime had confronted differently the problems posed by the social and cultural transformation of Iran, spreading an official nationalist ideology. To soften cultural resistance, institutions patronized by the queen and honoring Iranian traditions were created. Some intellectuals found in them an aseptic place to express themselves and to write reports that were put aside. In these institutions no one could discuss religion or politics.

The paradoxical evolution of Al-e Ahmad from socialism to a political Islam was reflected in splits among intellectuals. Some, like the sociologist Ehsan Naraghi, remained secular while allowing Islam a role in national identity.[25] Others sought an alternative to Westoxication in a deeper study of Islamic philosophy. Those closest to Al-e Ahmad's path chose political opposition.

Ulama in the Political Struggle

While some ulama intellectuals avoided politics and produced philosophical and theological works, others increasingly took public political positions. The most important among the politicized ulama, Ayatollah Ruhollah Musavi Khomaini, became a political figure of the first rank after the events of 1963, which put him in prison and then in exile, and especially in the revolution of 1978–79. Only his tenacious character and his critical thought could have led one to believe before the 1960s that this theologian would become anything but a high-ranking ayatollah.

He was born in September 1902 in Khomain (between Isfahan and Arak) into a religious family; his grandfather had traded in Kashmir (whence the accusation by Mohammad Reza Shah that he was an Indian paid by the British). His father was killed by a landlord before he was five months old, and he was raised by his mother. From his elder brother (Ayatollah Pasandideh, now living in Qom) he acquired a basic education. In 1919 he went to Soltanabad (Arak), where he became the disciple of Ayatollah Abdol Karim Ha'eri Yazdi, and two years later followed him to Qom. In 1927, after finishing the lower degrees of the theological course, he continued studying under Ha'eri, and on

Ha'eri's death in 1936, Khomaini became a respected mujtahid. In 1930 he married the daughter of a rich Tehran ayatollah, Mirza Mohammad Saqafi, who saw a bright future for this "village molla." Khomaini had two sons, both of whom became ayatollahs—Mostafa, killed perhaps by SAVAK in 1977 at Najaf, and Ahmad, who always accompanies his father—and three daughters.

In 1944 Khomaini first published criticisms of the Pahlavi regime: in an open letter to the ulama he asked them to unite against the immorality of public life, and especially to react against "a certain adventurer from Tabriz who is unjustly attacking your creed." He was certainly referring to the anticlerical intellectual, Ahmad Kasravi.[26] In a 1944 book, *Secrets Exposed,* Khomaini attacks *Secrets of a Thousand Years* by Kasravi's disciple A. A. Hakamizadeh. Khomaini explains that he is answering a writer (unnamed) who has betrayed his country by attacking the ulama. "We must realize that writings that attack religious leaders help to destroy the country and its independence."[27] *Secrets Exposed* consists of six parts: (1) Divine Unity (*tauhid*); (2) The Imamate; (3) The Role of the Ulama; (4) Government; (5) Law; and (6) Traditions (*hadith*). Each time, Khomaini cites a passage of the refuted writer, answers it, and gives his own doctrine.

When appropriate, he unsparingly attacks Reza Shah, seen as the enemy of religion. The idea of an Islamic government, dominated by mujtahids, is developed. He criticizes both the constituent assembly of 1925, which was forced at bayonet-point to install the new Reza Shah and the majles, which is used only to impose European laws and is unsuited to Iran. Only a sovereign elected by pious mujtahids, knowing divine commands and exercising justice without being prisoner to the pressures and ambitions of this world, can govern Iran with equity. The monarchy (*saltanat*) may even be suppressed, as "apart from the royalty of God, all royalty is against the interests of the people and oppressive; apart from the law of God, all laws are nul and absurd. A government of Islamic law, controlled by religious jurists (*faqih*) will be superior to all the iniquitous governments of the world."[28] On the other hand, other passages seem to accept limited monarchy.

One scholar says that Khomaini in the 1950s had a "quietist period" in which he gave lessons and became a leading disciple and confidant of the chief (and conservative) ayatollah, Borujerdi (d. 1961).[29] Around

1960 the course in ethics given by Khomaini in the Faiziyeh Madraseh in Qom attracted more and more sutdents. The teacher abandoned the traditional *minbar* of the mosque and spoke seated on the ground in a corner of the room, fascinating his audience by his criticism of the government's policies. He eventually became one of the successors of Borujerdi to the function of marja'-e taqlid (source of imitation), although some other ayatollahs were, in 1961–63, considered more important than he.

In 1962 Khomaini began direct combat against the Pahlavi regime. His exile from 1964 through 1978 after his 1963–64 battles with the regime did not stop Khomaini from continuing his struggles against the shah, imperialism, and Zionism via declarations and tape cassettes diffused, after he went to Najaf in 1965, by Iranian pilgrims to the holy cities in Iraq. In 1971, at the time of the royalist celebrations in Persepolis, he called upon the ulama to denounce political terror and the waste of Iran's resources. His refusal of all compromise with the regime constituted a revolution by contrast with many in the religious opposition who called only for constitutional reforms.

At this time was published from student notes the book *Islamic Government,* which puts forth three main ideas:

1. Monarchy is radically condemned. The Prophet, he says, asked the Byzantine emperor and the Sasanid Shah to abandon their illegitimate power. By means of war Islam was able to achieve a reign of justice. In Hosain's battle to keep Islam from degenerating into monarchy, he died a martyr. "Islam knows neither monarchy nor dynastic succession."[30]

2. Islam gives, in the Quran and Tradition (*sunna*), "all the laws and principles needed by man for his happiness and perfection."[31] These laws are just; they protect the oppressed and hungry against iniquitous rule. "The legislative power in Islam is limited to God alone."[32] That is why, in Islamic government, instead of having a "legislative assembly" one should have an assembly to apply Islamic law. In order to apply the law and preserve it from deformations, society needed the Prophet and the Imams. They are the only ones to know the law perfectly and to possess in full the virtue of justice ('adalat). After them it is the Muslim jurists (*faqih,* pl. *foqaha*) who should govern. "Authority must come officially from the jurists."[33]

3. Islam is in danger, corrupted by perverse doctrines —materialism, Christianity, Zionism—encouraged in Iran by the imperialist powers. The ulama must purify Islam, and publicize the political and economic aspects of the Quranic message. Islam must be made known, especially among those with university educations.[34] Among the ulama, there are many SAVAK agents and court mollas. Their turbans must be torn off and the religious milieu purified; only those who are soldiers of God should keep their religious dress, serving Islamic government. We must cut all ties to the administration of the demonic (*taghuti*) regime of the shah.

In another text, *The Great Holy War,* Khomaini addresses the ulama of the *hauzeh* (theological colleges) and exhorts them to correct their conduct in order to be examples to society. They are an avant-garde of the "Party of God."[35]

Ayatollah Khomaini is not the sole marja'-e taqlid, and the uncontested leadership he achieved in the revolution did not eclipse the political thought of others. Among the best known ayatollahs playing different roles in the revolution and its ideology were Ayatollah Shariatmadari in Qom, who was very influential in his home province of Azerbaijan and in Khorasan, and Ayatollah Taleqani of Tehran, especially influential in liberal and progressive circles.

A moderate constitutionalist before and after the revolution, Shariatmadari became a leader of many who could not follow Khomaini. Born in 1905 in Tabriz, he studied first there and at nineteen went to Qom, where Shaikh Abdol Karim Ha'eri Yazdi had revived Qom's theological studies. He was a co-disciple with Khomaini, and became a mujtahid. About 1935 he reached Najaf and continued higher studies there . He then taught for about fifteen years in Tabriz and experienced Pishevari's pro-Soviet autonomist Azerbaijan in 1946. Invited by Ayatollah Borujerdi to teach in Qom, he has stayed there ever since, while keeping his ties with Azerbaijan. During the 1962–63 risings Shariatmadari played a major role, and it is generally agreed that he, supported by other ulama, saved the life of Khomaini when he was threatened by the regime.

The Islamic revolution brought out the traditionalism of Shariatmadari's positions: without breaking with Khomaini, he kept his distance. At the beginning of the revolution he supported popular protests against the brutal oppression of the shah and at first demanded, as did most others, the strict application of the 1906–07 constitution, which foresaw a veto power on legislation by a committee of five mujtahids. He thus indicated that, unlike Khomaini, he was not against a constitutional monarchy with mujtahids participating in power. After the revolution, renouncing official posts, he gathered around him various currents—liberal, moderate, and conservative: bazaar traders unhappy with the recession, and Azerbaijani regionalists. The mainly Azerbaijani Muslim Republican People's party used his name, but he was too prudent to voice support, and even acquiesced in its self-dissolution after the December 1979 struggles in Tabriz. In this he was faithful to his principle that the ulama must abstain from direct intervention in politics.

Although he never published a book systematically presenting his religious and political thought, Shariatmadari expressed his ideas through interviews. He said that an Islamic government does not a priori exclude monarchy, though the injustices of the Pahlavi regime and its subservience to the West removed its legitimacy. Shariatmadari reproaches most Muslim revolutionaries with taking the means (constitution, revolution) for the end. Speaking of some "Islamic revolutionaries," he asks if it is right to admire Che Guevera more than Imam Hasan. He defends himself against the accusation of reformism: the criterion of political action is not Marxism or socialism, it is Islam, and we can say that if on certain questions the Prophet was revolutionary, on others (the fight against slavery, against usury, etc.) he was "reformist."

With his subtle, seductive personality and the patience with which he agrees to answer all questions, Shariatmadari contrasts with Khomaini. We will not detail the power struggles of these two leaders, whose positions are often divergent. Where Khomaini, an innovator, crystallizes all religion around political positions, Shariatmadari, a very learned theologian, concentrates on maintaining traditional Shi'i positions. Some have said that their quarrels are superficial, masking a corporate solidarity, with divergences allowing all Iranians to follow a leading theologian. But perhaps Shariatmadari's rallying of conservatives and moderates represents the schism between a high clergy for whom the revolution, while allowing them to gain prestige and power, can be a social threat, and a lower clergy with populist tendencies around Khomaini. The former group has recourse to the integrity of theological dogma as an arm to defend its shaky power. Reportedly, several top ayatollahs are in disagreement with Khomaini and closer to Shariatmadari, who was pressured into silence in 1980, and was reported in early 1981 to be under house arrest.

Another prominent ayatollah in the Islamic political movement, Mahmud Taleqani (d. September 1979), was very popular, while remaining less powerful than Khomaini. He had been, since the 1950s, one of the leading ideologists of the religious opposition to the Shah. He entered personally into political combat, and was jailed or kept in internal exile for many years. Born in 1910 in the valley of Taleqan, Mahmud Taleqani pursued theological studies at Qom. He began to teach in 1938 at the Sepahsalar theological school in Tehran, and was jailed for six months in 1939 for his opposition to the religious policies of Reza Shah. He struggled for Mosaddeq together with Mehdi Bazargan and Yadollah Sahabi. After the coup d'état of 1953 he was arrested for having hidden at his home Navvab Safavi, the leader of the Feda'iyan-e Islam. He was imprisoned several times in the 1960s, notably for having demanded the application of the constitution and for having struggled along with Bazargan and Sahabi in the Freedom Movement of Iran. In 1971 he was exiled to the Southeast. In mid–1977 he was arrested for having supported the leftist Muslim guerillas, the Mojahedin, and was only freed by popular pressure at the beginning of November 1978.

Taleqani played a prominent role in the 1978–79 Revolution, serving as a link between lay groups like the National Front and religious ones. He served similarly in several crises of the new regime, and led, by designation of Ayatollah Khomaini, the Friday prayers on the campus of Tehran University that began in Ramazan, 1979. Quite isolated among the ulama, he was nonetheless the most popular of them, winning by far the highest number of votes in the 1979 elections to the constituent assembly. Years of strain contributed to his ill health and he died of a heart attack on September 10, 1979.

Ayatollah Taleqani appeared as one of the most liberal and progressive among the Iranian ulama; Sunni minorities approached him with their requests, as did also leftist groups, as they knew that Taleqani would welcome them and remember their common struggles against the shah and SAVAK. Possibly his long stays in jail with the nonreligious opposition helped him understand them. In the last months of his life, until one final statement, he ceased his former public statements differing from Khomaini's policies.[36]

Among the works of Taleqani were commentaries on the Quran and the *Nahj al-Balagha* (a collection of sayings, sermons, and letters of Ali). Taleqani presents his doctrine in a plain style, within the limits of traditional doctrines.[37] His more original work treats socioeconomic problems. In 1955 he edited, with introduction and notes, a 1909 political treatise by Ayatollah Na'ini. In his introduction, taking up Na'ini's arguments, Taleqani says religion has always been a threat to dictators who, concentrating all power, make idols of themselves. Divine unity, *tauhid,* in struggling against this idolatry, liberates men from slavery and submits them only to God, who is absolute truth, justice, and wisdom. Government of men belongs (1) to god; (2) to divine law; (3) to the Prophets and Imans, whose thought and spiritual force are entirely at the service of divine law and who claim no monarchical title; and (4) to the just ulama and believers. Men's efforts to govern themselves like the Constitutional Revolution, democracy, and socialism, can be steps toward tauhid if people see that the aim is beyond them. People must continue the effort to better the regime and fight against dictatorship, in the sense of Na'ini's book.[38]

In his *Islam and Property, in Comparison to the Economic Systems of the West,* Taleqani developed his capacity for analysis. This is a response to contemporary problems presented in an historical context.[39] Taleqani discusses successively:

1. The evolution of property since the origins of humanity; the division of labor, exchange, money, laws, and the ideal community; the first economic theories, and the industrial revolution.

2. The appearance of workers' power: here he examines Marxism, class struggle, extreme forms of capitalism, the dictatorship of the proletariat, and classless society. He criticizes Marxism as naive, for thinking inequalities can be suppressed by giving special privileges to workers' rule and by suppressing metaphysics. He explains such excesses in the context of struggles against capitalism.

3. The economy in the light of faith: Eschatology gives Islamic doctrine a transhistoric view of the economy; the legislator must both take account of spiritual aims and detach himself from his class condi-

tioning. Human laws ('urf) are fragmentary, limited by history, and subject to change. They are easily diverted by a tyrannic power; are influenced by passions; and must be applied by coercion. Only Islam is the perfect legislator—it encourages reason to follow the path of God instead of misleading it; frees man from the slavery of human customs; teaches all to distinguish good from evil; and makes of a man controlled by passions a controller of himself. Because of these qualities, Islamic law (fiqh) is not accessible to all; only mujtahids can decide its application.

4. The economic bases of Islam and the roots of its precepts: God is the absolute owner of the goods confided to us; this is opposed to capitalism, for which property is absolutely free; and to socialism, which suppresses individual property. These two excesses permit the enslavement of man. The author applies this principle to analyzing the system of landownership and vaqf; in Islam, before Westerners came, feudalism (tuyuldari) never implanted itself durably. In Islam landownership is never absolute, and land reverts to the one who puts it under cultivation.

5. Money and the economic problems tied to it: Interest (riba) has created capitalism. Islam forbids hoarding but encourages commerce, which brings the distribution of riches. Utilizing a socialist slogan, Taleqani declares: One should take from everyone according to his abilities, and give to him according to his needs.

6. The specific features of the Islamic economy: Taleqani insists on the freedom of economic activity, of the production and distribution of goods. Natural resources belong to those who render them productive. But there are limits, whose control is assured by the state (especially mineral resources).

7. Class differences, privileges, and their origin: Class privileges are not necessarily tied to money: for example, in the military classes. Islam, while recognizing differences among men, refuses the privileges engendered by monarchical regimes. Taleqani gives a history and criticism of the French Declaration of the Rights of Man, which is hypocritically advocated by the very people who constantly violate it. Inviolability of the principle of property opens the door to all the abuses of capitalism.

Notable is the passage where Taleqani, aware of the harm a priestly class can do in some societies, affirms that no such thing esists in Islam, where the ulama have no privileges and must, as in the early days, sit at the same level as others in assemblies. However, as noted, only mujtahids can interpret Muslim law correctly. A mujtahid is recognized by his justice and his faculty of interpreting, but he, even more than others, is subject to the same law.[40] Taleqani was one of several thinkers who had written in favor of decentralizing the function of marja'-e taqlid and proposed the creation of a doctrinal council that would convene the most esteemed ulama of the different regions.[41]

Taleqani remained limited by his theological formation; his contact with the West and modern ideological systems was indirect, and he does not deal with certain important questions concerning the economy: taxes, nationalizations, the banking system, and so forth. However, his appeal to Islamic morality has progressive aspects and includes an appreciation of social problems. This helps explain his popularity among leftist Muslim groups, like the Mojahedin-e Khalq.

Other ayatollahs have expressed, in books and in the press, diverse positions on democracy and political problems, and there is a large and powerful conservative group whose writings repel any progressive or reformist tendencies and combat both communism and laicism.

Lay Shi'i Politico-Religious Thinkers

The most original Islamic thinkers are those who, not having had the training of traditional ulama, have had educational contact with the West, which allows them to voice clearly, and with a new vocabulary, a critique of what they oppose, and to define a new Islamic ideology. Here are discussed three of them: Mehdi Bazargan, Ali Shariati, and Abolhasan Bani Sadr.

Bazargan addresses chiefly middle classes, merchants, and lower civil servants, while Shariati and Bani Sadr became the ideologues of young revolutionary intellectuals. All three say Islam is not against progress and that it has an answer to materialist ideologies in its positive approach to modern science and technology—points that traditional theologians cannot demonstrate.

Mehdi Bazargan was one of the most important politico-religious leaders of the revolution. From the 1950s to the revolution he presented a modern image of Islam. He criticized traditionalists immersed in a theoretical theology focused on minor points of faith. He also utilized his reputation as an engineer and professor to show that Islam was in accord with scientific and technical progress. Islam, he said, is a pragmatic doctrine, adapted to the modern world. Bazargan tried to answer secular ideologies on their own ground.[42]

Born in 1905 into a family of Tabriz bazaar merchants, Bazargan completed his education at the Ecole Centrale in Paris.[43] Returning to Iran in 1936, he worked at the National Bank, and then taught thermodynamics at Tehran University. After World War II he became a close collaborator of Mosaddeq, who named him in 1951 to head the oil-nationalization committee. After the fall of Mosaddeq, Bazargan joined the secret resistance movement. In 1961 with Taleqani and Yadollah Sahabi he founded the Freedom Movement of Iran, which was later proscribed and brought all three prison terms. Prison did not silence Bazargan. An indefatigable speaker, he also wrote treatises presenting Islam in modern form, with a new vocabulary and examples taken from contemporary culture and technology.

A frequent theme in Bazargan's writings is a refusal to separate the spiritual and the temporal. This separation, a feature of Western Christian culture, is found in decadent Muslim society, whose theologians and philosophers turn aside from this world, which they leave to base men, while they deal only in words.[44] For Bazargan there is no frontier between religion and politics. Religion must control and inspire politics, and not the contrary. He critizes the shah's trinity of "God-Shah-Country," in which "Shah" occupied the central place.[45] Religion must set the aims and principles of politics; the means are a human problem.

Bazargan's attitude toward the West is mixed admiration and disgust. He sees the West as the example of technical and scientific civilization, and also of social and political principles in which faith does not enter, such as democracy, the rights of man, and humanism. Europeans do not despise religion, unlike the Westernized Iranian bourgeoisie. But Bazargan severely criticizes Christianity as unable to give believers directives for practical, social, and political life. Westerners have to turn for guidance to philosophic-political doctrines made into idols, like socialism, Marxism, and so on, which Islam does not need, as it is a complete religion.[46]

In politics, Bazargan is more concerned by the problem of justice than by concrete social struggles. In a small book on labor, one looks in vain for references to workers' problems or social legislation.[47] Bazargan's influence and his popularity among the Muslim petty bourgeoisie are due to his courageous political activity with Mosaddeq and his opposition to the shah. A prudent reformer, he sees Islam as in accord with democracy, reason, and science.[48] If he criticizes Islam's fossilized and often compromised theologians, he does not question Shi'ism. To meet injustices and tyranny while avoiding social conflict and communism, he asked the Shi'i ulama to take more interest in temporal affairs, and found welfare, cultural, economic, and political institutions to lessen social inequalities. If this had been done, he said in 1962, a truly egalitarian Islamic government could exist "without recourse to revolution or bloodshed."[49] Thus, the man who became the Islamic Republic's first prime minister in February 1979 is a modern and liberal Muslim, but seems to underestimate the immense social problems which agitate Iran.

Ali Shariati did the most to prepare Iranian youth for revolutionary upheaval. Events made this Muslim sociologist, shortly after his 1977 death, the ideologist of the revolt. In the opposition demonstrations, his portrait was carried beside that of Ayatollah Khomaini.

Ali Shariati was born in 1933 in Mazinan, a village near the desert, in Khorasan in northeast Iran. His father, Mohammad Taqi Shariati, is a well-known preacher. Shortly after Ali's birth, his family moved to Mashhad, the capital of Khorasan and center of Iranian Shi'i pilgrimage; there he received his secondary education. At seventeen he entered normal school and two years later became a teacher. He began to write and translate works on Shi'ism and became involved in the pro-Mosaddeq opposition.

At twenty-three he entered the Faculty of Letters at Mashhad. He wrote articles published by local journals. He also married a student companion and served his first prison term. In 1959, he received a bachelor's degree, and, as one of the top students, had the right to a scholarship abroad. He was not allowed to leave for a year, and then went to Paris, where he was a sympathizer of the Algerian liberation movement. He studied religious history and sociology, although his thesis, contrary to what is often said, was not in these fields but in Persian philology. Among those whose influence he notes were Louis Massignon, for whom he had a deep admiration and with whom he studied Fatima, daughter of Mohammad and wife of Ali; Frantz Fanon, whose *Wretched of the Earth* he translated; and Jean-Paul Sartre. In 1964 he returned to Iran with a doctorate. At the frontier he was arrested and held for several months.[50]

In 1965 he first taught in a large Khorasan village, then in a Mashhad high school. He soon became assistant at the University of Mashhad, where the content and success of his courses led to his dismissal. He then went to Tehran where his reputation as a lecturer spread quickly. He was frequently invited to talk, especially at the Hosainiyeh Ershad, a progressive Muslim institution created in 1969. His lectures were recorded and diffused by mimeograph. Late in 1973 the Hosainiyeh Ershad was closed by the regime. Shariati hid, but his father was imprisoned as a hostage. After a few months, Shariati gave himself up and was held for eighteen more months in solitary confinement. Upon release he returned to Mazinan under virtual house arrest. In the spring of 1977 he decided to leave Iran, which was made possible by the relative liberalization of the regime. However, the authorities at the last minute refused his wife authorization to join him, and when he came to the airport in London he found only two of his three daughters. He died shortly afterward on June 19, 1977.

There is as yet no complete bibliography of Shariati, and as many of his works were short mimeographed lectures, or transcriptions from cassettes, while others appeared under pseudonyms or in obscure reviews, it is hard to establish one. Since 1977 these short texts have been reproduced, sometimes brought together and sold openly.[51] Shariati often added notes to his texts, but the oral style remains evident except in a few rare works like the autobiography *Desert (Kavir)*, composed in lovely poetic language. The titles of his lectures suggest his major themes: "Ali, the Superman of History," "Man, Islam, and the Doctrines of the West," "Eqbal, Architect of the Renewal of Islamic Thought," "Community (*umma*) and Imamate," "The Sura *Rum*: A Message to Responsible Intellectuals," "Shi'ism, the Perfect Party," and so on. His works are being reedited and regrouped by the revived Hosainiyeh Ershad.

The style and the context of Shariati's lectures did not encourage literary or scientifically argued works. He was above all a great orator who profited from the short time he knew he had to hammer into the conscience of his audience certain key ideas. Their arrangement was less important than the need to say as much as possible without losing his audience's attention.

Shariati wished to be a politico-religious thinker in the context of the Third World liberation struggles. He felt acutely the problems of colonialism and neocolonialism and attacked especially cultural colonization, which alienates people from their roots. Iran is especially exposed to this danger: Al-e Ahmad had denounced fifteen years before this Iranian malady in his *Westoxication*, long forbidden by the censor. Shariati believed that the undermining of national culture had politico-economic consequences. Western ideologies paralyzed the indigenous reactions of Muslim peoples. Neither capitalist liberalism, which causes and profits from this illness, nor Marxist or socialist doctrines, which have lost their dynamism and envisage an antihumanist and antireligious levelling, can provide a way out. Shariati saw in Islamic humanism the sole ideology that could save Iran and all oppressed peoples. Islam should be followed, not in the degraded form found in contemporary Muslim societies, but in the form of Mohammad's ideal society, which the Umayyads had plunged into decadence and tyranny.

Faith gives the individual his determination to struggle and the group its cement. For Shariati atheistic societies are sad and unattractive, as material satisfactions are deceptive. A religious and somewhat mystic spirit, Shariati refers constantly to the early Shi'i heroes, to whom he devoted many lectures: Ali, Hosain, Abu Zarr Ghefari, Horr, and others. He sees two Shi'i principles as the motors of liberation: (1) The imamate, a systematization of "leadership," the spiritual and political domination of a leader over a people who accept him willingly. The community (*umma*; from the same Arabic root as "imam") is not, as in Christianity, united by the mystic presence (of Christ) but is united by its movement, around its leader. (2) Justice, which has been elevated by Shi'ism to the rank of a theological principle: God must be just, and the human community cannot accept a tyrannical law that killed the imams and plunged Islam into decadence.

In a group of lectures gathered in one volume, Shariati presented a strong distinction between "Alid Shi'ism" (from Ali, the first Imam) and "Safavid Shi'ism." Alid Shi'ism represents original Islam and is a movement of progress and revolution, with no division between intellectuals and the people—Islam in its progressive and dynamic phase. The Safavids, in making Shi'ism the state religion, degraded it into an institution, making it a means of political enslavement and turning it from its original aim—the search for justice and sacred duties. "Safavid Shi'ism" opposed Iranians to Ottomans; it mixed ethnocentrism and supernationalism with Shi'ism. Aberrant forms of worship were, says Shariati, borrowed from Christianity in Safavid times, like the theatrical plays on the martyrdom of Hosain (ta'ziyeh), which he says are copied from Christian "mysteries."

Shariati's Safavid Shi'ism is also Pahlavi Shi'ism, and today's "Safavid" ulama are those who play games of power. They renounce their role as awakeners, content themselves with futile debates, and make of Shi'ism a religion of the vanquished (the Moharram mournings), turning believers toward exterior forms and not toward a movement. They claim that in the absence of the Twelfth Imam any government is acceptable, thus becoming accomplices of Islam's atrophy and the separation of religion and power.

At the end of the book Shariati gives a table between the two Shi'isms, based on their main concepts, which we summarize:[52]

Alid Shi'ism	Safavid Shi'ism
vesayat	
The Prophet's recommendation, by divine order, to designate his family the most capable and meritorious on the basis of knowledge and purity.	The principle of a government, at first designated, then hereditary, perpetuated on the basis of race and kinship.
imamate	
Pure, honest, revolutionary conduct of the people and the correct foundation of society in terms of conscience, the expansion and independence of people's judgment. The coming of "superior men" incarnating	Belief in twelve pure, saintly, extraordinary names; supermen like angels; little gods next to the great God; the only recourse for intercession and obtaining grace.

the religious ideal to be taken as models.

'esmat

Belief in the purity of those spiritually and socially responsible. Negation of government by traitors, and dishonest clerics attached to the caliphate.

An exceptional quality of hidden beings not of the earthly human species, who cannot be in error; only the "Sinless Fourteen" (Mohammad, Fatima, and the twelve imams) had it. This belief makes infamous government natural, accepts dishonest theologians as they are not among the Sinless Fourteen.

velayat

Offering one's friendship to Ali and following his path, in his manner, under his guidance.

Love of Ali alone; feeling oneself totally irresponsible.

taqlid

A logical, scientific, natural, and necessary relationship between nonspecialists and specialist theologians, for practical and juridical problems that demand specialization.

Blind obedience to the ulama, from whom one accepts absolutely, without reserve or logic, belief and orders. Quasi-adoration of the ulama.

'adl

God is just; the world is based on justice and consequently society must also be based on it.

A problem concerning the attributes of God and the afterlife (Last Judgment). In this world justice is to be left to Shah Abbas (to monarchies) according to the principle "render to God what is God's and to Caesar what is Caesar's."

ghaibat

| Responsibility of men to decide their destiny, faith, and spiritual and social life, taking guidance from conscientious, responsible, pure men representing the leadership of the Imam. | Total irresponsibility; the uselessness of all action under the pretext of the Imam's absence—he is the only model to whom one is responsible. |

entezar

| Spiritual, moral, and doctrinal preparation for reform, revolution, and change. Firm belief in the fall of tyranny, the victory of justice, and the advent of the exploited classes to world revolution. | Spiritual, moral, and doctrinal submission to the present situation; justification of corruption, and seeing the divine decree in everything. Negation of responsibility, fear of reforms, and condemnation in advance of all movements. |

By systematizing the concept of Alid Shi'ism, Shariati attained a double result; he detached himself from the petrified official Islam rejected by idealistic youth, and he brought a new and combative meaning to Shi'i concepts. Even prayer in this renovated Islam took on a political meaning, tied to action. This insurrectional meaning of common prayer was particularly developed in the 1978–79 Revolution. Refusing the fanaticism of Safavid Shi'ism, Shariati advocated an accord between Shi'is and Sunnis, as before the Umayyad schism.

Shariati also devoted several lectures to the role of women, published as *Fatima is Fatima*. He criticized the Western model, seen as fabricating women-objects and utilizing sexuality without marital ties for commercial ends. The West, in claiming to "liberate" women in its colonies, is really only trying to affirm its power by breaking up the unity of the Muslim family. Shariati favors women's participation in public life and severely attacks traditional principles of women's seclusion. But, he says, liberation and egalitarianism are words that risk going against nature. Westernization, which made these words a slogan, offers only an individualism in which women must choose between sacrificing their femininity in the hard professional struggle, or overdeveloping femininity in useless roles. The decadence of Muslim society and its contempt for women demand a reevaluation of woman's role, a search for a new model. Shariati uses the example of Fatima, daughter of Mohammad and wife of Ali, who shared her father's trials, and also those of Ali and of her sons, Imams Hasan and Hosain. She was the center of a family of fighters. She took on responsibilities and became socially engaged, equally to men but in a different way.[53] The "separate but equal" doctrine of Shariati regarding women has become popular with many Muslims.

The really political thought of Shariati is not very developed in published texts, even though everything leads to it. His stress on the community following the imamate suggests that Shariati, while making implacable criticisms of totalitarianism, dreamed of an Islamic totalitarianism, the only one he saw as respecting completely the individual, not enslaving him to anyone but God, and not reducing his autonomy to that of an economic producer. Islam is, besides, he says, the only basis for an ideology of permanent progress and revolution —halting any attempt at a return to tyrannical powers and any degradation of political relationships.

Shariati sees Western democracy as rotten, because the power of money and not electors dominates politics. It is also rotten in principle, as universal suffrage, while claiming to create equality, in fact ensures the crushing of the progressive minority by the conservative majority. In "The Community and the Imamate" he defines the "directed" democracy he advocates:

It is the government of a group which, on the basis of a revolutionary progressive program that aims at changing individuals —their view of the world, their language, their social relations, and their level of living—and also at changing social forms in order to perfect them, has, with the above aims, an ideology, a well-defined doctrine, and a precise plan. Its aim is not that everyone by his vote or his acquiescence should be its partisan, but it is to make a society reach the level where, on the basis of this doctrine, it begins to move toward this most elevated goal and to realize its revolutionary objectives. If there are people who do not believe in this path, and whose conduct leads to a stagnation or corruption of society, and if there are some who abuse with their own power, with their own money, this liberty, and if there are social formations and traditions, which keep men in this stagnation, we must suppress these traditions, condemn these ways of thinking, and save society from its own fossilized molds, by any means possible.[54]

The immense appeal that Shariati had for students and young Muslims is partly to be explained by the originality of his position. Coming from a modest religious background he acquired, through his studies in France, knowledge of modern ideologies, including liberalism, capitalism, Marxism, and existentialism, without ceasing to be a believer. Speaking a language accessible to Iranians who had only recently come to modern studies and who wished to understand, in order to refute, the ideologies of Western aggressors, he became celebrated by meeting their needs. He became famous at the time when Iran experienced a great expansion in higher education and when new social groups, without ideological preparation, were confronted by new cultural problems—accelerated urbanization, Westernization, industrialization, spectacular speculation and corruption, and many other phenomena tied to Iran's dependence on the West. Demographic growth affected most the less Westernized, poorer classes, who were the most religious. His ties to Islam made Shariati, who was well equipped to respond to other ideologies, the rampart against the undermining of traditional values. Islam, the religion of the Algerian National Liberation Front, of the Palestinians, was the religion of anti-imperialist combat. Feeling stifled by the West, Iranians rediscovered an identity.

Iran's new intellectuals had earlier seen Islam as something disconnected from the modern world's needs. Islam had even a negative role, turning attention to the hereafter, underpinning the regime by its silence, and presenting the defeatist side of religious combat, as it encouraged Muslims to cry for poor Hosain, who died miserably. Young Iranian Muslim intellectuals found in Shariati a revolutionary

Iranian Shi'i response. No more the crying Hosain of the ta'ziyeh, but Hosain fighting and dying for a just cause.

Although Shariati's books were forbidden they circulated secretly, especially among Iranian students abroad. Among religious traditionalists a strong opposition to Shariati and the Hosainiyeh Ershad developed. The theologians' prestige was being defied by someone who had not studied theology who accused those who had of distorting religion for their own profit and contested the good faith of religious authorities' resistance to the monarchy. Their struggles were backward looking and defended their corporate interests and former privileges, whereas Shariati's struggle was radically revolutionary. Of the ulama's critiques of Shariati none, to our knowledge, was more than a polemic, usually with unfounded accusations (being an agent of Sunnism, of Wahhabism, or of Communism), with nothing constructive. Among the accusations of the great mujtahids against Shariati was that he wished to have an Islam without ulama and hence, by dividing Muslims on this point, to play the game of the anti-Muslim regime. Ayatollah Khomaini has attacked the Mojahedin-e Khalq, heavily inspired by Shariati, on similar grounds, saying that one cannot be a Muslim if one does not recognize the power of the ulama.[55]

From the summer of 1977 on, however, Shariati's books were sold everywhere, by the hundreds of thousands. In front of Tehran University, bookstores are full of them, and sidewalk vendors have made a living by selling practically nothing else. The same is true in quarters near the Tehran bazaar, of provincial towns (even those without bookstores), and in the religious towns of Qom and Mashhad. Shortly after his death Shariati became a mythical figure of militant Islam. In the third volume of posthumous homages published in 1978 are found the names of many celebrated oppositionist intellectuals.[56]

It is too soon to predict what will be Shariati's lasting influence. Here we will not try to judge his still incomplete publications, nor to evaluate a person whose courage and spiritual qualities demand respect. We will limit ourselves to a few remarks: Despite the importance Shariati gave in his lectures to a critique of Western society and his insistence on saving a humanism threatened by decadent Christianity and materialism (both capitalist and Communist), his knowledge of the West was schematic. Understandably, he did not expand before his audience his portrait of the Christian mystic Massignon, or expatiate on the democratic ideals of many Western countries, but some of his polemics indicate that Shariati was not interested enough in the systems he combatted to study them closely.

Shariati also neglects the history of Iran; he admits that in his studies he disliked history, perhaps because of the use made of it. He refers very little to it; what interests him is an ideal original Islam, not its historic compromises. Hence, his analysis of the relations of Shi'ism with the government since Safavid times lacks references to accessible texts and documents. The Iranian ulama's major role in the Constitutional Revolution of 1905–11 is not discussed, except to criticize the use of *mashrutiyat* for "constitution." We have found just one page on the role the ulama should have in politics:

> But at the time of the (Imam's) Occulation, as there was no prophet and the Imam was absent, the mission of the prophets and imams fell upon the people themselves, and it is the people themselves who should learn Islam, put in practice the fundamental ideas of Islam, form Islamic society, and guide the people. Muslims must defend Islam, its power and unity, against Jews, Christians, and other enemies, carry on holy war, make the effort of interpretation [ijtihad], and oblige one group among them to specialize in the theoretical knowledge of Islam, the deducing of Islamic laws, and the resolution of the problems of society and the events of the time. They should confide to this group social and ideological leadership as well as responsibility for people's destiny. This group can decide the best, most honorable, most conscientious, most enlightened, and purest person for their guidance. And they can elect from among themselves someone in place of the Imam—which is the place of the Prophet of Islam! And they would invest him. In the execution of his heavy responsibilities—which are those of the Imamate—the people feel a permanent and direct responsibility and build the government of wisdom, of engaged wisdom, as Plato wished. . . . That is to say that the one who was chosen by God in the period before the Occultation (i.e., the Prophet and the Imams), during the Occultation is chosen by the people.[57]

Shariati thus takes the traditional theory of ijtihad, mixing it with democratic principles, but makes no historical or theological analysis, so that it is hard to know his precise position. This lack of precision does not keep young Iranian intellectuals and others from rallying to Shariati. All find in his energetic thought an Iranian response to their problems as Iranian intellectuals. Shariati helps them to set off to conquer the modern world without renouncing their Muslim identity.

Abolhasan Bani Sadr is one of the more original political ideologists and theoreticians of the Iranian Islamic movement. After having been close to Ayatollah Khomaini at Neauphle-le-Château, he became a rising figure in the new regime, and in November 1979 became acting foreign minister. In January 1980 he was elected first president of the Islamic Republic. His works are less popular than those of Shariati; they are also clearer. He analyzes problems and uses economic arguments.

Born in 1933–34 into a family of Ayatollahs originating in Hamadan, Bani Sadr studied at the university first theology and then sociology. In this period he met the French Marxist sociologist Paul Vieille, whose collaborator he became. Bani Sadr was already a known opponent of the shah's regime and participated in meetings organized by the National Front and by political groups at Tehran University, when he was forced into exile to France, where he pursued studies in economics and sociology. Much influenced by the 1968 student movement, he became a leader of students abroad opposed to the shah's regime. From 1972 he was in direct contact with Ayatollah Khomaini in Najaf.

In Bani Sadr's works may be distinguished economic articles (some in French) from more doctrinal texts. Both are directed to struggle: they denounce economic policies seen as delivering Iran to the control of imperialism, and also construct an ideology to mobilize Iran's vital forces. Several texts are instruments of political struggle: *Iran's Situation and the Role of Modarres* begins a study of contemporary history stressing the role of religion in the struggle against the Pahlavis. *The Hypocrites from Our Viewpoint* unites texts about the Mojahedin-e Khalq and the strategy of revolutionary combat after the 1975 split between Marxists and Muslims in the Mojahedin. Bani Sadr affirmed his attachment to Ayatollah Khomaini and refuted attacks made against

Mehdi Bazargan based on truncated and misleading citations. *The Cult of Personality* is a treatise on ethics with a Quranic base, a critique of man's ambition and desire for power which, especially in economics and politics, are the main causes of oppression.[58]

Bani Sadr made himself a theorist of Islamic government in three other books: *The Economics of Unity (Tauhid)* is an attempt to construct a political theory dominated by the Quranic principle, "There is no god but God"; and hence there must not be economic domination of man by man. Islam returns to the principle that only God has the absolute right to property, a right delegated by the Prophet and the Imams to those in the community who deserve it, thanks to their labor. Before being a relationship between man and man, labor is a relationship of man to God.[59]

In a 1971–72 work, republished as *Manifesto of the Islamic Republic*, Bani Sadr sketches an Islamic political anthropology. The first part is a critique of the Pahlavi regime for putting Iran under the political, military, and economic domination of the West, and hence causing Iranians to lose identity and creativity and become consumers. The second part proposes solutions. In foreign policy one must ensure Iran's independence and reaffirm Mosaddeq's "principle of negative equilibrium." In domestic policy there must be true Islamic government, reviving the real structures of power, like mosques; suppressing harmful conflict between state and religion; and building a state without constraints. In economics Bani Sadr wishes to bring internal production and consumption back into balance. He thinks ending dependence on imperialists will bring a better distribution of wealth, greater justice, an end to the flight of intellectuals, and reduction in bureaucracy. Finally, the socioeconomic causes of alienation having ended, Iranians will no longer be in a passive dependent relation to world centers of decision. There will no longer be a schism between state and people, and a new Islamic society can be created. "Everyone is responsible for all; everyone is imam and guide of all"; such is the unity (tauhid) of society that religion has as its message.[60]

Finally, *The Fundamental Principles of Islamic Government* is a theoretical work concerning tomorrow's society, in the style of the great European nineteenth-century ideologues. The method used by the author is to analyze his subject according to categories identical to the five principles of Shi'ism. The first, divine unity, is a dynamic unification and a negation of polytheist trends (no one can be God's representative, or claim any participation in God's unity). This fundamental principle is the foundation of the other four. Because of this unity, one may condemn all human formations that oppress and divide people. "The principle of unity involves the negation of every sort of economic, political, ideological, or other bastion in which power can be concentrated."[61] The believer must try to achieve unity everywhere so that society will be in the image of the community desired by God. Devotions are a training to fight for this ideal: common prayer, fasting, pilgrimage (a sort of annual congress), and holy war (against evil impulses within) prepare one to combat oppression by making the everyday a constant rejection of all that is not God.

Thus, one must not adore any leader, neither Stalin, nor Hitler, nor de Gaulle, nor Mosaddeq, nor Khomaini, as the cult of men leads to enslavement and totalitarianism. With Bani Sadr this principle goes very far, as all power coming from men is condemned, even if it tries to justify itself by religion. Bani Sadr reacts against the idea of God as an arbitrary and absolute will—an idea that theology developed in the decadent period of the caliphate, and which allowed the imposition of illegitimate and irreligious governmental authority. All false human authorities, who divide men, must be overthrown. Society must not be divided into classes, into dominant and dominated; and excessive property is a negation of God. Economic resources must be controlled so they do not lead to concentrations of power, depriving most people of their capacity to produce. Slavery, meaning massive workers' migrations from poor to rich countries, must be abolished. In Islamic government, only work justifies ownership of the product of labor, which excludes capitalism. The economy belongs to everyone, not to one class. Luxury must be eliminated, as it means poverty for the majority.

To Marxists, who say that religion obstructs class consciousness by transforming into prayer the revolt of the exploited, Bani Sadr says that differences between men come from God and should not be denied. They can be kept from engendering classes by putting special talents at the service of society. Bani Sadr criticizes ideologies which, after having brought people to power, are used as instruments of domination. Any belief used for domination is an opiate of the people:

> But would not Islam become an opiate if one made of it an instrument of the system? Since Islam is a religion that rests on universal laws and one nature, and which envisages liberation from the traps of these perpetual realities, it is not possible for it to become the opiate of the masses, unless one makes of it a scourge, as the present regime (1975) has institutionalized it and made it a scourge.
>
>   Hence, in an Islamic government, belief must not be an instrument of government, but the government must be an instrument of Islamic belief. And this necessitates guarantees that it be the belief that governs.[62]

Islam was established on the basis of universal laws and human nature. The end does not justify the means.

The goal of Islamic government, to Bani Sadr, is not only to stop a person or group from monopolizing power; it is to suppress centralized power and the state as a form of oppression. Nationalism is a pretext to divide and oppress peoples; offensive armies should be abolished. Only a defensive army should be created, and should be organically based in society. Holy war is in reality a permanent revolution, in which there is no "model for imitation" (marja'-e taqlid); everyone must discover himself the cause for which he is fighting.

Two tendencies seem to dominate the writings of Bani Sadr; on the one hand a certain anarchist tendency, which pushes him toward rejecting any domination of man by man under any pretext, and toward rendering possible the installation of what he calls "organized spontaneity;" on the other hand a tendency to make (in his Persian more than his French writings) all analyses, even in the social or economic domain, enter the traditional theological categories of Shi'ism. These two features give Bani Sadr's thought a contradictory quality, but it is also thanks to these tendencies that he attracts numerous partisans, who are trying to reconcile a desire for liberty with the rigors of Islamic law.

Conclusion

Critical analyses of recent Shi'i political thought have been made elsewhere, and here only a few general remarks will be offered. [63] First, the above survey of Iranian political thought since the late nineteenth century suggests the frequent reappearance of certain similar themes, often found in both religious and secular thinkers. One of the most important is anti-imperialism, accompanied by a determination to free Iran from Western economic and cultural dominance. This took a reformed Islamic form with Sayyed Jamal ad-Din, a more secular form with Mossadeq and his main followers, and again a religious form in recent years. The Islamic nature of recent reactions even by many nonclerical leaders may in part be explained by the association of Western dominance with Western "cultural colonization," and of Pahlavi rule with secularism. Islam appeared, to those who rejected both liberalism and Marxism, as the natural ideological base from which to fight the West and the Pahlavis, especially as Islam was believed by, and familiar to, the great mass of Iranians. As with modernist and political adaptations of religion elsewhere, this utilization of Islam has involved new interpretations of old texts and practices, interpretations sometimes attacked by the more traditional and orthodox. It has also involved indiscriminate attacks on the West as a monolithic evil.

A more serious difficulty is that most modern Shi'i political thinkers have assumed that solutions to Iran's problems are essentially simple. They have tended to think that freeing Iran from foreign control and influence and setting up new and fairly simple political and economic institutions, for which they find an Islamic base, will solve Iran's problems, but this has not turned out to be the case. In essence, the new Islamic thought became a potent weapon in making a revolution, but had far less success in building up new institutions. The various books and pamphlets on Islamic politics and economics written in the past twenty years do not, even had they been followed in detail, provide an adequate basis for setting up a polity that could meet the widely recognized needs for social justice, mass participation in political and economic life, rights for minorities and women, a truly functioning economy, and so forth.

Intolerance by some leaders of ideas labeled "un-Islamic" or "counterrevolutionary" has narrowed the range of permissible discourse, even though this, as of 1980, remains broader than it was under the Pahlavis. Voices of the secularist left, including the Tudeh and the Feda'iyan-e Khalq as well as smaller leftist groups, of the left-Islamic Mojahedin-e Khalq, and of liberal secularists may still be heard, and to a degree published, in Iran today, and there are signs of widespread hostility toward the mollas and their policies. It may be that the dominance of thought couched in Islamic terms is not as durable a phenomenon as it now appears, and that Iran's long traditions of religious dissidence and skepticism, rationalist philosophy, and even secularism and anticlericalism will once again come to the fore. Whichever tradition is dominant in the foreseeable future, it is to be hoped that Iranians have learned that the "two cultures" split, which separates the religious from the secular and the masses from the elite, does not benefit Iran, and that each of the two culture groups may strive to understand, learn from, and see the needs and contributions of the other.

9 THE REVOLUTION

Secular and Guerilla Opposition Forces

The continuing growth of malaise and discontent among most sections of the Iranian population as despotism and repression increased in the 1970s, promised political and economic decentralization failed to materialize, and economic difficulties grew in 1976 and 1977, despite huge oil income, led to an outbreak of opposition beginning in 1977. The appearance of open opposition to the shah would likely have occurred soon in any case, but its form and timing were to some degree a consequence of the human-rights policy enunciated by President Carter, inaugurated in January 1977, which implied that countries guilty of basic human-rights violations might be deprived of American arms or aid. The influence of the human-rights policy was not due to any significant American pressures, however, but to the belief by both the shah and the opposition that the United States might act for human rights. This belief helped give some Iranians the courage to circulate open letters and petitions in the hope that they might be heeded and would surely not be as severely repressed as before. United States diplomats and policy makers, however, refused significantly to pressure the shah on human rights. The human-rights questions occasionally discussed with the shah were arrests and torture, not liberalization or civil rights, and no threats of reduced support were made. The sporadic mention by official Americans of human rights helped make the shah waver in his confidence regarding American backing and hence in his response to the opposition, but this was more a sign of his mentality than of any actual threat. The liberal opposition was in part encouraged to activity by Carter's words, even though they were backed by few deeds.

There may have been additional reasons, rarely mentioned, for the shah to tolerate criticisms in 1977 that he would not have allowed earlier. Among them was that he knew he was ill with cancer, and that the throne might pass to his minor son, with regency going to Queen Farah, according to a provision he had initiated. In the fall of 1977, as on some previous and later occasions, there was a period during which pictures of the shah's activities were noticeably absent from TV and the newspapers (presumably because of illness; when he did reappear he looked bad). Instead, one saw frequent pictures of the queen engaging in a series of public-minded activities throughout Iran. At the time of the queen's birthday, photos of the queen alone (without the father-son members of the universal trinity) were for the first time plastered all over Iran's cities; and, extraordinarily, they were severe, unglamorous photos, suggesting a woman of determination who could rule. It seems logical to attribute some easing of dictatorship and of ironclad restraints on open opposition in 1977 to the shah's recognition that his designated successors would not be able to start off their rule with his type of strong hand, but would have to enlist some cooperation from various elements of the population, including an increasingly vocal opposition. As the crisis progressed, some of the shah's weakness may have been due to his cancer and medication,[1] which either included strong tranquilizers or had the same effect. Also, reforms in the judiciary and in reducing torture may have been as much due to pressures from world opinion, particularly Amnesty International and the International Commission of Jurists, which began before the Carter administration, as to any United States action.

Interviews and statements do indicate, however, that professionals and intellectuals were determined to utilize the American human-rights policy to wedge an opening by publishing their grievances, hoping to widen the crack in order to change government policies. In the spring and summer of 1977 several petitions and open letters were circulated. The fact that these letters came from non-"extremist" types—neither the militants of the religious oppositon nor those on the left—should not be exaggerated, as it sometimes is, to imply that the "moderates" started the revolution and the "extremists" took it over. Radical petitions from either religious or Marxist elements could only circulate in greater secrecy, but this does not mean that these groups were inactive in 1977; and, on the other hand, the moderates were relatively too weak among the masses to keep leadership of the opposition.

Among the major 1977 letters were: a two-page open letter to the shah in June signed by leaders of the revived National Front—men whose association with the Front dated back to Mosaddeq: Karim Sanjabi, Shahpour Bakhtiar, and Daryush Foruhar. The letter criticized the failure of the shah's reforms and particularly the disregard for human rights, enshrined in both the Iranian constitution and the Universal Declaration of Human Rights. It attacked shortages, inflation, and the squandering of oil, and called for fulfillment of the constitution, release of political prisoners, freedom of the press, and free elections. The letter circulated widely, and was especially influential among the new middle classes, whose reformist constitutionalist trends it voiced. Shortly after this letter another was sent to Prime Minister Hoveyda signed by forty well-known writers and professors demanding an end to censorship, free meetings, and recognition for the Writers' Guild, which had been suppressed some years before.

In the same period a group of lawyers began a series of protests; in May they had protested rushed changes in the judicial system, and in July, 64 lawyers demanded an end to special courts and strict observance of law without constant encroachment by the executive upon the judiciary. After a further letter protesting the judicial system in September, 143 lawyers issued a manifesto in October stating their intention of forming a Jurists Association, which was to monitor observance of human rights. Finally, a series of poetry readings with political content at the Irano-German Institute in Tehran in October attracted unprecedented crowds and became virtual antiregime demonstrations.[2]

One influence of the Carter human-rights program was probably in encouraging intellectuals to send and circulate (although they could not publish) their protests, which in the past would probably have involved jail sentences. Now they brought no immediate punishment, and although such direct criticisms were not published in the press or elsewhere, they did circulate from hand to hand and abroad. At the same time as these intellectuals' protests circulated, pressure from foreign human-rights groups like Amnesty International and the International Association of Jurists, and from Iranian guerilla, religious, and other opposition groups kept up, while economic and social problems became increasingly acute. The shah thus made some gestures toward public opinion; in April 1977 for the first time a trial on antiregime charges was open to the public, the International Red Cross was permitted to inspect twenty prisons, torture was significantly reduced, and new laws, which were only partially improvements, were promulgated regarding military tribunals (before which political prisoners were tried). The writings of Ali Shariati, newly freed from censorship, now achieved vast sale.

In the face of growing public discontent and economic problems the shah removed Prime Minister Hoveyda in July 1977, but made him minister of court. The new prime minister, Jamshid Amuzegar, was a technocrat with high governmental experience as minister of interior; in economics and oil; and as leader of the official Rastakhiz party; his appointment indicated no basic change in political policy but at best a hope that a man with a better economic background could help solve Iran's growing economic problems. In fact, his attempts to cool off inflation and the overheated economy without reducing the huge sacrosanct military budget resulted in mass unemployment and other problems. Construction jobs in particular, which began falling in 1976, tumbled further and discontents increased.

In November 1977, the shah visited Washington, where he faced large hostile demonstrations; these were shown on Iranian television and made a great impression. Carter returned the visit, along with high praise of the shah, in December. In seems likely that, as the Iranian opposition believed, in return for Iran's moderating its stand on oil prices, the United States guaranteed continued arms supplies, diplomatic support, and a downplaying of the human-rights issue. In December Iran backed Saudi Arabia's oil-price-freeze policy, while American officials from then on played down human rights in Iran more than before.[3] From the end of 1977 on, also, there were numerous incidents of "mysterious" beatings and bombings of opposition leaders and protesters, generally attributed to the regime via SAVAK.

Once the door was opened to protest, however, it was not to be shut. There had already been far more protest in the years since the 1963–64 crackdown than a reading of the world press would lead one to suppose. Workers' strikes were quite frequent, even though opposed by officially supervised trade unions and confronted by threats of force.

Much of the regime's policy of favoring workers in large factories and industries with higher wages and bonuses was based on fear of a labor movement, even though a nationwide movement did not materialize, owing to strict SAVAK surveillance.

At least as great a political threat were students, both at home and abroad. Most students were too young and idealistic to have been co-opted by the regime, and they had many grievances. Within their lecture halls they could sense the strain between those technical or politically harmless new ideas they were permitted access to and the many others their teachers could not voice nor their booksellers sell. (Books in Persian by Marxists and Iranian oppositionists were forbidden sale, even in the few cases when they were published, and there remained from Reza Shah's days a law against any advocacy of "collectivism" or "socialism.") Some teachers were dismissed and others were warned or suspended. This aroused opposition from students. With rapidly expanding universities and a large influx of poorly educated secondary students, many from rural areas, academic and economic frustrations also grew. Also, the great majority of university applicants failed to get in, and those who did were often dissatisfied with academic, housing, and educational conditions, as well as political ones. Hence there were frequent major student protests and strikes over the years, particularly in the main cities, and many campuses remained closed for months at a time. Although for years student protests tended to be concentrated in campus areas, once the national protest movement broadened in 1977–78, students had the habits, inclination, and experience that helped make them important participants in the revolutionary movement. A variety of political persuasions were represented on campuses, most notably Marxist groups and religious leftists. There was a trend among some women students in the 1970s to return to the chador or to adopt a new costume, with a large headscarf covering hair and forehead, a knee-length smock, and loose trousers, all in plain neutral colors, a costume that has become a kind of uniform for the women of the Mojahedin-e Khalq. Some students who wore the new costume or the chador were genuinely religious; others wished to stress their protest against the regime.

In the 1970s probably over one hundred thousand Iranian students were abroad at a time, and many of them opposed the Iranian government. The strongest oppositional group was the Confederation of

Iranian Students, which grew out of earlier varied Iranian student groups abroad but coalesced in 1960 with considerable leftist and Tudeh party influence. Tudeh popularity among students dropped with the growing rapprochement between the Soviet Union, Eastern Europe, and Iran in the later 1960s (the Soviets built Iran's first steelmill and provided small arms, and in the same period economic relations with Eastern Europe developed). As Soviet policy toward Iran became conciliatory, the pro-Soviet Tudeh party lost much of its appeal to Iranian leftist oppositionists, including students. Some turned to a pro-Chinese group that split off from the main Tudeh party, although this group lost much of its credibility as the Chinese too, in the 1970s after the shah recognized the People's Republic, drew up trade and diplomatic agreements with Iran. As time went on the Confederation of Iranian Students became increasingly radicalized and included numerous admirers of the small guerilla groups operating in Iran, the most important of which were the Marxist Feda'iyan-e Khalq and the Islamic leftist Mojahedin-e Khalq.

In the 1970s Muslim students' associations, sometimes entirely Iranian and sometimes from different Muslim countries, also became as important abroad as they were in Iran. Some, as in France, had ties with groups using the name of the National Front and venerated both Mosaddeq and Khomaini. Islamically oriented lay leaders of the 1978–79 Revolution were often involved in, or leaders of, such movements, including notably Abolhasan Bani Sadr, Ibrahim Yazdi, and Sadeq Ghotbzadeh. Through their propaganda, Iranian student groups abroad were among the first to awaken some in the West to the activities of the shah and SAVAK and to help enlist Western support and pressure against human-rights violations. Although some ex-student oppositionists at home and abroad were bought off by official offers of good jobs, and others were scared off from returning by penalties for belonging to the Confederation and other activities abroad, still others continued their oppositional work before and during the Revolution both in Iran and abroad.

More important than their small numbers and few pre–1978 successes would indicate were the guerilla groups in Iran, recently studied by E. Abrahamian.[4] According to him, guerilla tactics were an outgrowth of the regime's bloody suppression of the 1963 riots, which made many think that open protests were sure to be violently suppressed. Militant students formed small secret groups, which translated and studied works by Mao, Guevera, and Fanon and discussed guerilla tactics. Three of these groups merged in 1970–71 under a name usually shortened as the Feda'iyan-e Khalq, whose best known theorist Bizhan Jazani was killed in prison in 1975; Hamid Ashraf, the leader who longest eluded the police, was killed in Tehran in 1976. Critical of Maoists and especially the pro-Soviet Tudeh, they hoped to create nuclei of armed struggle on the then popular model of Che Guevera and Regis Debray. They planned to spend a year in the mountains and forests of the Caspian province of Gilan, well situated for guerilla warfare and having a post–World War I history of such struggle. Two of their sympathizers were arrested, however, and the rest feared their plans might be revealed under torture. Hence they hastened Iran's first major guerilla operation in February 1971, attacking a gendarmerie post in Siahkal village and killing three gendarmes. Failing to find their two colleagues, they escaped into the Gilan mountains.

The shah reacted strongly, sending his brother to head a large well-equipped force which, after a manhunt that left several soldiers and thirty guerillas dead, captured eleven Feda'iyan. Ten were shot and the other died of torture. Despite the military failure, the Feda'iyan and other oppositionists looked to this day, which showed it was possible to shake the regime, as the beginning of a successful antishah movement. In the following weeks the government confirmed the importance of the Siahkal incident by arresting oppositionists, spreading anti-left propaganda, and outlawing the Confederation of Iranian Students abroad. Armed robberies, assassinations, and bombings followed, but by late 1976 some Feda'iyan thought that losses from such tactics outweighed gains, given the heavy toll in lives and the lack of mass struggles triggered by their acts, and this minority turned toward the Tudeh party. Both factions kept their weapons, and were able to use these, along with their training and experience, during the Revolution.

The other guerilla group, whose name is shortened to Mojahedin-e Khalq, also originated in the 1960s, but while the Feda'iyan came mostly from the Tudeh party and from Marxists in the National Front, the Mojahedin came mostly from the religious wing of that Front, particularly the Freedom Movement led since 1961 by Mehdi Bazargan and Ayatollah Mahmud Taleqani. The Freedom Movement was intended as a link between Shi'ism and modern ideas, but the government's brutality in 1963 caused some of its younger and more militant activists to leave the Movement and form a secret discussion group. The leaders of this group changed the Freedom Movement leaders' liberal interpretations of Shi'ism, deciding that true Shi'ism opposed not only despotism but also capitalism, imperialism, and conservative clericalism. As summarized by Abrahamian, one Mojahedin ideologist, Reza'i, argued that the realm of unity (or monotheistic order—*Nezam-e Tauhid*) the Prophet sought was a commonwealth fully united by virtue of being "classless" and striving for the common good as well as by the fact that it worships only one God:

> Reza'i further argued that the banner of revolt raised by the Shi'i Imams, especially 'Ali, Hassan, and Hussein, was aimed against feudal landlords and exploiting merchant capitalists as well as against usurping Caliphs who betrayed the *Nezam-i Towhid*. For Reza'i and the *Mujahidin* it was the duty of all Muslims to continue this struggle to create a 'classless society' and destroy all forms of capitalism, despotism, and imperialism. The *Mujahidin* summed up their attitude towards religion in these words: "After years of extensive study into Islamic history and Shi'i ideology, our organization has reached the firm conclusion that Islam, especially Shi'ism, will play a major role in inspiring the masses to join the revolution. It will do so because Shi'ism, particularly Hussein's historic act of resistance, has both a revolutionary message and a special place in our popular culture."[5]

Given these ideas, it was natural for the Mojahedin to be on good terms with Ali Shariati; although many of their theories preceded Shariati's public lectures and writings, it seems likely that each helped inspire the other. A series of individual acts of violence from 1971 on resulted in heavy Mojahedin losses via arrests and executions; as with the Feda'iyan, the Mojahedin did not see such individual acts as their ultimate goal but as the only means toward revolution in a period of extreme repression. Most Mojahedin were children of bazaaris or ulama, and came mainly from the physical sciences. The Feda'iyan, largely from modern middle-class backgrounds, included more women than the Mojahedin, drew from the arts and social-science faculties, and included a number of industrial workers.

Some Mojahedin began to study Marxism, and in 1975 a majority of leaders still free in Tehran voted to declare the organization Marxist-Leninist. The transformation is suggested in a letter by Mojtaba Taleqani, son of Ayatollah Taleqani, to his father: "to organize the working class, we must reject Islam, for religion refuses to accept the main dynamic force of history—that of the class struggle. Of course, Islam can play a progressive role, especially in mobilizing the intelligentsia against imperialism. But it is only Marxism that provides a scientific analysis of society and looks toward the exploited classes for liberation."[6] This change caused a major split; most provincial members refused to change ideology, accusing their rivals of murdering one of their leaders and betraying two to the police. The Mojahedin split into two groups, and both continued violent action, but by early 1976, like the Feda'iyan, they had such heavy losses that they switched more to propaganda; the Muslim Mojahedin mainly among students and the Marxist ones among workers. Thus, when revolutionary activities began in late 1977 there were two Mojahedin—Marxist and Muslim; and two Feda'iyan—pro-Tudeh and activist. All had organizations, weapons, underground publications, and revolutionary ideologies, equipping them for important roles in a revolutionary movement. Some had ties to the Palestinian resistance, particularly its left constituents, and this facilitated the entry of weapons from abroad after mid–1978.

Although several guerilla actions aroused horror among many—particularly assassinations of Iranian and American military and intelligence figures—there were peaceable Iranian oppositionists who argued that, given the atmosphere of repression, only such acts could indicate the vulnerability of the regime and keep alive hope for its eventual overthrow. It seems likely that the increase in jailings, torture, repression, and censorship in the 1970s was tied to the guerillas' activities, although repression was already strong previously.

The "Religious Opposition" and the Revolution

As suggested above, parts of various opposition groups—the predominantly middle-class and elderly remnants of the National Front, students inside and outside Iran, the workers, and the guerillas—had ties to the growing number of oppositionists who voiced their views in Islamic terms, here called the "religious opposition." The religious opposition can best be understood in terms of its own two major groups, even though they overlap the above groups; first, those with a traditional religious education and functions, and second, those with Western or Western-style educations who united modern and traditional ideas under an Islamic rubric. Many of these persons and particularly their ideas were discussed at some length in chapter 8—notably Ayatollahs Khomaini, Shariatmadari, and Taleqani among the first, and Bazargan, Shariati, and Bani Sadr among the second group, but here they will be related to the background and events of the Revolution.

A major grievance of the trained ulama against the Pahlavi regime was its continual whittling away at ulama power and influence, accompanied by the growing power of Western infidels and their ways. Reza Shah instituted examinations to qualify for wearing a turban and hence being one of the ulama; secularized the legal and educational systems, thus depriving many ulama of jobs; unveiled women; instituted university coeducation, and took other steps that weakened the ulama and their ideological hegemony. Mohammad Reza Shah moved further in the same directions, by trying to tame religion by setting up schools of theology in state universities, including the University of Tehran; by putting new controls on pilgrimages abroad; and by setting up a "religion corps" to parallel the literacy corps for the villages and teach an officially approved version of religion. Although no respecter of women, the shah came to see, partly under the pressure of the homogenized Women's Organization, that the encouragement of women in the labor force could help in Iran's economic growth. The Iranian Women's Organization, whose director Mahnaz Afkhami was made the Third World's first minister for women's affairs, headed a group that helped train women to read and to acquire other skills that might enable them to work for a living and to defend their legal rights, especially under the Family Protection Law of 1967/75. Both this law and the slowly spreading practice of coeducation were opposed in teaching and writing by Ayatollah Khomaini and some Islamic fundamentalists as were more obviously disturbing signs of Western-influenced "decadence," such as sexy films, dances, and music; forms of women's dress that not only went against old veiling norms but were often tight or revealing; open drinking and gambling (both against Muslim law); and others. Westernization seemed inextricably tied to a decline in Islamic practices, quite aside from its economic ill effects. There were several individual events from the mid–1970s that further aroused the ulama and their followers. One was the shah's scheme to redevelop the area around the holy shrine of the Imam Reza at Mashhad, which, like many shrines, was surrounded by a dense bazaar area that helped unify the bazaaris and the ulama. The plan was carried through and razed all buildings around the shrine, creating instead a green space and a broad traffic circle. It was so unpopular that bulldozers and construction equipment were often bombed or sabotaged, but it created something more attractive to "modern" taste. It dispersed Mashhad's bazaaris but further kindled their resentments. A related scheme for the Tehran bazaar, to cut through it with broad boulevards, which would, as in Mashhad, have dispersed potentially dangerous bazaaris, aroused so much opposition that it was not carried through. A drastic 1977 cut in government subsidies to the ulama for various purposes, carried out when Amuzegar was prime minister, also increased ulama discontent.[7]

Various attempts to create a monarchist ideology-mythology were also unpopular, both with the ulama and with other elements in the opposition. Although Iranian kings and rulers have had more of an ideological base than some recent works stressing ulama ideology would suggest, Iranian rulers since the rise of Islam did not go nearly as far as the Pahlavis in their attempts to glorify the monarchy—attempts that devalued Islam and were bound to arouse ulama. Reza Shah's identification with pre-Islamic kings was carried further by his son, who at a vastly wasteful 1971 celebration at Persepolis tried to give the world and Iranians the false impression that Iran had an uninterrupted twenty-five-hundred-year monarchical tradition (in fact there were a variety of titles for rulers—of areas that did not correspond to modern Iran—between the Muslim conquest and 1501, and again between 1722 and 1796). From abroad Ayatollah Khomaini denounced the celebration and monarchy itself.[8] The imposition of a new calendar dating from the pre-Islamic monarch Cyrus the Great instead of from Mohammad's *hijra* convinced many that the shah was out to uproot

Islam. The inclusion of some (though not most) vaqf land in land reform was also of some importance. The imprisonment of revered religious leaders, and their foreign or internal exile in the cases of Ayatollahs Khomaini and Taleqani, further aroused their colleagues and followers. It was also felt that the shah's downgrading of Islam was accompanied by his favoring of both foreigners and non-Muslim Iranians. In the case of the Baha'is, considered apostates from Islam by pious Muslims, this was a point that sometimes took on exaggerated proportions, while the words of some ulama occasionally went from anti-Zionism to anti-Semitism. A minority of Baha'is, Christians, and Jews had well-paying jobs and/or ties to foreigners or to the court; the importance of this was often exaggerated and so, like similar minorities elsewhere, these non-Muslims were sometimes resented. Officially the ulama and their partisans spoke and speak of protecting the recognized minorities. Resentment was also felt against reputed Freemasonic connections of some in the government and at court, as many considered Freemasonry anti-Islamic and pro-British.

The ending of Iraq-Iran cold and hot hostilities by treaty in 1975 resulted in a resumption of Iranian pilgrimages to Iraq in 1976, and an increasing number of tapes and writings reached Iran from Ayatollah Khomaini in Iraq. His uncompromising line gave courage to oppositional ulama within Iran, and much mosque preaching became increasingly hostile to the shah. Some within Iran, like Ayatollah Kazem Shariatmadari, took a more moderate line, but nonetheless eventually began to call for the full restoration of the 1906–07 constitution (meaning free elections, a government responsible to the majles, a weak shah, and a committee of mujtahids to veto bills not deemed in accord with Muslim law). The death of Khomaini's son Mostafa in Iraq in October 1977, assumed to be the work of SAVAK, added to the opposition.

In January 1978, the regime demonstrated the degree to which it miscalculated the strength of the religious opposition in taking one of its fatal missteps. Reportedly at the instigation of the shah, an article was published in the leading, semiofficial newspaper, *Ettela'at*, violently attacking and slandering Khomaini. The article emanated from Information Minister Daryush Homayun (one of several former oppositionist students abroad who rose high in the shah's regime). The two-column article was entitled "Iran and Red and Black Colonization" and signed with a pseudonym. After generalities on the White Revolution and "black reaction" (of the ulama), the article attacked a religious leader chosen to direct the movement: "an adventurer, without faith, and tied to the centers of colonialism . . . a man with a dubious past, tied to the more superficial and reactionary colonialists." This man was Ruhollah Khomaini, better known as "the Indian Sayyed." Although his ties to India had never been brought to light, it was clear that he had contacts with the British. In his youth he wrote love poems signed *Hindi* (the Indian). The article ended by saying that Khomaini was opposed to the shah's reforms, and suggested that he received large sums from the English (via an Arab) to continue his fight against the shah.

The promotion of such calumnies showed the concern of the regime to discredit Khomaini, but events proved it to be a bad miscalculation. The following day theological students in Qom staged a massive protest and sit-in, which was broken up by security forces. This brought on a violent confrontation, at least seventy were killed in two days, making this the bloodiest incident since 1963.

The newspaper attack on Khomaini and the Qom incident may be seen as a key point—January 1978—in which much of the initiative in the protest movement swung from the secular forces, with their letters, petitions, organizations, and political poetry readings, to the religiously led opposition. Even if the authorities had had the sense not to calumniate Khomaini, the religiously led movement would probably have developed as the leading oppositional force. The religious opposition, especially if one adds those who admired Shariati and the Mojahedin, appealed to far larger numbers than did the secular liberals, and in any mass protest it is virtually certain that these people would ultimately have been decisive and would have turned to the leaders they trusted most. The government had been largely successful over many years in suppressing secular protests and had left a clearer field for the less manageable religious opposition.

The ulama and bazaar leadership, sensing their new power and the grievances of their constituency, helped in 1978 to organize massive memorial demonstrations for those killed in previous incidents, taking place at traditional forty-day religious intervals. Here was a brilliant example of political use of Shi'i traditions; the government would risk truly massive demonstrations if it outlawed traditional mourning gatherings occurring at the proper and traditional intervals: such a prohibition would have been unheard of, even under the shah. In addition, the forty-day interval gave an excellent hiatus to regroup forces, spread the word orally, bring people together almost automatically without the need to argue about date and place, and to utilize spontaneous or ritual emotion to intensify opposition to the regime. At one of the first demonstrations, in Tabriz in February, many banks, shops, and cinemas were attacked and destroyed, and the cry, "Death to the shah," was first heard. These and other such acts of destruction continued in later protests. Human life was spared, even of those considered enemies, and except for rare incidents involving a very few persons at the high point of late revolutionary fervor, even American lives were inviolable. Banks, shops, and cinemas were considered symbols of dependence on the West and infidels (banks had a significant percentage of foreign capital, and cinemas showed mostly foreign, often sexy, films).

Among the followers both of Khomaini and of Shariati (whose ideas were rarely distinguished by the masses in 1978–79) were the bazaaris, meaning not only those who had shops in the bazaar but also those who carried on retail and export trade and manufacture of a traditional rather than a modern type. Bazaaris are not a class in the Marxist sense, as they have different relations to the means of production; the journeyman artisan or worker in a small bazaar factory is in a different position from a banker or moneylender, who may be quite wealthy; nonetheless the expression "bazaari" has meaning in its involvement with petty trade, production, and banking of a largely traditional or only slightly modernized nature, as well as its centering on bazaar areas and traditional Islamic culture. These people are sometimes called "petty bourgeois," but this term seems inadequate, as some are rich wholesalers and bankers and some are workers. Most of them are united in their resistance to dependence on the West and the spread of Western ways. Although Western goods are widely sold in the bazaars, the growth of supermarkets, department stores, large banks, and goods like machine-made carpeting that compete with Persian rugs added to Western control of Iran's economy and reduced the role of the bazaar.

Governmental favoring of nonbazaar trade and industry and various plans of "modernization" or dispersal of the bazaar, of which two have been discussed, were partly designed to weaken the bazaar's politico-economic cohesion and were seen as a threat. Among those who live much in the old way in the traditional economy, Western mores are often viewed with horror, and the "traditionalist" bazaar attitude along with the close family, financial, and cultural ties of the bazaar with the ulama, help explain the bazaar-ulama alliance that has been responsible for so much revolutionary activity in Iran since 1891. Religious taxes and gifts to the ulama for religious, educational, charitable, and political purposes come from bazaaris, account for a high percentage of ulama influence, and help cement the political ties between bazaar and mosque. In addition, bazaaris often held weekly "religious" meetings in homes, which provided an ideal network for discussing political problems and tactics. The extent and propinquity of small, open bazaar shops make the bazaar an easy area for rapid communication and organization.

Some in the modern economy who had recently moved from the bazaar were also attracted particularly by Shariati's blend of Islam with modern ideas. Despite the modernization of Iran, the bazaar remained a focal point of major political opposition movements from 1891 through 1979. This was partly due to the ease of organizing craft and religious circles that in time of crisis took on an increasingly political aspect. In addition, bazaaris have been closely tied to the ulama who, as noted, have given ideological leadership to many important opposi-tional movements. Most bazaaris are free of ties to the government, which might have made them hesitate (as did many in the modern middle class, often in governmental or quasi-governmental jobs) to join a really revolutionary movement. Although one tends to think of bazaaris as a group in decline, this is probably true only in a relative sense; the new middle class with Westernized educations and positions may have grown faster than they, but with the massive immigration from the countryside there is more need than ever before for petty retailers, bazaar wholesalers, and bazaar moneylenders and bankers, so that their numbers are considerable and have grown along with cities. According to Robert Graham, citing reliable estimates: "Despite the modernisation of the economy, the Bazaar still controls over two-thirds of domestic wholesale trade and accounts for at least 30 per cent of all imports . . . At the same time through its control of the carpet trade and other export items like nuts and dried fruits, the Bazaar has access to foreign exchange which has not been channelled through the official system. . . . One unofficial estimate puts Bazaari lending in 1976 at 15 per cent of private sector credit."[9]

Over the years the Pahlavis tried to reduce bazaar power by building new streets, shops, schools, and institutions away from it; by imposing grid patterns on bazaar streets, by controlling distribution, and by campaigns against "profiteers," chiefly bazaaris rather than the really rich, and by restricting cheap credit to bazaaris. Although a major shift in economic power to the modern sector occurred, bazaaris were neither cowed nor reduced in numbers.

One incident in the new militant bazaar-ulama alliance was a fight to keep Iran's most ubiquitous private bank, the Bank Saderat, considered by some to be the bazaaris' friend, from falling under the control of a Baha'i, Yazdani, who had acquired a 26 percent share in it. Working with ulama, bazaar merchants organized a campaign of withdrawals from the bank and Yazdani was forced to sell out. Bazaaris also helped to support families of victims of 1978's struggles, and provided financial support for the antiregime strikes that began in May 1978 among university students and teachers and in the fall spread to the workers and civil servants.

Another group important in the victory of the revolution was the subproletariat, often recent immigrants to town. These people lived in slums and shantytowns with few amenities; often left their families behind in the village; and suffered increasingly from the growing shortage of unskilled construction and other jobs from 1976 onward, combined with a rise in prices. Uprooted literally and culturally, and closer physically and culturally to the bazaar than to the modernized parts of town, they easily believed that drastic action should be taken to see that the oil billions they knew were streaming into Iran did something for them.

The key role of such rootless young males was first seen in the important Tabriz riot of February 1978, which began in commemoration of those killed in Qom in January but soon turned into a strong protest against the shah. The Azerbaijani police reportedly refused to act, and outside troops were called in, and began to shoot. A riot developed, led by youths, who attacked the banks, the headquarters of the shah's Rastakhiz party, cinemas, and liquor stores. Some Azerbaijani autonomist feeling and belief (based on facts) that the area was neglected by the center fed the movement. Radical students from Tabriz University also joined. According to some reports about one hundred people were killed and over six hundred arrested. This protest-to-riot pattern was to be repeated later in Iran's main cities. Although villagers living far from cities could not participate in such riots, many villagers who commuted to urban jobs did participate.[10]

Another important group of participants in the Iranian revolution, whose participation varied some by class and ideology but exceeded anything hitherto seen in Iran, were women. In the student movement within and outside Iran women had always played a role of some importance although, as in the West, most dominant leaders were men. Women were important among the guerillas even before 1977, and a number were jailed or died in shootouts. Since women's organizations had been homogenized into the official Iranian Women's Organization, women strongly opposed to the regime tended to shun such organizations and indeed generally avoided wholly feminist causes, which they mostly saw as divisive at a time when the main aim was to overthrow the shah and his regime. As in many revolutionary movements, many politically conscious women assumed that their participation in struggle and the victory of their cause would give to women what they desired. It should also be realized that many women did not consciously feel oppressed as women, and showed no interest in women's causes. Therefore, the moves of the shah's regime to modernize women's dress, education, and work patterns, which in any case mainly affected middle- and upper-class women, were not necessarily approved or even felt by the majority of Iran's women, while the entry of women into factory work or commercial carpetmaking added to their burden of labor. Women's participation in politics during and after the revolution was multiclass and gave many women a new sense of pride at their ability to organize, take action in the public sphere, and sometimes risk their lives.

In the cultural climate of the 1970s, those opposed to the shah's regime increasingly saw as bad everything the regime said was good.

Thus, as noted, we find the ironic phenomenon of some women university students from the mid–1970s on readopting Muslim modes of dress as a means of stressing their identity with Islam, seen as morally and politically superior to the ways of the regime, and/or of stressing their political opposition to the regime, whether or not they were believers. Even before the Revolution many tricky and important issues of principle regarding women were raised when Muslim and non-Muslim students tried to unite against the regime; on more than one occasion Muslim students demonstrated for sexually segregated dining halls and classes, and some women students were pressured into wearing the chador, while, on the other hand, university instructors or authorities reportedly sometimes refused admission to classes or examinations of chadored women.

Although women students played and play an important role in political demonstrations and activities, even more numerous in the demonstrations of 1978 were chadored bazaari women, who came out usually in separate ranks to participate in the mourning processions, where they had always been, but where their presence took on a new political meaning. As the threat of violence grew, women often marched bravely at the head of processions; participants recognized that this put the police and regime in a difficult position.

The size and courage of demonstrating crowds was again seen in Isfahan in July when three days of demonstrations led to numerous deaths and martial law. Aside from this there was a partial break in the pattern of escalating forty-day-interval demonstrations during June and July, and in the same period the shah made a number of promises of liberalization, including, notably, free elections with a variety of political parties to occur the following year. Westernized Iranians and foreigners present then can attest that this was a period of euphoria for Westernized liberals in Iran; they believed the liberal pressures and mass protests had sufficed to start the regime on a path of true liberalization from which it could not turn back, given the threat of renewed street action if it did. The possibility that street demonstrations might culminate in the shah's overthrow and a regime headed by Khomaini, still in exile, was scarcely discussed at this time by the new middle classes. Later in 1978 many of them were to join the revolution, but in June and July they almost universally miscalculated the situation.[11] (Those analysts who attribute the Iranian revolution to the "middle class" or "the bourgeoisie" without specifying which middle class or bourgeoisie are wide of the mark; modernized intellectuals were important to the verbal protests of 1977–78 but they and other Westernizers, aside from some of the students, were overshadowed by the active religiously oriented protests of 1978 until late in the year. Throughout 1978 most Westernizers misjudged the situation, first thinking that the shah's regime would stay in and reform, and later that the Revolution would allow them a significant postrevolutionary role.)

A lull on one summer day when demonstrations might have been expected to occur did not imply that things were quieting, as many intellectuals thought, but may have been a preparation for the holy month of Ramazan, when mass mobilization was easy. Already by early August the Shiraz International Festival, held under the auspices of the queen and considered by the religious a decadent sign of subservience to the non-Muslim West, was threatened with serious trouble and had to be canceled. Far more dramatic was the fire in the Rex Theatre in Abadan in August, in which hundreds were killed; the government tried to blame it on oppositional terrorists but the great majority of Iranians believed it to be a provocation by the shah via SAVAK. Although evidence points to gross incompetence and possible complicity by local authorities, it is questionable whether the shah, at a time of relative quiet which he hoped to preserve, would order an act that could only have the opposite effect. What counted, however, was what people thought, and the fire helped to rekindle active protests that would probably have occurred, if a bit later, in any case. (In 1980 a trial of one of the accused indicated that a religiously oriented group was responsible, possibly manipulated by police, and, according to some, perhaps had ties to higher clericals.)

In the face of vast protest, the shah tried to meet his problem with further concessions that still left power in his hands. He removed Amuzegar as premier and replaced him with Sharif-Emami, a longtime politician whom the shah had also used in 1960 to try to assuage the opposition. The shah allowed Sharif-Emami to widen political freedoms, but accompanied this with severe repression of active opposition. During Sharif-Emami's two-month premiership the press and majles debates became far freer, old political parties resurfaced, new ones were born, and orderly political demonstrations were allowed. A new ministry to protect religious affairs was created, casinos were closed, and the recent monarchy calendar that began with Cyrus the Great, not Mohammad's hijra, was abolished. A code to deal with royal family corruption was too little and too late. Sharif-Emami's reputation as a Freemason, a group that most Iranians associated with Western, and especially British, influence, added to his difficulties in attracting support.

In the same period repression became worse than ever. Although a peaceful demonstration that comprised over a million people occurred on September 5, three days later martial law was declared in the early morning hours, so that many did not hear of it, and on "Black Friday," September 8, those shot and killed in a massive but peaceful Tehran demonstration in Jaleh Square probably numbered from 500 to 900, though both higher and lower figures are given. This ended all real opportunity for an accommodation with the opposition, and two months later, in November, the shah ended the attempt and appointed General Gholam Reza Azhari prime minister in a new military government. (This followed riots and the burning of public buildings, which some think were caused by the army to force the shah to act.) Schools and universities were now closed, newspapers suspended, and meetings of over three persons in Tehran prohibited, although the new government was not as repressive as many had feared and did not cow the opposition. The arrest of ex-prime minister Hoveyda and ex-SAVAK head General Nasiri were widely regarded as scapegoating.

Throughout the 1977–78 period Khomaini's popularity grew. In this more than in previous revolutionary protest movements the urban poor and subproletariat were represented, and because of their large numbers they at first came out in greater strength than did factory workers and the middle classes, despite the latter's importance. For the urban poor Khomaini and his words were supreme guides, and as revolutionary anger, enthusiasm, and activity grew, Khomaini's refusal to make any compromise with the monarchy and his implication that problems could be solved by a return to Islamic ways had increasing appeal for the Muslim masses. Popular ayatollahs who stressed rather a return to full implementation of the 1906–07 constitution, whether the moderate Shariatmadari or the socially conscious Mahmud

Taleqani (whose arrest and imprisonment in the summer of 1977 was a further cause of discontent), were bound to lose influence to the more uncompromising Khomaini in revolutionary circumstances. In the fall there was the decisive entry of the industrial and salaried working classes, including the key oil workers, into the mass protest movement, and also of the new middle classes, represented chiefly by the revived coalition of some National Front elements, which was known as the National Front. Both groups, whatever the private views of some of their constituents, had little choice but to join forces with Khomaini. The latter, evidently in part because of Iranian pressure on Iraq, had been forced to leave Iraq and, after being refused entry to Kuwait, with permission from the shah to the French, took refuge near Paris in October 1978. This proved a foolish move by Iran's regime, as telephone, airplane, and cassette communication was easier than before, Iraqi controls on Khomaini ended, and worldwide television and press coverage of Khomaini vastly increased.

As people became increasingly fearless, enthusiastic, and aroused, even in the face of deaths in demonstrations, and as total opposition to the regime spread to new classes of people, there began the crucial stage of the revolution, with massive politico-economic strikes against the shah starting in late summer, lasting until the end of the Revolution, and virtually paralyzing the economy. In September began strikes in the Tehran oil refinery and at a large petrochemical complex at Bandar Shahpur, followed in days by a strike of NIOC workers at the main center of Ahwaz. Strikes then spread through the government and oil industry, so that by late October the production level had fallen to an average of 1.5 million barrels daily, about 28 percent of its former level. Leftist, liberal, and religious groups encouraged the strikes and discouraged acceptance of large wage settlements. By the time military government arrived few public services were functional. The military government pledged to end strikes, but instead they increased. Attempts to reimpose censorship were met by press strikes.

The return of oppositionists from abroad and the revival of protest in Iran encouraged open activity by guerilla groups, both in killing Iranian military and police leaders, and participating in oppositional demonstrations. Now the Feda'iyan and the Mojahedin were able to apply united front tactics effectively and to attract open members and followers. In the course of 1978 they became sizable movements, largely of young people, who were attracted partly by the more visible activity of these groups than of either the pro-Soviet or pro-Chinese Communist groups. (The Soviets and especially the Chinese refrained from criticizing the shah until the very end.) On the other hand, late 1978 also saw an increase in grassroots organization by the Khomaini supporters. All these groups as well as many others published newspapers, pamphlets, and posters that were widely and eagerly read and helped spread and influence revolutionary ideas.

From France, Khomaini's refusal to compromise with either the shah or the liberal constitutional monarchists, which was wholly consistent with his nature and ideology, was also just what his style of revolution needed. Karim Sanjabi visited him in the name of the National Front and emerged with a joint declaration that spoke of both Islam and democracy as basic principles; once the Revolution was won, however, Khomaini explicitly refused to put the same word, democracy, into either the title of the Republic or its constitution—a position consistent with his view that democracy was a Western import and Islam sufficed. Khomaini's statements in France convinced many secularists that he would support their rule. His indications that he did not want to rule directly were probably based on the false assumption that others would rule just as he wanted them to. The apparent democratic nationalist tone of many of his statements from France was largely due to the advice of his Western-educated entourage there—Bani Sadr, Ghotbzadeh, and Yazdi. Many revolutionaries knew only these French statements and not the theocratic ideas of his *Hokumat-e Islami*.

The Sanjabi-Khomaini visit and agreement were of great importance to the outcome of the Revolution, as they concluded a Khomaini-National Front alliance and probably foreclosed the possibility of a solution midway between the monarchy and the Islamic Republic and sealed the later failure of Shahpour Bakhtiar to implement such a solution.

The shah's failure either to win over or cow the growing opposition was shown in massive peaceful demonstrations in several cities, with probably over a million people in Tehran, on December 11, 1978, to mark Ashura, the anniversary of the death of Imam Hosain, seen as a martyred victim of autocracy. In this demonstration a resolution was passed asking Khomaini to lead Iran and calling on Iranians to struggle until the shah was overthrown. The shah tried to appease the opposition by finding a moderate oppositional prime minister and got Shahpour Bakhtiar, a signer of the 1977 National Front letter for civil liberties, to agree on December 30 to form a new constitutional government, provided the shah leave Iran indefinitely and a Regency Council be set up. Bakhtiar was denounced by his National Front colleagues, now allied with Khomaini, and was not redeemed by his release of political prisoners, his announced dismantlement of SAVAK, or promised changes in the economy and foreign relations.

Until late fall top American policy makers in Washington and Tehran, misled in part by their limited Iranian contacts and their reliance on SAVAK and Iranian officials for their knowledge of the opposition, were sure the shah's regime would last. By fall some in the State Department and in Iran were changing their views, and from early November Ambassador Sullivan cabled home his doubts that the shah, and later Bakhtiar, could win out. The embassy began secret contacts with the antileftist parts of the pro-Khomaini opposition, including National Front leaders, Bazargan, and some clericals, especially Ayatollah Mohammad Beheshti, a Khomaini follower recently returned from Europe. Many American policy makers thought, on the basis of Khomaini's recent statements and political inexperience, that in the event of a revolutionary victory Khomaini might step into the background and allow moderates to rule. The State Department seems to have approved a late, abortive plan for a National Front-Clerical ruling alliance with the shah effectively to bow out. (The shah's refusal to abdicate and the opposition's refusal to settle for less was one stumbling block.) This was the probable context of Ambassador Sullivan's plan to send an American envoy to meet with Khomaini, which was apparently blocked by National Security Adviser Brzezinski, who opposed the State Department's approach and actively promoted a hard line, which he thought could keep the shah in power.

Carter followed no clear policy but did send General R. Huyser to Iran in early January 1979 to report on the state of the armed forces and work to keep them unified and intact. If either Bakhtiar or a largely moderate government won out it was seen as important to keep the army intact as a conservative, anti-Communist, and potentially pro-

American force. Huyser worked to unify the generals behind Bakhtiar, with armed force or a coup as final options, but in the end key generals saw the cause was lost and did not fight. The unexpectedly rapid march of events and the continuing indecisiveness of the shah forestalled any possibility of a coup and paved the way for Khomaini's accession in February 1979. Neither the embassy nor most of Washington policy makers considered a coup a viable possibility by 1979, given the overwhelming strength of the revolutionaries. By late 1978 many in the embassy and State Department were convinced the shah could not last and were in contact with secular and religious figures who might enter a governmental coalition with which the American government could deal. American military intervention was not a serious possibility given the united strength of Iran's revolutionary movement, not to mention American post-Vietnam wariness of dubious military adventures.

American contacts with the opposition and lack of intervention for the shah made many anti-Khomaini Iranians believe that the United States was responsible for Khomaini's victory. It appears rather that the State Department was trying to make the best of what it saw as a bad situation; near the end there was no feasible way to stop the Khomaini movement, and so Americans tried to contact it and encourage its moderates in the hope of lessening its anti-American tone. No aid was given to the opposition, and apart from one late statement by Carter indicating uncertainty that the shah's rule would last, verbal and moral support for the shah, including regular counsel from Ambassador Sullivan, continued until the end. Brzezinski's hawkish proshah policies could not succeed, given the shah's lack of internal support and his objections to using massive force at a time he feared he would not live long and thought his young son should not inherit after a bloodbath.[12]

It seems unlikely that a different American policy in 1978–79 could have significantly changed the course of events. Neither of the two sides that alternately influenced Carter had much chance of influencing the Revolution: there was no practical way to save the shah, nor is there reason to think that Sullivan's people could have achieved their ends had they increased American contact with Khomaini and his coalition. Probably only a very different set of policies over the previous twenty-seven years could have led to different results.

As to the shah's vacillating carrot-and-stick behavior during the crisis it may first be said that, as in the case of United States attitudes and policy, there is no proof that different behavior in 1978 would have maintained his throne. Iranians had in the past heard many words and promises regarding freedom and especially economic betterment, and were now so resentful about autocracy, corruption, jailings, torture, and terrorization (which went far beyond those plotting against the regime), that they were unlikely to be impressed by promised concessions. This was all the more so in that palpable concessions by the shah in 1978 did not include sharing political power with the populace or even choosing a prime minister with a large popular base and freedom of action. The opposition feared that concessions like the promised future free elections could always be withdrawn as long as the shah remained anything more than a Western type of constitutional ruler, as envisaged in the 1906–07 constitution. The shah's concessions were always a step or more behind popular demands, and at the end the constitutional monarchy favored by some of the opposition was no longer acceptable to its pro-Khomaini majority. The shah did show himself weaker and more indecisive than most people expected. This was not only due to cancer and drugs, but echoed his weakness until 1953, which later remained hidden only when he was sure he was in command. Megalomania and insecurity went together, as with many similar ruling figures. His insecurity and suspicion extended to the United States, and he was unsure of American support, particularly if he should opt for harsh policies.

The possibility of the shah's using more military force throughout also posed several problems. First, before fall it would have seemed extreme, whereas by fall soldiers were refusing to fire on crowds and some even fraternized with them, especially conscripts and others who revered Khomaini and identified with the protestors; the shah did not want to risk more of this. Second (and this affected more than the military sphere), it seems likely that the shah long believed much of his own propaganda and also his toadying aides who assured him he was vastly popular and that the demonstrators were a minority of agitators who had misled people; he therefore long retained hope of regaining popularity by concessions, and did not wish to alienate more people by massacres. Third, the shah wished history to regard him as a great ruler who had beneficially transformed Iran, and massive slaughters (although one such was allowed in September) could only tarnish this image and make his son's succession, which he expected to be near, more difficult. Fourth, the shah's massive armed forces and secret police were not well trained for the situation they faced; they were designed on the one hand to give Iran the posture of an international great power, able to police areas beyond its borders, and on the other, in the case of the secret police, to infiltrate and hunt down small numbers of oppositionists. Weapons and training for crowd control had not been given priority—another sign of the shah's misreading his people. In a sense the shah was caught in the same situation as his American official sponsors; while it might at one time have been possible to suppress demonstrations and strikes by military force (though probably not without American aid), this would result in a government far more unpopular and repressive than that which began in 1953, given the far greater scope, revolutionary devotion, and unity of different political parties and groups in 1978 than in 1953.

The shah's growing megalomaniac self-confidence in the 1970s did not equip him to deal in a new and flexible way with unanticipated mass opposition, while his cancer, the drugs he was taking, and probably his doubts about American and British intentions, added to his tendency to withdraw and collapse in face of opposition, seeking his salvation from frequent advisory sessions with the American and British ambassadors rather than taking a strong and firm-sounding stand of any sort. The recent deaths of confidants Asadollah Alam and Manuchehr Eqbal added to his confusion.[13] The shah's turn to the American and British ambassadors indicates how much the system he had built had deprived him of supporters whose words he trusted and suggests his dependence on outside powers.

The new premier, Bakhtiar, to effect the kind of transition the moderates preferred, negotiated the shah's "temporary" departure on January 16, with a regency council of which he was a member. He ordered the release of all political prisoners and the dismantlement of SAVAK, began a review of all important foreign contracts, refused oil sales to Israel and South Africa, and declared he would make major cuts in military and nuclear-plant expenditures. None of this won him oppostion support, however, not even from the National Front, which had expelled him as a traitor.

Khomaini's followers were clamoring for his return from Paris; Bakhtiar stalled by closing the Tehran airport, but soon had to allow Khomaini's return to a massive welcome, on February 1, 1979. Four days later Khomaini appointed Mehdi Bazargan as the "real" prime minister, creating a situation known in some other revolutions as "dual power." For several days there was a standoff; according to some sources, Bazargan was secretly negotiating on behalf of Khomaini with the United States, SAVAK, and the army chiefs for an orderly transition of power. A showdown, however, began on the evening of February 9 when units of the elite Imperial Guard tried to suppress a Tehran rebellion of prorevolutionary air-force cadets and technicians (*homafars*), who resisted strongly. When word of the struggle reached the Feda'iyan and Mojahedin, as well as some other armed groups, they mobilized, distributed guns among members and sympathizers, and moved to support the struggling cadets and technicians. Successfully fending off the Imperial Guards, the fighters spent February 10 and 11 opening up prisons, police stations, armories, and Tehran's major military bases. Similar events occurred in the provinces. Hundreds of lives were lost but in two days power was effectively transferred. Guerillas and homafars, with the aid of religiously led groups, had routed the elite Imperial Guard. The crucial role of the guerillas was noted both in the Western and Iranian press.[14]

Robert Graham mentions "numerous mullah-led local committees" in the movement "led by the main guerilla groups,"[15] and oral sources also note molla-led groups, but there seems no doubt (despite occasional denials) that the leftist guerilla groups were of major importance in the military victory, as were the homafars themselves. This brought the transfer of power on February 11, 1979, to the coalition of Khomaini and his followers, including clericals, lay religious figures led by Barzagan, and, for a time, a few lay National Front and other ministers, notably Dr. Karim Sanjabi.

Numerous eyewitnesses have commented on the almost universal enthusiasm, discipline, mutual cooperation, and organization which not only added to the esprit and extent of the last months of the revolution and distributed supplies and heating oil during the revolutionary strikes, but helped make it impossible to break off one group from the others. Spontaneous or directed councils and committees to organize revolutionary guards, urban quarters, factories, and other institutions began in this period, and many continued after February when, however, prerevolutionary unity increasingly broke down.

The Revolution in Power: A Brief Survey

The main political events after the February 1979 Revolution largely followed the pre–1978 line of Khomaini and his clerical followers and increasingly destroyed or eroded the power and position of other groups, whether conservatives and liberals in the National Front and related groups; the secular or Muslim leftists; the national minorities (who in the case of the primarily Sunni Kurds, Turkomans, and Baluchis feared Shi'i theocracy); or even some high religious critics of Khomaini, notably Ayatollah Shariatmadari. Many in these groups opposed the desire of Khomaini and his followers for a straight referendum allowing people to choose between monarchy and an "Islamic Republic," either because the latter was undefined, because Khomaini explicitly refused to add the word "democratic" to the title, or because there should have been a wider range of better defined choices, with time for debate. Khomaini's forces won and the referendum was held in late March, with an overwhelming vote for the Islamic Republic. In Sunni Kurdish, Baluchi, and Turkoman areas, however, there were boycotts and some active fighting at the time of the referendum.

A similar, though more complex, fate attended the republic's new constitution; a draft less theocratic than many lay groups had feared was composed which, after disaccords on procedure, was presented in the summer of 1979 to an elected assembly of experts dominated by clerical and pro-Khomaini forces. The resulting document gave virtually all ultimate power though almost no defined duties to a faqih (religious jurist), that is, Khomaini during his lifetime, and either another religious leader or a religious committee in the future. This individual or group controlled the armed forces, could ratify the dismissal of the elected president, and had a number of similar veto powers should he wish to exercise them. The constitution also includes a prime minister and cabinet, an elected Parliament, and some libertarian and egalitarian language, but is capable of being interpreted in an authoritarian way. Despite fairly widespread opposition, including over-whelming boycotting of the referendum on the constitution in Kurdis-tan and a heavy boycott in Azerbaijan, which contributed to a much lower total vote than before, the constitution was heavily approved in late 1979.[16]

Early in 1980 Abolhasan Bani Sadr was elected president with 75 percent of the vote, but he, a lay Muslim recently returned from long exile in France, had built no organization to match that of the conserva-tive clerical wing of Khomaini supporters, and some observers feel that his then semianarchist views helped make him organizationally ineffec-tual. Well-organized Khomaini supporters, led by Ayatollah Beheshti and the Islamic Republican party (IRP), came out far ahead in the parliamentary elections of the spring of 1980 and dominated the Parliament. At that time, sections of the left and the minorities made up the main serious opposition to the regime. Although his views and pronouncements are closer to the clericals, Khomaini has not, as of early 1981, consistently supported either Beheshti or Bani Sadr, and has tried with scant success to dampen their escalating feud. In June 1980 Khomaini urged the conservatives to compromise with the Bani Sadr moderates in order to reverse Iran's disintegration, but later he scolded Bani Sadr for inaction. Khomaini's early 1981 statements indicate a desire that the two sides could stop their conflict, but no clear view of how to accomplish this. Khomaini was probably surprised as well as troubled by the disagreements among his followers, and hesi-tated to be seen as the unqualified supporter of either the IRP or Bani Sadr.

Despite their services to the Revolution and their mass following, especially in Tehran and the northern provinces, at no time were the guerillas or the Tudeh allowed to play a role in the government; religion did not lead Khomaini to accept the Mojahedin any more than secularism led the National Front to like the Feda'iyan. Official hostility to the Soviet Union and to communism were and are very strong. Both guerilla and nonguerilla leftists were deprived of govern-mental influence on all levels to the degree the government could do this. Although there were some periods of substantial free press and assembly, there were increasing crackdowns on the left's headquarters, their sale of literature, and their meetings, often carried on by bands of thugs who called themselves The Party of God (*Hezbollahis*) but had no open form of official identification. The first such concerted attack came in August–September 1979, when the fasting month of Ramazan and the government's military attacks on Kurdish autonomists created heightened feelings and a favorable opportunity for the government to crack down. Later, after some liberalization of the press and other spheres beginning in October 1979, attacks began again in late March 1980. Then a number of statements by Khomaini excoriated the left and helped inspire physical attacks on major university campuses in April, aimed at getting rid of "leftist" professors, silencing leftist students, and ousting left organizations which, after being removed from their headquarters in the summer, had taken refuge on campuses. In the first days this resulted in at least a thousand people wounded and many killed.

The violent renunciation of the left has extended sporadically to the Tudeh party, desperately wanting to keep its legality, which it saw as possible only if it essentially supported Khomaini and his followers. The Tudeh does not share the belief in the efficacy under some circumstances of illegal guerilla tactics held by the Mojahedin and some Feda'iyan, having suffered a great loss of influence during the years it was illegal and scarcely operated in Iran. Tudeh leaders, including the derisively nicknamed "Ayatollah" Kianuri, have continually defended Khomaini and his policies, citing the progressivism of ending the monarchy and expecially of the anti-imperialist break in dependence on the United States, as well as measures to help the poor.[17] The majority faction of the Feda'iyan followed a similar line in 1980 and early 1981. Tudeh leaders speak of wishing to avoid the errors they made under Mosaddeq, when they continued to attack him until quite late and did not support him on the crucial final day, but to some it seems that their desire for legality and open operation outweighs any attempt at serious Marxist analysis of Khomaini and those around him. The underlying analysis seems to be that Khomaini represents the "petty bourgeois nationalist" phase of a revolution that may move to the left. In the summer of 1979 the Tudeh succeeded in reestablishing their "mistakenly" suppressed newspaper, but it is not clear that even their current line will continue to save them. Ironically, the "Islamic" Mojahedin are in much greater conflict with the clerical rulers than are the main secular leftist groups, and their criticisms of the regime are closer to those of some smaller Marxist groups than are the writings of the Tudeh.

If left forces were those most rapidly and quickly attacked by the Revolutionary government (though not, as of February 1981, with such force as yet to send them back to the underground, guerilla or otherwise), a rather similar fate awaited some other elements of the coalition, even if their treatment was sometimes more genteel. The Revolution in 1979 retained a system of "dual government" with a prime minister and cabinet appointed provisionally, pending parliamentary elections and a new constitution, while a provisional "revolutionary council," whose membership was long secret, and a series of local *komitehs* (from French, *comité*) generally wielded real power, under the direction of Ayatollah Khomaini's close followers. The first provisional prime minister, Bazargan, included in his cabinet National Front secularists, notably Foreign Minister Karim Sanjabi, but these soon found they had no power and their acts were countermanded. They resigned and the National Front, a largely elderly and moderate constitutionalist group, went into eclipse. Only the breakoff left-liberal National Democratic Front, under the leading democratic lawyer and grandson of Mosaddeq, Hedayatollah Matin-Daftari, continued active, but its demonstrations and writings supporting suppressed newspapers and its support for demands by minorities like the Kurds, Turkomans, Arabs, and Baluchis brought its suppression in the summer of 1979, when Matin-Daftari had to go into hiding. Other lay liberals, notably another prominent lawyer, Hasan Nazih, who was made head of the NIOC but then fired, and Rahmatollah Moqaddam Maraghe'i, a prominent liberal activist, also went into hiding, on the basis of very dubious charges, as did the popular ex-presidential candidate Admiral Madani (all later escaped abroad). Although freedom of speech, assembly, and the press remain, as of February 1981, somewhat above what they were under the shah, they are far from what liberals or other opposition groups and parties expected and hoped for. Khomaini's December 1980 agreement to Bani Sadr's demand for an investigation into torture and 1981 references to torture by some leaders and signed petitions indicate its revival, while arbitrary executions are notorious. In 1979 SAVAK was essentially reconstituted as

SAVAMA, apparently with the advice of the ex-shah's friend since boyhood, the turncoat former director of the Imperial Inspectorate, Hosain Fardust.

The lay religious members of Khomaini's coalition have suffered a major diminution in power since the Revolution, accompanied by an increase in power for the clericals. Medhi Bazargan, provisional prime minister from February to November 1979, has described how difficult it was to accomplish anything when, on the one hand, he was not told in advance by Khomaini what would be acceptable but, on the other, his orders might be countermanded by Khomaini at any time.[18] Similar problems were faced by his foreign minister, Ibrahim Yazdi, who replaced Sanjabi, and later by Bani Sadr as president. (Despite his ties to Khomaini and his relative radicalism, Bani Sadr has often found himself as powerless in face of the clericals and Khomaini as did Bazargan.) By many Iranians, extending beyond the organized left, Bazargan, Yazdi, Ghotbzadeh and, by some, Bani Sadr, are seen as "Liberals" who would return Iran to dependence on the United States.

The November 4, 1979, taking of the American embassy and hostages by pro-Khomaini students with a go-ahead by at least one high clerical and approval at least after the fact by Khomaini was apparently only in part a response to admission of the ex-shah to a United States hospital on October 22. It also had other motives and gave clericals and radicals a means to forestall American attempts to increase military, political, and business ties to Iran and a tool to force the resignation of Bazargan and Yazdi, who were prevented from taking action against the students. Their fall was precipitated by their being shown on TV shaking hands with Brzezinski in Algiers, thus implying that they were tools of the Americans. Although anti-imperialists and leftists may have found reasons to rejoice at this and at further breaks with the United States, there seems no doubt that the hostage crisis both postponed serious dealing with Iran's desperate unemployment and other economic problems and, at least as of February 1981, redounded more to the benefit of Khomaini and the clericals than to that of the left or liberals. Just as imperialist and Kurdish threats were used to suppress the left in the summer of 1979, so in 1980 similar threats were used to rally support around Khomaini and further to put down the left, liberals, and the minorities. As had already happened to Bazargan and Yazdi, pragmatic lay religious politicians were put into the line of fire; the popular Bani Sadr and his foreign minister, Ghotbzadeh, had to make statements about the hostages and other matters based on their guesses or hopes of what the revolutionary council or Khomaini might do; often they guessed wrong and could take no action. American and international efforts to end the hostage crisis early in 1980 foundered largely on the impotence of Bani Sadr and Ghotbzadeh. (The ex-shah's death in July changed little.)

This mode of government keeps Khomaini above the battle; his constitutional position of faqih, confirmed by the plebiscite on the new constitution late in 1979, gives him most powers but no specific responsibilities. Similarly, powerful clericals like Beheshti could remain largely behind the scenes, encouraging a sort of backward mode of political operation. Instead of a consultative body including the chief executive making a decision that the executive announces and executes, there were numerous instances, concerning the hostages and other matters, of the president or foreign minister announcing a policy, the revolutionary council either vetoing it or splitting, and in some cases Ayatollah Khomaini making a pronouncement at the end that killed the whole policy. Khomaini has hoped for unity around his views but lacks the approach to practical politics necessary to encourage effective government. In 1980–81 effective power passed to the IRP parliamentary majority and its leaders, who named prime minister Raja'i and refused Bani Sadr a say in naming a cabinet.

Not only Ayatollah Shariatmadari, who spoke out against governmental policies throughout 1979, but most of the other older clerical leaders called "Great Ayatollahs" are reputed to oppose, on various grounds and to various degrees, Khomaini's policies and ideas, but it is hard for them to speak up as long as Khomaini is alive. In February 1981 Ayatollah Shirazi did make an open critical statement, however. Khomaini's top clerical followers come mainly from the ranks of his ex-students and disciples a generation below him, like Ayatollahs Montazeri and Beheshti, and do not have the religious stature of the Great Ayatollahs. Some Great Ayatollahs are more conservative than Khomaini on such questions as land reform and women's participation in politics, but most apparently oppose direct clerical rule.

Even though it is fairly normal for revolutionary regimes to set up new governing organs and to have trouble in starting things moving again, Iran seems to have had more difficulties than most in this direction, despite (and also because of) the fact that until the Iran-Iraq war that began in September 1980, Iran continued to produce enough oil to make $10–20 billion in oil-export income, given increased prices. (By early 1981 oil exports nearly regained their prewar level.) After the Revolution fewer efforts were made than in China, Eastern Europe, or some Third World socialist countries to retain managerial and technical talent in Iran by promising continued jobs with decent pay and conditions, and great numbers fled abroad. These individuals were not nearly offset by revolutionaries who returned home. Though some welfare measures were taken for the poor, for orphans, and for ex-prostitutes and others, there was no program to expand jobs, which in fact declined with the closing or reduced production of many large industries, so that unemployment is now about 3 million in a country with an economically active population of 11–12 million. Only agriculture experienced partial benefits, mainly from good weather, increased grain subsidies, the ending of controls that had helped urban dwellers and foreigners, and some new measures of land reform coming from below. Good statistics are lacking, but grain production has apparently risen, while that of some other important crops has fallen. The optimistic campaign to draw people back to villages cannot be expected to flourish unless both agricultural and nonagricultural employment are expanded in the villages. Tribespeople have reverted to more migrating, which is probably a net gain to the economy, but cannot be expected in itself to make a major contribution to production, given high population growth, even higher demand for meat, and the small number of nomads.[19] The nationalization of banks and many other companies and the reduced role of foreigners could be used to build up a more self-suff\u200bicent economy, but only if a means is achieved of operating them efficiently and for the benefit of the people within the framework of a functioning national economy. The government has been forced into continuing wage increases, generally to already favored sectors of labor, and into paying wages to workers in nonfunctioning enterprises. Capital flight, which began well before the Revolution with the buying of real estate and other investments and purchases abroad, has been huge. It goes far into the upper and upper middle classes, including both those who have fled Iran and those who have relatives abroad. Efforts to stop or slow it have been relatively ineffectual.

With all this, Khomaini retains considerable personal popularity, especially among the lower bazaar and poorer classes in the urban areas in regions where Persian is the first language. Movements for minority rights are strong among border linguistic minorities (all of whom have related groups across the borders)—the predominantly Sunni Kurds, Turkomans, and Baluchis, and the predominantely Shi'i Azerbaijanis and Arabs. The Kurds have been the most militant, and the government has used arms to combat them both in the summer of 1979 and more than once in 1980–81. The Azerbaijanis, at about 10 million, many of them outside the two Azerbaijan provinces, are a potential problem. When they were beginning to fight in Tabriz in December 1979, their spiritual leader Ayatollah Shariatmadari refused to voice support and agreed to the dissolution of the political party that represented their demands. In 1980 he was effectively silenced, but both he and the Azerbaijanis may reemerge. (In early 1981 Shariatmadari was reported to be receiving renewed visits and money.) The Arabs are a problem because they live in the oil-rich province of Khuzistan where the Abadan refinery is located, even though they no longer make up a majority of that province. A revival of bad relations and border incidents with Iraq meant that the Iraqis, even before their invasion of Khuzistan in September 1980, were suspected of backing both Arab and Kurdish minorities, which they clearly did after the invasion. The Arabs and Iraqis were logical suspects in numerous peacetime incidents against oil pipelines. Both the Arabs of southwest Iran and the Baluchis of the southeast are impoverished, which creates another grievance. There was not, however, the mass Iranian Arab defection to Iraq that the Iraqis expected.

These and other minorities for whom Persian is a second language apparently constitute slightly over half of Iran's population, but they again are not united with each other. The Persians are more united. Some among the minority peoples support Khomaini, but his real support comes from lower-class Persians, and also from religious students and ulama. Khomaini decreed a number of measures for the poor early in the Revolution that would abolish or lower their costs of electricity, gas, and housing; and although most of this has remained on paper, there have been some serious efforts to house the poor and keep them fed, and this is appreciated by the masses. The "Manichaean" world outlook long held by many Iranians, in which all that is good can be attributed to God and his representatives and all that is bad to satanic forces (American, royalist, Zionist, or some other) helps maintain Khomaini's position and virtue, as does the political system described above that deflects criticism onto lay subordinates. The legacy of prerevolutionary policies provides continuing problems for Iran, but the continuing focus on these problems and on supposed CIA, United States, and allied "liberal" activity at a time when internal analysis, planning, and reconstruciton are desperately needed seems dangerous to Iran's future. It also encourages the association of internal critics with foreign enemies, and hence the silencing of such critics. Two of Khomaini's June 1980 speeches stressing the internal causes of Iran's troubles broke with the dominant trend, but the Iraqi invasion was made the occasion to blame the war and other problems on the United States. While anti-American feeling is comprehensible in view of events since 1953, it often substitutes sloganeering and internal witch-hunting for serious analysis and constructive action.

There are still too many contradictory tendencies in the Iranian Revolution to predict even the general lines of its future, but it is relevant to note that both in major lines of foreign and domestic policy discussed above and in its "Islamic" steps—suspension of the Family Protection Law, outlawing of coeducation and of women magistrates, Islamization of education at all levels, reestablishment of Islamic law and judges, outlawing of liquor and gambling and of much music and dance, and in its severe punishments—it appears to be headed now very much on the lines adumbrated by Ayatollah Khomaini a decade ago. To the degree consistent with modern technological civilization (which Khomaini does not oppose per se) Islamic law is being reestablished. However, Khomaini's anti-imperialist and anti-Western sentiments sometimes outweigh his respect for Islamic law. Islamic law both Shi'i and Sunni, as Khomaini must know, supports the inviolability of diplomats visiting a Muslim country from abroad, but this point of Muslim law was not raised in Iran during the hostage crisis. (As on many legal questions, however, there are enough varying precedents and latitude for interpretation that a new interpretation could be given were it felt necessary.)[20] In both the hostage crisis and in prewar verbal provocation of Iraq, the Iranian regime created for itself more problems than it solved in the name of Islam and anti-imperialism. Anti-imperialist and antiforeign slogans have been used to bolster rule by inexperienced and impractical clerics.

Anti-imperialism, focused on the United States and secondarily Israel and the Soviet Union, is an important point in Khomaini's outlook, accounting for much of his past and present popularity even beyond the borders of true believers. Relations with Israel stopped immediately, relations with the Palestine Liberation Organization stepped up, and relations with the United States deteriorated and continued at a low point throughout 1980, mainly because of the lengthy hostage crisis. Another point of Khomaini's policy was its opposition to kings in general and the Pahlavis in particular. Although from the outside it may appear that this point lost its force once Khomaini took power, this is not the view of many Iranians. Basing themselves on frequent foreign, and especially American, intervention in favor of dictators and royal families, many Iranians believe that the United States will intervene to reinstate either the ex-shah's son, General Oveissi, or Shahpour Bakhtiar (whose supporters include many wealthy people with former ties to the shah, and who has openly called for United States support). Bakhtiar and Oveissi were, however, widely discredited by their dealings with Iraq. Khomaini, whose political efficacy against kings and their supporters has been demonstrated, is still seen as an effective defender against foreign-backed counter-revolutionary plots. As long as Khomaini is ascetic and anti-imperialist, most Iranians will not compare him to the shah, although the modern middle class, the minorities, many leftists, and a growing discontented group may have different views. As noted, Khomaini continually associates himself with the needs of the poor or "dispossessed" and has taken steps to implement this identification, which adds to his popularity. (This analysis avoids, only because they are so frequently noted, his personal charisma, his political shrewdness in getting what he wants, and the deep religious veneration felt for him by many of his followers.) It should be noted, however, that he has been most effective as one who said *no* to things people did not want: to the shah, to American influence or control, to the wholesale renunciation of Irano-Islamic culture in favor of Western fads, to the ever widening income gap and conspicuous consumption by the Westernized elite, to flaunted immorality, and so forth. Even two years after the Revolution, nay-saying is more prominent and effective than yea-saying.

Reports from on-the-scene observers in 1980–81 say, however, that complaints against the regime, against hardships, and against mollas are heard everywhere.[21] The buildup of antigovernmental demonstrations and riots beginning in November and December 1980, just when the war was in some ways unifying people to defend Iran's territory, is significant. As of early 1981, the clerical party has more power than Bani Sadr's, but this may change. Bani Sadr has considerable support in the army and among various political groups ranging from left to right. Whether Bani Sadr or someone else with practical ideas on how to build up a functioning, nondependent, more egalitarian economy will have an opportunity to mobilize people who can pull Iran together and create a new economy and society remains to be seen. It is not to be excluded that a popular exile like Admiral Madani or even a relative unknown may emerge after Khomaini's death, or that an IRP leader may come to rule more effectively at that time; on the other hand, civil strife or a coup are also possible.

On the level of class analysis, there have been as many differences of opinion among analysts of this Revolution as among historians of other great revolutions. There were clearly few classes or groups whose support of the ex-shah was solid enough to withstand the onslaught of a large popular movement. Businessmen and bureaucrats who had profited from his regime were not willing to risk their lives or money to save it, and even the army proved less united and decisive than might have been predicted. Classes that had felt some benefits from the regime, including many civil servants and professionals, businessmen, and skilled factory workers, also had major grievances, such as lack of freedom to speak and organize. Many of them came late to the revolution but were ready to join into nonrevolutionary protests, and in the end, into the Revolution itself, where massive strikes ultimately became crucial. The bulk of the demonstrations in the first half of 1978 came from groups not usually identified as social classes but still identifiable as meaningful entities—the bazaar classes, secular and religious students, the urban subproletariat, and clericals. Politically one may roughly identify the National Front and its related groups with the "new" middle class; the clerical groups and parties with the bazaaris (many now dissatisfied), the subproletariat, and some students; and the secular and religious leftist groups with many students, workers, and intellectuals. There are also regional differences, with the left strong among the Kurds and across the north. As many of the minority areas are poorer, and have a less flourishing middle class, than the majority Persian areas, there is also a class or social element in many of the minorities' demands for greater autonomy and equality of treatment in practice as well as theory.

Trends since the Revolution may also be seen partly in social or class terms, although here too the subject is controversial and not clearcut. Events since February 1979 include some acts of economic and political revolution that are defeats for the business classes (including some wealthy bazaaris as well as men in the newer business class). The role of private enterprise and management has been greatly reduced by large-scale nationalizations of industries and banks. Salary reductions at the higher levels, along with raises on the lower levels, have been attempted with some success. Many Iranians believe that the reduced power of top business elements and the end of the court apparatus and its policies have greatly reduced the chance that Iran will return to its former dependence on outside powers like the United States and their policies, and this could prove true if a popularly oriented, more self-sufficient economy were built up.

During and after the Revolution many in the popular classes scored gains by their own efforts: many nomads went back to a more economically rational and productive migratory system; some peasants occupied land they were tilling, and in many cases succeeded in holding onto it; and widespread strikes brought increased wages and greater worker participation in the running of industry, including many factory committees that exercized varying degrees of power. As elsewhere, the authorities tend to discourage such autonomous revolutionary efforts, preferring to aid the poor rather than let them control their own destinies. Inflation, unemployment, the lack of a planned or really functioning economy, and government efforts to stop strikes and other unauthorized popular steps make it problematic whether the Revolution will ultimately bring gains in participation and living standards for the popular classes, however. Many leading clericals lack Khomaini

and Bani Sadr's concern for the masses. Many politically powerful
mollas (generally supported by Parliament) are more concerned in
practice with restoring Muslim law, enforced by Muslim judges, and
with putting down those considered dissidents—whether leftists, liberals, or national minorities—and by these and other means increasing
their own power and wealth than with allowing President Bani Sadr or
others to rebuild an economy and society to meet the basic needs of
Iranians. In addition, the problems of the urban industrial economy are
even more complex than are those of the rural economy, and unlikely to
be met only by self-management or by simple breaks with the ex-shah's
policies. The industrial economy requires planning, technically trained
personnel and management, and, if exports are to grow to meet the
inevitable decline in oil production, wages and inflation cannot continue to race ahead of productivity. All this requires well-thought-out
adjustments between the needs of Iran as a whole and the demands of
workers. Since the Revolution the modern sector of the economy has
functioned very badly, many plants are closed, and the sector produces
at about one-third of capacity.

Before the Iraqi invasion, anticlerical feeling was increasingly being
expressed even in the big cities that had supported Islamic ideology.
Although the first months of the war for a time revived the strength of
Islamic forces, complaints resumed and the IRP's future is problemati-
cal as long as major economic, social, and cultural problems remain.[22]

The suicidal hostage rescue attempt by the American government in
April 1980 probably set back negotiations for the hostages' liberation,
but unofficial negotiations resumed in the summer before the Iraqi
invasion of Iran. The war apparently interrupted negotiations, but
agreement was finally reached, on terms almost wholly favorable to the
United States, that did not meet any of Iran's original demands. The
final resolution of the American hostage crisis after long, interrupted
negotiations in which a turning point was Khomaini's advocacy of
more realistic terms in September 1980, and the release of the hostages
on President Reagan's inauguration day, January 20, 1981, had mixed
effects in Iran. It appears to have encouraged open criticism of the
ruling IRP, with Bani Sadr noting that their prolongation of the crisis
and its final terms brought a net loss for Iran, while other intellectuals

made more open criticisms of Iran's de facto IRP rulers than they had done before. Petitions were circulated signed by prominent antishah writers criticizing the regime for torture and limits on human rights. One hopes that both the hostage crisis and Iran's continuing economic and political problems have created a renewed sense of realism among many Iranians, and that the enthusiasm and independent action which inspired many of them during and after the Revolution may be channeled from simplistic solutions and sloganeering into the hard work of building a society that more fully meets the needs and desires of most Iranians.

As of March 1981, however, what is notable is not the unity or realism of Iranians, but growing discontent and disunity. Pro-Bani Sadr and anti-IRP meetings, not only in Tehran and other cities, but in small towns, are often broken up by Hezbollahis or other thugs. At one Tehran pro-Bani Sadr meeting in early March 1981 the Hezbollahis were counterattacked and identifications indicating official governmental ties were reportedly found on them; this was followed by threats in parliament to remove and try Bani Sadr.[23] At about the same time the first hints were made that the Iranian government may not be as uncompromising as it has always said about not negotiating the Iran-Iraq war until all Iraqi troops leave, or about making no concessions. In that war there have developed two rival military forces: First, the regular army using regular military tactics backed by Bani Sadr, who is frequently at the front; the army has regained much prestige from its creditable performance in the war. Second, there are the *pasdaran*, revolutionary guards, created during the Revolution and following largely guerilla tactics, backed by the IRP and various Islamic radicals. Following Khomaini's death, civil strife, with possible exile participation, cannot be ruled out.

The current political lineup is confusing in political and religious, as well as class terms. The IRP has both rightist and radical Muslim backing, and qualified backing from the secular leftist Tudeh and Feda'iyan majority; the opposition includes rightists, secular liberals, Islamic Third Worldists like Bani Sadr, and the Islamic leftist Mojahedin and some smaller leftist groups, as well as Sunnis, minorities, and some Shi'i ulama. Very few wish to return to the old regime, and many still hope that the élan and positive aims of the Revolution may be regained in order to achieve a society with popular participation, organized government and institutions, and a functioning and more egalitarian economy. Most who participated in the Revolution were fighting, not for clerical rule, but for an ideological vision of Islam that embodied ideals of a just society that the secularists voiced in other terms. These ideals remain alive, however great disillusionment with clerical government may be.

CONCLUSION

A major thread tying together many aspects of nineteenth- and twentieth-century Iranian history has been Iran's relations with Western countries—both as they existed in reality and as they were and are perceived by Iranians and Westerners. Already in the early nineteenth century many Iranians were concerned with the presence of French and British advisers and especially with the two wars against the Russian "infidels." These wars not only lost important territories, initiated the series of unequal treaties including extraterritoriality with Westerners, and helped incite Iran's first major antiforeign incident, against Griboyedov, but they also put new financial burdens on the government and on the Iranians they taxed. The cheap entry of foreign manufactures, supported by treaty limitations on tariffs, brought complaints from Iranian artisans and merchants from at least the 1830s onward. In the course of the nineteenth century, Iran's trade relations with the West grew, and Iran's exports changed from primarily wool, silk, and textiles, to the newer cash crops of opium, cotton, tobacco, dried fruits and nuts, and others, which were often grown on land bought by merchants. As detailed above, many poor peasants and artisans suffered from these changes, while even some merchants who profited resented the privileged treaty position of Western merchants. These were among the causes leading to growing economic discontent in the nineteenth century.

The Qajar government, plagued by the decentralizing forces of geography, nomadism, and independent ulama and bazaar classes, accomplished little of the centralizing "reform from above" seen in Mediterranean countries like Turkey, Egypt, and Tunisia. In addition to the difficulties of reforming Iran, the Qajars lacked many promising reformers; Prince Abbas Mirza, who modernized Azerbaijan's army and encouraged modern education in Azerbaijan early in the century, died before his accession. The later reforming prime ministers, Amir Kabir, Moshir ad-Dauleh, and Amin ad-Dauleh, were all dismissed before they could carry through their reform programs—largely because of the hostility of decentralizing or vested interests that would have been hurt by centralizing reform. No Qajar shah was a consistent reformer, and none was even effective in trying to build up a strong, centralized army.

In Iran, as in many Third World countries, the official reformers from above were followed by critics of the government, some of whom held official posts at times, but many of whom did not. Among the former group the best known is Malkom Khan, who worked for governmental reorganization, the rule of law, and sometimes constitutionalism, and who published a newspaper against the government after his dismissal as an official in 1889. Among the unofficial critics the best known is Jamal ad-Din "al-Afghani"; although he spent few of his adult years in Iran, in the 1886–91 period, he had considerable influence in awakening Iranians to the use of propaganda, leaflets, and speeches against the government's sale of Iran to foreigners. It was the spate of Qajar concessions to Westerners, which rose dramatically after 1888, that aroused the bazaar classes, the ulama, and intellectuals against the government and foreigners, and culminated in a successful movement against a British tobacco concession, 1890–92. The growth of secular and religiously led opposition to the government led to the Constitutional Revolution of 1905–11, which gave Iran a Western-style constitution. In this period the ulama were upset about direct Western encroachments in the land of Islam, but they were not then concerned over Western intellectual borrowings, which had not taken on the overwhelming importance that they did under the Pahlavis. Between 1911 and 1960 most critical writers were secularists, but then came the revived Islamic opposition.

In the years before the 1905-11 revolution Russia was seen as the biggest threat to Iranian independence, and liberals and even some ulama placed hope in Great Britain, long Russia's biggest rival, to help protect Iran and its fledgling revolution against Russian hostility. When Great Britain and Russia signed their 1907 entente dividing Iran into spheres of influence, however, Iranians felt bitterly betrayed, and believed the British had sold out them and their revolution. Feelings against Great Britain after this were stronger than feelings against Russia, as nothing had been expected of Russia, whereas Great Britain had been seen as more of a supporter of Iran's independence and integrity. When Great Britain backed the Russo-British ultimatum that ended in Iranian Revolution in 1911 these feelings intensified, as they did again with Britain's proposed 1919 treaty that would have made Iran a virtual protectorate. Further anti-British feeling was enflamed by the oil issue, where Iranians could see that after the British concession and the discovery of oil in 1908 by far the lion's share of profit from a wasting resource was going to Great Britain. These feelings were already expressed in the dispute of 1932, and came out much more strongly in the postwar disagreements that culminated in the nationalization of oil and the Mosaddeq period.

If the British, once regarded by many as relatively friendly, were transformed for many into an enemy after the Constitutional Revolution, a similar fate befell the Americans after the Mosaddeq period, and for similar reasons. Americans had generally been well regarded early in the twentieth century, when individual Americans helped in the Constitutional Revolution and in founding schools, and Morgan Shuster had made valiant efforts to help build up an independent Iranian economy and enforce tax collection. Even more mixed figures like Millspaugh were not objects of widespread dislike, and it was only beginning in World War II when Americans, backed by their government, became heavily involved with military and gendarmerie training that doubts arose. The real change in widespread Iranian nationalist feeling about American policy, however, came when the Americans, after indicating support for Iranian grievances against the Anglo-Iranian Oil Company, gradually changed their position, and went along with the worldwide blockade on Iranian oil initiated and partially enforced by the AIOC. Feelings against the United States government became far stronger when it rapidly became known that the United States was heavily involved in the 1953 overthrow of Mosaddeq. American support over twenty-five years for the Shah's dictatorship and nearly all its ways added to this anti-American feeling. Hence, in both the British and American cases, however exaggerated and paranoid some charges by some Iranians may be, suspiciousness and hostility have their roots in real and important occurrences; chiefly, participation in the overthrow of popular revolutionary movements and support of unpopular governments. This antirevolutionary participation was all the more traumatic for Iranians in that it involved a power hitherto considered largely friendly, or at least a clear lesser of evils, so that distrust of anything said by the representatives of either America or Britian (or by others in their behalf) increased. (For every strange-seeming Iranian character trait, as with "mistrust" or "paranoia," one can nearly always find partially explanatory causes in Iranian history.)

Iranians see foreign powers, which recently meant mainly the Americans, as using them for their own purposes: always for Iran's strategic role, with the hope of scoring gains and stopping gains by others, chiefly the Russians; in the twentieth century for oil; and by the Americans also as a gendarme of the region against Soviet or Communist advance. Foreign governments have also promoted exports, investments, construction of infrastructure, and banking by their nationals or governments in Iran. As noted, huge American sales of arms, agricultural equipment, high technology, and consumer goods inadvertently helped destabilize Iran's economy and contributed to the Iranian Revolution. However wrong and self-defeating have been many of the methods and policies used in Iran since that Revolution, one may understand the Iranians' widespread desire to demonstrate their release from foreign control and foreign ways and to build up an economy, society, and culture that are independent or freely interdependent, rather than subordinate to Western powers.

NOTES

Chapter 1

1. See W. Montgomery Watt, *Muhammad at Mecca* (Oxford, 1953) and *Muhammad at Medina* (Oxford, 1956); Maxime Rodinson, "The Life of Muhammad and the Sociological Problem of the Beginnings of Islam," *Diogenes,* 20 (Winter 1957); 28–51, and *Mohammad,* trans. A. Carter (London, 1971).

2. On Shi'i history see A. Bausani, *Persia Religiosa* (Milan, 1959); M. G. S. Hodgson, *The Order of Assassins* (The Hague, 1955); B. Lewis, *The Origins of Isma'ilism* (Cambridge, 1940), and *The Assassins* (New York, 1968); W. M. Watt, *Islam and the Integration of Society* (London, 1961) and the works below.

3. W. M. Watt, "The Reappraisal of Abbasid Shi'ism," in G. Makdisi, ed., *Arabic and Islamic Studies in Honour of Hamilton A. R. Gibb* (Leiden, 1965).

4. Watt, "Reappraisal," p. 653.

5. On these groups see especially John K. Birge, *The Bektashi Order of Dervishes* (London, 1937); C. Huart, *Textes persans relatifs a la secte des Houroufis* (Leiden, 1909); Michel M. Mazzaoui, *The Origins of the Safawids* (Wiesbaden, 1972); V. Minorsky, *Notes sur la secte des Ahle-Haqq* (Paris, 1921); and C. Cahen, "Le problème du shi'isme dans l'Asie Mineure turque préottomane," in *Le Shi'isme imamite* (Paris, 1970).

6. Hasan-i-Rumlu, *Ahsanu't-Tawarikh,* C. N. Seddon, trans. (Baroda, India, 1934), p. 27.

7. (In order): Hanna Sohrweide, "Der Sieg der Safaviden in Persien und seine Rückwirkungen auf die Schiiten Anatoliens im 16. Jahrhundert," *Der Islam,* 41 (1965): 106–09; C. Grey, ed. and trans., *A Narrative of Italian Travels in Persia, in the Fifteenth and Sixteenth Centuries* (London, 1873), accounts by C. Zeno, p. 59, an Anonymous Merchant, p. 172, and V. d'Alessandri, p. 223; J. Chardin, *Voyages de Monsieur le Chevalier Chardin en Perse et autres lieux de l'Orient* (Amsterdam, 1711), 2: 52, 275–81.

8. See E. G. Browne, *A Literary History of Persia,* 4 (Cambridge, 1928, reprinted 1953): 73–78. See also J. Aubin, "La Politique religieuse des Safavides," in *Le Shi'isme imamite.*

9. See Grey, ed., *Italian Travels,* pp. 206–23, and Z. V. Togan, "Sur l'origine des Safavides," in *Mélanges Louis Massignon,* 3 (Damascus, 1957): 345–57.

10. As some scholars have maintained that political claims by the mujtahids are very recent, it is worth repeating at some length what Chardin says in the late seventeenth

century: "many of them [mujtahids] maintain that it is not at all true that the Succession of Imams was lost, and that there is nobody today who has at least part of the charge; and that it is even impossible that this occur, but one must believe on the contrary that the succession of Imams continues always and that there is always someone who has the charge of Lieutenant of God on earth. . . . They teach that the *Imam* should be sought particularly among the . . . *Mujtahid*(s)" (*Voyages,* 2: 337). And "The People of the church . . . and all those who profess the strict observation of religion, hold that in the absence of the Imam, the royal place should be filled by a Mujtahid . . . 'How is it possible,' say the people of the Church, 'that these impious . . . Kings, drinkers of wine, consumed by passion, be the vicars of God, and that they have communication with heaven? . . . Our kings being iniquitous and unjust men, their domination is a tyranny, to which God has subjected us to punish us, after having taken from the world the legitimate successor of his Prophet. The supreme throne of the universe belongs only to a mujtahid, or man who possesses sanctity and science above most people. It is true that since the mujtahid is holy, and consequently a man of peace, there must be a king who carries a sword for the exercise of justice, but he must be only like his minister and dependent on him." (Chardin, *Voyages,* 2: 207–08.) Playing down the ulama's premodern political claims are J. Eliash, "Misconceptions Regarding the Juridical Status of the Iranian 'Ulama,' " *International Journal of Middle East Studies,* vol. 10 no. 1 (1979): 9–25; and S. A. Arjomand, "Political Action and Legitimate Domination in Shi'ite Iran: Fourteenth to Eighteenth Centuries A.D.," *Archives Européennes de Sociologie,* vol. 20 no. 1 (1979): 59–109.

11. The Twelver Creed by al-Allama al-Hilli, *al-Babu'l-Hadi 'Ashar,* trans. W. M. Miller (London, 1928), praises the Mu'tazilites, stresses the rationality and comprehensible justice of God, and says that men have free will and that certain things are incumbent on God. See also W. Madelung, "Imamism and Mu'tazilite Theology," in *Le Shi'isme Imamite.* Thanks to N. Keddie's 1979–80 graduate seminar, especially to J. Cole and T. Shimamoto, for aiding in this analysis.

12. See Comte de Gobineau, *Religions et philosophies dans l' Asie Centrale* (Paris, 1957), pp. 35–39.

Chapter 2

1. On the contrasting centralizing role of cannons and decentralizing role of good handguns see H. Inalcik, "The Socio-Political Effects of the Diffusion of Fire-arms in the Middle East," in V. Parry and M. Yapp, eds., *War, Technology, and Society in the Middle East* (London and New York, 1975). The point on the importance of rifles to the resurgence of tribes in eighteenth-century Iran was suggested to me on the basis of research in progress by Robert McDaniel. Among the works showing significant eighteenth-century socioeconomic change are T. Naff and R. Owen, eds., *Studies in Eighteenth Century Islamic History* (Carbondale, Ill. 1977); N. Berkes, *The Development of Secularism in Turkey* (Montreal, 1964); and A. Hourani, "The Changing Face of the Fertile Crescent in the Eighteenth Century," *Studia Islamica,* 8 (1957): 89–122.

2. The estimates are by C. Issawi, ed., *The Economic History of Iran: 1800–1914* (Chicago, 1971), p. 20. A detailed study of a shorter period is G. G. Gilbar, "Demographic Developments in Late Qajar Persia, 1810–1906," *Asian and African Studies* vol. 11, no. 2 (1976): 125–56.

3. More detailed analyses of the role of tribes in Iran and the Middle East are found in articles by N. R. Keddie, "Is There a Middle East?" *International Journal of Middle East Studies*, vol. 4, no. 3 (1973): 255–71; "Socio-Economic Change in the Middle East since 1800: A Comparative Analysis," in A. Udovitch, ed., *The Islamic Middle East, 700–1900: Studies in Social and Economic History* (Princeton, Darwin Press, 1981); and "Pre-Capitalist Structures in the Middle East," in N. R. Keddie, *The Middle East and Beyond* (London, 1981). There is a large recent literature on Iranian tribes by authors including G. R. Garthwaite and J. P. Digard on the Bakhtiaris; L. G. Beck and P. Oberling on the Qashqa'i; W. Irons on the Turkomans; P. Saltzman and B. Spooner on the Baluchis; R. and N. Tapper on the Shahsevan; G. Chaliand, ed. *People Without a Country: The Kurds and Kurdistan* (London, 1980), and M. Van Bruinessen on the Kurds, and D. Bradburd and L. Helfgott on theoretical questions.

4. On the Qajar bureaucracy see the article by A. R. Sheikholeslami in A. Banani, ed., *State and Society in Iran* (special issue of *Iranian Studies*, 1978); and S. Bakhash, *Iran: Monarchy, Bureaucracy, and Reform under the Qajars, 1858–1896* (London, 1978). In the literature important men are known either by their given names, often preceded by the honorific "Mirza" and followed by the honorific "Khan," or by titles, which may change, or as here by the name followed by the title. In the latter case we italicize the title to distinguish it from the name. Most titles were abolished under Reza Shah, who also introduced family names. (The word "Mirza" *before* a name means an educated man; *after* a name it keeps its original meaning of a royal prince.)

5. On the disruptive economic impact of opium see the important article by Roger Olson in M. Bonine and N. Keddie, eds., *Modern Iran: The Dialectics of Continuity and Change* (paperback, *Continuity and Change in Modern Iran*) (Albany, 1981). Overviews of nineteenth- and twentieth-century agricultural changes are in N. R. Keddie, "Stratification, Social Control, and Capitalism in Iranian Villages, before and after Land Reform," *Rural Politics and Social Change in the Middle East*, ed. R. Antoun and I. Harik (Bloomington, Ind., 1972), reprinted in N. R. Keddie, *Iran: Religion, Politics and Society* (London, 1980), and A. K. S. Lambton, *Landlord and Peasant in Persia* (London, 1953, reprinted 1969).

6. This is suggested to us by the studies of leading families in Maragheh by M. J. Good and in Shiraz by Wm. Royce in M. Bonine and N. Keddie, eds., *Modern Iran*, which suggest considerable long-term continuity until at least the Reza Shah period, as does the ongoing study of mobility in various social strata in Shiraz being done by Ahmad Ashraf and Ali Banuazizi. This contrasts to the high mobility in Tehran elite families, most of whom came from elsewhere, revealed by the ongoing work of Constance Cronin on Tehran.

7. There has yet to be a book-length study of women's religious lives or women mollas, although Judith Goldstein and other women have done fieldwork in this area and several Western women including myself have witnessed women's ceremonies.

Research in Iran was largely inspired by the first Western work to deal extensively with Shi'i women's religious ceremonies and mollas, E. W. Fernea's enthralling account of life in a Iraqi village, *Guests of the Sheik* (Garden City, N.Y., 1965).

8. On the harem as a center of useful work and management see A. L. Marsot, "The Revolutionary Gentlewomen in Egypt," in L. Beck and N. Keddie, eds., *Women in the Muslim World* (Cambridge, Mass., 1978).

9. J. Atkinson, trans., *Customs and Manners of the Women of Persia* (New York, 1971; reprint of 1832 ed.); A. Chodzko, "Code de la femme chez les persans," unidentified offprint at the Institut Nationale des Langues Orientales Vivantes in Paris.

Chapter 3

1. G. Curzon, *Persia and the Persian Question*, 2 (London, 1892), 470–71, "Formerly the Crown only claimed one-tenth; but this proportion was doubled by Fath Ali Shah. In practice it is found that the assessment frequently amounts to thirty percent, and twenty-five percent may perhaps be taken as a fair average. The system, however, varies absolutely in different parts of the country, and even in different parts of the same province."

2. See N. R. Keddie, "Stratification, Social Control, and Capitalism in Iranian Villages, before and after Land Reform," *Rural Politics and Social Change in the Middle East*, ed. R. Antoun and I. Harik (Bloomington, Ind., 1972), reprinted in N. R. Keddie, *Iran: Religion, Politics and Society* (London, 1980).

3. Mid-nineteenth-century appeals by merchants to the government to limit or prohibit European imports are noted in various sources, among them one reported by a British consul in 1844, cited in C. Issawi, ed., *The Economic History of Iran: 1800–1914* (Chicago, 1971), p. 76. By the late nineteenth and early twentieth centuries merchants and nationalists were forming companies to boycott Western goods and promote Iranian ones. Even merchants who profited from foreign trade often saw opportunities for greater profit if European privileges were ended.

4. See the account in H. Algar, *Religion and State in Iran 1785–1906* (Berkeley and Los Angeles, 1969), pp. 94–99, which challenges standard Western accounts.

5. See H. Algar, "The Revolt of Agha Khan Mahallati and the Transference of the Isma'ili Imamate to India," *Studia Islamica*, 29 (1969): 55–81. A recent scholar has studied the small Isma'ili community in contemporary Iran.

6. See N. R. Keddie, "Religion and Irreligion in Early Iranian Nationalism," *Comparative Studies in Society and History*, vol. 4, no. 3 (1962): 265–95, and the sources cited therein (reprinted in N. R. Keddie, *Iran: Religion, Politics and Society* (London, 1980). On Shaikhism and Babism see M. Bayat-Philipp, "Mysticism and Dissent in Socio-religious Thought in Qajar Iran," forthcoming.

7. See Roger Olson, "Persian Gulf Trade and the Agricultural Economy of Southern Iran," in M. Bonine and N. Keddie, eds., *Modern Iran: The Dialectics of Continuity and Change* (Albany, 1981). G. Gilbar, "Persian Agriculture in the Late Qajar Period, 1860–1906," *Asian and African Studies*, vol, 12, no. 3 (1978): 363, while

noting price rises in basic foodstuffs, speaks of a more diversified peasant diet, but cites only sugar, tea, opium, and tobacco. His article is, however, factually informative. Nineteenth-century economic decline is argued in H. Katouzian, *The Political Economy of Modern Iran* (London, 1981), chap. 3.

   8. A partial translation of this work is found in W. M. Floor's mimeographed Ph.D. thesis, "The Guilds in Qajar Persia," (Leiden, 1971).

   9. There is now controversy over the helpful or harmful impact of Western trade on Iranian nineteenth-century living standards. The primarily optimistic views represented by hitherto unpublished papers presented by Gad Gilbar and Guity Nashat at a 1978 congress in Babolsar, Iran, and Gilbar, "Persian Agriculture," appear to be based too heavily on assumptions found in pro-British documentation, whereas V. Nowshirvani's paper at Babolsar was more balanced. W. Floor spoke at a 1980 congress at Harvard of general nineteenth-century immiserization, a view supported by H. Katouzian, *Political Economy.* Olson, "Persian Gulf Trade," indicates that the commercialization of agriculture concentrated wealth in the hands of a few while leaving the majority more vulnerable. When one looks at similar long controversies about prerevolutionary France or postindustrial-revolution England it seems clear that not even the unearthing of better statistics and more sophisticated arguments is likely to solve this question to everyone's satisfaction.

   10. Curzon, *Persia,* 1: 480.

   11. On Mirza Hosain Khan see A. Karny, "Mirza Hosein Khan Moshir od-Dowle and His Attempts at Reform in Iran, 1871–1873" (unpublished Ph.D. dissertation, UCLA, Los Angeles, 1973), and G. Nashat, *The Beginning of Modern Reform in Iran* (Urbana, Ill., 1981).

   12. See F. Kazemzadeh, *Russia and Britain in Persia, 1864–1914* (New Haven, 1968), chaps. 2-3: L. E. Frechtling, "The Reuter Concession in Persia," *Asiatic Review*, 34 (1938); E. Taimuri, *Asr-e bikhabari ya tarikh-e emtiyazat dar Iran* (Tehran, Eqbal, 1953–54).

   13. Kazemzadeh, *Russia and Britain,* and Denis Wright, *The English amongst the Persians* (London, 1977).

Chapter 4

   1. On Malkom Khan see H. Algar, *Mirza Malkum Khan: A Study in the History of Iranian Modernism* (Berkeley and Los Angeles, 1973), the newspaper *Qanun,* and M. Tabataba'i, *Majmu'eh-ye asar-e Mirza Malkam Khan* (Tehran, 1948–49). *Qanun* has been reprinted as a book in Iran.

   2. On Afghani see N. R. Keddie, *Sayyid Jamal ad-Din "al-Afghani": A Political Biography* (Berkeley and Los Angeles, 1972); *An Islamic Response to Imperialism: Political and Religious Writings of Sayyid Jamal ad-Din "al-Afghani"* (Berkeley and Los Angeles, 1968); and H. Pakdaman, *Djamal-ed-Din Assad Abadi dit Afghani* (Paris, 1969), and the Persian and Arabic works referred to therein.

   3. N. R. Keddie, *Religion and Rebellion in Iran: The Tobacco Protest of 1891–1892* (London, 1966), and the sources in several languages referred to therein.

4. On the late nineteenth century see E. G. Browne, *The Persian Revolution of 1905–1909* (Cambridge, 1910), C. Issawi, ed., *The Economic History of Iran: 1800–1914* (Chicago, 1971); and S. Bakhash, *Iran: Monarchy, Bureaucracy and Reform under the Qajars* (London, 1978).

5. See N. R. Keddie, "The Origins of the Religious-Radical Alliance in Iran," *Past and Present*, 34 (July 1966): 70–80, and "Religion and Irreligion in Early Iranian Nationalism," in N. R. Keddie, *Iran: Religion, Politics and Society* (London, 1980).

6. On the British and Russian role in these years see F. Kazemzadeh, *Russia and Britain in Persia, 1864–1914* (New Haven, 1968); N. R. Keddie, "British Policy and the Iranian Opposition 1901–1907," *Journal of Modern History*, vol. 39, no. 3 (1967): 266–82, and "Iranian Politics 1900–1905: Background to Revolution," *Middle Eastern Studies*, vol. 5, nos. 1, 2, 3 (1969): 3–31, 151–67, 234–50; all make extensive use of available British, Persian, and Russian documents.

7. On prerevolutionary oppositional writing see H. Kamshad, *Modern Persian Prose Literature* (Cambridge, 1966), and E. G. Browne, *The Press and Poetry of Modern Persia* (Cambridge, 1914). The Persian books and newspapers mentioned have been consulted in reprints or in libraries.

8. On the probable participation of both the shah and leftists in the Atabak's assassination see N. R. Keddie, "The Assassination of the Amin as-Sultan (Atabak-i A'zam), 31 August 1907," in C. E. Bosworth, ed., *Iran and Islam* (Edinburgh, 1971).

9. On the revolution see Browne, *Persian Revolution;* W. M. Shuster, *The Strangling of Persia* (New York, 1912); R. A. McDaniel, *The Shuster Mission and the Persian Constitutional Revolution* (Minneapolis, 1974); and several articles by E. Abrahamian and A. K. S. Lambton. Among the best Persian books on the revolution are Nazem ol-Eslam Kermani, *Tarikh-e bidari-ye Iranian,* 2nd ed. (Tehran, 1332/1944); A. Kasravi, *Tarikh-e mashruteh-ye Iran,* 12th ed. (Tehran, 2535/1977); M. Malekzadeh, *Tarikh-e enqelab-e mashrutiyat-e Iran,* 7 vols. (Tehran, 1328–32/1949–53); and Sayyed Hasan Taqizadeh, *Tarikh-e avva'el-e enqelab-e mashrutiyat-e Iran* (Tehran, 1338/1959–60). A vast literature and documentation exists on the subject in Persian and English especially.

10. See M. Bayat-Philipp, "Women and Revolution in Iran, 1905–1911," in L. Beck and N. Keddie, eds., *Women in the Muslim World* (Cambridge, Mass., 1978).

11. On the Bakhtiaris and their relations with the British see the forthcoming Cambridge University Press book and several articles by Gene R. Garthwaite, including that in M. Bonine and N. Keddie, eds., *Modern Iran: The Dialectics of Continuity and Change* (Albany, 1981), and "The Bakhtiyari Khans, the Government of Iran, and the British, 1846–1915," *International Journal of Middle East Studies* vol. 3, no. 1 (1972): 24–44.

Chapter 5

1. See F. S. Cocks, ed., *The Secret Treaties and Understandings* 2nd ed. (London, 1918), pp. 15–25.

2. G. Lenczowski, *Russia and the West in Iran, 1918–1948* (Ithaca, N.Y., 1949), pp. 54–55.

3. See the discussions of these movements in R. W. Cottam, *Nationalism in Iran: Updated Through 1978* 2nd ed. (Pittsburgh, 1979).

4. J. M. Balfour, *Recent Happenings in Persia* (Edinburgh and London, 1922), p. 23.

5. J. C. Hurewitz, ed., *The Middle East and North Africa in World Politics: A Documentary Record* 2nd. ed., 2 (New Haven and London, 1979), pp. 182–83.

6. United States, Department of State, *Papers Relating to the Foreign Relations of the United States,* Caldwell to Lansing, August 16, 1919; 1919, 2 (Washington, D.C., 1934), p. 699 (henceforth called U.S. *Papers*).

7. Colby to Caldwell, August 16, 1920, U.S. *Papers,* 1920, 3 (Washington, D.C., 1936), p. 354.

8. F. A. C. Forbes-Leith, *Checkmate: Fighting Tradition in Central Persia* (London, [1927]), p. 44.

9. For fine discussions of this period and Ironside's key role, see R. H. Ullman, *Anglo-Soviet Relations 1917–1921,* 3 (Princeton, 1972), chap. 9; and D. Wright, *The English amongst the Persians* (London, 1977), pp. 180–84. Ironside's diary is the main document.

10. Hurewitz, *Middle East* p. 244.

11. Ibid., pp. 242–43.

12. On these postwar movements see especially Cottam, *Nationalism.*

13. Engert to Hughes, June 21, 1921, U.S. *Papers,* 1921, 2 (Washington, D.C., 1936), p. 635.

14. See the documents in U.S. *Papers,* 1927, 3 (Washington, D.C., 1942), pp. 523–24.

15. On Millspaugh's mission see, in addition to the secondary works covering the period, A. C. Millspaugh, *The Financial and Economic Situation of Persia, 1926* (New York, 1926).

16. On the Sinclair negotiations and their ultimate failure see U.S. *Papers,* 1923, 2 (Washington, D.C., 1938), pp. 711–36, and 1924, 2 (Washington, D.C., 1939), pp. 539–52.

17. On Millspaugh's resignation see U.S. *Papers,* 1927, 3 (Washington, D.C., 1942), pp. 549–54.

18. V. Sheean, *The New Persia* (London, 1927), pp. 231–32.

19. R. N. Gupta, *Oil in the Modern World* (Westport, Conn., 1976; reprint of Allahabad: Kitab Mahal, 1949), gives production figures, p. 60.

20. L. P. Elwell-Sutton, *Modern Iran* (London, 1941), pp. 131–33.

21. Badr ol-Molk Bamdad, *From Darkness into Light: Women's Emancipation in Iran,* ed. and trans. F. R. C. Bagley (Hicksville, N.Y., 1977).

22. More optimistic interpretations are found in the best summary work on the period, A. Banani, *The Modernization of Iran, 1921–1941* (Stanford, 1961), in various writings by D. Wilber, and L. P. Elwell-Sutton, "Reza Shah the Great: Founder of the Pahlavi Dynasty," in G. Lenczowski, ed., *Iran under the Pahlavis* (Stanford, 1978). An

interpretation as critical as mine, albeit with partly different emphases, is in H. Katouzian, *The Political Economy of Modern Iran* (London, 1981).

23. These codes, which were partly provisional and altered in later years, are discussed in Banani, *Modernization*, pp. 70–84.

24. A. K. S. Lambton, *Landlord and Peasant in Persia* (reprinted London, 1969), p. 189.

25. Ibid., p. 197.

26. Ibid., p. 209.

27. Banani, *Modernization*, p. 108. See also I. Sadiq, *Modern Persia and Her Educational System* (New York, 1931). A slightly higher percentage is shown in the table in J. Bharier, *Economic Development in Iran 1900–1970* (London, 1971), p. 65.

28. Badr ol-Molk Bamdad, *From Darkness into Light*.

29. Banani, *Modernization*, pp. 80–84.

30. D. N. Wilber, *Iran: Past and Present* (Princeton, 1948), pp. 143–44; R. N. Gupta, *Iran, an Economic Study* (New Delhi, 1947); and with different details, Bharier, *Economic Development*, pp. 194–98.

31. Banani, *Modernization*, pp. 133–35; H. Soheily, *Essai sur l'industrialisation de l'Iran* (Montreux, 1950), pp. 75–78; Bharier, *Economic Development*, pp. 202–07.

32. L. P. Elwell-Sutton, *Modern Iran*, pp. 93–94, and Wilber, *Iran*, p. 147.

33. Wilber, *Iran*, p. 132. Bharier, *Economic Development*, pp. 172–80, gives official figures that are divided somewhat differently.

34. Wilber, *Iran*, pp. 132–33.

35. On tariff levels see E. B. Yagenegi, *Recent Financial and Monetary History of Persia* (New York, 1934), pp. 55–57; on inflation see Bank Melli Iran, Bulletin de la Banque Mellie Iran, 12 (June 1937): 43–49.

36. Bank Melli Iran, *Bulletin* 55 (Dec. 1941–Jan. 1942): 312.

37. Elwell-Sutton, *Modern Iran*, pp. 115–16.

38. Bharier, *Economic Development*, pp. 65–66, using official figures for expenditures by ministries.

39. Elwell-Sutton, *Modern Iran*, p. 117, gives budgets for two years, 1940–41 and 1941–42. See also the ministry budgets 1928–48 in Bharier, *Economic Development*, pp. 65–66.

40. K. Sandjabi, *Essai sur l'economie rurale et le regime agraire de la Perse* (Paris, 1934), pp. 117, 127, 138.

41. Ibid., pp. 143–62.

42. Ibid., pp. 169–73.

43. Ibid., pp. 186–89.

44. Ibid., pp. 202–05.

45. Ibid., p. 110, and A. Esfandiary, *Les Propriétés et enterprises de l'etat iranien* (Geneva, 1945), pp. 44–45.

46. Lambton, *Landlord*, pp. 246–49.

47. Wilber, *Iran*, pp. 99–100.

48. Bank Melli Iran, *Bulletin*, 2 (March 1934): 2–4.

49. R. W. Davenport, "Soviet Economic Relations with Iran, 1917–1930" (Ph.D.

diss., Columbia University, 1953), p. 141. See also the text and tables on trade in Bharier, *Economic Development*, pp. 102–16.

50. Great Britain, Department of Overseas Trade, *Economic Conditions in Persia* (London, 1930), pp. 13–14.

51. D. S. Zavriev, *Vneshniaia torgovlia za gody krizisa* (Tiflis, 1934), p. 10.

52. A. Amini, *L'institution du monopole du commerce exterieur en Perse* (Paris, 1932), pp. 144–47. On exchange controls see Bharier, *Economic Development*, pp. 123–26.

53. Bank Melli Iran, *Bulletin*, 2 (March 1934): 1–2.

54. See Great Britain, Department of Overseas Trade, *Economic Conditions in Iran (Persia)* (London, 1935), pp. 4–5, 23.

55. Bank Melli Iran, *Bulletin*, 2 (March 1934): 3.

56. Wilber, *Iran*, p. 136.

57. Bank Melli Iran, *Bulletin*, 55 (Dec. 1941–Jan. 1942): 326.

58. Elwell-Sutton, *Modern Iran*, p. 142.

59. Ibid., pp. 141–42.

60. M. W. Thornburg, "An Economic Study of the Near East with Particular Reference to Oil Revenues" (unpublished study, 1944), pp. 25–29.

61. Hedley V. Cooke, *Challenge and Response in the Middle East* (New York, 1952), p. 238. Bharier, *Economic Development*, pp. 58–59, indicates a rise in per capita GNP under Reza Shah but there are no income statistics to indicate how this rise was divided and a variety of evidence indicates that most of it went to upper- and middle-class groups.

Chapter 6

1. G. Lenczowski, *Russia and the West in Iran, 1918–1948* (Ithaca, N.Y., 1949), p. 168.

2. Ibid., p. 175.

3. A. Millspaugh, *Americans in Persia* (Washington, D.C., 1946), pp. 85–86.

4. Bank Melli Iran, *Bulletin*, 56, (Feb.–March 1942): p. 470.

5. Millspaugh, *Americans*, p. 47. On American wartime and postwar relations with and interests in Iran see Barry Rubin, *Paved with Good Intentions* (New York, 1980), and B. Kuniholm, *The Origins of the Cold War in the Middle East* (Princeton, 1980).

6. Millspaugh, *Americans*, pp. 61, 83.

7. The most complete English-language work covering the Tudeh is S. Zabih, *The Communist Movement in Iran* (Berkeley and Los Angeles, 1966). E. Abrahamian has a forthcoming book *Iran between Two Revolutions* (Princeton, 1982), with additional information on the Tudeh.

8. Zabih, *Communist Movement*, chap. 3, and L. P. Elwell-Sutton, "Political Parties in Iran: 1941–1948," *Middle East Journal*, vol. 3 no. 1 (1949): 48.

9. E. Abrahamian, "The Strengths and Weaknesses of the Labor Movement in Iran, 1941–53," in M. Bonine and N. Keddie, eds., *Modern Iran: The Dialectics of Continuity and Charge* (Albany, 1981).

10. Millspaugh, *Americans*, p. 45, and Elwell-Sutton, "Political Parties," p. 50.
11. Lenczowski, *Russia*, pp. 250–53.
12. Millspaugh, *Americans*, pp. 113, 152.
13. Ibid., pp. 96–152.
14. United States, Department of State, *Treaties and other International Agreements of the United States of America 1776–1949*, 8, "Military Mission with Iranian Gendarmerie" (Washington, D.C., U.S. G.P.O., 1971), 1286–89.
15. R. N. Frye, *Iran* (New York, 1953), pp. 113–14. On Allied contributions to inflation see H. Katouzian, *The Political Economy of Modern Iran* (London, 1981), pp. 142–43.
16. United Nations, Department of Economic Affairs, *Public Finance Information Papers: Iran* (New York, 1951), p. 21.
17. Great Britain, Department of Overseas Trade, *Persia: Review of Commercial Conditions* (London, 1945), pp. 21–29.
18. Lenczowski, *Russia*, p. 246, and interviews with Sayyed Zia and others, 1960.
19. Of the several works on the politics of Iranian oil, probably the best is L. P. Elwell-Sutton, *Persian Oil: A Study in Power Politics* (London, 1955). Among works with further information are F. Fesharaki, *Development of the Iranian Oil Industry* (New York, 1976); A. Sampson, *The Seven Sisters* (New York, 1975); M. W. Thornburg, "An Economic Study of the Near East with Particular Reference to Oil Revenues" (unpublished, 1944); and J. M. Blair, *The Control of Oil* (New York, 1976).
20. T. C. Young, "The National and International Relations of Iran," in T. C. Young, ed., *Near Eastern Culture and Society* (Princeton, 1951), p. 202.
21. Zabih, *Communist Movement*, chap 3; Lenczowski, *Russia*, p. 195.
22. E. Abrahamian, "Communism and Communalism in Iran: The *Tudah* and the *Firqah-i Dimukrat*," *International Journal of Middle Eastern Studies*, vol. 1 no. 4 (1970): 291–316; Zabih, *Communist Movement*, chap. 3.
23. Zabih, *Communist Movement*, chap. 3.
24. Wm. Eagleton, Jr., *The Kurdish Republic of 1946* (London, 1963), and M. M. Karadaghi, "The Kurdish Question," (unpublished thesis, Berkeley, 1955), pp. 137–54.
25. Terms in Lenczowski, *Russia*, p. 302.
26. Iran, Ministre du Travail, *La Loi du travail* (Tehran, 1946).
27. International Labour Office, *Labour Conditions in the Oil Industry in Iran* (Geneva, 1950), pp. 28–29.
28. Lenczowski, *Russia*, 308.
29. M. Thornburg, "Communism (Persia)" (unpublished, n.d.), p. 3.
30. Lenczowski, *Russia*, pp. 313–14.
31. A. K. S. Lambton, *Landlord and Peasant in Persia* (London, 1953), pp. 379–81.
32. Overseas Consultants, Inc., *Report on Seven Year Development Plan for the Plan Organization of the Imperial Government of Iran*, vol. 3 (New York, 1949), 8.
33. L. J. Hayden, "Living Standards in Rural Iran: A Case Study," *Middle East Journal*, vol. 3 no. 2 (1949): 143. An unpublished Iranian study, with Ford Foundation aid, showed very low incomes but also income variation from the relatively prosperous

northwest to the incredibly impoverished southeast, and indicated income and status variation within each village. See N. R. Keddie, "The Iranian Village before and after Land Reform," *Journal of Contemporary History,* vol. 3, no. 3 (1968): 69–91, reprinted in H. Bernstein, ed., *Underdevelopment and Development: The Third World Today* (Harmondsworth, 1973); and N. R. Keddie, "Stratification, Social Control and Capitalism in Iranian Villages, before and after Land Reform," in I. Harik and R. Antoun, eds., *Rural Politics and Social Change in the Middle East* (Bloomington, Ind., 1972), reprinted in N. R. Keddie, *Iran: Religion, Politics and Society* (London, 1980).

34. OCI, *Report,* 3: 13; and R. N. Gupta, *Iran: An Economic Study* (New Delhi, 1947), p. 45.

35. United Nations, *Public Finance Information Papers: Iran* (New York, 1951); and M. Thornburg, "Rising Prices, High Cost of Living, and Fall in Value of the Rial" (unpublished, 1948), pp. 5–6. Sometimes customs duties are listed separately from indirect taxation, but in effect they were a form of indirect taxation, hitting especially items of mass consumption.

36. Thornburg, "Rising Prices," p. 4.

37. A. Moarefi, *The Iranian Seven Year Plan and Its Monetary Effects* (Washington, D.C., 1950), pt. 3, p. 85.

38. Lambton, *Landlord,* p. 244.

39. Ibid., p. 289.

40. Ibid., p. 262–63.

41. OCI, *Report,* 1: 47.

42. M. Thornburg, "Conversation with Agha Firoughzadeh" (unpublished, Tehran, 1949), p. 103.

43. United Nations, Department of Economic Affairs, *Review of Economic Conditions in the Middle East, 1951–1952* (New York, 1953), p. 40.

44. OCI, *Report,* 4: 8.

45. Ibid., p. 18.

46. Ibid., pp. 149, 189.

47. See T. C. Young, "The Social Support of Current Iranian Policy," *Middle East Journal,* vol. 6, no. 2 (1952): 125–43.

48. Ibid., pp. 130–31.

49. On working-class and trade-union activity see especially Abrahamian, "The Strengths and Weaknesses of the Labor Movement in Iran"; see also Gupta, *Iran,* p. 83.

50. OCI, *Report,* I: 35–38.

51. M. Naficy, "Preliminary Report on the Persian Seven Year Plan" (unpublished, Tehran, 1947), p. 3.

52. Quoted in Moarefi, *Seven Year Plan,* pt. 6, p. 2.

53. M. Thornburg, "The Seven Year Plan" (unpublished speech, Tehran, October 19, 1947), p. 3.

54. OCI, *Report,* 1: 5.

55. Moarefi, *Seven Year Plan,* pt. 3, p. 87.

56. Thornburg, "The First Year of the Plan" (unpublished speech, Tehran, April 5, 1950), p. 4.

57. Thornburg, "Statement on behalf of O.C.I." (unpublished, June 24, 1950): 3–6.

58. See *Middle East Economist,* 5 (May 1951): 8.

59. On Iranian grievances see especially Elwell-Sutton, *Persian Oil,* chaps. 13–14.

60. Among the sources for this is J. Kimche, *Seven Fallen Pillars: The Middle East 1945–1952* (London, 1953), pp. 341, 348, 354.

61. Elwell-Sutton, *Persian Oil,* chaps, 17–20.

62. *Middle East Economist,* 6 (September 1952): 8. The best English-language treatment of Mosaddeq is in R. W. Cottam, *Nationalism in Iran: Updated through 1978* (Pittsburgh, 1979).

63. As early as July 1951, Max Thornburg recommended to Secretary of State Dean Acheson a "bold course" supported by the United States to establish a "responsible" government that would reach an oil settlement. Thornburg, "Notes for Discussion with Dean Acheson: 5 July, 1951, Washington, D.C." (unpublished).

64. United Nations, Department of Economic Affairs, *Summary of Recent Economic Developments in the Middle East 1952–1953* (New York, 1954), p. 25. For the dramatic improvement in exports, and the balance of trade see the official statistics reproduced in Katouzian, *Political Economy,* p. 184.

65. United Nations, *Summary,* p. 32.

66. Max W. Thornburg to Clare Booth Luce (unpublished, Rome, May 7, 1953). Mrs. Luce's zeal in pressuring the Italians about buying Iranian oil was brought up against her in the Senate when she was confirmed as ambassador to Brazil.

67. Harry N. Howard, "The Development of United States Policy in the Near East, South Asia, and Africa during 1953: Part 1" *The Department of State Bulletin* vol. 30, no. 765 (February 22, 1954), p. 279.

68. Kermit Roosevelt, *Countercoup: The Struggle for the Control of Iran* (New York, 1980). This work was reportedly approved both by the then shah, to whom Roosevelt represented that it was better to tell the true story than to have false or partly false stories believed, and by the CIA. After publication in the fall of 1979, it was recalled from bookstores in early November and all copies that the publisher (McGraw-Hill) had or recovered were destroyed. According to reliable sources, British Petroleum (ex-AIOC) objected because British secret service activities were attributed to it. (Internal evidence in the book shows the author often uses false names and identifications without warning the reader.) There has also been speculation that the Carter administration, having decided to let the ex-shah into the United States for medical treatment and knowing it might cause trouble, did not want further publicity given to America's role in the 1953 coup. Clearly proud of his Iran activity, Roosevelt represents Iran as threatened by Russia and communism, and the majority of Iranians as behind the shah, not Mosaddeq. A 1980 edition corrects the point on BP. Reliable oral sources state that Roosevelt was not as much in charge of the Iranian operation as he says and that he misstates some facts such as the sum of money spent and his description of the Iranians involved.

69. Loy Henderson's statement is in Saikhal, *The Rise and Fall of the Shah* (Princeton, 1980), p. 215, n. 70. My 1980 interviews with involved parties confirm a figure of several million dollars.

70. For further information on Mosaddeq's overthrow see S. Zabih, *Communist Movement*, pp. 199–207. Andrew Tully, *C.I.A.: The Inside Story* (New York, 1962), chap. 7, and D. Wise and T. B. Ross, *The Invisible Government* (New York, 1964), pp. 110–13, gave the essence of the story before Roosevelt's detailed account. R. W. Cottam, *Nationalism in Iran*, stresses internal Iranian forces in the overthrow, but in Cottam's more recent "The Imperial Regime of Iran: Why it Collapsed?" in *L'Iran d'heir et de demain* (Quebec, 1980), he says, "As Dr. Mossadeq had been informed by Soviet Intelligence, his dismissal was the first act of a coup d'état organized by the American CIA and British MI-6 to make General Fazlollah Zehedi prime minister and dictator in Iran." He goes on to say, "The western governments provided the money and direction of eliminating Mossadeq. The purchase of mercenary mob support proved to be the critical element in achieving success on August 19, 1953." This account may be presumed to supersede Cottam's better known earlier one. The detail about Soviet intelligence we have not seen elsewhere and may come from inside information, although a reliable Iranian oral source speaks rather of a Tudeh military officer who was to participate in the coup as having warned Mosaddeq.

Chapter 7

1. R. W. Cottam, *Nationalism in Iran: Updated through 1978* (Pittsburgh, 1979), chap. 16. For details and analysis of the whole post–1953 period see H. Katouzian, *The Political Economy of Modern Iran* (London, 1981), and B. Rubin, *Paved with Good Intentions* (New York, 1980).

2. On the shah's security methods, see especially M. Zonis, *The Political Elite of Iran* (Princeton, 1971), chaps. 3, 4, and passim.

3. Statistics from Bank Melli *Bulletins* cited in John Marlowe, *Iran: A Short Political Guide* (London, 1963), chap. 7, especially p. 107.

4. This was discovered in interviews with officials involved in a Ford Foundation-sponsored village survey in Iran in the 1950s, some of whose unpublished written work is reported in N. R. Keddie, "The Iranian Village before and after Land Reform," *Journal of Contemporary History*, vol. 3, no. 3 (1968): 69–91, reprinted in H. Bernstein, ed., *Underdevelopment and Development: Third World Today* (Harmondsworth, 1973).

5. Ibid.; A. K. S. Lambton, *The Persian Land Reform 1962–1966* (Oxford, 1969), chap. 2; and a forthcoming article by W. Floor in *International Journal of Middle East Studies (IJMES)*, which documents ulama opposition to the 1960 reform and its effects.

6. W. Floor, *IJMES*, forthcoming.

7. H. Algar, "The Oppositional Role of the Ulama in Twentieth-Century Iran," in N. R. Keddie, ed., *Scholars, Saints, and Sufis* (Berkeley and Los Angeles, 1972), p. 246, lists four "real targets of Khumayni's criticism of the regime in 1963," two of which are "the proposal to grant capitulatory rights to American advisors and military personnel in Iran and their dependents; [and] the contracting of a $200 million loan from the United States for the purchase of military equipment," and on p. 249 speaks of Khomaini as having been exiled in June 1963. In fact, however, as is documented both in Floor, *IJMES*, forthcoming, and in Zonis, *Political Elite*, chap. 3, both the

immunity bill and the loan were passed in late 1964 (although there was earlier discussion of the former) and Khomaini, who was not exiled in 1963 but twice imprisoned up to May 1964, attacked the above-mentioned bills late in 1964, after which he was exiled. Although Algar is correct in saying Khomaini opposed the two bills, this was mainly in 1964, not 1963 as he says. More research is needed on Khomaini's 1963 speeches, as some say he did attack land reform, and others say he did not.

8. Floor, *IJMES*, forthcoming, gives ulama writings on land reform and woman suffrage; although Khomaini and Shariatmadari seem not to have written against land reform (although some claim Khomaini spoke against it), opposition by several other important ulama is documented by Floor.

9. See the paper by W. Millward, "The Islamic Political Theory and Vocabulary of Ayatullah Khumayni," presented at Middle East Studies Assocation meeting, Salt Lake City, November 1979.

10. Quoted in Algar, "Oppositional Role," p. 247.

11. On capitalism in Iran see especially Fred Halliday, *Iran: Dictatorship and Development* (New York, 1979), chaps. 5ff. On the shah's use of reforms to strengthen his political power see J. A. Bill, *The Politics of Iran: Groups, Classes and Modernization* (Columbus, Ohio, 1972), chap. 6.

12. See especially R. Looney, *The Economic Development of Iran* (New York, 1973).

13. This policy was proposed by, among others, Hossein Mahdavy in an unpublished paper delivered at Harvard in 1965.

14. See the calculations in Keddie, "The Iranian Village."

15. See the calculations from Plan Organization and Central Bank data in J. and A. Carey, "Iranian Agriculture and Its Development: 1952–1973," *IJMES*, vol. 7 no. 3 (1976): 359–82. On land reform and its results see, in addition to the works cited in notes 4, 5, and 11–14 above, and 16–18 below, M. G. Weinbaum, "Agricultural Policy and Development Politics in Iran," *Middle East Journal*, vol. 31, no. 4 (1977); Paul Vieille, *La Féodalité et l'etat en Iran* (Paris, 1975); T. Brun and R. Dumont, "Iran: Imperial Pretensions and Agricultural Dependence," *MERIP Reports*, 71 (1978); D. R. Denman, "Land Reforms of Shah and People," in G. Lenczowski, ed., *Iran under the Pahlavis* (Stanford, 1978); A. K. S. Lambton, "Land Reform and the Rural Cooperative Societies," in E. Yar-Shater, ed., *Iran Faces the Seventies* (New York, 1971); and N. R. Keddie, "Oil, Economic Policy and Social Conflict in Iran," *Race and Class*, vol. 21, no. 1 (1979): 13–29. E. J. Hooglund's fine dissertation, "The Effects of Land Reform on Rural Iran, 1962–1972" (Johns Hopkins, 1975) has been revised and will be published by the University of Texas Press, Austin.

16. M. A. Katouzian, "Oil versus Agriculture: A Case of Dual Resource Depletion in Iran," *The Journal of Peasant Studies*, vol. 5, no. 3 (1978): 347–69 and the cited unpublished Oxford University dissertation by Fatemah Etemad Moghadam, "The Effects of Farm Size and Management System on Agricultural Production in Iran," Somerville College, 1978.

17. Calculations from official figures in J. and A. Carey, "Iranian Agriculture," p.

359, and Halliday, *Iran,* p. 130. The Careys' statement that over 8 percent of Iran's total population went from rural to urban areas in 1972–73 can be reconciled with the fact of rising rural population only if 1972–73 was an exceptional year. Both statements are based on official statistics, but these are often in error, as noted in T. Walton, "Economic Development and Revolutionary Upheavals in Iran," *Cambridge Journal of Economics* vol. 4, no. 3 (1980), where the increase in rural-urban migration in the 1966–76 census period is analyzed. The migration figures in Halliday, *Iran,* for 1956–76 are compatible with the slight increase in those employed in agriculture that he cites; clearly the migration rate was higher in the 1970s than before.

18. See Lois Beck, "Economic Transformations among the Qashqa'i Nomads, 1962–1977," in M. Bonine and N. Keddie, eds., *Modern Iran: The Dialectics of Continuity and Change* (Albany, 1981); and Dan Morgan, *Merchants of Grain* (New York, 1979).

19. G. B. Baldwin, *Planning and Development in Iran* (Baltimore, 1967).

20. Much of the above analysis is based on private conversations or unpublished reports by Iranian and international organizations. Among the most useful published works are R. Looney, *Economic Development;* International Labour Organization, *Employment and Income Policies for Iran* (Geneva, 1973); D. Housego, "Quiet Thee Now and Rest," *The Economist,* August 28, 1976; R. Graham, *Iran: The Illusion of Power,* Revised ed. (London, 1979); and Halliday, *Iran.*

21. M. H. Pesaran and F. Gahvary, "Growth and Income Distribution in Iran," in R. Stone and W. Peterson, eds., *Econometric Contributions to Public Policy* (London, 1978). Pesaran has done excellent studies on income distribution, as has F. Mehran; most of the latter were distributed in mimeo by the ILO. On income distribution see also Looney, *Economic Development,* and his *Income Distribution Policies and Economic Growth in Semiindustrialized Countries* (New York, 1975), and ILO *Employment.*

22. Graham, *Illusion of Power,* chap. 5.

23. See Keddie, "Oil, Economic Policy and Social Conflict."

24. See A. Sampson, *The Arms Bazaar: From Lebanon to Lockheed* (New York, 1977), chap. 14, "The Arming of the Shah." On the 1960s see J. C. Hurewitz, *Middle East Politics: The Military Dimension* (New York, 1969), chap. 15, "An American Client: Iran."

25. On Iranian women 1960–77 see the introduction and articles by L. Beck, M. Fischer, M. Good, J. and M. Gulick, B. Pakizegi, N. Tapper, and P. Vieille, in L. Beck and N. Keddie, eds., *Women in the Muslim World* (Cambridge, Mass., 1978).

26. On the secular opposition see Halliday, *Iran,* chap. 8. *MERIP Reports,* 86 (Mar.–Apr. 1980) is entitled "The Left Forces in Iran," and in addition to articles and interviews by Fred Halliday contains a major article by E. Abrahamian, "The Guerrilla Movement in Iran, 1963–1977," pp. 3–15.

27. See M. Fischer, *Iran: From Religious Dispute to Revolution* (Cambridge, Mass., 1980), chap. 6, and S. Akhavi, *Religion and Politics in Contemporary Iran* (Albany, 1980), chaps. 5–6.

Chapter 8

1. On ta'ziyeh the most recent work is P. J. Chelkowski, *Ta'ziyeh: Ritual and Drama in Iran* (New York, 1979). Women's ceremonies have been witnessed by the author in Isfahan, 1977, and elsewhere.

2. On popular theatre, see W. Beeman, "A Full Arena: The Development and Cultural Meaning of Popular Performance Traditions in Iran," in M. Bonine and N. Keddie, eds., *Modern Iran: The Dialectics of Continuity and Change* (Albany, 1981). I saw several of these plays at the Shiraz Festival, 1976.

3. This is based on oral presentations and a forthcoming article by Kaveh Safa Esfahani on Iranian women's theatre games.

4. See especially the discussion of the dissident tradition since Safavid times by Mangol Bayat-Philipp, "Tradition and Change in Iranian Socio-Religious Thought," in Bonine and Keddie, *Modern Iran*.

5. See N. R. Keddie, *Sayyid Jamal ad-Din "al-Afghani": A Political Biography* (Berkeley and Los Angeles, 1972). On other thinkers see H. Algar, *Mirza Malkum Khan: A Study in the History of Iranian Modernism* (Berkeley and Los Angeles, 1973); E. G. Browne, *The Persian Revolution of 1905–1909* (Cambridge, 1910) and *The Press and Poetry of Modern Persia* (Cambridge, 1914); and a forthcoming book by M. Bayat-Philipp.

6. In addition to the above works see H. Kamshad, *Modern Persian Prose Literature* (Cambridge, 1966).

7. Interview with Mohammad Ali Jamalzadeh, Geneva, summer, 1961; discussed also in N. R. Keddie, "Religion and Irreligion in Early Iranian Nationalism," reprinted in N. R. Keddie, *Iran: Religion, Politics and Society* (London, 1980).

8. See Keddie, "Religion and Irreligion," and E. G. Browne, *Materials for the Study of the Babi Religion* (Cambridge, 1918), p. 221. Confirmation of those listed by Browne as men who were reputed to be Azali Babis (for at least a large part of their lifetime) was given me orally by Sayyed Hasan Taqizadeh in 1960, although he did not want to be listed as a source during his lifetime: the most important were Mirza Aqa Khan Kermani; Shaikh Ahmad Ruhi (and his brothers); Malek al-Motakallemin; and Mirza Jahangir Khan.

9. See H. Algar, "The Oppositional Role of the Ulama in Twentieth-Century Iran," in N. R. Keddie, ed., *Scholars, Saints, and Sufis* (Berkeley and Los Angeles, 1972), and A.-H. Hairi, *Shi'ism and Constitutionalism in Iran* (Leiden, 1977).

10. See M. C. Hillmann, "Furugh Farrukhzad, Modern Iranian Poet," in E. W. Fernea and B. Q. Bezirgan, eds., *Middle Eastern Muslim Women Speak* (Austin, Texas, 1976).

11. See Kamshad, *Modern Persian Prose*, pt. 2, and Sadeq Hedayat, *Haji Agha*, trans. G. W. Wickens, introduction by Lois Beck (Austin, Texas, 1979).

12. Kamshad, *Modern Persian Prose*, chap. 12.

13. See S. Behrangi, *The Little Black Fish and Other Modern Persian Stories*, trans, E. and M. Hooglund (Washington, D.C., 1976); R. Baraheni, *The Crowned Cannibals: Writings on Repression in Iran* (New York, 1977); "Iran: Contemporary Persian Literature," special issue of *Literary Review*, ed. T. M. Ricks, vol. 18, no. 1 (1974).

14. See E. Abrahamian, "Kasravi: The Integrative Nationalist of Iran," in E. Kedourie and S. G. Haim, eds., *Towards a Modern Iran* (London, 1980), and the sources cited therein.

15. See Jalal Al-e Ahmad, *Khasi dar miqat* (Tehran, 1977) and the discussion of it in a forthcoming article by Brad Hanson, "The Westoxication of Iran: Depictions and Reactions of Al Ahmad, Behrangi, and Shariati," delivered at Middle East Studies Association, Washington, D.C., 1980. See also the discussion of Shariati in S. Akhavi, *Religion and Politics in Contemporary Iran* (Albany, 1980), and M. Bayat-Philipp, "Shi'ism in Contemporary Iranian Politics: The Case of Ali Shari'ati," in Kedourie and Haim, eds., *Towards a Modern Iran.*

16. On Khalil Maleki and on Iranian political ideas and programs in the Pahlavi period see H. Katouzian, *The Political Economy of Modern Iran* (London, 1981).

17. See M. Rodinson, *Marxisme et monde musulman* (Paris, 1972).

18. See A. Abdel-Malek, "Political Islam—Positions," unpublished text, Round Table on Socialism in the World, 1978, Cavtat, September, 1978.

19. The phrase "Gharbzadegi" was popularized by Al-e Ahmad, but he borrowed it from Ahmad Fardid; see J. Al-e Ahmad, *Gharbzadegi*, 2nd ed. (Tehran, 1979), p. 16.

20. The best biography of Al-e Ahmad is that which he himself wrote in 1967–68, "Masalan sharh-e ahvalat," *Jahan-e Nau*, vol. 26, no. 3 (Tehran, 1348/1969), 4–8.

21. Brad Hanson, "The Westoxication of Iran," notes that in his pilgrimage diary, *Khasi dar miqat,* Al-e Ahmad *tries* to be a Muslim, but observes what is around him at Mecca with a very detached and critical eye.

22. Al-e Ahmad wrote, after citing Shariati at length, that in January 1969 he "had the honor to meet two or three times the great Ali Shariati while I was in Mashhad, and I was impressed. We spoke at length on the subject of intellectuals in our society, and I am happy that on these questions we walk on the same path." (*Dar khedmat va khiyanat-e raushanfekran,* 3rd ed. [Tehran, 1977–78], p. 51, n. 1).

23. See n. 19, above.

24. Fazlollah Nuri has generally been considered by historians as a reactionary; hence Al-e Ahmad was bold in contradicting the received ideas of intellectuals.

25. Naraghi, a sociologist known in the West, was for some years with UNESCO. He was particularly concerned with problems of cultural colonialism and the flight of intellectuals. Born into a family of Kashan ulama, Naraghi speaks of Islam as an institution, a spiritual tradition defending national identity against materialist levelling. Religion, however, is not central to his cultural sociology. See E. Naraghi, *L'Orient et la crise de l'Occident,* trans. B. Simon (Paris, 1977), pp. 167–85.

26. See M. Fashkhami, *Talkhisi az zendegi-ye qa'ed-e a'zam Emam Khomaini* (Tehran, 1357/1978), pp. 13–15.

27. Ruhollah Khomaini, *Kashf al-asrar* (n.p., 1323/1944), p. 2.

28. Ibid., pp. 185–86, 222.

29. W. G. Millward, "The Islamic Political Theory and Vocabulary of Ayatullah Khumayni, 1941–1963," unpublished, presented to MESA, Salt Lake City, 1979.

30. Ruhollah Khomaini, *Hokumat-e eslami* (Najaf, 1971), p. 13. There are several recent editions, sometimes as *Velayat-e faqih.*

31. *Hokumat-e eslami,* p. 33.

32. Ibid., p. 53.
33. Ibid., p. 60.
34. Ibid., p. 177.
35. *Jehad-e akbar,* published together with *Hokumat-e eslami.* It is undated, but must come from the years of exile in Najaf.
36. As leader of the great outdoor prayers at Tehran Univeristy, Ramazan, 1979, he attacked the Kurdish and Arab autonomy movements as inspired by outside leftists, but in his last statement in September 1979 he restated his former sympathy with minority desires. Possibly he feared Iran might fall apart, which caused him for some months to mute his criticisms of the government (n.k.).
37. See M. Taleqani, *Tarjomeh va sharh-e Nahj al-balagha* (n.p., n.d.); Taleqani, *Partovi az Qor'an,* 4 vols. (recently reprinted, Tehran).
38. M. H. Na'ini, *Tanbih al-omma va tanzih al-mella; ya hokumat az nazar-e Eslam,* introduction, notes, and commentary by M. Taleqani (n.p., 1955). On this book see A. Hairi, *Shi'ism and Constitutionalism in Iran* (Leiden, 1977).
39. M. Taleqani, *Eslam va malekiyat dar moqayeseh ba nezamha-ye eqtesadi-ye gharb* (n.p., n.d.). The mention of "gharbzadegi" (p. 167) suggests that this book may date from the 1960s.
40. Ibid., pp. 282, 297, 141, 283.
41. See Taleqani's article in *Bahsi dar bareh-ye marja'iyat va ruhaniyat* (Tehran, 1341/1962), and A. K. S. Lambton, "A Reconsideration of the Position of the marja' al-taqlid and the Religious Institution," *Studia Islamica,* 20 (1964): 125ff. Taleqani was the sole religious leader who openly approved of Shariati; see his speech of 26 Ordibehesht (1358/1979) in *Majmu'eh-ye chand sokhanrani dar Daneshgah-e Tehran be monasebat-e ruz-e Shariati* (n.p., n.d.).
42. See M. Bazargan, "Peragmatizm dar Eslam," in *Bi-nehayat kuchekha* (Tehran, 1357/1978).
43. See the "portrait" of Bazargan in *Le Monde,* February 7, 1979.
44. See M. Bazargan, *Marz bain-e din va siyasat,* speech of September 12, 1962 (n.p., n.d.), p. 8.
45. Ibid., p. 46.
46. *Mazhab dar Orupa,* lecture of 1942, ed. and notes by M. Khosraushahi, recent reedition (Tehran, n.d.).
47. *Kar dar Eslam va dar Iran,* lecture, April 1946 (Qom, 1347/1968).
48. See, for example, *Bad va baran dar Qor'an* (Qom, 1344/1965).
49. M. Bazargan, "Entezar-e mardom az maraje'," in *Bahsi dar bareh-ye marja'iyat,* pp. 126ff.
50. The existing short biographies of Shariati disagree about dates. See "Zistnameh-ye Doktor Shari'ati," In *Yadnameh-ye Doktor 'Ali Shari'ati be monasebat-e chehelom-e u* (Tehran, 2536 shah/1977); "Salnameh-ye zendegi va asar-e Doktor 'Ali Shari'ati," *Yadnameh-ye salgard-e hejrat-e "Abu Zarr-e zaman" Ostad Doktor 'Ali Shari'ati* (Tehran, 1978). Shariati's Sorbonne thesis for a university doctorate, which both authors of this book have seen, was a philological one under the direction of Professor G. Lazard: an edition, translation, and introduction to a classical Persian text, the *Faza'el-e Balkh.*

51. A preliminary bibliography of Shariati by Y. R[ichard] is in *Abstracta Iranica,* 1 and 2, Tehran–Leiden, 1978, 1979. Hamid Algar has translated some texts in *On the Sociology of Islam* (Berkeley and Los Angeles, 1979). These are among the least specifically Shi'i texts of Shariati. Other translations include *Hajj* by A. Behzadnia and N. Denny (Bedford, 1978), and several booklets in English published in Tehran by the Hosainiyeh Ershad, the Shariati Foundation, and the Hamdani Foundation. The oratorical style for Shariati and the rapid analyses he sometimes made before his enthusiastic public render translation difficult.

52. A. Shariati, *Tashayyo'-e 'alavi va tashayyo'-e safavi* (n.p., n.d.), pp. 320ff. An independent translation is in Shahrough Akhavi, *Religion and Politics in Contemporary Iran* (Albany, 1980), pp. 231–33. Akhavi's book appeared after this chapter was written; it contains additional useful information about the men and trends discussed herein.

53. A. Shariati, *Fatima Fatima ast,* lecture delivered in 1350/1971, recently reprinted.

54. A. Shariati, *Ommat va emamat* (n.p., n.d.), pp. 179–80.

55. A series of fatvas (religious decrees) has recently been reproduced in Qom without a title page, but with the original handwriting photocopied to prove authenticity, containing condemnations and warnings of leading mujtahids against Shariati. Included are Ayatollah Khomaini, who never names Shariati but points to his ideas in decrees of 1964, 1977, 1978, and 1979; Ayatollah Shariatmadari, and Ayatollahs Najafi, Kho'i, Qomi, Milani, Esfahani, Abdollah Shirazi, Mar'ashi, and others. Khomaini almost surely did not direct a 1964 decree against the then unknown Shariati, but it may have been included to indicate that Khomaini was the first to see the danger of one who wished to divide the ulama. (Shariati was in France during Khomaini's 1962–64 political activities, and his works do not refer to Khomaini, whereas Al-e Ahmad praises Khomaini and reproduces his speech against capitulations in October 1964 in his *Dar Khedmat,* pp. 7ff.)

56. *Yadnameh-ye salgard-e hejrat.*

57. A. Shariati, *Tashayyo'-e 'alavi* pp. 273–74.

58. A. Bani Sadr, *Mauqe'iyat-e Iran va naqsh-e Modarres,* vol. 1 (n.p., 1356/1977); and *Monafeqin az didgah-e ma,* recently reprinted n.p., n.d.; and *Kish-e shakhsiyat* (n.p., 1355/1976).

59. *Eqtesad-e tauhidi* (Tehran, 1357/1978).

60. A. Bani Sadr, *Bayaniyeh-ye jomhuri-ye eslami* (Tehran, 1358/1979), p. xi. On the ties between Shariati and Bani Sadr, see the three texts of Bani Sadr in the collection *Vizhenameh (-ye Shari'ati), yekomin salgard* (n.p., n.d.). Through his favorable reflections on Shariati's work one may discern Bani Sadr's position—more subtle than that of his predecessor, but very close, notably on the problem of the place of theologians in society. He writes: "We must not expect anything from the "traditional" masters who are the guardians of cultural institutions. In two centuries they have been deprived of the foundations of thought and action, and this deprivation continues. Sometimes they make a little formal protest before submitting. Among them, it is true, have been found Sayyed Jamal ("Afghani"), Modarres, Khomaini, and Taleqani. But

these same traditional masters have kept these persons from conquering their enemies"
(pp. 131–32).

61. A. Bani Sadr, *Osul-e payeh va zabeteha-ye hokumat-e eslami* (n.p., 1975).

62. Ibid., pp. 51–52.

63. Critical studies of recent Islamic thought in Iran are found in articles by W.
Floor, H. Katouzian, and others in *Mardomnameh* (Berlin, 1981), which will later be
published in English. Other critical studies include N. Keddie, "L'Ayatollah, est-il
integriste?" *Le Monde,* August 22, 1980, and "Islamic Revival as Third Worldism"
(forthcoming in a festschrift for M. Rodinson, ed. J.-P. Digard). Translations from the
writings of Bani Sadr and selections from his French writings are in Abol-Hassan
Banisadr, *Quelle revolution pour l'Iran?* (Paris, 1980). A survey of traditional and modern
Shi'i thought is Y. Richard, *Le Shi'isme en Iran* (Paris, 1980).

Chapter 9

1. Many of the above conclusions about the shah's illness and its political effect are
based on my own observations and newspaper reading in Iran in the summers of 1977
and 1978 and on interviews 1978–81. The role of the shah's cancer in weakening him in
1978 is discussed in M. A. Ledeen and W. H. Lewis, "Carter and the Fall of the Shah:
The Inside Story," *Washington Quarterly,* vol. 3 no. 2 (1980): 3–40. Conclusions on the
role of the human-rights program are based on observations and interviews, and on B.
Rubin, *Paved with Good Intentions* (New York, 1980), chap. 7, and R. Cottam,
"Goodbye to America's Shah," *Foreign Policy,* 34 (Spring 1979): 3–14.

2. R. Graham, *Iran: The Illusion of Power,* rev. ed. (London, 1979), has good brief
coverage of the revolution in chapter 12, which ends in March 1979. (Readers should
beware of the new chapter in the American edition by St. Martin's Press, however, as it
has many errors and the footnotes are undecipherably out of order.) In addition to books
and articles specifically mentioned below, for the Revolution and its background I have
used numerous interviews, regular newspaper reading, especially of *Le Monde,* the *New
York Times,* the *Washington Post,* and the *Los Angeles Times,* as well as regular reading of
magazines and journals, including the 1979 Iranian journal *The Iranian* and many
others. See also M. Fischer, *Iran: From Religious Dispute to Revolution* (Cambridge, Mass.,
1980), esp. chap. 6.

3. Graham, *Iran,* p. 212, and newspaper coverage at the time.

4. E. Abrahamian, "The Guerrilla Movement in Iran, 1963–1977," *MERIP
Reports,* 86 (Mar.–Apr. 1980): 3–21.

5. Ibid, pp. 9–10.

6. Ibid., p. 11.

7. This has been reported in several sources, but the most interesting may be
Fereydoun Hoveyda, *The Fall of the Shah,* trans. Roger Liddell (New York, 1980).
Although apologetic and often inaccurate about himself and his brother, Hoveyda has
some good information about the 1970s. On pp. 84–85, after discussing Amuzegar's
abrupt credit squeeze, Hoveyda says: "In his relentless drive to cut spending,
Amuzegar abruptly canceled the funding that my brother had made available for

religious purposes, amounting to about eleven million dollars a year. This money, charged against the secret budget of the Prime Minister, was used to finance the upkeep of the country's mosques and Koranic schools as well as for various other expenses. . . . These grants were for the benefit of all the clergy, including the supporters of Khomeini." Hoveyda goes on to note Amuzegar's announcement of the plan to extend the Tehran north-south expressway to go through the bazaar giving rise to "rumors that the shah wanted to destroy their tradespeople's shops and disperse them. After the Amuzegar government's drastic cuts and the announcement of this plan, discontent spread among religious circles, the middle classes, and the tradesmen in the bazaars." Hoveyda's views are, however, contested by a few Iranians interviewed, who feel that the acts described were the fault of the shah rather than Amuzegar.

8. Ruhollah Khomaini, *Nehzat-e Eslami 3: Tazadd-e Eslam ba shahanshahan va rezhim-e shahanshahi* (n.d., n.p.). (The text of a talk given on June 22, 1971, in Najaf directed against the shah's celebration of the 2500th anniversary of the Persian monarchy).

9. R. Graham, *Iran*, p. 224.

10. See E. Hooglund, "Rural Participation in the Revolution," *MERIP Reports*, 87 (May 1980): 3–6.

11. This is based on extensive interviewing of Iranian liberals in Iran in June and July 1978, and subsequently.

12. On the above points aside from newspapers see Rubin, *Paved with Good Intentions;* W. Sullivan, "Dateline Iran: The Road Not Taken," *Foreign Policy*, 40 (Fall 1980); M. Ledeen and W. Lewis, "Carter and the Fall of the Shah"; and R. Shaplen, "The Eye of the Storm," *New Yorker*, pts. 1 and 2, June 2 and 9, 1980.

13. The above conclusions are based on my analysis of numerous sources, including those mentioned in note 12, above, and on interviews with several involved parties.

14. Abrahamian, "Guerrilla," p. 13.

15. Graham, *Iran*, p. 240.

16. The *New York Times* and other major newspapers covered the events surrounding the new constitution. Its text is translated in *Constitution of the Islamic Republic of Iran*, Foreign Broadcast Information Service (Springfield, Va., Dec. 6, 1979, Supplement); this translation is reprinted in *Middle East Journal*, vol. 34, no. 2 (1980). See also H. Algar, trans., *Constitution of the Islamic Republic of Iran*. Berkeley: Mizan Press, 1981.

17. Several reports in *Le Monde* describe and analyze the Tudeh's position, and a typical interview of Kianuri is found in *The Iranian*, vol. 1, no. 2. (July 4, 1979), "Islamic Regime Is Enacting Tudeh Program." The "Ayatollah" nickname is partly a play on Kianuri's descent from Shaikh Fazlollah Nuri, who during the Constitutional Revolution of 1905–11 was considered a monarchist reactionary but who has recently been rehabilitated as a defender of Islam.

18. See especially Bazargan's interview with Oriana Fallaci, "Everybody Wants to Be Boss," *New York Times Magazine*, Oct. 28, 1980.

19. See Lois Beck, "Revolutionary Iran and Its Tribal Peoples," *MERIP Reports*, 87 (May 1980): 14–20.

20. See R. P. Mottahedeh, "Iran's Foreign Devils," *Foreign Policy*, 38 (Spring 1980): 19–34.

21. For an excellent summary and analysis of this and other aspects of Iran in 1980 see E. Rouleau, "Khomeini's Iran," *Foreign Affairs,* vol. 59, no. 1 (1980): 1–20.

22. The problems of the Iranian Revolution, particularly as seen by Bani Sadr and those around him, are well expressed in the 1979 and 1980 reports in *Le Monde,* particularly those by Eric Rouleau. Other important articles that deserve wider readership in the English-speaking world are found in successive issues beginning in 1979 of *Peuples Méditerranéens/Mediterranean Peoples,* especially two interviews: Paul Vieille, "La Révolution iranienne en panne, entretien avec A. H. Banisadr," 9 (Oct.–Dec. 1979): 73–83; and F. Khosrokhavar, "Hassan K., paysan-dépaysanné parle de la révolution iranienne," 11 (Apr.–June 1980): 3–30.

Among the best of several useful analyses of the Revolution in English are those by Shaul Bakhash, especially "The Iranian Revolution," *New York Review of Books,* June 26, 1980. See also the predominantly English articles in *L'Iran d'hier et de demain* (Québec, 1980), and A. Jabbari and R. Olson, eds., *Iran: Essays on a Revolution in the Making* (Lexington, Ky., 1981). The French have published numerous general books on the revolution, of which the best is probably P. Balta and C. Rulleau, *L'Iran insurgé* (Paris, 1979). *Iran in der Krise,* intro. by M. Domitra and The-Quyen Vu (Bonn, 1980), has articles in English by J. Bill, S. Chubin, R. Graham, K. Hunt, N. Keddie, A. Whitley, V. Yorke, and M. Zonis. Whitley's article in it, "The Approach of the Islamic Republic of Iran to Economic Policy," pp. 151–59, is particularly useful.

23. By mid-June, Bani Sadr's newspaper was closed and he was removed as military commander-in-chief, leaving his presidency ceremonial and his future in doubt. Execution of Baha'is also increased.

SELECT BIBLIOGRAPHY OF
BOOKS IN ENGLISH

General

Alexander, Yonah and Allan Nanes, eds. *The United States and Iran: A Documentary Hisotry.* Frederick MD: University Publications of America, 1980.

Aramajani, Yahya. *Iran.* Englewood Cliffs, NJ: Prentice-Hall, 1972.

Avery, Peter. *Modern Iran.* New York: Praeger, 1965.

Banani, Amin, ed. *State and Society in Iran. Iranian Studies,* special issue, vol. 11 (1978).

Bausani, Alessandro. *The Persians: From the Earliest Days to the Twentieth Century.* Trans. J. B. Donne. London: Elek Books, 1971.

Bosworth, C. E., ed. *Iran and Islam: In Memory of the late Vladimir Minorsky.* Edinburgh: Edinburgh University Press, 1971.

The Cambridge History of Iran. Cambridge: The University Press, 1968–1975.
Vol. 1: *The Land of Iran,* William B. Fisher, ed.
Vol. 4: *The Period from the Arab Invasions to the Saljuqs,* Richard N. Frye, ed.
Vol. 5: *The Saljuq and Mongol Periods,* John A. Boyle, ed.
Forthcoming volumes on later periods.

Chaliand, Gerard, ed. *People Without a Country: The Kurds and Kurdistan.* Translated by Michael Pallis. London: Zed Press, 1980.

Cottam, Richard W. *Nationalism in Iran: Updated through 1978.* 2nd ed. Pittsburgh: University of Pittsburgh Press, 1979.

Frye, Richard Nelson. *Iran.* New York: Holt, 1953; revised ed., London: Allen and Unwin, 1968.

Keddie, Nikki. *Iran: Religion, Politics and Society.* London and Totowa, N.J.: Frank Cass, 1980.

————, ed. *Scholars, Saints and Sufis: Muslim Religious Institutions Since 1500.* Berkeley and Los Angeles: University of California Press, 1972.

Lambton, Ann K. S. *Landlord and Peasant in Persia: A Study of Land Tenure and Land Revenue Administration.* London and New York: Oxford University Press, 1953, reprinted 1969.

Ramazani, Rouhollah K. *The Foreign Policy of Iran: A Developing Nation in World Affairs, 1500–1941*. Charlottesville: University Press of Virginia, 1966.

Upton, Joseph M. *The History of Modern Iran: An Interpretation*. Harvard Middle Eastern Monographs 2. Cambridge, Mass.: Harvard University Press, 1960.

Watt, W. Montgomery. *Islam and the Integration of Society*. London: Routledge and Kegan Paul, 1961.

Wilber, Donald. *Iran: Past and Present*. 8th ed. Princeton: Princeton University Press, 1948; revised ed., 1978.

Wright, Denis. *The English amongst the Persians*. London: Heinemann, 1977.

Iran: 1400–1796

Grey, Charles, ed. and trans. *A Narrative of Italian Travels in Persia, in the Fifteenth and Sixteenth Centuries*. The Hakluyt Society Series, no. 49, pt. 2. London: The Hakluyt Society, 1873.

Hanway, Jonas. *An Historical Account of the British Trade over the Caspian Sea*. 4 vols. London: Dodsley, 1753.

————. *The Revolutions of Persia*. London: Dodsley, 1753.

Holod, Renata, ed. *Studies on Isfahan: Proceedings of the Isfahan Colloquium. Iranian Studies*, special issue, vol. 7 (1974).

Lockhart, Laurence. *The Fall of the Safavi Dynasty and the Afghan Occupation of Persia*. Cambridge: Cambridge University Press, 1958.

————. *Nadir Shah: A Critical Study Based Mainly upon Contemporary Sources*. London: Luzac, 1938.

Mazzaoui, Michel M. *The Origins of the Safawids: Si'ism, Sufism, and the Gulat*. Wiesbaden: F. Steiner, 1972.

Minorsky, Vladimir, ed. and trans. *Tadhkirat al-Muluk: A Manual of Safavid Administration*. London: Luzac, 1943.

Perry, John R. *Karim Khan Zand: A History of Iran, 1747–1779*. Chicago and London: University of Chicago Press, 1979.

Ross, Edward D. *Sir Anthony Sherley and His Persian Adventure*. London: Routledge and Sons, 1933.

Savory, Roger M. *Iran under the Safavids*. Cambridge: Cambridge University Press, 1980.

Woods, John. *The Aqquyunlu: Clan, Confederation, Empire*. Minneapolis: Bibliotheca Islamica, 1976.

The Qajar Period: 1796–1925

Algar, Hamid. *Mirza Malkum Khan: A Study in the History of Iranian Modernism.* Berkeley and Los Angeles: University of California Press, 1973.
_____. *Religion and State in Iran, 1785–1906.* Berkeley and Los Angeles: University of California Press, 1969.

Bakhash, Shaul. *Iran: Monarchy, Bureaucracy, and Reform under the Qajars, 1858–1896.* London: Ithaca Press for the Middle East Centre, St. Antony's College, 1978.

Browne, Edward G. *Materials for the Study of the Babi Religion.* Cambridge: Cambridge University Press, 1918.
_____. *The Persian Revolution of 1905–1909.* Cambridge: Cambridge University Press, 1910.

Curzon, George N. *Persia and the Persian Question.* 2 vols. New ed. London: Frank Cass, 1969.

Entner, Marvin L. *Russo-Persian Commercial Relations, 1828–1914.* Gainesville: University of Florida Press, 1965.

Forbes-Leith, F. A. C. *Checkmate: Fighting Tradition in Central Persia.* London: Harrap, 1927.

Gupta, Raj Narain. *Iran: An Economic Study.* New Delhi: Indian Institute of International Affairs, 1947.

Issawi, Charles, ed. *The Economic History of Iran: 1800–1914.* Chicago and London: The University of Chicago Press, 1971.

Kazemzadeh, Firuz. *Russia and Britian in Persia, 1864–1914: A Study in Imperialism.* New Haven: Yale University Press, 1968.

Keddie, Nikki R. *An Islamic Response to Imperialism: Political and Religious Writings of Sayyid Jamal ad-Din "al-Afghani".* Berkeley and Los Angeles: University of California Press, 1968.
_____. *Religion and Rebellion in Iran: The Tobacco Protest of 1891–1892.* London: Frank Cass, 1966.
_____. *Sayyid Jamal ad-Din "al-Afghani:" A Political Biography.* Berkeley and Los Angeles: University of California Press, 1972.

McDaniel, Robert A. *The Shuster Mission and the Persian Constitutional Revolution.* Minneapolis and Chicago: Bibliotheca Islamica, 1974.

Malcolm, Sir John. *The History of Persia.* 2 vols. London: J. Murray, 1815.
_____. *Sketches of Persia: From the Journals of a Traveller in the East.* 2 vols. London: J. Murray, 1827.

Shuster, William Morgan. *The Strangling of Persia.* New York and London: The Century Company, 1912.

Sykes, Christopher. *Wassmuss, "The German Lawrence."* London: Longmans, Green, 1936.

Watson, Robert G. *A History of Persia from the Beginning of the Nineteenth Century to the Year 1858.* London: Smith, Elder, 1866.

Yeselson, Abraham. *United States–Persian Diplomatic Relations: 1883–1921.* New Brunswick: Rutgers University Press, 1956.

The Pahlavi Period: 1925–1979

Abrahamian, Ervand. *Iran between Two Revolutions.* Princeton: Princeton University Press, 1982.

Akhavi, Shahrough. *Religion and Politics in Contemporary Iran: Clergy-State Relations in the Pahlavi Period.* Albany: S.U.N.Y. Press, 1980.

Amirsadeghi, Hossein and R. W. Ferrier, eds. *Twentieth Century Iran.* London: Heinemann, 1977.

Amuzegar, Jahangir and M. Ali Fekrat. *Iran: Economic Development under Dualistic Conditions.* Chicago and London: University of Chicago Press, 1971.

Arfa, General Hassan. *Under Five Shahs.* London: John Murray, 1964.

Baldwin, George B. *Planning and Development in Iran.* Baltimore: The Johns Hopkins University Press, 1967.

Bamdad, Badr ol-Moluk. *From Darkness into Light: Women's Emancipation in Iran.* Ed. and trans. F. R. C. Bagley. Hicksville, N.Y.: Exposition Press, 1977.

Banani, Amin. *The Modernization of Iran, 1921–1941.* Stanford: Stanford University Press, 1961.

Barth, Fredrik. *Nomads of South Persia: the Basseri Tribe of the Khamseh Confederacy.* Oslo: University Press; London: Allen and Unwin, 1961.

Bayne, Edward A. *Persian Kingship in Transition: Conversations with a Monarch Whose Office Is Traditional and Whose Goal Is Modernization.* New York: American Universities Field Staff, 1968.

Beck, Lois and Nikki Keddie, eds. *Women in the Muslim World.* Cambridge, Mass. and London: Harvard University Press, 1978.

Benedick, Richard Elliot. *Industrial Finance in Iran: A Study of Financial Practice in an Underdeveloped Economy.* Boston: Division of Research, Graduate School of Business Administration, Harvard University, 1964.

Bharier, Julian. *Economic Development in Iran, 1900–1970.* London and New York: Oxford University Press, 1971.

Bill, James Alban. *The Politics of Iran: Groups, Classes and Modernization.* Columbus, Ohio: Charles E. Merrill, 1972.

Binder, Leonard. *Iran: Political Development in a Changing Society*. Berkeley and Los Angeles: University of California Press, 1962.

Blair, John M. *The Control of Oil*. New York: Pantheon Books, 1976.

Bonine, Michael and Nikki R. Keddie, eds. *Modern Iran: The Dialectics of Continuity and Change*. Paperback edition, *Continuity and Change in Modern Iran*. Albany: S.U.N.Y. Press, 1981.

Chubin, Shahram and Sepehr Zabih. *The Foreign Relations of Iran: A Developing State in a Zone of Great-Power Conflict*. Berkeley and Los Angeles: University of California Press, 1974.

Douglas, William Orville, *Strange Lands and Friendly People*. New York: Harper and Brothers, 1951.

Eagleton, William, Jr. *The Kurdish Republic of 1946*. London and New York: Oxford University Press, 1963.

Elwell-Sutton, L. P. *Persian Oil: A Study in Power Politics*. London: Lawrence and Wishart, 1955.

English, Paul Ward. *City and Village in Iran: Settlement and Economy in the Kirman Basin*. Madison: Univeristy of Wisconsin Press, 1966.

Fesharaki, Fereidun. *Development of the Iranian Oil Industry: International and Domestic Aspects*. New York: Praeger, 1976.

Gupta, Raj Narain. *Oil in the Modern World*. Westport, Conn.: Hyperion Press, 1976; reprint ed., Allahabad, India: Kitab Mahal Allahabad, 1949.

Hoveyda, Fereydoun. *The Fall of the Shah*. New York: Simon and Schuster, 1980.

International Labour Organization. *Employment and Income Policies for Iran*. Geneva, 1973.

Katouzian, Homa. *The Political Economy of Modern Iran*. London: Macmillan, 1981.

Kedourie, Elie and Sylvia Haim, eds. *Towards a Modern Iran*. London: Frank Cass, 1980.

Kuniholm, Bruce R. *The Origins of the Cold War in the Middle East: Great Power Conflict and Diplomacy in Iran, Turkey, and Greece*. Princeton: Princeton University Press, 1980.

Lambton, Ann K. S. *The Persian Land Reform, 1962–1966*. Oxford: Clarendon Press, 1969.

Lenczowski, George, ed. *Iran under the Pahlavis*. Stanford: The Hoover Institution, 1978.

———. *Russia and the West in Iran, 1918–1948: A Study in Big-Power Rivalry*. Ithaca: Cornell University Press, 1949.

Looney, Robert. *The Economic Development of Iran: A Recent Survey with Projections to 1981*. New York: Praeger, 1973.

_____. *Income Distribution Policies and Economic Growth in Semiindustrialized Countries: A Comparative Study of Iran, Mexico, Brazil and South Korea.* New York: Praeger, 1975.

Marlowe, John. *Iran: A Short Political Guide.* London: Pall Mall Press, 1963.

Mehdevi, Anne Sinclair. *Persia Revisited.* New York: Knopf, 1964.

Millspaugh, Arthur Chester. *The American Task in Persia.* New York and London: The Century Company, 1925.

_____. *Americans in Persia.* New York: Da Capo Press, 1976, reprint ed.; Washington: Brookings Institution, 1946.

_____. *The Financial and Economic Situation of Persia, 1926.* New York: Imperial Persian Government, 1926.

Morgan, Dan. *Merchants of Grain.* New York: Viking Press, 1979.

Nirumand, Bahman. *Iran: The New Imperialism in Action.* Trans. Leonard Mins. New York and London: Monthly Review Press, 1969.

Oberling, Pierre. *The Qashqa'i Nomads of Fars.* The Hague: Mouton, 1974.

O'Donnell, Terence. *Garden of the Brave in War.* New Haven, Conn.: Ticknor and Fields, 1980.

Overseas Consultants, Inc. *Report on Seven Year Development Plan for the Plan Organization of the Imperial Government of Iran.* 5 vols. New York, 1949.

Pahlavi, Mohammad Reza. *Answer to History.* Briarcliff Manor, N.Y.: Stein and Day, 1980.

_____. *Mission for My Country.* New York: McGraw-Hill, 1961.

Ramazani, Rouhollah K. *Iran's Foreign Policy 1941–1973: A Study of Foreign Policy in Modernizing Nations.* Charlottesville: University Press of Virginia, 1975.

Roosevelt, Kermit. *Countercoup: The Struggle for the Control of Iran.* New York: McGraw-Hill, 1979, 1980.

Rubin, Barry. *Paved with Good Intentions: The American Experience and Iran.* New York and Oxford: Oxford University Press, 1980.

Sadiq, Issa Khan. *Modern Persia and Her Educational System.* New York: Teachers College, Columbia University, 1931.

Saikhal, Amin. *The Rise and Fall of the Shah.* Princeton: Princeton University Press, 1980.

Sampson, Anthony. *The Arms Bazaar: From Lebanon to Lockheed.* New York: Bantam Books, 1977.

_____. *The Seven Sisters: The Great Oil Companies and the World They Shaped.* New York: Bantam Books, 1975.

Stork, Joe. *Middle East Oil and the Energy Crisis.* New York: Monthly Review Press, 1975.

Wilber, Donald. *Riza Shah Pahlavi: The Resurrection and Reconstruction of Iran.* Hicksville, N.Y.: Exposition Press, 1975.

Yeganegi, Esfandiar Bahram. *Recent Financial and Monetary History of Persia.* Published Ph.D. dissertation, Columbia University, 1934.

Yar-Shater, Ehsan, ed. *Iran Faces the Seventies.* New York: Praeger, 1971.

Zabih, Sepehr. *The Communist Movement in Iran.* Berkeley and Los Angeles: University of California Press, 1966.

Recent Events

Albert, David H., ed. *Tell the American People: Perspectives on the Iranian Revolution.* Philadelphia: Movement for a New Society, 1980.

Bakhash, Shaul. *Khomaini's Revolution.* London: Sidgwick and Jackson, forthcoming.

Fischer, Michael M. J. *Iran: From Religious Dispute to Revolution.* Cambridge, Mass. and London: Harvard University Press, 1980.

Graham, Robert. *Iran: The Illusion of Power,* Revised ed. London: Croom Helm, 1979.

Halliday, Fred. *Iran: Dictatorship and Development.* New York: Penguin, 1979.

Kazemi, Farhad, ed. special issue of *Iranian Studies* on the Iranian Revolution, forthcoming.

MERIP Reports. Issues on Iran:

No. 37 (May 1975). "Iranian Nationalism and the Great Powers."

No. 40 (September 1975). "America's Shah, Shahahshah's Iran."

No. 43 (December 1975). "Land Reform and Agribusiness in Iran."

No. 69 (July–August 1978). "Iran: Political Challenge, Economic Contradictions."

No. 71 (October 1978). "Iran: The Political Crisis, Trade Unions, Agricultural Dependence."

No. 75/76 (March–April 1979). "Iran in Revolution."

No. 86 (March–April 1980). "The Left Forces in Iran."

No. 87 (May 1980). "Iran's Revolution: The Rural Dimension."

No. 88 (June 1980). "Iran's Revolution: The First Year."

Nobari, Ali-Reza, ed. *Iran Erupts.* Stanford, Calif.: Iran-America Documentation Group, 1978.

Race & Class. Special Issue on the Iranian Revolution. Vol. 21 (Summer 1979).

Zonis, Marvin. *The Political Elite of Iran.* Princeton: Princeton University Press, 1971.

Intellectual Trends: Political, Religious, and Literary

Al-e Ahmad, Jalal. *The School Principal.* Trans. John K. Newton. Minneapolis and Chicago: Bibliotheca Islamica, 1974.

Baraheni, Reza. *The Crowned Cannibals: Writings on Repression in Iran.* New York: Vintage Books, 1977.

Behrangi, Samad. *The Little Black Fish and Other Modern Persian Stories.* Trans. Eric and Mary Hooglund. Washington, D.C.: Three Continents Press, 1976.

Browne, Edward G. *A Literary History of Persia.* 4 vols. 2nd ed. Cambridge: The University Press, 1928–1929.

————. *The Press and Poetry of Modern Persia.* Cambridge: the University Press, 1914.

Chelkowski, Peter J. *Ta'ziyeh: Ritual and Drama in Iran.* New York: New York University Press, 1979.

Esfandiary, F. M. *The Day of Sacrifice.* New York: McDowell, 1959.

————. *Identity Card.* New York: Grove Press, 1966.

Hedayat, Sadeq. *Hedayat: An Anthology of Short Stories.* Edited by Ehsan Yarshater. Boulder: Westview, 1979.

————. *The Blind Owl.* Trans. D. P. Costello. New York: Evergreen, 1959.

————. *Haji Agha: Portrait of an Iranian Confidence Man.* Trans. G. M. Wickens, intro. Lois Beck, Middle East Monographs, no. 6, Center for Middle Eastern Studies, University of Texas at Austin, Austin, Texas, 1979.

Kamshad, Hassan. *Modern Persian Prose Literature.* Cambridge: Cambridge University Press, 1966.

Karimi-Hakkak, Ahmad, comp. and trans. *An Anthology of Modern Persian Poetry.* Boulder: Westview, 1978.

Khomeyni, Ayatollah Ruhollah. *Islamic Government.* Springfield, Va.: National Technical Information Service, 1979.

Lambton, Ann K. S. *Theory and Practice in Medieval Persian Government.* London: Variorum Reprints, 1980.

The Literary Review. "Iran." 18, no. 1 (1974).

Literature East and West. "Major Voices in Contemporary Persian Literature." Michael C. Hillmann, ed., vol. 20 (January–December 1976), actual date of publication, June 1980.

Pelly, Sir Lewis. *The Miracle Plays of Hasan and Husain. Collected from Oral Tradition by Colonel Sir Lewis Pelly.* 2 vols. Ed. by Arthur N. Wollaston. Farnborough (Hants.): Gregg International, 1970; 1st ed. London: W. H. Allen, 1879.

Rahman, Munibur. *Post-Revolution Persian Verse.* Aligarh: Institute of Islamic Studies, Muslim University, 1955.

Shari'ati, Ali. *Marxism and Other Western Fallacies: An Islamic Critique.* Trans. R. Campbell, Berkeley: Mizan Press, 1980.

_____. *On the Sociology of Islam*. Trans. Hamid Algar, Berkeley: Mizan Press, 1979.
Southgate, Minoo, ed. and trans. *Modern Persian Short Stories*. Washington, D.C.: Three Continents Press, 1980.
Tabataba'i, M. H. *Shi'ite Islam*. Trans. Hossein Nasr. Albany: S.U.N.Y. Press, 1975.
Vaughan, Leo. *The Jokeman*. London: Eyre and Spottiswoode, 1962.

Supplement

Bayat, Mangol. *Mysticism and Dissent: Socioreligious Thought in Qajar Iran*. Syracuse: Syracuse University Press, forthcoming.
Beck, Lois, and Nikki Keddie. *The Qashqa'i People of Southern Iran*. Los Angeles: UCLA Museum of Cultural History, 1981.
Garthwaite, Gene. *Khans and Shahs: The Bakhtiari in Iran*. Cambridge: Cambridge University Press, forthcoming.
Helms, Cynthia. *An Ambassador's Wife in Iran*. New York: Dodd, Mead, 1981.
Hooglund, Eric. *Reform and Revolution in Rural Iran*. Austin: University of Texas Press, forthcoming.
Iran in der Krise. Bonn: Verlag Neue Gesellschaft, 1980; includes eight articles in English.
Jabbari, Ahmad and Robert Olson, ed. *Iran: Essays on a Revolution in the Making*. Lexington, Ky.: Mazda Publishers, 1981.
Ledeen, Michael, and William Lewis. *Debacle: The American Failure in Iran*. New York: Knopf, 1981.
McManus, Doyle. *Free at Last!* New York: New American Library, 1981.
Said, Edward. *Covering Islam*. New York: Pantheon, 1981.
The journals *Iranian Studies, The Iranian,* and *RIPEH* contain useful articles and texts, as does *The Iran Times*.

INDEX

Malcolm, John, 41
Malek al-Motakallemin (Mirza Nasrollah Esfahani), 72, 76, 193
Maleki, Khalil, 201
Malekzadeh, Mehdi, 193
Malkom Khan, Mirza, 63–64, 66, 67, 72, 187, 190, 204
Manichaeism, 3, 265
Mansur, Hasan Ali, 178
Mardom (People's) party, 150
marja'-e taqlid, 149, 157, 207, 208, 213, 228
marriage, 33–34, 35, 98, 109, 179–180
Marxism, 195, 198, 201, 209, 211, 214, 217, 225, 227–228, 235, 236, 239, 260–261
mashruteh, 73
Massignon, Louis, 215, 224
Matin-Daftari, Hedayatollah, 201, 261
Mazdak, 3, 192
Mecca, 5, 6
Medina, 5
Mehrjui, Daryush, 198
Melliyun (Nationalist) party, 150
merchants, 13, 28, 29, 32, 45, 58, 67, 70, 72, 73, 93, 107
messianism, 7, 48–52
middle class, 93, 111, 128, 268–269
Milani, Ayatollah Mohammad Hadi, 157
military, 25, 57–58, 89, 93, 104, 125, 126, 139–140; modernization of, 29–30, 31, 41, 43–44, 47, 53, 59, 60, 68, 88, 94–95, 106, 107, 172, 176–177; U.S. involvement in, 116, 122, 142, 144, 146, 150, 155, 157, 159, 176–177. See also weapons and military equipment
Millspaugh, A. C., 90, 114, 115–116
mineral exploitation concessions, 38, 58, 61
Mir Damad, 19, 199
Mission for My Country (Mohammad Reza Shah), 179

Modarres, Sayyed Hasan, 91, 92, 93
modernization: by Mohammad Reza Shah (after 1950), 143; Qajar efforts for, 29–30, 31, 39, 44, 47, 53–54, 59; by Reza Shah (1925–30), 93, 94–105, 110–112
Mohammad, Prophet, 5, 6, 50
Mohammad Ali Shah (Qajar), 69, 73, 74–76, 193–194
Mohammad Mirza, 47
Mohammad Reza Shah Pahlavi, 113–182; abdication demanded of, 253; attempts on life of, 179; autobiographies by, 179; cancer condition of, 232; dictatorial role of (after 1953), 142–181; fortune of, 149, 172, 178, 180; marriages of, 152; Revolution 1978–79 and, 231, 234, 249–250, 253, 255–256
Mohammad Shah (Qajar), 47, 48, 51
Morier, James, 72, 193
Mojahedin, in 1905–11 Revolution, 76
Mojahedin-e Khalq, 181, 210, 213, 223, 225, 230, 235, 236, 237–239, 251–252, 257, 259, 260–261
mollas, 31, 32, 72, 73, 185–186, 230, 270
Mongols, 8, 11, 25
monopolies, governmental, 107, 114, 123–124, 127, 131, 132. See also state capitalism
Monopoly of Foreign Trade Law (1931), 106
Montazeri, Ayatollah Hosain Ali, 263
Moqaddam Maraghe'i, Rahmatollah, 261
Morrison-Knudson firm, 130
Mosaddeq, Mohammad, 91, 92, 94, 117, 118, 132–141, 200, 201, 203, 210, 214, 215, 226, 229, 260
Moshir ad-Dauleh (1920), 84
Moshir ad-Dauleh. See Hosain Khan, Mirza
Mossad, Israeli, 144
Mozaffar ad-Din Shah (Qajar), 69–74